Chicago

"All you've got to do is decide to go
and the hardest part is over.

So go!"

TONY WHEELER, COFOUNDER – LONELY PLANET

D1018605

THIS EDITION WRI,
Karla Zimmerman

Contents

(left) Deep-dish pizza (p75)

(above) Navy Pier (p69)

(right) City views from North Avenue Beach (p108)

Welcome to Chicago

Steely skyscrapers, top chefs, rocking festivals – the Windy City will blow you away with its low-key cultured awesomeness.

Art & Architecture

It's hard to know what to gawp at first. High-flying architecture is everywhere, from the stratospheric, glass-floored Willis Tower to Frank Gehry's swooping silver Pritzker Pavilion to Frank Lloyd Wright's stained-glass Robie House. Whimsical public art studs the streets; you might be walking along and wham, there's an abstract Picasso statue that's not only cool to look at, you're allowed to go right up and climb on it. For art museums, take your pick: impressionist masterpieces at the massive Art Institute, psychedelic paintings at the mid-sized National Museum of Mexican Art or outsider drawings at the small Intuit gallery.

Chowhounds' Delight

Loosen your belt – you've got a lot of eating to do. On the menu: peanut-butter-and-banana-topped waffles for breakfast (at Stephanie Izard's Little Goat); a chicken, apple and cranberry hot dog for lunch (at Hot G Dog); and 20 courses of centrifuged, encapsulated molecular gastronomy for dinner (at Grant Achatz' Alinea).

You can also chow down on a superb range of ethnic eats from Vietnamese pho to Mexican *carnitas,* Polish pierogi and Swedish almond tarts. Still hungry? Order a late-night deep-dish pizza.

Sports Fanatics

Chicago is a maniacal sports town, with a pro team for every season (two teams, in baseball's case). Watching a game is a local rite of passage, whether you slather on the blue-and-orange body paint for a Bears football game, join the raucous baseball crowd in Wrigley Field's bleachers, or plop down on a bar stool at the neighborhood tavern for whatever match is on TV. Count on making lots of spirited new friends. Should the excitement rub off and inspire you to get active yourself, the city's 26 beaches and 580 parks offer a huge array of play options.

Rollicking Festivals

Chicago knows how to rock a festival. Between March and September it throws around 200 shindigs. The specialty is music. Blues Fest brings half a million people to Grant Park to hear guitar notes slide and bass lines roll, all for free. During the three-day Lollapalooza mega-party, rock bands thrash while the audience dances in an arm-flailing frenzy. Smaller, barbecue-scented street fests take place in the neighborhoods each weekend – though some rival downtown for star power on their stages (oh, hey, Olivia Newton-John at Northalsted Market Days).

Why I Love Chicago

By Karla Zimmerman, Writer

I've lived in this city for 25 years, and I never get bored. There's something groovy going on any night of the week. Like tonight: should I see the Grant Park Orchestra playing Shostakovich's Fifth Symphony in Millennium Park, or a guitar-drum duo called Earring at Empty Bottle? I love that Tibetan dumplings, Mexican *carnitas* and crème brûlée doughnuts are all equally, easily accessible from local eateries. I love how total strangers sitting next to each other in a bar watching a Blackhawks game become high-fiving pals by evening's end. Chicago really is my kind of town.

For more about our writers, see p320.

Above: Pritzker Pavilion (p47)

Chicago's
Top
10

Art Institute of Chicago (p49)

1 The second-largest art museum in the country, the Art Institute houses a treasure trove from around the globe. The collection of impressionist and post-impressionist paintings is second only to those in France, and the number of surrealist works is tremendous. Wander the endless marble and glass corridors, and into rooms stuffed with Japanese prints, Grecian urns, suits of armor, Grant Wood's *American Gothic,* Edward Hopper's *Nighthawks* and one very big, dotted Seurat. The Modern Wing dazzles with Picassos and Mirós.

⊙ *The Loop*

Millennium Park (p46)

2 The playful heart of the city, Millennium Park shines with whimsical public art. Go head, walk under Anish Kapoor's *Cloud Gate* – aka 'the Bean' – and touch its silvery smoothness. Let the human gargoyles of Jaume Plensa's Crown Fountain gush water on you to cool down in summer. Unfurl a blanket by Frank Gehry's swooping silver band shell as the sun dips, wine corks pop and gorgeous music fills the twilight air. Or try to find the secret garden abloom with prairie flowers and a wee, gurgling river.

RIGHT: PRITZKER PAVILION (P47)

⊙ *The Loop*

Sky-High Views *(p51)*

3 For superlative seekers, Willis Tower is it: the city's tallest building (and one of the world's loftiest). Breathe deeply during the ear-popping, 70-second elevator ride to the 103rd-floor Skydeck, then stride to one of the glass-enclosed ledges that juts out in mid-air. Look down some 1400ft. Crikey. The lakeside John Hancock Center also rises high in the sky. Ascend to the 96th-floor Signature Lounge, order a cocktail and watch the city sparkle around you. It's especially lovely at night. TOP LEFT: VIEW FROM WILLIS TOWER (P51)

👁 *The Loop*

Architecture Cruises *(p263)*

4 Who cares if all the backward neck-bending causes a little ache? There's no better way to feel Chicago's steely power than from low on the water looking up while cloud-poking towers glide by and iron bridges arch open to lead the way. The skyline takes on a surreal majesty as you float through its shadows on a river tour, and landmark after eye-popping landmark flashes by. Guides' architecture lessons carry on the breeze, so you'll know your beaux arts from International style by day's end.

🏃 *Transportation*

Wrigley Field *(p111)*

5 A tangible sense of history comes alive at this 100-plus-year-old baseball park, thanks to the hand-turned scoreboard, iconic neon entrance sign, legendary curses and time-honored traditions that infuse games played here. No matter that the hapless Cubbies haven't won a championship since 1908 – shoveling down hot dogs and drinking beer in the raucous bleachers makes for an unforgettable afternoon. No tickets? No worries. Peep in the 'knot-hole,' a garage-door-sized opening on Sheffield Ave, to watch the action for free.

🏃 *Lake View & Wrigleyville*

Public Art (p53)

6 You can't walk two blocks downtown without bumping into an extraordinary sculpture. The granddaddy is Picasso's *Untitled* (what the heck is it – an Afghan hound?), set smack in Daley Plaza. Jean Dubuffet's abstract creation is officially titled *Monument with Standing Beast* but everyone calls it 'Snoopy in a Blender.' Marc Chagall's grand mosaic *Four Seasons* is more recognizable, depicting Chicago scenes. And Alexander Calder's hulking, red-pink *Flamingo* does indeed look like the namesake bird, but only after you've had a few beers. BELOW: ALEXANDER CALDER'S *FLAMINGO* (P53)

👁 *The Loop*

Comedy & Theater (p105)

7 A group of jokesters began performing intentionally unstructured skits in a Chicago bar a half-century ago, and voilà – improv comedy was born. Second City still nurtures the best in the biz, though several other improv theaters also work from booze-fueled suggestions that the audience hollers up. Among the city's 200 theaters are powerhouse drama troupes such as Hollywood-star-laden Steppenwolf, and heaps of fringey, provocative 'off-Loop' companies. The coolest ones base admission cost on a dice roll, or let you pay what you can. TOP RIGHT: UP COMEDY CLUB (P106)

⭐ *Lincoln Park & Old Town*

Blues & Rock *(p188)*

8 In Chicago no genre is as iconic as the blues – the electric blues, to be exact. When Muddy Waters and friends plugged in their amps c 1950, guitar grooves reached new decibel levels. Hear it in clubs around town, such as Buddy Guy's Legends, where the icon himself still takes the stage, or Rosa's Lounge, where it's a bit more down and dirty. The blues paved the way for rock and roll, so no surprise cool little clubs hosting edgy indie bands slouch on many a street corner. LEFT: BUDDY GUY'S LEGENDS (P188)

⭐ *South Loop & Near South Side*

Global Eats (p26)

9 During the last decade chefs such as Grant Achatz, Rick Bayless, Stephanie Izard and many others put Chicago on the culinary map. They won a heap of James Beard awards, and suddenly international critics were dubbing Chicago one of the globe's top eating destinations. The beauty here is that even the buzziest restaurants are accessible: they're visionary yet traditional, pubby at the core and decently priced. You can also fork into a superb range of ethnic eats in Chicago's neighborhoods, from Puerto Rican *jibaritos* to Indian samosas to Polish pierogi.

✗ *Chicago Dining*

Navy Pier (p69)

10 Stretching away from the skyline and into the blue of Lake Michigan, half-mile-long Navy Pier is Chicago's most-visited attraction. Its charms revolve around the cool breezes and sweet views, especially from the stomach-turning, 196ft Ferris wheel. High-tech rides, splash fountains, big boats and greasy snacks blow the minds of young ones. Live music, Shakespearean theater and whopping fireworks displays entertain everyone else. A smart renovation is bringing an ice rink and additional amusements.

◉ *Near North & Navy Pier*

What's New

The 606

This elevated cycling and walking path runs along a repurposed train track for 2.7 miles through Wicker Park and Logan Square. It offers a great peek at neighborhood life. (p137)

Stony Island Arts Bank

Local artist Theaster Gates saved a South Side bank building from demolition and revamped it into an African American cultural center with quirky collections such as DJ Frankie Knuckles' vinyl trove. (p195)

Maggie Daley Park

Next door to Millennium Park, this space entertains kids with its imaginative free playgrounds, and all ages get in on the action at the summer rock-climbing wall and winter ice-skating ribbon. (p53)

West Loop

Trendy brands such as Google, Nobu and Ace Hotel are joining the slew of stylish bars and restaurants that seem to open almost every day in Chicago's meatpacking district. (p43)

Chicago Design Museum

Hidden in a downtown mall, the Design Museum puts on cool free exhibitions about contemporary and historical design. One month it might be about Irish architecture, the next about environmental graphic design. (p58)

Forbidden Root

Chicago's brewery scene has exploded in recent years, but nothing's quite like Forbidden Root, which uses bark, spices, flowers and more in its unusual beers. (p147)

Navy Pier

OK, so Navy Pier opened in 1916. What's new here is a multi-million-dollar renovation with a new theater, ice rink, hotel, and upgraded eating and drinking options. Oh, and a taller, scarier Ferris wheel too. (p69)

Riverwalk

The city continues to put a big effort (and big bucks) into expanding downtown's Riverwalk with the addition of waterfront seats, outdoor cafes, wine bars, and bike and kayak rentals. (p55)

Chicago Architectural Biennial

Chicago has long been an architecture innovator. In 2015 it launched the biennial to bring together designers from around the world for a three-month architecture confab. The next one is in 2017. (p23)

Pullman National Monument

Pullman, a far South Side community famed for its urban design and utopian ideals, came under the National Park Service umbrella in 2015. It offers a fascinating walkabout. (p201)

For more recommendations and reviews, see **lonelyplanet. com/chicago**

Need to Know

For more information, see Survival Guide (p259)

Currency
US dollar ($)

Language
English

Visas
Generally not required for stays of up to 90 days.

Money
The US dollar ($) is the currency.

Cell Phones
Europe and Asia GSM 900/1800 standard does not work in the USA. Consider buying a cheap local phone with a pay-as-you-go plan.

Time
Central Standard Time (GMT/ UTC minus six hours)

Tourist Information
Visitor Center (www.choose chicago.com; 111 N State St; ⊘10am-8pm Mon-Thu, to 9pm Sat, 11am-7pm Sun; Ⓜ Brown, Orange, Green, Purple, Pink Line to Randolph) This isn't a particularly useful place; has a smattering of brochures and maps. Concierges can answer basic questions. Located in Macy's basement.

Daily Costs

Budget:
Less than $100
➡ Dorm bed: $35–$40
➡ Lunchtime specials: $10–$15
➡ Transit day pass: $10
➡ Discount theater or blues-club ticket: $10–$25

Midrange:
$100–$300
➡ Hotel or B&B double room: $150–$250
➡ Dinner in a casual restaurant: $20–$30
➡ Architecture boat tour: $44
➡ Cubs bleacher seat: $40–$60

Top end:
More than $300
➡ Luxury hotel double room: $400
➡ Dinner at Alinea: $265
➡ Lyric Opera ticket: $200

Advance Planning
Three months before Book your hotel. Reserve at mega-hot restaurants such as Alinea, and Girl & the Goat.

Two weeks before Reserve ahead at your other must-eat restaurants, and book tickets for sports events and blockbuster museum exhibits.

One week before Check www. hottix.org for half-price theater tickets. Check www.chicago reader.com to see entertainment options and make bookings.

Useful Websites
Lonely Planet (www.lonely planet.com/chicago) Destination information, hotel bookings, traveler forum and more.

Choose Chicago (www.choose chicago.com) Official tourism site with sightseeing and event info.

Chicagoist (www.chicagoist. com) Quirky take on food, arts and events.

DNA Info Chicago (www. dnainfo.com/chicago) Detailed news about sights, bars, restaurants and events, broken down by neighborhood.

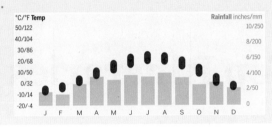

WHEN TO GO

Peak season is June through August when it's warm. It's freezing between November and March, so bargains abound. December twinkles with festivities.

°C/°F **Temp**   **Rainfall** inches/mm
J F M A M J J A S O N D

Arriving in Chicago

O'Hare International Airport
The Blue Line El train ($5) runs 24/7. Trains depart every 10 minutes or so; they reach the city center in 40 minutes. Shuttle vans cost $32, taxis around $50.

Chicago Midway Airport The Orange Line El train ($3) runs between 4am and 1am. Trains depart every 10 minutes or so; they reach downtown in 30 minutes. Shuttle vans cost $27, taxis cost $35 to $40.

Union Station All trains arrive here, and Megabus arrives a block away. For transportation onward, the Blue Line Clinton stop is a few blocks south (not a great option at night). The Brown, Orange, Purple and Pink Line station at Quincy is about a half-mile east. Taxis queue along Canal St outside the station entrance.

For much more on **arrival** see p260

Getting Around

The El (a system of elevated/subway trains) is the main way to get around. Buses are also useful. Buy a day pass for $10 at El stations. The Chicago Transit Authority (p260) runs the transport system.

➡ **Train** El trains are fast, frequent and ubiquitous. Red and Blue Lines operate 24/7; others between 4am and 1am.

➡ **Bus** Buses cover areas that the El misses. Most run at least from early morning until 10pm, some go later. Some don't run on weekends.

➡ **Taxi** Easy to find downtown, north to Andersonville and west to Wicker Park/ Bucktown. But costly.

➡ **Boat** Water taxis travel along the river and lakefront and offer a fun way to reach the Museum Campus or Chinatown.

➡ **Bicycle** Abundant rental shops and the Divvy bike-share program make cycling a doable option.

For much more on **getting around** see p261

Sleeping

Accommodations will likely be your biggest expense in Chicago. The best digs are groovy, wired-up boutique hotels, especially those set in architectural landmarks. Several independent hostels have popped up over the past few years in fun, outlying neighborhoods such as Wicker Park and Wrigleyville. Enormous business hotels cater to conventioneers in the Loop and Near North. Low-key B&Bs are scattered in Wicker Park and Lake View and are often cheaper than hotels.

Useful Websites

➡ **Lonely Planet** (www.lonelyplanet.com/hotels) Recommendations and bookings.

➡ **Chicago Bed & Breakfast Association** (www.chicago-bed-breakfast.com) Represents some 15 properties.

➡ **Hotel Tonight** (www.hoteltonight.com) National discounter with last-minute deals; book via the free app.

➡ **Choose Chicago** (www.choosechicago.com) Options from the city's official website.

For much more on **sleeping** see p215

Top Itineraries

Day One

The Loop (p44)

 You might as well dive right in with the big stuff. Take a boat or walking tour with the **Chicago Architecture Foundation** and ogle the most sky-scraping collection of buildings the US has to offer. Saunter over to **Millennium Park** to see 'the Bean' reflect the skyline and to splash under Crown Fountain's human gargoyles.

> **Lunch** The Gage (p61) dishes Irish-tinged grub with a fanciful twist.

The Loop (p44)

Explore the **Art Institute of Chicago**, the nation's second-largest art museum. It holds masterpieces aplenty, especially impressionist and post-impressionist paintings (and paperweights). Then head over to **Willis Tower**, zip up to the 103rd floor and step out onto the glass-floored ledge. Yes, it is a long way down.

> **Dinner** Taxi or El to the West Loop to Duck Duck Goat (p171).

Near West Side & Pilsen (p163)

 The West Loop parties in the evening. Sit on the glittery patio sipping a glass of bubbly at **RM Champagne Salon**. **Haymarket Pub & Brewery** pours great beers and has the Drinking and Writing Theater inside. Or down an unusual brew at celeb chef Rick Bayless' *cervecería* **Cruz Blanca**.

Day Two

Near North & Navy Pier (p67)

 Take a stroll on Michigan Ave – aka the **Magnificent Mile** – where big-name department stores ka-ching in a glittering row. Mosey over to **Navy Pier**. Wander the half-mile promenade and take a spin on the high-in-the-sky Ferris wheel.

> **Lunch** Heft a mighty slice of pizza at Giordano's (p76).

South Loop & Near South Side (p178)

Spend the afternoon at the **Museum Campus** (the water taxi from Navy Pier is a fine way to get there). Miles of aisles of dinosaurs and gemstones stuff the **Field Museum**. Sharks and other fish swim in the kiddie-mobbed **Shedd Aquarium**. Meteorites and supernovas are on view at the **Adler Planetarium**.

> **Dinner** Hop the Blue Line to Damen for Dove's Luncheonette (p141).

Wicker Park, Bucktown & Ukrainian Village (p135)

 Wander along Milwaukee Ave and take your pick of booming bars, indie-rock clubs and hipster shops. **Quimby's** shows the local spirit; the bookstore stocks zines and graphic novels, and is a linchpin of Chicago's underground culture. The **Hideout** and **Empty Bottle** are sweet spots to catch a bad-ass band.

Jaguar at Lincoln Park Zoo (p98)

Day Three

Lincoln Park & Old Town (p95)

 Dip your toes in Lake Michigan at **North Avenue Beach**. Amble northward through the sprawling greenery of **Lincoln Park**. Stop at **Lincoln Park Zoo** to see lions and tigers and bears (the polar kind). Pop into **Lincoln Park Conservatory** to smell exotic blooms.

> **Lunch** Munch a char-dog and cheddar fries at Wieners Circle (p103).

Lake View & Wrigleyville (p109)

 Make your way north to **Wrigley Field** for an afternoon baseball game. The atmospheric, century-old ballpark hosts the Cubs, a team that has been cursed for a century but whose luck just might be changing. Afterward practice your home-run swing (and beer drinking) at **Sluggers**, one of many high-fiving bars that circle the stadium.

> **Dinner** Mmmm, mussels and *frites* (fries) at Hopleaf (p129).

Andersonville & Uptown (p125)

Andersonville has several fine taverns to hang out at and sink a pint, like **Simon's**. Or see what's on at the **Neo-Futurists** theater. Jazz hounds can venture to the **Green Mill**, a timeless venue to hear jazz, watch a poetry slam or swill a martini. Al Capone used to groove on it.

Day Four

Hyde Park & South Side (p191)

 The **Museum of Science & Industry** isn't kidding around with its acres of exhibits. There's a German U-boat, mock tornado and exquisite dollhouse for starters. Groovy university bookstores like **57th Street Books** and **Powell's** offer shelves of weighty tomes.

> **Lunch** Colorful cafe Medici (p202) makes a mean thin-crust pizza.

Hyde Park & South Side (p191)

Linger in Hyde Park, as there's more to do. Architecture buffs can tour **Robie House**, Frank Lloyd Wright's Prairie-style masterpiece. Check out the **Nuclear Energy sculpture**, where the atomic age began. Make your way north to the Kenwood neighborhood to see **Obama's house** and Muhammad Ali's former pad.

> **Dinner** Sip whiskey while waiting for a table at Longman & Eagle (p160).

Logan Square & Humboldt Park (p152)

 Nightlife options abound in Logan Square. Knock back slurpable beers at **Revolution Brewing**. See what arty band is playing for free at wee **Whistler**. Or imbibe at **Scofflaw**, a true gin joint where juniper is treated with reverence.

If You Like...

Famous Museums

Field Museum of Natural History Explore collections of dinosaurs, gems, mummies and enormous taxidermied lions. (p180)

Art Institute of Chicago Gawp at Monets, modern works, paperweights and much more at the nation's second-largest art museum. (p49)

Adler Planetarium Journey to the nether regions of outer space at this lakeside gem. (p181)

Museum of Science & Industry Geek out at the largest science museum in the western hemisphere. (p193)

Offbeat Museums

International Museum of Surgical Science Amputation saws, iron lungs and a roomful of cadaver murals cram a creepy old mansion. (p85)

Money Museum You'll emerge with a take-home bag of shredded currency and a photo with the million-dollar briefcase. (p53)

Busy Beaver Button Museum Thousands upon thousands of groovy pin-back buttons. (p154)

Leather Archives & Museum Scholarly displays about leather, fetish and S&M subcultures, including relics like the Red Spanking Bench. (p37)

Chicago Sports Museum The Cubs' infamous Bartman ball and Sammy Sosa's corked bat fill displays inside Harry Caray's tavern. (p85)

Lion statue at the entrance of the Art Institute of Chicago (p49)

Frank Lloyd Wright

Robie House The low eves and graceful lines of Wright's Hyde Park masterpiece were emulated around the world. (p194)

Rookery Wright gave the atrium a light-filled, Prairie-style renovation that features 'floating' staircases. (p54)

Frank Lloyd Wright Home & Studio See where the master lived and worked for the first 20 years of his career. (p207)

Charnley-Persky House Only 19 years old when he designed it, Wright declared the 11-room abode the 'first modern building.' (p86)

Contemporary Art

Museum of Contemporary Art Consider it the Art Institute's brash, rebellious sibling: a collection that always pushes boundaries. (p84)

Millennium Park Jaume Plensa's video-screen, glass-block Crown Fountain leads the pack of whimsical artworks throughout the park. (p46)

Untitled Baboon, dog, woman? You decide what Pablo Picasso's public artwork is. (p53)

Museum of Contemporary Photography Tidy and engaging (and free), it's a great stop in the South Loop. (p181)

Pilsen Mural Tours Locals lead you through the neighborhood's trove of art-splashed buildings. (p177)

Mars Gallery It's pop art presided over by a kitty cat (he's the assistant manager). (p165)

Stony Island Arts Bank African American cultural center and gallery that puts on thought-provoking exhibitions. (p195)

Skyscrapers

Willis Tower Chicago's tallest building lets you ascend 103 floors, then peer straight down from a glass-floored ledge. (p51)

Aqua Tower Jeanne Gang's wavy, 82-story beauty is the world's tallest building designed by a woman. (p55)

360° Chicago Get high at the John Hancock tower's 94th-floor observatory or 96th-floor lounge. (p83)

Trump Tower The Donald built Chicago's second-tallest building and made it into a glassy, uber-luxe hotel. (p74)

Tribune Tower This neo-Gothic cloud-poker is inlaid with stones from the Taj Mahal, Parthenon, Lincoln's Tomb and more. (p70)

Marina City The groovy corncob towers look like something from a *Jetsons* cartoon. (p70)

Kluczynski Building Ludwig Mies van der Rohe launched the modern skyscraper look with this boxy, metal-and-glass structure. (p54)

Photo Ops

Chicago Theatre Sign What's more perfect than a six-story-high neon sign spelling out the city's name? (p63)

Cloud Gate The awesomely mirrored sculpture lets you take a self-portrait with a skyline background. (p46)

Art Institute Lions The iconic beasts guard the entrance and wear special gear for holidays and big events. (p49)

Wrigley Field Entrance The red, art-deco-style marquee makes an especially fine backdrop when neon-lit at night. (p111)

Mr Beef Sign Snap a photo under the dumpy sign before indulging in the city's best Italian beef sammie. (p74)

For more top Chicago spots, see the following:
- ➡ Eating (p26)
- ➡ Drinking & Nightlife (p29)
- ➡ Entertainment (p31)
- ➡ Shopping (p33)
- ➡ Sports & Activities (p35)
- ➡ Gay & Lesbian Chicago (p37)

PLAN YOUR TRIP IF YOU LIKE...

Gangster Sites

Green Mill Al Capone's favorite speakeasy; the tunnels where he hid the booze are still underneath the bar. (p133)

Biograph Theater Where the 'lady in red' betrayed 'public enemy number one' John Dillinger. (p99)

Union Station Fans of *The Untouchables* can see where the baby carriage bounced down the stairs. (p55)

St Valentine's Day Massacre Site Where Capone's men, dressed as cops, killed seven members of Bugs Moran's gang. (p99)

Untouchable Gangster Tours Hokey but fun bus ride taking in famed mob sites around town. (p264)

Parks & Gardens

Lincoln Park Chicago's largest green space is where the city comes out to play. (p97)

Lurie Garden Find Millennium Park's secret garden and you'll be treated to a prairie's worth of wildflowers. (p46)

Garfield Park Conservatory Pretty plants under glass, plus the Monet Garden re-creates the impressionist painter's French flower patch. (p166)

Humboldt Park Zigzagging paths, an iris-edged lagoon, a makeshift beach and Puerto Rican food trucks comprise the 207 acres. (p154)

Northerly Island This prairie-grassed nature park offers a tranquil escape from the nearby Museum Campus. (p181)

Palmisano Park It's carved from an old quarry and reveals skyline views from walkways made of recycled debris. (p200)

Lincoln Park Conservatory The small but potent dose of tropical blooms is especially welcome during winter. (p98)

Windy City Icons

Billy Goat Tavern Subterranean dive where newspaper reporters have long boozed; also famous for spawning the Curse of the Cubs. (p74)

Buddy Guy's Legends The top spot in town to hear the blues, especially when Mr Guy himself takes the stage. (p188)

Wrigley Field More than 100 years old and still going strong with its hand-turned scoreboard and raucous bleacher seats. (p111)

Pizzeria Uno Deep-dish pizza was invented here in 1943, although the claim to fame is hotly debated. (p76)

Second City Launched the improv comedy genre and the careers of funny folk like Bill Murray and Tina Fey. (p105)

Pop Culture

Daley Plaza Site of the *Blues Brothers* epic car-crashing chase scene. (p52)

Marina City The strangely charming, corn-cob-shaped towers show up everywhere from *Ferris Bueller's Day Off* to Wilco album covers. (p70)

Original Playboy Mansion Hugh Hefner launched the magazine and began wearing his all-day pajamas here. (p85)

Route 66 Sign The famous Mother Road starts downtown by the Art Institute. (p55)

Hilton Chicago Ground zero for the 1968 Democratic Convention riots, where police threw protesters through the plate-glass windows. (p230)

Buckingham Fountain The water spout featured in the opening credits of the classic TV comedy *Married...with Children*. (p52)

History

Chicago History Museum Tells the city's story with artifacts such as Prohibition-era booze stills; also offers themed history tours in neighborhoods. (p98)

DuSable Museum of African American History The nation's first independent museum for African American art, history and culture; it's Smithsonian-affiliated. (p195)

National Museum of Mexican Art Politically charged pieces reveal Mexico's turbulent history and revolutionary leaders. (p166)

Graceland Cemetery A who's who of famous Chicagoans, including Ludwig Mies van der Rohe and Marshall Field. (p127)

Haymarket Square Site where the world's labor movement began after a riot. (p165)

Kid-Friendly Activities

Navy Pier The whirling swing, sky-high Ferris wheel, musical carousel – all here, plus boats. (p69)

Maggie Daley Park Imaginative playgrounds where kids can swing and climb for hours, plus rock climbing and mini golf. (p53)

Lincoln Park Zoo Swinging chimps, roaring lions and a barnyard full of farm animals to feed. (p98)

Peggy Notebaert Nature Museum The butterfly haven, bird garden and marsh full of frogs provide gentle thrills. (p98)

Chicago Children's Museum The slew of building, climbing and inventing exhibits keep young ones busy. (p70)

North Avenue Beach Pint-sized waves are perfect for pint-sized swimmers. (p108)

Ethnic Neighborhoods

Pilsen Chicago's Mexican community clusters here, where the salsas scald and the tortillas are fresh from the neighborhood factory. (p43)

Chinatown Small but bustling, its charms are nibbling chestnut cakes, sipping tea and slurping noodles. (p185)

Argyle Street The fishy-smelling heart of 'Little Saigon,' good for bubble tea, pho and exotic Asian wares. (p127)

Paseo Boricua The 'Puerto Rican Passage' is a half-mile-long stretch of Division St in Humboldt Park. (p155)

Devon Avenue It's mostly a mash-up of Indian and Pakistani businesses, with Russian and Orthodox Jewish shops mixed in. (p128)

Andersonville The Swedish American Museum Center and Swedish Bakery give a feel for what life was once like here. (p43)

Month By Month

January

It's the coldest month, with temperatures hovering around 22°F (-6°C), and the snowiest month, with around 10in total. Everyone stays inside and drinks.

✯✯ Chinese New Year Parade

Crowds amass on Wentworth Ave in Chinatown to watch dragons dance, firecrackers burst and marching bands bang their gongs during this parade (www.chicagochinatown.org). The exact date varies according to the lunar calendar, but it's typically in late January or early to mid-February.

March

Will the sun ever shine again? Windy City-zens fret during the grayest and windiest month, when temperatures linger at 37°F (3°C). Some fun events take the edge off.

✯ Chiditarod

The Chiditarod (www.chiditarod.org) is a crazy-costume, Burning Man–esque version of the Iditarod (the Alaskan sled-dog race) that swaps humans for huskies and shopping carts for sleds. Teams haul canned food for local pantries along the Near West Side route. Held on the first Saturday in March.

✯✯ St Patrick's Day Parade

It's a city institution: the local plumbers' union dyes the Chicago River shamrock green (pouring in the secret, biodegradable coloring near the N Columbus Dr bridge), and then a big parade follows along S Columbus Dr. Held the Saturday before March 17.

May

Finally, the weather warms and everyone dashes for the parks, lakefront trails, baseball stadiums and beer gardens. Beaches open over Memorial Day weekend. Hotels get busy.

✯✯ Cinco de Mayo Festival & Parade

This three-day, family-friendly bash draws thousands to Douglas Park near Pilsen with food, music and carnival rides the first weekend in May. Sunday's colorful parade along Cermak Rd (beginning at Damen Ave) marks the finale.

✯ Bike the Drive

The last Sunday in May, cars are banned from Lake Shore Dr, and 20,000 cyclists take to the road during Bike the Drive (www.bikethedrive.org). Riding 30 miles along the lakefront as the sun bursts out is a thrill. Pancakes and live music follow in Grant Park.

June

Schools let out. Beaches get busy. Festival season ramps up. The temperature hangs at an ideal 69°F (21°C). Alas, it rains a third of the days.

✯✯ Printers Row Lit Fest

This popular free event (www.printersrowlitfest.org), sponsored by the *Chicago Tribune,* features thousands of rare and not-so-rare books for sale, plus author readings. The browsable booths line the 500 to 700 blocks of S Dearborn St in early June.

☆ Chicago Blues Festival

It's the globe's biggest free blues fest (www.chicago bluesfestival.us), with three days of the electrified music that made Chicago famous. More than 500,000 people unfurl blankets by the multiple stages that take over Grant Park in mid-June.

☆ Grant Park Music Festival

The Grant Park Orchestra, composed of top musicians from symphonies around the globe, plays free concerts in Millennium Park's Pritzker Pavilion on Wednesday, Friday and Saturday evenings from mid-June through mid-August during this festival (www.grantparkmusicfes tival.com). It's a summer ritual to bring wine and a picnic.

🎆 Pride Parade

On the last Sunday in June, colorful floats and risqué revelers pack Halsted St in Boystown. It's the LGBT community's main event (http://chicagopride.go pride.com), and more than 800,000 people come to the party.

July

The month Chicagoans wait for all year. Festivals rock the neighborhoods every weekend. Millennium Park has concerts downtown nightly. Fireflies glow everywhere. It can be hot and humid, but who cares?

🍴 Taste of Chicago

The mid-month, five-day food festival (www.tasteof chicago.us) in Grant Park draws hordes for a smorgasbord of ethnic, meaty, sweet and other local edibles – much of it served on a stick. Several stages host free live music, including big-name bands.

☆ Pitchfork Music Festival

It's sort of Lollapalooza Jr (http://pitchforkmusicfes tival.com), for bespectacled alternative-music fans. Wilco, Digable Planets and other taste-making acts shake up Union Park for three days in mid-July. A day pass costs $65.

August

Ah, more awesome summer: warm weather, concerts, festivals, baseball games, beach frolicking. Tourists are still here en masse, so lodging prices are high and lines can be long.

☆ Lollapalooza

This mega rock festival (www.lollapalooza.com) once traveled city to city; now its permanent home is in Chicago. It's a raucous event, with 130 bands – including many A-listers – spilling off eight stages in Grant Park the first Friday to Sunday in August. A day pass costs $120.

☆ Chicago Air & Water Show

The third weekend in August, windows rattle as the latest military planes buzz the lakefront from Fullerton Ave south to Oak St during this event (www. chicagoairandwatershow. us). North Ave Beach is the epicenter. Two million people attend.

September

Kids go back to school and beaches close after Labor Day weekend. Peak season begins to wind down.

☆ Chicago Jazz Fest

Chicago's longest-running free music fest (www.chica gojazzfestival.us), well into its fourth decade, attracts top names on the national jazz scene. The brassy notes bebop over Labor Day weekend on multiple stages in Millennium Park and the Chicago Cultural Center.

🎆 EXPO Chicago

Top galleries from around the globe show off their contemporary and modern art on Navy Pier during EXPO Chicago (www.expo chicago.com), held over a long weekend in mid-September. Local galleries get in on the action by offering special tours and programs concurrently.

October

Temperatures drop, to an average of 53°F (12°C). Baseball is over, but basketball and hockey begin at month's end. The Bears and tailgate parties are in full swing.

🏃 Chicago Marathon

More than 45,000 runners compete on this 26-mile course (www.chicago marathon.com) through the city's heart, cheered on by a million spectators. Held on a Sunday in October (when

(Top) Christkindlmarket
(Bottom) Pride Parade

JON HICKS/GETTY IMAGES ©

CAFEBEANZ COMPANY/SHUTTERSTOCK ©

the weather can be pleasant or freezing), it's considered one of the world's top five marathons.

◉ Chicago Architecture Biennial

The three-month biennial (www.chicagoarchitecturebiennial.org) brings together designers from around the world for free exhibitions, tours and public programs about groovy architecture. It takes place from October through December, every two years. The next biennials are in 2017 and 2019.

☆ Chicago International Film Festival

Showing a few big-name flicks among myriad not-so-big-name flicks, this festival (www.chicagofilmfestival.com) brings a few big-name Hollywood stars to town to add a glamorous sheen to the proceedings. It unspools over two weeks, starting in mid-October, at varying venues.

December

'Tis the holiday season, and the city twinkles with good cheer. Michigan Ave bustles with shoppers and shines with a million lights. The ice rinks open. Hotel bargains abound.

🛍 Christkindlmarket

A traditional German holiday market (www.christkindlmarket.com) takes over Daley Plaza all month, selling sausages, roasted nuts and spiced wine along with Old World handicrafts. It starts around Thanksgiving and goes until Christmas Eve.

With Kids

Ferocious dinosaurs at the Field Museum, an ark's worth of beasts at Lincoln Park Zoo, lakefront boat rides and sandy beaches are among the top choices for toddlin' times. Add in magical playgrounds, family cycling tours and lots of pizza, and it's clear Chicago is a kid's kind of town.

Maggie Daley Park (p53)

Outdoor Activities

Parks

Millennium Park (p46) is a hot favorite. Kids love to run underneath and touch 'the Bean' sculpture, while Crown Fountain (p46) serves as a de facto water park to splash in. Nearby Maggie Daley Park (p53) offers imaginative playgrounds where kids can swing and climb for hours. Lincoln Park (p97) has a free zoo where lions roar and apes swing. At the southern end of the zoo, kids can get up close to goats, ponies, cows and chickens at the Farm-in-the-Zoo, and they can also see ducks along the Nature Boardwalk. The train ride and the carousel (each around $3 per ride) – with its wood-carved pandas, cheetahs and tigers – bring squeals of delight.

Beaches

Sand and swimming! Lifeguards patrol the city's 26 lakefront beaches throughout the summer. Waves are typically pint-sized – perfect for pint-sized swimmers. North Avenue Beach (p108) is the most crowded (and you do have to share it with skimpy-suited 20-somethings), but the selling point is the location near both downtown and Lincoln Park Zoo. The steamboat-shaped beach house is totally kid friendly, serving ice cream and burgers, and it has bathrooms and lockers. Montrose Beach (p134) is further flung, but it also has bathrooms and a snack bar. It's less crowded and more dune-packed and nature-filled. Remember to check the beach website (www.cpdbeaches.com) before you head out to make sure the water isn't off-limits due to high winds or bacteria levels.

Navy Pier

Amusements abound on the half-mile-long wharf (p69). A giant whirling swing, the sky-high Ferris wheel, a musical, hand-painted carousel, remote-control boats, a fun-house maze are all here, and then some. Popcorn, ice cream, burgers and other treats add to the carnival atmosphere.

Cycling

Bobby's Bike Hike (p262) and Bike Chicago (p262) rent children's bikes and bikes with child seats. Both also offer child-friendly tours. Try Bobby's 'Tike Hike,' which rolls by

FLIPHOTO/SHUTTERSTOCK ©

Lincoln Park Zoo and a statue of Abe Lincoln. Kids aged 10 and under are welcome on the 4.5-mile route. Bike Chicago's 'Lincoln Park Adventure' is also suitable for kids.

Boat Rides

The schooner *Windy* (p263) departs from Navy Pier and offers a pirate-themed cruise on most days, plus kids can help sail the boat. Water taxis offer another wind-in-your-hair experience. The boats that toddle along the lakefront between Navy Pier and the Museum Campus are popular with families.

> **NEED TO KNOW**
> ➡ For kid-friendly happenings, see **Chicago Parent** (www.chicagoparent.com), **Chicago Kids** (www.chicagokids.com) and **Time Out Chicago Kids** (www.timeoutchicagokids.com).
>
> ➡ **American Childcare Services** (☑312-644-7300; www.americanchildcare.com; per hour $35) provides professional babysitters who will come to your hotel (four-hour minimum service). Book at least 24 hours in advance.

Kid-Friendly Museums

Chicago Children's Museum

It is the reigning favorite, geared to kids aged 10 and under, with a slew of hands-on building, climbing and inventing exhibits. Bonus: it's located on Navy Pier (p70).

Field Museum of Natural History

Bring on the dinosaurs! The Crown Family PlayLab (p180), on the ground floor, lets kids excavate bones and make loads of other discoveries. It's open Thursday to Monday from 10am to 3pm.

Museum of Science & Industry

Families could spend a week here (p193) and not see it all. Staff conduct 'experiments' in various galleries throughout the day, like dropping things off the balcony and creating mini explosions. The Idea Factory lets scientists aged 10 and under 'research' properties of light, balance and water pressure.

Peggy Notebaert Nature Museum

This museum (p98) is somewhat overlooked, but its butterfly haven and marsh full of frogs provide gentle thrills. Bonus: it's located in Lincoln Park by the zoo.

Art Institute of Chicago

The Ryan Learning Center (p49) provides interactive games and art-making activities.

Theater & TV

Chic-A-Go-Go (www.facebook.com/chicagogo) is a cable-access TV show that's like a kiddie version of *Soul Train*. Check the website for taping dates and locations to join the groovy dance party.

Chicago Children's Theatre (p92) puts on terrific shows. The stories are often familiar, as they're frequently adapted from kids' books. Many use puppets or music. Performances take place at the Ruth Page Center for Arts in the Gold Coast.

Emerald City Theatre Company (p121) is another kid-focused troupe. It presents well-known shows such as *School House Rock Live,* as well as original, lesser-known works like *Three Little Kittens.* Performances are at the group's on-site theater, as well as the Apollo Theater in Lincoln Park.

Festivals

Chicago Kids & Kites Festival

On a Saturday in early May, hundreds of kites soar and dip around Montrose Beach (p134). The city supplies free kite-making kits, and professional flyers demonstrate how to harness the wind. Face painting and balloon artists round out the fun.

Kidzapalooza

Lollapalooza (www.lollapalooza.com; day pass $120; ☉early Aug) isn't just for arm-flailing, mosh-pit-thrashing adults. Kidzapalooza is a festival within the giant rock festival.

Magnificent Mile Lights Festival

During the free **Magnificent Mile Lights Festival** (☉late Nov), held the Saturday before Thanksgiving, Mickey Mouse and a slew of family-friendly musicians march in a parade and flip on Michigan Ave's one million twinkling lights.

Deep-dish pizza (p75)

Eating

Chicago has become a chowhound's hot spot. For the most part, restaurants here are reasonably priced and pretension-free, serving masterful food in come-as-you-are environs. You can also fork into a superb range of ethnic eats, especially if you break out of downtown and head for neighborhoods such as Pilsen or Uptown.

Eat Streets

Randolph Street, West Loop Chicago's best and brightest chefs cook at downtown's edge.

Clark Street, Andersonville Nouveau Korean, traditional Belgian and sweet Swedish.

Division Street, Wicker Park Copious sidewalk seating spills out of hip bistros and cafes.

Argyle Street, Uptown Thai and Vietnamese noodle houses steam up this little corridor.

18th Street, Pilsen Mexican bakeries and taquerias mix with hipster cafes and barbecue joints.

Tours

Chicago Food Planet Tours (☏312-818-2170; www.chicagofoodplanet.com; 3hr tours $45-55) Go on a guided walkabout where you'll graze through five or more neighborhood eateries.

Chicago Beer Experience (☏312-818-2172; www.chicagobeerexperience.com; tours $60) The three-hour walking tours visit Lincoln Park, Wicker Park or downtown and hit four bars over the course of a mile or so.

Chicago Pizza Tours (☏312-221-8502; www.chicagopizzatours.com; tours $60-80) These

3½-hour tours are by bus or on foot, and take in four pizzerias (all food included in price).

A Foodie's Perfect Day

Start the morning at a farmers market; Green City Market (p98), the city's largest, has cooking demos by top chefs. Next go on a graze with Chicago Food Planet Tours (p26). For dinner, go upscale in West Loop (part of the Near West Side – try Girl and the Goat; p172) or laid-back at Logan Square (Longman & Eagle; p160).

Food Trucks

Food trucks generally prowl office-worker-rich hot spots, such as the Loop and Near North around lunchtime, and then Wicker Park and Lake View toward evening. Chicago Food Truck Finder (www.chicagofoodtruckfinder.com) amalgamates many truck locations on one map. Daley Plaza hosts several trucks on Fridays at lunchtime.

Eating by Neighborhood

➧ **The Loop** Lunch spots for office workers, not much late night. (p58)

➧ **Near North & Navy Pier** Huge variety, from deep-dish pizza to ritzy seafood. (p74)

➧ **Gold Coast** Epicenter of sceney steakhouses and swanky eateries. (p87)

➧ **Lincoln Park & Old Town** A smorgasbord, from elite Alinea to cute French bakeries and student bites. (p99)

➧ **Lake View & Wrigleyville** Good-time midrange places for vegetarians and global food lovers. (p113)

➧ **Andersonville & Uptown** Cozy, international array in Andersonville; noodle houses in Uptown's Little Saigon. (p127)

➧ **Wicker Park, Bucktown & Ukrainian Village** Dense with nouveau comfort food and cafes. (p138)

➧ **Logan Square & Humboldt Park** Inventive foodie mecca, sans reservations. (p155)

➧ **Near West Side & Pilsen** West Loop for Chicago's hottest chefs; Greektown, Little Italy and Pilsen for ethnic fare. (p166)

➧ **South Loop & Near South Side** Cheap eats for students give way to Chinatown flavors. (p186)

➧ **Hyde Park & South Side** Far-flung hipster chow in Bridgeport, earthy cafes in Hyde Park. (p202)

NEED TO KNOW

Price Ranges

The following price ranges refer to the cost of a main dish at dinner.

$ less than $15

$$ $15–$25

$$$ more than $25

Opening Hours

Most restaurants: breakfast 7am or 8am to 11am, lunch 11am or 11:30am to 2:30pm, dinner 5pm or 6pm to 10pm Sunday to Thursday, to 11pm or midnight Friday and Saturday.

Reservations

➧ Make dinner reservations for eateries in the midrange and upper price brackets, especially on weekends.

➧ There are exceptions, ie megahot restaurants that require serious pre-planning or places that don't take reservations at all.

➧ Many restaurants let you book online through **OpenTable** (www.opentable.com).

Customs

Many restaurants are BYOB, so it's fine to bring your own wine or beer. Occasionally there's a corkage fee of a few dollars.

Tipping

Tipping 15% of the total bill is the minimum. If service is good, 20% is the norm.

Credit Cards

Almost all restaurants accept credit cards, aside from a smattering of budget places.

Websites

➧ **LTH Forum** (www.lthforum.com) Local chowhounds rant and rave.

➧ **Happy Cow** (www.happycow.net) Vegetarian options.

➧ **Chicago Farmers Markets** (www.chicagofarmersmarkets.us) Where to find them.

Lonely Planet's Top Choices

Hopleaf (p129) Locals pile in for the mussels, *frites* and 200-strong beer list.

Dove's Luncheonette (p141) Sit at the retro counter for Tex-Mex dishes, pie and whiskey.

Lou Mitchell's (p166) Route 66 diner where waitstaff call you 'honey' without irony.

Little Goat (p167) *Top Chef* Stephanie Izard's delicious comfort-food diner.

Irazu (p138) Chicago's lone Costa Rican eatery whips up distinctive, peppery fare.

Best by Budget

$

Publican Quality Meats (p167) Beefy sandwiches straight from the butcher's block.

Xoco (p74) Celeb chef Rick Bayless' Mexican street-food hut.

Big Star Taqueria (p139) Tacos for Wicker Park foodies.

Kuma's Corner (p155) Hulking burgers with a side of heavy metal.

Honey Butter Fried Chicken (p155) Sweet and salty bird.

$$

Parachute (p160) Michelin-starred spin on Korean street food, set in an off-the-beaten-path location.

Longman & Eagle (p160) Michelin-starred, shabby-chic tavern for breakfast, lunch or dinner.

Avec (p171) Communal tables, noisy chatter and bacon-wrapped dates.

Saint Lou's Assembly (p171) Retro cafeteria set up for modern comfort foods, cocktails and bocce.

$$$

Girl & the Goat (p172) Rockin' ambience and dishes starring the titular animal.

Fat Rice (p160) A wild Portuguese-Indian-Chinese mash-up with *Bon Appétit* approval.

Boeufhaus (p145) Wee, European-style steakhouse and butcher shop.

Alinea (p103) Molecular gastronomy at one of the world's best restaurants.

Best by Cuisine

Modern American

Blackbird (p172) West Loop trendsetter known for fantastic desserts.

Schwa (p144) Apple-pie soup and other inventive dishes form the multicourse menu.

Dusek's (p174) Michelin-starred gastropub in Pilsen serving beer-inspired dishes.

Latin

Topolobampo/Frontera Grill (p77) Rick Bayless' flavor-packed signature restaurants.

mfk (p118) Romantic hole-in-the-wall for unfussy Spanish seafood.

Cafecito (p58) Fat Cuban sandwiches.

Asian

Duck Duck Goat (p171) Festive ambience and Chinese-inspired food from celeb chef Stephanie Izard.

Crisp (p113) Cheerful cafe for Korean fried chicken and mixed vegetable bowls.

Le Colonial (p87) Banana-leaf-wrapped fish that will transport you to Saigon.

Andy's Thai Kitchen (p113) Real-deal, hot-spiced fare from a Thai master.

Vegetarian

Mana Food Bar (p141) Swanky all-veg eatery that makes dishes from around the globe.

Victory's Banner (p113) New Age, meat-free bliss (and a great brunch).

Chicago Diner (p113) The local scene's long-standing all-veg linchpin.

Green Zebra (p145) Chicago's highfalutin veg-out spot.

Handlebar (p139) Bike messenger hangout with many meat-free dishes on the menu.

Pizzerias

Giordano's (p75) It's like deep-dish on steroids, with awesomely bulked-up crusts.

Pequod's Pizza (p99) Sweet sauce and caramelized cheese.

Pizano's (p60) Makes a great thin crust to supplement the deep dish.

Hot Dogs

Hot G Dog (p128) Goes beyond gourmet weenies, with a killer Chicago-style dog too.

Vienna Beef Factory Store & Cafe (p140) Franks at the factory with the folks who made 'em.

Wieners Circle (p103) Char-dogs, cheddar fries and lots of unruly swearing.

Best Neighborhood Gems

Ruxbin (p145) Teeny spot where passionate chefs cook artful dinners.

Duck Inn (p203) Cozy gastro-pub on a working-class block in Bridgeport.

Home Bistro (p116) Nouveau comfort food in Boystown's center.

Drinking & Nightlife

Chicagoans love to hang out in drinking establishments. Blame it on the long winter, when folks need to huddle together somewhere warm. Blame it on summer, when sunny days make beer gardens and sidewalk patios so splendid. Whatever the reason, drinking in the city is a widely cherished civic pastime.

Beer

Chicago has long been a beer-drinking town. You can get a bottle of rank-and-file favorites Pabst and Old Style, but an explosion of craft brewers means you can drink much better. Watch the taps for Half Acre, Revolution, 5 Rabbit, Metropolitan, Two Brothers and 3 Floyds, all brewed locally.

Cocktails

The craft cocktail craze is in full swing. Mixologists do their thing using small-batch liqueurs and fresh-squeezed juices. It may sound pretentious, but most of the bars are actually pretty cool.

How to Find a Real Chicago Bar

To discover classic, character-filled bars on your own, look for the following: an Old Style beer sign swinging out front; a well-worn dartboard and/or pool table inside; patrons wearing ballcaps with the logos of the Cubs, White Sox, Bears or Blackhawks; and sports on TV.

Clubs

Clubs cluster in three main areas: River North and West Loop, where the venues tend to be huge and luxurious, with dress codes; Wicker Park and Ukie Village, where they're typically more casual; and Wrigleyville and Boystown, where they fall somewhere in between. Most clubs use social media to provide discounts on admission, so check before heading out.

Drinking & Nightlife by Neighborhood

➡ **The Loop** Rooftop hotel bars, Riverwalk cafes, not much after 10pm. (p61)

➡ **Near North & Navy Pier** Scores of options from dives to champagne bars; also a club hub. (p78)

➡ **Gold Coast** Martini lounges for folks on the prowl. (p91)

➡ **Lincoln Park & Old Town** Student saloons around Lincoln and Halsted Sts; quirky gems in Old Town. (p104)

➡ **Lake View & Wrigleyville** Sports bars around Wrigley Field, dance clubs in Boystown. (p118)

➡ **Andersonville & Uptown** Awesome beer bars and low-key LGBT drinkeries. (p132)

➡ **Wicker Park, Bucktown & Ukrainian Village** Cocktail lounges and wine bars, peppered with mom-and-pop joints. (p146)

➡ **Logan Square & Humboldt Park** Hipster dive bars, microbreweries, gin lounges and tiki bars. (p161)

➡ **Near West Side & Pilsen** Fancy cocktails in West Loop, artist hangouts in Pilsen. (p174)

➡ **South Loop & Near South Side** Neighborhood pubs, patios and taprooms. (p187)

➡ **Hyde Park & South Side** Sip alongside locals in Bridgeport. (p203)

NEED TO KNOW

Opening Hours

➡ Bars: 5pm to 2am (3am on Saturday); some licensed until 4am (5am on Saturday).

➡ Nightclubs: 10pm to 4am; often closed Monday through Wednesday.

Tipping

Per round 15%, minimum per drink $1.

Door Policies

➡ Some clubs don't allow blue jeans, tennis shoes or baseball caps. However, there are also many places where you can come as you are.

➡ The drinking age is 21. Take your driver's license or passport out at night: you will be asked for ID.

Credit Cards

Most bars and clubs will run a tab on your credit card, though small neighborhood taverns may be cash only.

Average Costs

➡ Bottle of Old Style beer: $3

➡ Pint of local microbrew: $6

➡ Glass of wine: $8

➡ Craft cocktail: $13

➡ Cup of coffee: $2.50

Websites

➡ **Chicago Reader** (www.chicagoreader.com) Bar and club listings.

Lonely Planet's Top Choices

Old Town Ale House (p104) Trendy tipplers and grizzled regulars sip under bawdy paintings.

Revolution Brewing (p161) Industrial-chic brewpub pouring righteous ales.

Signature Lounge (p91) Ascend to the Hancock Center's 96th floor and gawp.

RM Champagne Salon (p174) Twinkling West Loop spot that feels like a Parisian cafe.

Best Beer

Delilah's (p104) Spirited punk bar with all kinds of odd ales (and whiskeys too).

Forbidden Root (p147) Botanical brewery making eclectic beer from roots, spices and flowers.

Map Room (p146) Globe-laden tavern with 200 worldly brews.

Half Acre Tap Room (p118) Local craft brewer that cooks up fine suds.

Maria's Packaged Goods & Community Bar (p203) Artsy neighborhood gathering spot with excellent microbrews.

Best Cocktails

Violet Hour (p146) Beard Award–winning cocktails in a hidden bar.

Matchbox (p147) Teensy space with big gimlets.

Aviary (p174) Molecular gastronomy applied to booze.

Lost Lake (p161) Cool, refreshing tiki concoctions.

Billy Sunday (p161) Impeccable libations and Things in Jars.

Best Local Scene

Simon's (p132) Neighborhood stalwart with a ballsy jukebox and Swedish spiced wine in winter.

Happy Village (p147) Festive boozing and camaraderie playing table tennis.

Skylark (p175) Where Pilsen's underground goes for cheap drinks and tater tots.

Clark Street Ale House (p78) Join postshift workers over pretzels and microbrews in the back beer garden.

Best Views

Cindy's (p62) Loop rooftop with vistas of Millennium Park.

J Parker (p105) The lake and skyline look sweet from this Lincoln Park rooftop.

Cyrano's Cafe & Wine Bar (p62) Riverside tables to watch boats gliding by.

Best Dance Clubs

Smart Bar (p119) Intimate club that's serious about its DJs.

Late Bar (p161) Groovy, new-wave club that draws an uber-mixed crowd.

Berlin (p120) Welcome-one, welcome-all space to dance your ass off.

Best Sports Bars

Sluggers (p120) Sidestep the Cubs revelers and head for the batting cages.

Murphy's Bleachers (p120) Traditional watering hole steps from Wrigley Field's bleacher seats.

Best Coffee

Intelligentsia Coffee (p62) Local roaster known for strong java.

Dollop (p78) Baristas do caffeinated wonders in the sunny space.

Entertainment

Finding something to do in Chicago on any given night is effortless, and the spectrum of entertainment that's available in every price range is overwhelming. Just flip through the city's news weekly, the Reader, with its pages of theater openings and concert announcements, and Chicagoans' insatiable appetite for nocturnal amusement becomes apparent.

Music

Blues and jazz have deep roots in Chicago, and indie rock clubs slouch on almost every corner. Besides mega-bashes such as Blues Fest, Lollapalooza and Pitchfork, the following are a must for any music fan's calendar:

Riot Fest (www.riotfest.org) Big-name punk bands scream in Douglas Park for three days in mid-September.

Hideout Block Party (www.hideoutchicago.com) The taste-making indie rock club hosts a two-day party in early September with the hippest of bands.

World Music Festival Musicians from around the globe descend for two weeks of performances, anchored by the Chicago Cultural Center (p52). Held in mid-September.

Theater

Beyond the flashy Theater District in the Loop, Chicago has many adventurous small stages known as 'off-Loop' theaters. Keep an eye out for troupes such as **Theater Oobleck** (www.theateroobleck.com) and House Theatre (p148).

Film

Movies in the Parks is a summer tradition. The Chicago Park District (www.chicagopark district.com) has the nightly schedule. The **Chicago International Film Festival** (www. chicagofilmfestival.com) is the city's star event; it rolls in October.

Entertainment by Neighborhood

➡ **The Loop** The neon-lit Theater District, everything classical and free concerts in Millennium Park. (p62)

➡ **Near North & Navy Pier** Shakespeare, jazz and blues. (p79)

➡ **Gold Coast** Smattering of theater, jazz. (p92)

➡ **Lincoln Park & Old Town** Second City, iO improv, blues, outdoor theaters, indoor theaters. (p105)

➡ **Lake View & Wrigleyville** Heaps of rock, improv and little jazzy clubs. (p120)

➡ **Andersonville & Uptown** Historic venues like the Green Mill cluster in Uptown. (p133)

➡ **Wicker Park, Bucktown & Ukrainian Village** Best area for cool-cat rock clubs. (p148)

➡ **Logan Square & Humboldt Park** Artsy, far-reaching music and theater venues. (p162)

➡ **Near West Side & Pilsen** A nifty vintage concert hall in Pilsen. (p175)

➡ **South Loop & Near South Side** Big for blues, jazz and dance. (p188)

➡ **Hyde Park & South Side** A remote theater and a soul and funk venue in Hyde Park. (p204)

NEED TO KNOW

Ticket Shops

➜ **Hot Tix** (www.hottix. org) sells same-week drama, comedy and performing-arts tickets for half price (plus a $5 to $10 service charge). The selection is best early in the week.

➜ Book online or at the three Hot Tix outlets: 72 E Randolph St, 108 N State St (p66) and 163 E Pearson St (p92).

Websites

➜ **Chicago Reader** (www.chicagoreader. com) Great listings for music, arts and film.

➜ **Chicago Music** (www. chicagomusic.org) Tuneful listings across genres.

➜ **Broadway in Chicago** (www.broadwayin chicago.com) Touring show info.

➜ **See Chicago Dance** (www.seechicagodance. com) Covers all things dance-related.

➜ **Goldstar** (www. goldstar.com) Half-price offers from national ticket broker.

Lonely Planet's Top Choices

Green Mill (p133) Listen to jazz or a poetry slam while sipping martinis with Al Capone's ghost.

Hideout (p148) Feels like your grandma's basement but with alt-country bands and literary readings.

Buddy Guy's Legends (p188) The iconic bluesman's club puts the best bands on stage.

Second City (p105) The group that invented improv is still the best in the biz.

Metro (p120) Bands on the way up thrash here first.

Best Blues

Buddy Guy's Legends (p188) Sick licks fill the air day and night.

Rosa's Lounge (p162) Unvarnished joint where dedicated fans feel the blues.

BLUES (p106) Small, crackling club with seasoned local players.

Blue Chicago (p79) Handy Near North spot with good local acts.

Kingston Mines (p106) Hot and sweaty late-night venue with two stages jamming daily.

Best Jazz

Green Mill (p133) Big names in bebop at this timeless tavern.

Whistler (p162) Artsy little club where indie bands and jazz trios brood.

Jazz Showcase (p188) Elegant room where national acts blow their horns.

Constellation (p121) Intimate spot for progressive jazz and improvised music.

Best Rock

Metro (p120) Cool buzz bands smash through sets.

Empty Bottle (p148) Go-to club for edgy indie rock.

Lincoln Hall (p106) Indie bands love to play the intimate room with pristine acoustics.

Best Comedy

Second City (p105) The improv bastion that's launched many a jokester's career.

iO Theater (p105) This good-time, four-theater improv house has sent many on to stardom.

Annoyance Theatre (p121) Naughty and absurd shows for late-night chuckles.

CSz Theater (p121) Two teams compete for your laughs.

Best Theater

Steppenwolf Theatre (p105) Drama club of Malkovich, Sinise and other Hollywood stars.

Goodman Theatre (p63) Excellent new and classic American plays.

Neo-Futurists (p133) Original works make you ponder.

Best Classical & Opera

Grant Park Orchestra (p62) Everyone's favorite group to picnic with at Pritzker Pavilion.

Chicago Symphony Orchestra (p63) World-renowned, with a smokin' brass section.

Lyric Opera (p63) High Cs in a chandeliered venue.

Best Dance

SummerDance (p188) Locals come out for free world music concerts and dance lessons.

Hubbard Street Dance Chicago (p63) Foremost modern troupe in town.

Joffrey Ballet (p64) Famed dancers leap through the classical repertoire.

Best Cinema

Music Box Theatre (p121) Art-house palace with a sense of humor.

Facets Multimedia (p106) Offbeat stuff you won't see anywhere else.

Shopping

From the glossy stores of the Magnificent Mile to the countercultural shops of Lake View to the indie designers of Wicker Park, Chicago is a shopper's destination. It has been that way from the get-go. After all, this is the city that birthed the department store and traditions such as the money-back guarantee, bridal registry and bargain basement.

Specialties

Music is big. Independent record stores flood Chicago's neighborhoods, supported by the thriving live-music scene in town. Vinyl geeks will find heaps of stacks to flip through. Vintage and thrift fashions are another claim to fame. Folks here don't throw out their old bowling shirts, pillbox hats, faux-fur coats and costume jewelry. Instead, they deposit used duds at vintage or secondhand stores, of which there are heaps. Art- and architecture-related items are another Chicago specialty.

Locally Made Wares

Several stores proffer handbags, pendants, dresses and journals that city artisans have stitched, sewed and glue-gunned themselves. You're pretty much guaranteed a one-of-a-kind item to take home. The Indie Designer Market (inside the massive Randolph Street Market) is the epicenter of such craftiness.

Chicago-Style Fashion

It's difficult to find 'Chicago style' fashions to take home, mostly because there isn't a distinct Chicago style. If anything, it's casual, comfortable and defined by cold weather. That's not to say there aren't trendsetters. Thanks to the Art Institute and its fashion program, a lot of budding designers do their own thing. Shops like Logan Square's Wolf-bait & B-girls carry their wares.

Shopping by Neighborhood

➡ **The Loop** National chains, plus souvenir and arts-and-crafts winners. (p65)

➡ **Near North & Navy Pier** Home to the Magnificent Mile, lined with sleek big-name retailers. (p79)

➡ **Gold Coast** Oak St offers luxury brand boutiques, while malls rise on Michigan Ave. (p93)

➡ **Lincoln Park & Old Town** Urban living chains throng Halsted and Clybourn Sts; posh shops around Armitage Ave. (p107)

➡ **Lake View & Wrigleyville** Shops for kitschy hipsters and rock-and-roll types around Clark and Belmont Sts; naughty stuff in Boystown. (p122)

➡ **Andersonville & Uptown** Quality antiques, fashion and locally made wares along Clark St. (p133)

➡ **Wicker Park, Bucktown & Ukrainian Village** Vintage, hip fashion, book and record shops on Milwaukee Ave; crafters on Division St. (p149)

➡ **Logan Square & Humboldt Park** Far-flung indie shops with stylish goods for hipsters. (p162)

➡ **Near West Side & Pilsen** Where the markets are, plus funky vintage shops in Pilsen. (p175)

➡ **South Loop & Near South Side** Student-made arts in the South Loop; inexpensive homewares and trinkets in Chinatown. (p189)

➡ **Hyde Park & South Side** Bookstores galore. (p204)

NEED TO KNOW

Opening Hours

➜ Shops: 11am to 7pm Monday to Saturday, noon to 6pm Sunday.

➜ Malls: 10am to 8pm or 9pm Monday to Saturday, 11am to 6pm Sunday.

Taxes

Sales tax on goods (excluding food) is 10.25%.

Websites

➜ **Chicago Magazine** (www.chicagomag.com/ style-shopping) Publishes a roundup of sales and new store openings on a week-by-week basis via its 'sales check' newsletter.

Lonely Planet's Top Choices

Chicago Architecture Foundation Shop (p65) Pick up a mini Willis Tower model or skyline poster.

Strange Cargo (p122) Huge array of iconic T-shirt iron-ons, from Coach Ditka to a Chicago-style hot-dog diagram.

Quimby's (p149) Ground zero for comics, zines and underground culture.

Logan Hardware (p162) Awesome vinyl, plus vintage arcade games to get your *Donkey Kong* on.

Woolly Mammoth Antiques & Oddities (p133) That jar of old dentures? Here, beside the stuffed wallaby.

Best Music

Dusty Groove (p149) Killer stacks of vinyl hold rare soul and funk beats.

Reckless Records (p149) Great place to get the scoop on local indie rock bands.

Dave's Records (p107) *Rolling Stone* magazine dubbed it one of the nation's best stores.

Best Souvenirs

Art Institute of Chicago (p49) Posters and note cards of the collection's masterpieces.

Garrett Popcorn (p79) The sweet and salty mix will haunt your dreams.

Sports World (p123) Heavy on Cubs gear, but other Chicago teams get their dues, too.

Best Fashion & Vintage

Una Mae's (p149) Emerge looking all Jackie O in your new old hat.

Knee Deep Vintage (p176) Groovy garb and homewares from the 1920s to the 1970s.

Wolfbait & B-girls (p162) Local designers sew wares on-site.

Best Books

Seminary Co-op Bookstore (p204) Brainy shop beloved by Nobel Prize winners.

57th Street Books (p204) Lose yourself in the labyrinth.

Open Books (p175) Welcoming used bookstore with a whopping selection.

Best Markets

Randolph Street Market (p176) Scads of antiques and indie designer wares in a festival ambience.

Maxwell Street Market (p176) Historic market for socks and hubcaps, now known for Mexican food stalls.

Handmade Market (p150) Monthly DIY crafters' fair held at a bar.

Best for Kids

American Girl Place (p93) Have tea and get a new hairdo with your doll.

Hershey's (p93) Chocolate, chocolate and more chocolate.

Wicker Park Secret Agent Supply Co (p149) Supercool gear for junior spies.

Lego Store (p93) So many cool things to build at the hands-on tables.

Best Arts & Crafts

ShopColumbia (p189) Goods from Columbia College's arty students.

Andersonville Galleria (p134) Three floors of craftiness from local indie vendors.

Greenheart Shop (p107) Ecofriendly, socially conscious wares from around the globe.

Sports & Activities

Chicago is a rabid sports town, and fans of the pro teams are famously die-hard. It's not all about passively watching sports, though. Chicago offers plenty of places to get active via its city-spanning shoreline, 26 beaches and 580 parks. After a long, cold winter, everyone goes outside to play.

Spectator Sports

The football-playing Bears ignite the most fervor. They're followed by baseball's cursed Cubs; basketball's try-hard Bulls; hockey's young, Stanley Cup–winning Blackhawks; the up-and-down White Sox, the second baseball team in town; and the soccer-playing Fire.

Water Sports

Visitors often don't realize Chicago is a beach town, thanks to mammoth Lake Michigan lapping its side. There are 26 official strands of sand patrolled by lifeguards in summer. Swimming is popular, though the water is pretty freaking cold. Beaches at Montrose and North Ave have rental places offering kayaks and stand-up paddleboards. Other kayak companies have set up shop along the Chicago River.

Cycling

The flat, 18-mile lakefront trail is a beautiful ride along the water, though on nice days it's jam-packed. The trail starts at Hollywood Ave and rolls all the way down to 71st St. The **Active Transportation Alliance** (www.activetrans. org) publishes a bike trail map and provides local trail condition updates. **Chicago Critical Mass** (www.facebook.com/ChicagoCriticalMass) sponsors popular, traffic-disrupting rides in several neighborhoods.

Running

Tons of runners use the lakefront trail and paths in Lincoln Park. **The Chicago Area Runners Association** (www.cararuns.org) has the lowdown on races and free daily fun runs around town.

Sports & Activities by Neighborhood

➡ **The Loop** Cycling, ice-skating and kayaking options; free workouts in Millennium Park. (p66)

➡ **Near North & Navy Pier** Bike rentals near Navy Pier. (p80)

➡ **Gold Coast** Busy Oak St Beach fringes the skyscrapers; kayaking at the neighborhood's western edge. (p94)

➡ **Lincoln Park & Old Town** The masses play in Lincoln Park and at North Avenue Beach. (p108)

➡ **Lake View & Wrigleyville** Pro baseball at Wrigley Field, plus bowling and golfing. (p124)

➡ **Andersonville & Uptown** Montrose Beach is the surfing and skateboarding hot spot. (p134)

➡ **Wicker Park, Bucktown & Ukrainian Village** The 606 trail rambles along a repurposed train track, perfect for walking or cycling. (p137)

➡ **Logan Square & Humboldt Park** The 606 trail continues here, plus walking paths in Humboldt Park.

➡ **Near West Side & Pilsen** Pro basketball and hockey at United Center. (p177)

➡ **South Loop & Near South Side** Pro football and sledding at Soldier Field, walking and cycling paths on Northerly Island. (p189)

➡ **Hyde Park & South Side** Pro baseball at US Cellular Field; beaches and lagoon-filled Jackson Park. (p204)

NEED TO KNOW

Opening Hours

➡ Parks: 6am to 11pm.

➡ Beaches: 11am to 7pm late May to early September for swimming; same hours as parks otherwise.

Tickets

You can try to buy tickets to games direct from team websites or stadiums, or from scalpers outside the venues. Or you can try online providers; some charge an inconvenient 'convenience' fee.

➡ **Ticketmaster** (www. ticketmaster.com)

➡ **TicketExchange by Ticketmaster** (www. ticketexchangebyticket master.com)

➡ **StubHub** (www.stub hub.com)

➡ **Goldstar** (www.gold star.com)

➡ **Craigslist** (https:// chicago.craigslist.org)

Websites

➡ **Chicago Beaches** (www.cpdbeaches.com) Info on swim advisories due to currents or water pollution.

➡ **Chicago Park District** (www.chicagopark district.com) Lowdown on all the parks and their facilities and events.

➡ **Chicago Park District Golf** (www.cpdgolf.com) Book tee times.

Lonely Planet's Top Choices

Chicago Cubs (p124) It's hard to beat a day at Wrigley Field, beer in hand in the sun-splashed bleachers.

The 606 (p137) Elevated trail rambles along a repurposed train track through Wicker Park and Logan Square.

McCormick Tribune Ice Rink (p46) Sublime skating set between 'the Bean' and Michigan Ave.

Bobby's Bike Hike (p262) Friendly guides lead the way on South Side and hot-dog-eating rides.

Montrose Beach (p134) Lovely stretch of sand, surf, dunes and a beach bar.

Best Bike Rides

Bobby's Bike Hike (p262) Groovy tours for children, and pizza and beer lovers.

Bike Chicago (p262) Excellent tours from Lincoln Park to Obama's house.

Divvy (p262) Stations around the city rent bicycles for quick trips.

Best Beaches

Montrose Beach (p134) Bird-watching and kitesurfing add to the usual beachy sports.

North Avenue Beach (p108) Party time at the boathouse and on the volleyball courts.

63rd St Beach (p205) Regal beach house and fun fountains for kids.

Oak Street Beach (p94) Sandbox in the shadow of skyscrapers.

Best Paddling

Wateriders (p94) Slither past downtown's skyscrapers on a river kayaking tour.

Kayak Chicago (p134) Learn to paddleboard at Montrose Beach.

Urban Kayaks (p66) Rentals and fireworks tours launch downtown from the Riverwalk.

Best Winter Activities

McCormick Tribune Ice Rink (p66) The city's most popular and atmospheric rink.

Maggie Daley Park (p53) The ice ribbon makes for fine skating.

Sledding Hill (p190) Big slope by Soldier Field with snowmaking machine.

Best Golf

Diversey Driving Range (p108) Hit buckets of balls in Lincoln Park.

Sydney R Marovitz Golf Course (p124) Nine-hole course with killer skyline views.

Jackson Park Golf Course (p205) The only city-run course with 18 holes.

GLOW IMAGES, INC/GETTY IMAGES ©

Gay & Lesbian Chicago

Exploring kinky artifacts in the Leather Archives & Museum, or playing a game of naughty Twister at a rollicking street fair? Shopping for gay literature, or clubbing alongside male go-go dancers? Chicago's flourishing gay and lesbian scene in party-hearty Boystown and easygoing Andersonville offers plenty of choices.

Festivals

The main event on the calendar is the **Pride Parade** (http://chicagopride.gopride.com), held the last Sunday in June. It winds through Boystown and attracts more than 800,000 risqué revelers. **Northalsted Market Days** (www.northalsted.com), another wild time in Boystown, is a steamy two-day street fair in mid-August. Crafty, incense-wafting vendors line Halsted St, but most folks come for the drag queens in feather boas, Twister games played in the street and disco divas (Gloria Gaynor!) on the main stage. The **Interna-**

tional Mr Leather (www.imrl.com) contest brings out lots of men in, well, leather, in late May. Workshops and parties take place around town, with the main event happening at a downtown hotel or theater.

Museums & Tours

The **Leather Archives & Museum** (☏773-761-9200; www.leatherarchives.org; 6418 N Greenview Ave; $10; ⊗11am-7pm Thu & Fri, to 5pm Sat & Sun; ▣22) holds all sorts of fetish and S&M artifacts, from the Red Spanking Bench to the painting *Last Supper in a Leather Bar with Judas Giving Christ the Finger*. It's inside a

NEED TO KNOW

Opening Hours

➡ Bars: 11am to 2am (3am on Saturday), some bars until 4am (5am on Saturday).

➡ Clubs: 9pm to 2am (3am on Saturday), some clubs until 4am (5am on Saturday).

Websites

➡ **Windy City Times** (www.windy citymediagroup.com) LGBT newspaper, published weekly. Website is the main source for events and entertainment.

➡ **Purple Roofs** (www.purpleroofs.com) Website listing queer accommodations, travel agencies and tours.

➡ **Chances Dances** (www.chances dances.org) Organizes queer dance parties at clubs around town.

repurposed synagogue north of Andersonville. Chicago Greeter (p264) offers free, guided sightseeing trips through the city's gay neighborhoods. You must reserve at least 10 days in advance.

Theater

Keep an eye out for **About Face Theatre** (📞773-784-8565; www.aboutfacetheatre.com), an itinerant ensemble that stages plays dealing with gay and lesbian themes at theaters around Chicago. Comedies, dramas and musicals all get their due. It's well regarded and has won Jeff Awards (sort of like the local Tony Award) for its work.

Community Center

The mod, glassy Center on Halsted (p113) is the Midwest's largest LGBT community center. It's mostly a social service organization for locals, but visitors can use the free wi-fi and reading library, plus there's a Whole Foods grocery store inside.

Gay & Lesbian by Neighborhood

➡ **Lake View & Wrigleyville** Home to Boystown, dense with bars and clubs on N Halsted St between Belmont Ave and Grace St. (p113)

➡ **Andersonville & Uptown** Chicago's other main area of LGBT bars, but in a more relaxed, less party-oriented scene. (p132)

Pride Parade (p37)

Lonely Planet's Top Choices

Big Chicks (p132) Super-friendly, all-inclusive bar with cheap drinks, a beer garden and rockin' weekend DJs.

Sidetrack (p120) Thumping dance music, show tune sing-alongs and prime people-watching.

Hamburger Mary's (p132) Cabaret, karaoke, burgers and a booze-soaked outdoor patio for good times.

Unabridged Bookstore (p123) Shelves of gay fiction and queer spirituality.

Spyner's (p120) A lady-heavy dive bar that shines during karaoke nights.

Best Bars

Big Chicks (p132) It's often called the friendliest gay bar in Chicago.

Hamburger Mary's (p132) Swill the housemade brews and watch the action from the patio.

Crew (p132) One of the few sports bars that also hosts underwear contests for guys.

Best Dance Clubs

Sidetrack (p120) It's massive and packed with frisky boys in tight jeans.

Berlin (p120) For more than three decades it's been where party people dance until the wee hours.

Hydrate (p120) Guys, just take off your shirt and boogie.

Best Shops

Unabridged Bookstore (p123) Well-curated stacks on hard-to-find LGBT topics; good sci-fi, too.

Women & Children First (p134) Feminist-focused tomes, children's books and big-name author readings.

Egoist Underwear (p123) Naughty knickers including a sublime selection of G-strings.

Best Restaurants

Home Bistro (p116) Bring your own wine and settle in for nouveau comfort food in Boystown's center.

Tweet (p129) Decadent organic breakfasts next door to Big Chicks bar.

Best for Lesbians

Spyner's (p120) Get ready to belt out that Alanis Morissette tune after a few brews.

Closet (p120) A small, laid-back bar for ladies until the boys crash late night.

Best Gay Stays

Best Western Hawthorne Terrace (p227) Reasonably priced hotel steps from Boystown's main vein.

Villa Toscana (p227) Silky B&B on Halsted St, smack in Boystown's midst.

PLAN YOUR TRIP GAY & LESBIAN CHICAGO

Explore Chicago

CHICAGO'S TOP SIGHTS

Neighborhoods at a Glance

W Peterson Ave

Rosehill Cemetery

ANDERSONVILLE

6

Edens Expwy

W Foster Ave

East River Park

W Lawrence Ave

LINCOLN SQUARE

UPTOWN

Waveland Park

W Irving Park Rd

Horner Park

W Montrose Ave

W Addison St

W Belmont Ave

WRIGLEYVILLE

5 ◉ *Wrigley Field*

LAKE VIEW

Lake Michigan

S Kedzie Ave

N Western Ave

N Lincoln Ave

N Milwaukee Ave

N Clybourn Ave

W Fullerton Ave

Hanson Park

LOGAN SQUARE

8

BUCKTOWN

John F Kennedy Expwy

North Branch Chicago River

4

LINCOLN PARK

N Lake Shore Dr

W Grand Ave

W North Ave

WICKER PARK

HUMBOLDT PARK

7

Lincoln Park ◉

OLD TOWN

Goose Island

360° Chicago

3

OAK PARK

W Chicago Ave

UKRAINIAN VILLAGE

W Grand Ave

NEAR NORTH

2 ◉ *Navy Pier*

🏛 *Museum of Contemporary Art*

Lake St

WEST LOOP

THE LOOP

Millennium Park

Columbus Park

W Madison St

GREEKTOWN

◉

1

S Central Ave

Eisenhower Expwy

S Ogden Ave

LITTLE ITALY

Willis Tower

Art Institute of Chicago

W Roosevelt Rd

Douglas Park

9

Field Museum of Natural History 🏛

MUSEUM CAMPUS

W Cermak Rd

W Ogden Ave

S Kedzie Ave

PILSEN

10

CICERO

S Cicero Ave

Sanitary Drainage and Ship Canal

W Cermak Rd

CHINATOWN

Adlai Stevenson Expwy

McKinley Park

S Archer Ave

W 31st St

W 35th St

BRONZEVILLE

S Martin Luther King Jr Dr

S Lake Shore Dr

BRIDGEPORT

W Pershing Rd

11

S Archer Ave

W 47th St

Dan Ryan Expwy

S Drexel Blvd

KENWOOD

W 55th St

Sherman Park

W Garfield Blvd

Washington Park

HYDE PARK

E 55th St

Museum of Science & Industry 🏛

W 59th St

Robie House ◉

N 0 — 5 km / 0 — 2.5 miles

① The Loop p44

The Loop is Chicago's center of action, named for the elevated train tracks that lasso its streets. The Art Institute, Willis Tower, Theater District and Millennium Park are top draws among the skyscrapers. The city's biggest festivals also rock the area.

② Near North & Navy Pier p67

The Near North packs in hotels, deep-dish pizza parlors, art galleries and so many upscale stores that its main vein – Michigan Ave – has been dubbed the 'Magnificent Mile.' Navy Pier unfurls a half-mile-long wharf of tour boats and carnival rides.

③ Gold Coast p81

The Gold Coast has been the address of Chicago's wealthiest residents for more than 125 years. The cloud-poking 360° Chicago and provocative Museum of Contemporary Art are the top attention grabbers. At night, Rush St entertains with swanky steakhouses and piano lounges.

④ Lincoln Park & Old Town p95

Lincoln Park – the green space – is the city's premier playground of lagoons, footpaths, beaches and zoo animals. Lincoln Park – the surrounding neighborhood – adds topnotch restaurants and lively music clubs to the mix. Next door, stylish Old Town hangs on to its free-spirited past with artsy bars and improv-comedy bastion Second City.

⑤ Lake View & Wrigleyville p109

Wrigley Field, both cursed and hallowed, draws baseball pilgrims. The bar-filled neighborhood around it parties hard and collides with the rainbow banners of Boystown, the nearby gay district. Kicky eateries and shops cater to the masses.

⑥ Andersonville & Uptown p125

Vestiges of Andersonville's Swedish past remain, but today the area is about foodie taverns, funky boutiques, and gay and lesbian bars. Uptown offers historic jazz houses like the Green Mill (Al Capone's fave), along with the thriving eateries of 'Little Saigon.'

⑦ Wicker Park, Bucktown & Ukrainian Village p135

These three neighborhoods are hot property. Hipster record stores, thrift shops and cocktail lounges have shot up, though vintage Eastern European dive bars linger on many street corners. The restaurant and rock-club scene is unparalleled.

⑧ Logan Square & Humboldt Park p152

Logan Square is Chicago's current 'it' neighborhood, the place to go for the hippest tiki lounge or all-the-rage fried-chicken cafe. Gastronoms flock to Michelin-starred Parachute and Longman & Eagle, plus several other hot spots. Puerto Rican stronghold Humboldt Park is the place to sample a *jibarito,* the local sandwich specialty.

⑨ Near West Side & Pilsen p163

The meatpacking West Loop buzzes with hot-chef restaurants and on-trend bars. Development continues here big-time. Greektown and Little Italy serve ethnic fare nearby. In Pilsen, Mexican culture mixes with Chicago's bohemian underground, and colorful murals, taquerias and cafes result.

⑩ South Loop & Near South Side p178

In the South Loop, the Field Museum, Shedd Aquarium and Adler Planetarium huddle at the Museum Campus. Historic buildings dot the area, including Chess Records, the seminal blues label. Chinatown bustles with noodle shops and exotic wares.

⑪ Hyde Park & South Side p191

Brainy Hyde Park holds bookstores galore and sights like Frank Lloyd Wright's Robie House and the Museum of Science & Industry. Irish enclave Bridgeport has blossomed with bars and galleries, while Bronzeville has architecture and jazzy African American–history shrines.

The Loop

Neighborhood Top Five

❶ Millennium Park (p46) Exploring this arty park, where freebies beckon all day long, from morning yoga classes to afternoon splashes in Crown Fountain and evening concerts at Frank Gehry's swooping silver band shell.

❷ Art Institute of Chicago (p49) Admiring color-swirled Monets, Renoirs and one very big Seurat, plus unexpected delights such as the miniature rooms and glass paperweight collection.

❸ Chicago Architecture Foundation (p53) Gaping at sky-high ingenuity on an architecture tour by boat or on foot.

❹ Willis Tower (p51) Stepping onto the glass-floored ledge and peering a longgg way down.

❺ Chicago Cultural Center (p52) Popping in to see free art exhibitions, concerts and the world's largest Tiffany glass dome.

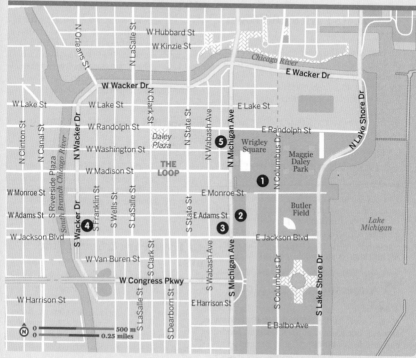

For more detail of this area see Map p286 ➡

Explore The Loop

The Loop is Chicago's hub – its financial and historic heart – and it pulses with energy. Tumultuous tides of pin-striped businessfolk rush the sidewalks, while clattering El trains roar overhead. Above the melee, a towering forest of steel and stone soaks in the sun (or snow, as the case may be).

But it's not all work, work, work here. The Loop is also Chicago's favorite playground. Grant Park unfurls as a sprawling green buffer between the skyscrapers and Lake Michigan. Millennium Park is Grant's crown jewel, sparkling in the northwest corner. Both host bashes galore, especially in summer, when everything from Blues Fest and Lollapalooza to the Grant Park Orchestra makes sweet music for the masses.

The Loop is also home to big-ticket attractions such as the Art Institute, the neon-lit Theater District and the city's world-famous architecture and public art. So count on spending significant time in the neighborhood. Take in the parks, art and cloud-scraping towers by day, then see a theater show or free Millennium Park concert at night. Despite the evening entertainment, the Loop clears out by 9pm or so.

Local Life

→ **Amish donuts** Downtown workers throng the Thursday farmers market at Daley Plaza (p52). Keep an eye out for the Amish ladies who tempt passersby to their baked-goods stand with offers of free donuts.

→ **German fests** It's tradition to visit the Berghoff (p61) in December when it's festooned with old-world Christmas decorations. It's also a ritual to *prost* beers during Berghoff's Oktoberfest, which takes over the plaza at Adams and Dearborn Sts in mid-September.

→ **Happy-hour hangout** Off-duty office workers and the occasional local TV reporter can be found in Monk's Pub (p61) when the day is done.

→ **Hidden falafel** Middle Eastern restaurant Oasis (p60) is a local secret, tucked away behind diamond sellers in the jewelers' mall.

Getting There & Away

→ **El** All lines converge in the Loop. Clark/Lake is a useful transfer station between them all. Randolph station is handy for the parks, Quincy station for Willis Tower.

→ **Metra** Trains going south to Hyde Park and on into Indiana depart from Millennium Station; most other regional trains depart from Ogilvie or Union Stations.

→ **Car** Meters cost $6.50 per hour. Parking lots cost around $40 per day. **Millennium Park Garage** (www.millenniumgarages.com; 5 S Columbus Dr; per 3/24hr $28/35) is one of the cheapest.

Lonely Planet's Top Tip

Pack a picnic and meander over to Millennium Park to hear a free concert. Indie rock, jazz or classical performers take the stage nightly, including many big-name musicians. Pastoral (p60) and Toni Patisserie (p61) can set you up with deli goods and wine.

 Best Places to Eat

→ Gage (p61)

→ Nando's Peri-Peri (p58)

→ Cafecito (p58)

→ Pastoral (p60)

→ Pizano's (p60)

→ Oasis (p60)

For reviews, see p58 →

 Best Places to Drink

→ Berghoff (p61)

→ Toni Patisserie & Cafe (p61)

→ Monk's Pub (p61)

→ Cindy's (p62)

For reviews, see p61 →

☆ **Best Entertainment**

→ Grant Park Orchestra (p62)

→ Hubbard Street Dance Chicago (p63)

→ Goodman Theatre (p63)

→ Lyric Opera of Chicago (p63)

For reviews, see p62 →

THE LOOP

TOP SIGHT
MILLENNIUM PARK

Chicago's showpiece shines with whimsical public art. Where to start amid the mod designs? Pritzker Pavilion, Frank Gehry's swooping silver band shell? Jaume Plensa's Crown Fountain, with its human gargoyles? Anish Kapoor's silvery sculpture *Cloud Gate* (aka 'the Bean')? Or maybe someplace away from the crowds, like the veiled Lurie Garden abloom with prairie flowers.

The Magic Bean

The park's biggest draw is 'the Bean' – officially titled *Cloud Gate* – Anish Kapoor's 110-ton, silver-drop sculpture. It reflects both the sky and the skyline, and everyone clamors around to take a picture and to touch its silvery smoothness. Good vantage points for photos are at the sculpture's northern and southern ends. For great people-watching, go up the stairs on Washington St, on the Park Grill's northern side, where there are shady benches.

The Bean wasn't always so well-loved. Kapoor was still polishing and grinding the 168 stainless-steel plates that comprise the sculpture when the city first showed it to the public in 2004. The surface was supposed to be seamless – and it is now. But it wasn't then, and soon after its debut it went back under wraps. It didn't re-emerge until 2006.

Splashy Crown Fountain

Jaume Plensa's Crown Fountain is another crowd-pleaser. Its two, 50ft-high, glass-block towers contain video displays that flash a thousand different faces. The people shown are all native Chicagoans and they all agreed to strap into Plensa's special dental chair, where he immobilized their heads for filming. Each mug puckers up and spurts water, just like

DON'T MISS

➡ Skyline photo with the Bean
➡ Getting wet in Crown Fountain
➡ Concert and picnic at Pritzker Pavilion
➡ Lurie Garden tour
➡ Winter ice-skating

PRACTICALITIES

➡ Map p286
➡ ☎312-742-1168
➡ www.millennium park.org
➡ 201 E Randolph St
➡ ⊙6am-11pm
➡ 👬
➡ Ⓜ Brown, Orange, Green, Purple, Pink Line to Randolph

the gargoyles atop Notre Dame Cathedral. A fresh set of nonpuckering faces appears in winter, when the fountain is dry.

On hot days the fountain crowds with locals splashing in the streams to cool off. Kids especially love it. Bring a towel to dry off.

Pritzker Pavilion

Pritzker Pavilion is Millennium Park's acoustically awesome band shell. Architect Frank Gehry designed it and gave it his trademark swooping silver exterior. Supposedly it's inspired by gefilte fish, a classic Jewish dish that as a child Gehry watched his grandma make every week; he was struck by the fish's shape and movement before she hacked it to death. The pipes that crisscross over the lawn are threaded with speakers, so that's where the sound comes from.

The pavilion hosts free concerts at 6:30pm most nights June to August. There's indie rock and new music on Monday, world music and jazz on Thursday, and classical music on Wednesday, Friday and Saturday. On Tuesday there's usually a movie beamed onto the huge screen on stage. Seats are available up close in the pavilion, or you can sit on the grassy Great Lawn that unfurls behind.

For all shows – but especially the classical ones, which the top-notch Grant Park Orchestra performs – folks bring blankets, picnics, wine and beer. There is nothing quite like sitting on the lawn, looking up through Gehry's wild grid and seeing all the skyscraping architecture that forms the backdrop *while* hearing the music. If you want a seat up close, arrive early.

The pavilion hosts daytime action, too. Concert rehearsals take place Tuesday to Friday, usually from 11am to 1pm, offering a taste of music if you can't catch the evening show. Each Saturday free exercise classes turn the Great Lawn into a groovy fitness center. Instructors backed by live music-makers lead tai chi at 7am, yoga at 8am, Pilates at 9am and Zumba dance at 10am.

The Secret Garden

If the crowds at the Bean, Crown Fountain and Pritzker Pavilion are too much, seek out the peaceful **Lurie Garden** (www.luriegarden.org), which uses native plants to form a botanical tribute to Illinois' tall-grass prairie. Visitors often miss the area, because it's hidden behind a big hedge. Yellow coneflowers, poet's daffodils, bluebells and other gorgeous blooms carpet the 5-acre oasis; everything is raised sustainably and without chemicals. A little river runs through it, where folks kick off their shoes and dangle their feet.

TOURS

Volunteers provide free walking tours of the park at 11:30am and 1pm daily from late May to mid-October. Departure is from the Chicago Cultural Center's visitor center, across the road at 77 E Randolph St. Space is limited to 10 people on a first-come, first-served basis.

Millennium Park is actually a rooftop garden – the world's largest, they say. A busy parking garage and Metra rail's Millennium Station lie underneath.

FAMILY FUN

The Family Fun Tent in the park's northwest corner offers free arts, crafts and games for kids from 10am to 2pm daily in summer.

Concessions, bathrooms and a gift shop are available at McCormick Tribune Plaza (by the outdoor cafe/ice rink) on Michigan Ave.

From mid-May to mid-September, volunteers lead free tours through the garden on Thursdays and Fridays between 11am and 1:15pm, and on Sundays between 11am and 2:15pm. They last 20 minutes and depart every 15 to 20 minutes. No reservations are required, just show up at the south end of the boardwalk. Staff also offer free workshops on topics such as how to make lip balm using herbs from the garden. These require advance registration; sign up online. The garden is at the park's southeastern end.

BP Bridge & Nichols Bridgeway

In addition to Pritzker Pavilion, Frank Gehry also designed the snaking **BP Bridge** (Map p286) that spans Columbus Dr. The luminous sheet-metal walkway connects Millennium Park (from the back of the Great Lawn) to the new Maggie Daley Park (p53), which has ice-skating and rock climbing among its activity arsenal. The bridge offers great skyline views, too.

The **Nichols Bridgeway** (Map p286) is another pedestrian-only span. Renzo Piano designed this silver beauty. It arches from the park over Monroe St to the Art Institute's 3rd-floor contemporary sculpture terrace (which is free to view). Piano, incidentally, also designed the museum's Modern Wing, which is where the sculpture terrace is located.

Cycling & Ice Skating

The **McDonald's Cycle Center** (239 E Randolph St; ⊘6:30am-7pm), in the park's northeastern corner near the intersection of Randolph St and Columbus Dr, is the city's main facility for bike commuters, with 300 bike-storage spaces plus showers. It's also a convenient place to pick up rental bikes from Bike Chicago (p66), including road, hybrid, tandem and children's bikes.

Tucked between the Bean sculpture and the twinkling lights of Michigan Ave, the McCormick Tribune Ice Rink (p66) fills with skaters in winter. It operates from late November to late February and it is hands down the city's most scenic rink. Admission is free; skate rental costs $12. In summer the rink morphs into the Park Grill's alfresco cafe.

Wrigley Square & Boeing Galleries

The big plaza at the corner of Michigan Ave and Randolph St is Wrigley Square. The Greek-looking structure rising up from it is the **Millennium Monument**. It is a replica of the original peristyle that stood here between 1917 and 1953. The semicircular row of Doric columns shoots up nearly 40ft. It juxtaposes oddly with the modern art throughout the rest of the park, but it's meant to tie past and present together. The lawn in front is dandy for lolling.

The two Boeing Galleries flank the park on the north and south sides. The outdoor spaces display changing exhibits of contemporary sculpture and photo-murals.

Park History

Millennium Park was originally slated to open in 2000 to coincide with the millennium (hence the name), but construction delays and escalating costs pushed it back. The whole thing seemed headed for disaster, since the original budget was $150 million, yet costs were rising far in excess of that. The final bill came to $475 million. Private donors – families such as the Pritzkers and Crowns, and corporate donors such as Boeing – ended up paying $200 million to complete the project.

TOP SIGHT
ART INSTITUTE OF CHICAGO

The second-largest art museum in the country, the Art Institute houses a treasure trove from around the globe. The collection of impressionist and post-impressionist paintings is second only to those in France, and the number of surrealist works is tremendous. The Modern Wing dazzles with Picassos and Mirós. Japanese prints, Grecian urns and suits of armor stuff endless rooms beyond.

Must-See Works: Floor 2

This floor is where the majority of the museum's celebrated highlights hang.

Get close enough to Georges Seurat's *A Sunday Afternoon on the Island of La Grande Jatte* (Gallery 201) for the painting to break down into its component dots and you'll see why it took Seurat two long years to complete his pointillist masterpiece. The painting sometimes resides in Gallery 240.

The Bedroom (Gallery 241) by Vincent van Gogh depicts the sleeping quarters of the artist's house in Arles. It's the second of three versions of the painting, executed during Van Gogh's 1889 stay at an asylum.

Claude Monet's *Stacks of Wheat* (Gallery 243) – paintings of the 15ft-tall stacks located by the artist's farmhouse in Giverny – were part of a series that effectively launched his career when they sold like hotcakes at a show he organized in 1891.

Nighthawks (Gallery 262), Edward Hopper's lonely, poignant snapshot of four solitary souls at a neon-lit diner, was inspired by a Greenwich Ave restaurant in Manhattan.

Grant Wood, a lifelong resident of Iowa, used his sister and his dentist as models for the two stern-faced farmers in his iconic painting *American Gothic* (Gallery 263).

DON'T MISS

➡ *American Gothic*
➡ *Nighthawks*
➡ *A Sunday Afternoon on the Island of La Grande Jatte*
➡ *America Windows*
➡ Lions guarding the entrance

PRACTICALITIES

➡ Map p286
➡ ☎312-443-3600
➡ www.artic.edu
➡ 111 S Michigan Ave
➡ adult/child $25/free
➡ ⊙10:30am-5pm Fri-Wed, to 8pm Thu
➡ 🛜🚻
➡ Ⓜ Brown, Orange, Green, Purple, Pink Line to Adams

LION SCULPTURES

The beloved lions guarding the entrance may seem identical, but they actually have different stances, expressions and measurements. Their creator, Edward Kemeys, described the south lion as closely watching something in the distance, while the north lion has his back up and is ready to spring. They remain regal and dignified, even when the museum plops fiberglass Blackhawks helmets on their heads when the team is in the Stanley Cup (or Bears helmets when the team is in the Super Bowl, etc).

The museum offers a full slate of children's programming. Stop by the Ryan Learning Center (on Level 1 in the Modern Wing) to see what hands-on activities staff are conducting.

Must-See Works: Floors 1 & 3

America Windows (Gallery 144) – huge, blue stained-glass pieces – were created by Marc Chagall to celebrate the USA's bicentennial.

The elongated figure of *The Old Guitarist* (Gallery 391) by Pablo Picasso is from the artist's Blue Period, reflecting not only Picasso's color scheme but his mindset as a poor, lonely artist in Paris in the early years.

Salvador Dalí's *Inventions of the Monsters* (Gallery 396) was painted in Austria immediately before the Nazi annexation. The title refers to a Nostradamus prediction that the apparition of monsters presages the outbreak of war. The artist's profile is visible in the lower left corner, along with that of his wife, Gala.

Other Intriguing Sights

The Thorne Miniature Rooms (Lower Level, Gallery 11) and Paperweight Collection (Lower Level, Gallery 15) are awesome, overlooked galleries. The Modern Wing, dazzling with natural light, allows works by Miró, Brancusi, Warhol and the like to shine and provides gallery space for new, cutting-edge multimedia work.

Outdoor Freebies

You can see a fair bit of art without even entering the museum. The north garden (enter from Michigan Ave) has Alexander Calder's *Flying Dragon*, a little buddy to his *Flamingo* (p53) in the Loop. The Stock Exchange Arch, a revered architectural relic, rises up on the museum's northeast side. The 3rd-floor contemporary sculpture terrace provides cool city views and connects to Millennium Park via the modern, pedestrian-only Nichols Bridgeway.

Top Tips

➡Allow two hours to browse the museum's highlights; art buffs should allocate much longer.

➡Advance tickets are available, but unless there's a blockbuster exhibit going on they're usually not necessary. The entrance queue moves fast.

➡Ask at the information desk about free talks and tours once you're inside.

➡Download the museum's free app, either at home or using the on-site wi-fi. It offers more than 50 tours through the collection (divided by theme, time available etc).

➡The museum's main entrance is on Michigan Ave, but you can also enter via the Modern Wing on Monroe St.

TOP SIGHT
WILLIS TOWER

For superlative seekers, Willis Tower is it: Chicago's tallest skyscraper, rising 1450ft into the heavens. Built in 1973 as the Sears Tower, the black-tubed behemoth reigned as the world's tallest building for almost 25 years. It still wins the prize for views from its 103rd-floor Skydeck, where glass-floored ledges jut out in midair and give a knee-buckling perspective straight down.

Before ascending, there are factoid-filled murals to ponder and a factoid-filled movie to watch. You'll learn about the 43,000 miles of phone cable used, the 2232 steps to the roof, and how the tower height is the equivalent of 313 Oprahs (or 262 Michael Jordans). Then it's time for the ear-popping, 70-second elevator ride to the top. From here, the entire city stretches below and you can see exactly how Chicago is laid out. On good days you can see for 40 to 50 miles, as far as Indiana, Michigan and Wisconsin. On hazy or stormy days you won't see much at all, so don't bother.

The four ledges are on the deck's west side. They're like glass-encased boxes hanging out from the building's frame. If crowds are light, you can sprawl out on one for the ultimate photo op. If the ledges crack – which they did in 2014 when some folks stepped on them – fear not: that's not the glass cracking, but the protective coating covering the 1.5-inch-thick glass. You won't fall. Really. So don't even think about it.

Fazlur Khan came up with the design of nine bundled tubes after looking at cigarettes in their pack. The structure lost its 'world's tallest' crown in 1996 to Malaysia's Petronas Twin Towers. It lost its 'USA's tallest' crown in 2013 to New York's One World Trade Center.

Avoid peak times in summer, between 11am and 4pm Friday to Sunday, when queues can surpass an hour.

DON'T MISS

➡ The ledges
➡ Sunset views
➡ Skyscraper trivia during the elevator ride
➡ Feeling the tower sway

PRACTICALITIES

➡ Map p286
➡ ☎312-875-9696
➡ www.theskydeck.com
➡ 233 S Wacker Dr
➡ adult/child $22/14
➡ ⊙9am-10pm Apr-Sep, 10am-8pm Oct-Mar
➡ Ⓜ Brown, Orange, Purple, Pink Line to Quincy

⊙ SIGHTS

MILLENNIUM PARK   PARK
See p46.

ART INSTITUTE OF CHICAGO   MUSEUM
See p49.

WILLIS TOWER   TOWER
See p51.

**CHICAGO CULTURAL
CENTER**   NOTABLE BUILDING
Map p286 (☏312-744-6630; www.chicagocul
turalcenter.org; 78 E Washington St; ⊙9am-7pm
Mon-Thu, to 6pm Fri & Sat, 10am-6pm Sun; 🛜;
Ⓜ Brown, Orange, Green, Purple, Pink Line to Randolph) **FREE** This block-long building houses
terrific art exhibitions (especially the 4th-
floor Yates Gallery), as well as jazz, classical and electronic-dance-music concerts
at lunchtime (12:15pm Monday, Wednesday and most Fridays). It also contains the
world's largest Tiffany stained-glass dome.
InstaGreeter tours of the Loop depart from
the Randolph St lobby (11am to 2pm Friday
through Sunday year-round), as do Millennium Park tours (11:30am and 1pm daily in
summer). And it's all free!

Oh, and there's more. Free foreign films
screen on Wednesday at 6:30pm from June
through September. StoryCorps' recording
studio (where folks tell their tale, get a CD
of it and have it preserved in the Library
of Congress) operates on Thursday (noon to
6pm) and Saturday (10am to 4pm). Check
the daily schedule posted at the entrances
(at both Randolph and Washington Sts) to
see what else is going on.

The exquisite, beaux-arts building began its life as the Chicago Public Library in
1897. The Gilded Age interior mixes white
Carrara and green Connemara marble
throughout. The gorgeous Tiffany dome is
on the 3rd floor, where the library circula-
tion desk used to be. The building's splen-
dor was meant to inspire the rabble toward
loftier goals. You can explore on your
own, or take a free building tour (1:15pm
Wednesday, Friday and Saturday), which
departs from the Randolph St lobby. There's
also free wi-fi and seating areas throughout
the building.

BUCKINGHAM FOUNTAIN   FOUNTAIN
Map p286 (301 S Columbus Dr; Ⓜ Red Line to Harrison) Grant Park's centerpiece is one of the
world's largest squirters, with a 1.5-million-
gallon capacity and a 15-story-high spray.
It lets loose on the hour from 9am to 11pm
mid-April to mid-October, accompanied at
night by multicolored lights and music.

Wealthy widow Kate Sturges Buckingham gave the magnificent structure to the
city in 1927 in memory of her brother, Clarence. She also wisely left an endowment
to maintain and operate it. The central
fountain symbolizes Lake Michigan, with
the four water-spouting sea creatures rep-
resenting the surrounding states.

DALEY PLAZA   PLAZA
Map p286 (50 W Washington St; Ⓜ Blue Line to
Washington) Picasso's eye-popping untitled
sculpture marks the heart of Daley Plaza,
which is the place to be come lunchtime,
particularly when the weather warms up.
You never know what will be going on –
dance performances, bands, ethnic festivals, holiday celebrations – but you do
know it'll be free. A farmers market sets up
on Thursdays (7am to 3pm) and food trucks
add to the action on Fridays (11am to 3pm,

LOCAL KNOWLEDGE

THE PEDWAY

Come wintertime, when the going gets tough and icy sleet knifes your face, head
down to the Pedway. Chicago has a 40-block labyrinth of underground walkways, built
in conjunction with the subway trains. The system isn't entirely connected (ie it would
be difficult to walk from one end of the Loop to the other underground), and you'll find
that you rise to the surface in the oddest places – say, an apartment building, a hotel
lobby or Macy's. The walkways are also hit-or-miss for amenities: some have coffee
shops and fast-food outlets tucked along the way, some have urine smells, but they're
an interesting place to soak up local life. The city posts 'Pedway' signs above ground
at points of entry. City Hall is a good place to dive under. Chicago Detours (p264) provides a free map to download from its website for DIY jaunts. The company also offers
guided excursions that include the passageways.

BEST PUBLIC ART

Several mind-blowing public artworks have popped up in the Loop over the decades. **Untitled** (Map p286; 50 W Washington St; M Blue Line to Washington) Pablo Picasso's work, which everyone just calls 'the Picasso,' is the granddaddy of Chicago's public art. The artist was 82 when the work was commissioned. The US Steel Works in Gary, Indiana, made it to Picasso's specifications and erected it in 1967 in Daley Plaza. When Chicago tried to pay Picasso for the work, he refused, saying the sculpture was meant as a gift to the city. At the time, many locals thought the abstract piece was hideous and should be torn down and replaced with a statue of Cubs legend Ernie Banks.

Miró's Chicago (Map p286; 69 W Washington St; M Blue Line to Washington) Originally called *The Sun, The Moon and One Star*, Joan Miró's monument sits across the street from Daley Plaza. Miró hoped to evoke the 'mystical force of a great earth mother' with the 40ft sculpture, made of various metals, cement and tile in 1981.

Monument with Standing Beast (Map p286; 100 W Randolph St; M Brown, Orange, Green, Purple, Pink, Blue Line to Clark/Lake) French sculptor Jean Dubuffet created this piece, which some call 'Snoopy in a Blender.' The 1984 white fiberglass work looks a little like inflated puzzle pieces and has a definite Keith Haring–esque feel to it. As you can see by the large number of kids crawling around inside, it's a hands-on piece of art.

Four Seasons (Map p286; 10 S Dearborn St; M Blue Line to Monroe) Russian-born artist Marc Chagall loved Chicago and in 1974 he donated this grand mosaic to the city. Using thousands of bits of glass and stone, the artist portrayed six scenes of the city in hues reminiscent of the Mediterranean coast of France, where he kept his studio. Chagall continued to make adjustments, such as updating the skyline, after the work arrived in Chicago.

Flamingo (Map p286; 50 W Adams St; M Blue Line to Jackson) Alexander Calder's soaring red-pink sculpture provides some much-needed relief from the stark facades of the federal buildings around it. Calder dedicated the sculpture in October 1974 by riding into the Loop on a bandwagon pulled by 40 horses, accompanied by a circus parade.

For the locations of more public artworks stashed around the city, check the website www.cityofchicago.org/publicart. And don't forget to visit the Bean (p46), the reigning Loop fave.

March to late October). City Hall rises to the plaza's west over Clark St.

Daley Plaza remains a pilgrimage site to many as the film location where the Blues Brothers drove through and crashed into the Daley Center's plate-glass windows.

MAGGIE DALEY PARK PARK

Map p286 (www.maggiedaleypark.com; 337 E Randolph St; ⊙6am-11pm; ⊕; M Brown, Orange, Green, Purple, Pink Line to Randolph) Families love the park's fanciful free playgrounds in all their enchanted-forest and pirate-themed glory. There's also a rock-climbing wall, 18-hole mini-golf course (which becomes an ice-skating ribbon in winter) and tennis courts; these features have fees. Multiple picnic tables make the park an excellent spot to relax. It connects to Millennium Park via the pedestrian BP Bridge.

CHICAGO ARCHITECTURE FOUNDATION GALLERY

Map p286 (CAF; ☑312-922-3432; www.architecture.org; 224 S Michigan Ave; ⊙9am-9pm, reduced hours in winter; M Brown, Orange, Green, Purple, Pink Line to Adams) **FREE** CAF is the premier keeper of Chicago's architectural flame. Dip in to check out the galleries in the atrium (behind the shop). The 'Chicago Model City' display provides a cool 3-D overview of local skyscrapers. You can also get the lowdown on CAF's extensive roster of boat and walking tours (p263) and make bookings; many tours depart from here.

The foundation's shop (p65) sells stacks of books about local buildings and architects if you prefer to do it yourself.

MONEY MUSEUM MUSEUM

Map p286 (☑312-322-2400; www.chicagofed. org; 230 S LaSalle St; ⊙8:30am-5pm Mon-Fri;

FAMOUS LOOP ARCHITECTURE

Ever since Chicago presented the world with the first skyscraper in 1885, it has thought big with its architecture and pushed the envelope of modern design. The Loop is ground zero for gawking.

Monadnock Building (Map p286; www.monadnockbuilding.com; 53 W Jackson Blvd; M Blue Line to Jackson) Architecture buffs go gaga at the Monadnock, two buildings in one that delineate a crucial juncture in skyscraper development. The north half is the older, traditional design from 1891 (with thick brick walls and a plain facade), while the south is the newer, more modern half (with a steel frame that allows for jazzier-looking walls and bigger windows).

Rookery (Map p286; www.flwright.org; 209 S LaSalle St; 9:30am-5:30pm Mon-Fri; M Brown, Orange, Purple, Pink Line to Quincy) The 1888 Rookery looks hulking and fortresslike outside, but it's light and airy inside thanks to Frank Lloyd Wright's atrium overhaul. Step inside and have a look. Tours ($7 to $12) are available at 11am and noon on weekdays. Pigeons used to roost here, hence the name.

Marshall Field Building (Map p286; 111 N State St; 10am-8pm Mon-Thu, to 9pm Sat, 11am-7pm Sun; M Brown, Orange, Green, Purple, Pink Line to Randolph) Weep all you want over the old Marshall Field's becoming Macy's; the building remains a classic no matter who's in it. The iconic bronze corner clocks on the outside have given busy Loop workers the time for more than 100 years now. Inside, a 6000-sq-ft dome designed by Louis Comfort Tiffany caps the north-side atrium; 50 artists toiled for 18 months to make it.

Sullivan Center (Map p286; www.thesullivancenter.com; 1 S State St; M Red Line to Monroe) Louis Sullivan designed this ornate building in 1899. For a century it was home to the Carson Pirie Scott & Co department store. Check out the superb metalwork around the main entrance at State and Madison Sts, and try to find Sullivan's initials amid the flowing botanical and geometric forms. A Target store now occupies the building's main space.

Marquette Building (Map p286; www.marquette.macfound.org; 140 S Dearborn St; 7am-10pm; M Blue Line to Monroe) The architects behind the Marquette Building made natural light and ventilation vital components. While that's nice, the most impressive features are the sculptured panels and mosaics that recall the exploits of French explorer Jacques Marquette; look for them above the entrance and in the lobby.

Reliance Building (Map p286; 1 W Washington St; M Blue Line to Washington) With its 16 stories of shimmering glass, framed by brilliant white terra-cotta details, the Reliance Building is a breath of fresh air. The structure's lightweight internal metal frame supports a glass facade that gives it a feeling of lightness, a style that didn't become universal until after WWII. Today the Reliance houses the chic Hotel Burnham (p218). Added historical bonus: Al Capone's dentist drilled teeth in what's now room 809.

Santa Fe Building (Map p286; 224 S Michigan Ave; M Brown, Orange, Green, Purple, Pink Line to Adams) Architect Daniel Burnham kept his offices in this 1904 terra-cotta beauty. Enter the lobby and look up at the vast light well Burnham placed in the center – he gave this same feature to the Rookery. Appropriately enough, the Santa Fe Building now houses the Chicago Architecture Foundation.

Kluczynski Building (Map p286; 230 S Dearborn St; M Blue Line to Jackson) Last, but certainly not least, no discussion of famed Loop architecture is complete without mentioning the mod, boxy, metal-and-glass style of Ludwig Mies van der Rohe. His 1974 Kluczynski Building, part of the Chicago Federal Center, is a prime example. He designed many more buildings at the Illinois Institute of Technology in Bronzeville.

M Brown, Orange, Purple, Pink Line to Quincy) FREE This small museum in the Federal Reserve Bank of Chicago is fun for a quick browse. The best exhibits include a giant glass cube stuffed with one million $1 bills (they weigh 2000lb) and a counterfeit display differentiating real bills from fakes. Learn why we call $1000 a 'grand,' and snap a sweet photo clutching the million-dollar-stuffed briefcase.

You'll also get a free bag of shredded currency to take home. The museum is a school-group favorite. At 1pm there's a 45-minute guided tour. When you enter the building, look for the 'visitors center' sign (it doesn't say 'Money Museum'), and note you'll have to go through a metal detector.

ROUTE 66 SIGN   HISTORIC SITE

Map p286 (E Adams St, btwn S Michigan & Wabash Aves; Ⓜ Brown, Orange, Green, Purple, Pink Line to Adams) Attention Route 66 buffs: the Mother Road's starting point is here. Look for the sign that marks the spot on Adams St's south side as you head west toward Wabash Ave. From Chicago the route moseys 2400 miles onward to Los Angeles, past neon signs, mom-and-pop motels and pie-filled diners.

AQUA TOWER   ARCHITECTURE

Map p286 (225 N Columbus Dr; Ⓜ Brown, Orange, Green, Purple, Pink Line to State/Lake) Aqua made waves when it appeared in 2009. Local architect Jeanne Gang designed the 82-story tower, the world's tallest created by a woman. Dramatic undulating balconies curve out from the core, interspersed with reflective glass that forms 'pools' shimmering from the white rippled tiers. The Radisson Blu Aqua Hotel (p219) takes up floors 1 to 18; the remaining floors hold multi-million-dollar apartments and offices.

GRANT PARK   PARK

Map p286 (Michigan Ave, btwn E Roosevelt Rd & Randolph St; ⊘ 6am-11pm; Ⓜ Brown, Orange, Green, Purple, Pink Line to Adams) Grant Park hosts the city's mega-events, such as Taste of Chicago, Blues Fest and Lollapalooza. Buckingham Fountain (p52) is the park's centerpiece. The skateboard park in the southwest corner draws a cool-cat crowd. Other features include a rose garden and loads of baseball diamonds.

RIVERWALK   WATERFRONT

Map p286 (Chicago River waterfront along Wacker Dr, btwn N Lake Shore Dr & W Lake St; Ⓜ Brown, Orange, Green, Purple, Pink, Blue Line to State/Lake) Clasping the Chicago River's south side along Wacker Dr, this 1.25-mile-long promenade is slowly being developed as a local hangout. Access it from the stairs at any bridge. Outdoor cafes, wine bars, fountains, and bike and kayak rental shops dot the way. There's also a Vietnam veteran's memorial (near N Wabash Ave), a small river history museum (at N Michigan Ave) and sightseeing boats sprinkled in. It's a fine spot to escape the crowds and watch boats glide by.

CHICAGO BOARD OF TRADE   ARCHITECTURE

Map p286 (141 W Jackson Blvd; Ⓜ Brown, Orange, Purple, Pink Line to LaSalle) The Board of Trade is a 1930 art-deco gem. Inside, manic traders swap futures and options – or they used to. There aren't many left these days, as most trading is now done by computer versus guys yelling on the trading-pit floor. Outside, check out the giant statue of Ceres, the goddess of agriculture, that tops the building.

The Chicago Architecture Foundation (p263) offers tours ($15) of the building's interior three times per month.

UNION STATION   FILM LOCATION

Map p286 (☎ 312-655-2385; www.chicagounion station.com; 225 S Canal St; Ⓜ Blue Line to Clinton) This wonderfully restored 1925 train station looks like it stepped right out of a gangster movie. In fact, it has been used to great effect in exactly this way. Remember director Brian De Palma's classic *The Untouchables,* when Eliot Ness loses his grip on the baby carriage during the shoot-out with Al Capone's henchmen? And the carriage bounces down the stairs in slow motion? Those steps are here.

They're the north ones from Canal St to the waiting room. The steps were recently restored and look Hollywood-sharp now in photos. Come during the day when Amtrak and Metra riders stride through the space, which is dappled with bright shafts of sunlight from the banks of windows.

HAROLD WASHINGTON
LIBRARY CENTER   LIBRARY

Map p286 (☎ 312-747-4300; www.chipublib.org; 400 S State St; ⊘ 9am-9pm Mon-Thu, to 5pm Fri & Sat, 1-5pm Sun; 🛜; Ⓜ Brown, Orange, Purple, Pink Line to Library) This grand, art-filled building with free internet terminals and wi-fi is Chicago's whopping main library. Major authors give readings here and exhibits constantly show in the galleries. The light-drenched, 9th-floor Winter Garden is a sweet spot for reading, writing or just taking a load off, though it's a bit of a hike to get there.

Take the escalators to the 3rd floor (home of the browsable newspapers and computer commons), then transfer to the elevator to go up six more floors. And those green-copper creatures staring down from the exterior roof? They're wise old owls.

The Loop – Architecture

When the Great Fire of 1871 burned down the city, it created the blank canvas that allowed Chicago's mighty architecture to flourish. The city presented the world with the first skyscraper soon after, and it has been home to big ideas in modern design ever since. The Loop is ground zero for gawking.

FELIX LIPOV/SHUTTERSTOCK ©

1. Reliance Building (p54)
This glass-paneled beauty set the precedent for modern skyscraper design.

2. Marquette Building (p54)
Mosaics in the entrance illustrate the adventures of explorer Jacques Marquette.

3. Marshall Field Building (p54)
Pose for a photo under the iconic, 7.5-ton Old Marshall Field's Clock, a timepiece for more than 100 years.

4. Door detail, Marquette Building (p54)
Explore the ornate designs of this 1895 building.

RICHARD I ANSON/GETTY IMAGES ©

AMANDA HALL/ROBERTHARDING/GETTY IMAGES ©

CHICAGO DESIGN MUSEUM — MUSEUM

Map p286 (☎312-894-6263; www.chidm.com; 108 N State St, 3rd floor; ☺noon-7pm Tue-Sat; Ⓜ Blue Line to Washington) FREE This small industrial space in the Block 37 mall puts on nifty free exhibitions about contemporary and historical design. The shows change every four months, so you'll see something new each time you visit. It shuts down when new exhibitions are being installed, so call ahead first.

FINE ARTS BUILDING — ARTS CENTER

Map p286 (☎312-566-9800; www.fineartsbuilding.com; 410 S Michigan Ave; ☺7am-10pm Mon-Fri, to 9pm Sat, 10am-5pm Sun; Ⓜ Brown, Orange, Purple, Pink Line to Library) This building has been a haven for artists for more than a century. Today you'll hear opera voices and piano music drift out of the rooms, and you'll see studios for violin makers and photographers. Its 10 floors make for quirky exploration. Be sure and take the vintage elevator – the last one in the city that an attendant operates manually.

✖ EATING

NANDO'S PERI-PERI — FAST FOOD $

Map p286 (☎312-589-7432; www.nandosperiperi.com; 22 S Wabash Ave; mains $9-15; ☺11am-10pm Sun-Thu, to 11pm Fri & Sat; Ⓜ Red, Blue Line to Monroe) South African chain Nando's is about hot-spiced, flame-grilled chicken. Peri peri, for the uninitiated, is a vinegary, chili-laden sauce in which they marinate the meat. Choose the spice level you want (it ranges from plain to tongue-scorching), order at the counter (including beer and wine), and staff bring the meal to your table. It's akin to fast food, but a winning step up.

A colorful mosaic and cool artworks dominate the big, boisterous room. Nando's has equally crowded branches in the West Loop, Lincoln Park and Lake View.

CAFECITO — CUBAN $

Map p286 (☎312-922-2233; www.cafecitochicago.com; 26 E Congress Pkwy; mains $6-10; ☺7am-9pm Mon-Fri, 10am-6pm Sat & Sun; ☎; Ⓜ Brown, Orange, Purple, Pink Line to Library) Attached to the HI-Chicago hostel and perfect for the hungry, thrifty traveler, Cafecito serves killer Cuban sandwiches layered with citrus-garlic-marinated roasted pork and ham. Strong coffee and hearty egg sandwiches make a fine breakfast.

🚶 Neighborhood Walk
A Postcard Perspective

START PICASSO SCULPTURE
END WILLIS TOWER
LENGTH 2.25 MILES; FOUR HOURS

Why buy postcards when you can make your own? A camera, comfortable shoes, a day spent clicking away at Loop sights and you'll have your own picture-postcard perspective of the city.

Begin at Daley Plaza scratching your head over Picasso's untitled **❶ sculpture** (p53). The artist never would say what the 1967 iron work represents. Most people believe it's the head of a woman. But Picasso also drew pictures of his dog that look similar. Then there's the baboon theory... Whatever it is, it has become a well-known Chicago symbol. The most intriguing perspective may just be laying face-up, camera angled, looking at the nose of the beast.

For more landmark public art, cross the street to **❷ Miró's Chicago** (p53). Spanish artist Joan Miró unveiled his robot/pagan fertility-goddess-like sculpture in 1981, on his 88th birthday. He originally titled it *The Sun, the Moon and One Star*. The star is the fork projecting off the top. The moon is the sphere at the center. The sun is... Oh, never mind. Just snap.

What could be more postcard perfect than a six-story-high lighted sign spelling the town's name? Any time is fine to capture the 1920s marquee for the **❸ Chicago Theatre** (p63), but if your tour falls on a cloudy day, that would eliminate harsh shadows.

'Meeting under the clock' has been a Chicago tradition since 1897, when retailer Marshall Field installed the **❹ Old Marshall Field's Clock** at Washington and State Sts outside his department store (now Macy's). The elaborate timepiece weighs more than 7.5 tons. A photo beneath the clock is a must.

The 38ft-diameter Tiffany dome, the world's largest, at the **❺ Chicago Cultural Center** (p52), is well worth photographing (as is the 1897 building's hodgepodge of Greek, Roman and European architectural styles). But you're really here to get inspiration from the

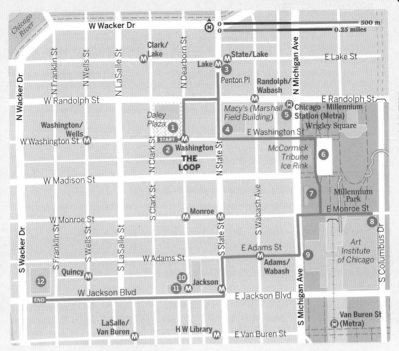

architectural photos in the Landmark Chicago Gallery. The ongoing exhibition shows 72 black-and-white images of prominent structures by well-known local shutterbugs such as Richard Nickel (more on him to come...).

Plenty of Kodak moments happen at 24-acre Millennium Park. Your first stop is the sculpture Chicagoans call 'the Bean', officially known as **6 Cloud Gate** (p46). Stand on the west side of the giant mirrored blob, hold your camera at waist level and you can take a self-portrait with a skyline background.

Mosey onward to the human gargoyles puckering up at the **7 Crown Fountain** (p46). Geysers spout from the ground in front of two 50ft LED screens projecting images of peoples' faces. When an open-mouthed guy or gal appears, the fountain spews water so it looks like they're spitting. Use a fast shutter speed and stick to a side view unless you've got a waterproof camera.

Many of renowned architect Louis Sullivan's buildings have been demolished. But you can get up close to his exquisite terracotta ornamentation at the **8 Chicago Stock Exchange Arch**, which was rescued and placed outside the Art Institute (on the northeast side). A telephoto lens can isolate the detail. Your arch pictures will be considerably less risky than those Richard Nickel took. While the Stock Exchange was abandoned and awaiting demolition in 1972, the famed photographer entered to document the scene. The building collapsed, taking his life.

Around the front of the Art Institute stand two 1894 bronze **9 lions** (p50) – city mascots of sorts. They wore Blackhawks helmets when the team won the 2010, 2013 and 2015 Stanley Cup, and they donned White Sox caps during the 2005 World Series win. They wear wreathes around their necks at Christmastime. Zoom in for a striking profile shot silhouetted against city buildings.

Alexander Calder's **10 Flamingo** (p53) is another easily recognized piece of monumental public art in Chicago. That bright-red paint job should photograph well, especially if you frame it against Mies van der Rohe's groundbreaking 1974 glass-and-steel **11 Kluczynski Building** (p54) in the Chicago Federal Center.

Aligning the building's edge on a slight diagonal will add dynamism to a shot of the **12 Willis Tower** (p51), one of the world's tallest buildings. A final photo from the 103rd-floor Skydeck sums it up: high-rises galore, lake beyond – that's the Loop.

FRENCH MARKET

The **French Market** (Map p286; www.frenchmarketchicago.com; 131 N Clinton St; mains $6-12; ☻10am-6:30pm Mon-Fri, to 4pm Sat; ☎; Ⓜ Green, Pink Line to Clinton), located in the Ogilvie train station, is a favorite of local chowhounds. They equate it to a food-truck pod, with eclectic vendors specializing in a couple of high-quality dishes each. The Euro-style hall with tables is not particularly atmospheric, but no one seems to mind when everything costs less than $12. Sniff around the aisles and see what appeals. Our favorites:

Saigon Sisters They are indeed two sisters and they ladle out Vietnamese pho (noodle soup) and *banh mi* (baguette sandwiches). Try the Sun Tanned Cow, with coconut-milk-braised beef ribs, lime leaves and ginger.

Fumare Meats Revered for its Montreal-style smoked-meat sandwiches.

Pastoral A branch of the artisan deli chain wafts its wares.

Vegan Now Makes heaping plates of tofu barbecue, corn bread and other vegan soul food.

Aloha Poke Co One of the market's most popular stalls, with people queued up for Hawaiian *poke* (raw fish and rice bowls).

Frietkoten Belgian fries in a paper cone slathered in one of 20 sauces. The stall sells European and craft brews to help wash the *frites* down.

PASTORAL
DELI $

Map p286 (☑312-658-1250; www.pastoralartisan. com; 53 E Lake St; sandwiches $8-12; ☻10:30am-8pm Mon-Fri, 11am-6pm Sat & Sun; ☑; Ⓜ Brown, Orange, Green, Purple, Pink Line to Randolph or State/Lake) Pastoral makes a mean sandwich. Fresh-shaved serrano ham, Basque salami and other carnivorous fixings meet smoky mozzarella, Gruyère and piquant spreads on crusty baguettes. Vegetarians also have options. There's limited seating; most folks take away for picnics in Millennium Park (call in your order a few hours in advance to avoid a queue). The shop sells bottles of beer and wine, too.

Pastoral has another branch in the Loop's French Market, plus others in Lakeview and Andersonville.

PIZANO'S
PIZZA $

Map p286 (☑312-236-1777; www.pizanoschicago.com; 61 E Madison St; 10in pizzas from $16; ☻11am-2am Sun-Fri, to 3am Sat; ☎; Ⓜ Red, Blue Line to Monroe) Pizano's is a good recommendation for deep-dish newbies, since it's not jaw-breakingly thick. The thin-crust pies that hit the checker-clothed tables are good, too, winning rave reviews for crispness. Some of the wait staff are characters who've been around forever, which adds to the convivial ambience. It's open late-night (with a full bar), which is a Loop rarity.

OASIS
MIDDLE EASTERN $

Map p286 (☑312-443-9534; 21 N Wabash Ave; mains $5-9; ☻10am-5pm Mon-Fri, 11am-3pm Sat; Ⓜ Brown, Orange, Purple, Pink, Green Line to Randolph) Walk past diamonds, gold and other bling in the jewelers' mall before striking it rich in this cafe at the back. Creamy hummus, crisp falafel and other Middle Eastern favorites fill plates at bargain prices. Eat in or carry out to nearby Millennium Park.

NATIVE FOODS CAFE
VEGAN $

Map p286 (☑312-332-6332; www.nativefoods. com; 218 S Clark St; mains $9-11; ☻10:30am-9pm Mon-Sat, 11am-7pm Sun; ☑; Ⓜ Brown, Orange, Purple, Pink Line to Quincy) 🍴 If you're looking for vegan fast-casual fare downtown, Native Foods is your spot. The meatball sandwich rocks the seitan, while the scorpion burger fires up hot-spiced tempeh. Local beers and organic wines accompany the wide-ranging menu of Greek, Asian, Mexican and Italian-inspired dishes. Soy-free, gluten-free and nut-free menus are available for allergy sufferers.

SHAKE SHACK
BURGERS $

Map p286 (☑312-646-6005; www.shakeshack. com; 12 S Michigan Ave; mains $5-10; ☻11am-11pm; Ⓜ Brown, Orange, Green, Purple, Pink Line to Adams) The NYC chain has come to Chicago. This burger spot is beloved for its well-griddled patties under a sweet-and-tangy

Shake Sauce, crinkle-cut fries and milkshakes made with creamy custard (with local doughnuts and pie blended in). Are the shakes really the nation's best? The endless crowd of happy slurpers provides the answer.

WASHBURNE CAFE
SANDWICHES $

Map p286 (www.washburneculinary.com; 226 W Jackson Blvd; mains $4-6; ☺7:30am-3:30pm Mon-Fri; Ⓜ Brown, Orange, Purple, Pink Line to Quincy) Grab a healthy sandwich, pomegranate smoothie or red-velvet cupcake made by culinary students at the Washburne Cafe.

DO-RITE DONUTS
BAKERY $

Map p286 (www.doritedonuts.com; 50 W Randolph St; donuts $2-3; ☺6:30am-2pm Mon-Fri, 7am-2pm Sat & Sun; Ⓜ Blue Line to Washington) At Do-Rite's shoebox-size shop office workers clamor for peanut butter banana, coffee cream and chocolate-ganache-dripping Boston cream doughnuts to jump-start their day. They're typically served warm (small fryers mean frequent, hot-off-the-press batches). A gluten-free option is always on the menu.

SEVEN LIONS
AMERICAN $$

Map p286 (☏312-880-0130; www.sevenlionschicago.com; 130 S Michigan Ave; mains $15-29; ☺11am-11pm Mon-Fri, 10am-11pm Sat & Sun; Ⓜ Brown, Orange, Green, Purple, Pink Line to Adams) Across from the Art Institute, this buzzy but conversation-friendly restaurant wafts a meaty menu of crowd-pleasers with an inventive edge. Fried chicken skins and pickles and squid-ink spaghetti hit the tables along with fab desserts (mmm, toffee corn puffs) and terrific wines. Sit indoors in casually elegant, tufted brown leather booths, or outdoors at the hoppin' sidewalk cafe.

★GAGE
MODERN AMERICAN $$$

Map p286 (☏312-372-4243; www.thegagechicago.com; 24 S Michigan Ave; mains $18-36; ☺11am-10pm Mon, to 11pm Tue-Fri, 10am-midnight Sat, to 10pm Sun; Ⓜ Brown, Orange, Green, Purple, Pink Line to Adams) This always-hopping gastropub dishes up fanciful grub, from Gouda-topped venison burgers to mussels vindaloo to Guinness-battered fish and chips. The booze rocks, too, including a solid whiskey list and small-batch beers that pair with the food.

Ask the knowledgeable servers about what will work best with your meal. Note the bar stays open later, usually until 2am.

The Scotch-egg appetizer – a sausage-encased, deep-fried, hard-boiled beast with the girth of a softball – has earned quite a following.

TRATTORIA NO 10
ITALIAN $$$

Map p286 (☏312-984-1718; www.trattoriaten.com; 10 N Dearborn St; mains $20-36; ☺11:30am-9pm Mon-Thu, to 10pm Fri, 5-10pm Sat; Ⓜ Blue Line to Washington) This clubby bistro is just steps from the Loop theater district and fills up fast with ticket-holders. The straightforward menu provides exceptionally flavorful takes on familiar items such as ravioli (try the one filled with crab and mascarpone) and risotto with chicken and sweet Gorgonzola cheese. Gluten-free pasta is available. Reservations are a good idea.

🍷 DRINKING & NIGHTLIFE

★BERGHOFF
BAR

Map p286 (☏312-427-3170; www.theberghoff.com; 17 W Adams St; ☺11am-9pm Mon-Fri, 11:30am-9pm Sat; Ⓜ Blue, Red Line to Jackson) The Berghoff dates from 1898 and was the first spot in town to serve a legal drink after Prohibition (ask to see the liquor license stamped '#1'). Little has changed around the antique wood bar since then. Belly up for frosty mugs of the house-brand beer and order sauerbraten, schnitzel and other old-world classics from the adjoining German restaurant.

TONI PATISSERIE & CAFE
CAFE

Map p286 (☏312-726-2020; www.tonipatisserie.com; 65 E Washington St; ☺7am-7pm Mon-Fri, 8am-7pm Sat, 9am-5pm Sun; Ⓜ Brown, Orange, Green, Purple, Pink Line to Randolph or Madison) Toni's provides a cute refuge for a glass of wine. The Parisian-style cafe has a small list of French reds, whites and sparkling wines to sip at the close-set tables while you try to resist the éclairs, macaroons and tiered cakes tempting from the glass case. It also sells bottles for take away (handy for park picnics).

MONK'S PUB
PUB

Map p286 (☏312-357-6665; www.monkspubchicago.com; 205 W Lake St; ☺9am-11pm Mon-Fri, 11am-5pm Sat; Ⓜ Blue, Brown, Orange, Green, Purple, Pink Line to Clark/Lake) Grab the brass handles on the huge wooden doors and enter a dimly lit Belgian beer cave. Old barrels, vintage taps and faux antiquarian books set the mood, accompanied by a whopping international brew selection and free, throw-your-shells-on-the-floor peanuts. Office workers and the occasional TV weatherman are the main folks hanging out at Monk's, which also serves good, burger-y pub grub.

CINDY'S
BAR

Map p286 (☑312-792-3502; www.cindysrooftop. com; 12 S Michigan Ave; ⊘11am-2am Mon-Fri, 10am-3am Sat, to midnight Sun; Ⓜ Brown, Orange, Green, Purple, Pink Line to Adams) Cindy's unfurls awesome views of Millennium Park and the lake from atop the Chicago Athletic Association Hotel. Sit at one of the long wood tables under twinkling lights and sip snazzy cocktails with ingredients such as mugolio pine sap. Alas, everyone wants in on the action, so try to come early to avoid having to wait for a seat.

It's also worth checking out the other bars in the building, including the Cherry Circle Room (like a handsome, low-lit supper club) and the Game Room (with pool, foosball, checkers and chess among the stash).

MILLER'S PUB
PUB

Map p286 (☑312-263-4988; www.millerspub. com; 134 S Wabash Ave; ⊘11am-4am; Ⓜ Brown, Orange, Green, Purple, Pink Line to Adams) The beauty of Miller's isn't so much literal, though it's attractive enough with dark-wood furnishings, stained glass and nostalgic sports photos and oil paintings adorning the walls. The real beauty comes from the late-night hours in an area where most places close by 10pm. Even better: Miller's pours a whopping selection of craft and Belgian brews and serves a big, meaty menu.

CYRANO'S CAFE & WINE BAR
CAFE

Map p286 (☑312-616-1400; www.cyranos cafeontheriver.com; Riverwalk, 233 E Wacker Dr; ⊘11am-10pm early May-Oct; Ⓜ Brown, Orange, Green, Purple, Pink Line to State/Lake) Cyrano's casual tables sit amid a jumble of bright-hued flowers along the Riverwalk. Swirl a glass of beer, Champagne, Beaujolais, Riesling or Cotés de Gascogne from the French owner's list while watching the boats drift by. Sandwiches, cheese plates and ice cream supplement the drinks.

INTELLIGENTSIA COFFEE
COFFEE

Map p286 (☑312-920-9332; www.intelligentsia coffee.com; 53 E Randolph St; ⊘6:30am-8pm Mon-Sat, 7am-7pm Sun; Ⓜ Brown, Orange, Green, Purple, Pink Line to Randolph) Intelligentsia is a local chain that roasts its own beans and percolates good strong stuff. The modern, industrial coffee-bar makes a good pre- or post–Millennium Park fuel up. There's another Loop outlet in the Monadnock Building.

ARGO TEA
TEAHOUSE

Map p286 (☑312-324-3899; www.argotea.com; 16 W Randolph St; ⊘6:30am-10pm Mon, to 11pm Tue-Fri, 8am-11pm Sat, to 9pm Sun; 🛜; Ⓜ Brown, Orange, Green, Purple, Pink Line to State/Lake) This whimsical, Bavarian-looking tea shop is a great place to get some work done while energizing with an exotic beverage. Grab a maté latte (South American–style tea and milk) or ginger-root-infused Japanese green tea, then head to the quiet 2nd-floor tables and settle in to use the free wi-fi. Coffee drinks and healthy sandwiches are available, too.

PLAZA AT PARK GRILL
CAFE

Map p286 (☑312-521-7275; www.parkgrillchicago. com/plaza; 11 N Michigan Ave; ⊘11am-10pm mid-May–early Oct; Ⓜ Brown, Orange, Green, Purple, Pink Line to Madison) If you want lively people-watching in the thick of it all, hit the Plaza. Set in Millennium Park between the Bean sculpture and Michigan Ave, the summer-only bar sprawls where the ice-skating rink is during colder months. It can be pricey and cheesy (cover bands!), but it's the neighborhood's hot spot for alfresco boozing.

☆ ENTERTAINMENT

★ GRANT PARK ORCHESTRA
CLASSICAL MUSIC

Map p286 (☑312-742-7638; www.grantpark musicfestival.com; Pritzker Pavilion, Millennium Park; ⊘6:30pm Wed & Fri, 7:30pm Sat mid-Jun–mid-Aug; Ⓜ Brown, Orange, Green, Purple, Pink Line to Randolph) It's a summertime must-do. The Grant Park Orchestra – composed of top-notch musicians from symphonies worldwide – puts on free classical concerts at Millennium Park's Pritzker Pavilion. Patrons bring lawn chairs, blankets, wine and picnic fixings to set the scene as the sun dips, the skyscraper lights flicker on and glorious music fills the night air.

If you can't catch the evening show, rehearsals take place Tuesday to Friday, usually from 11am to 1pm. The orchestra played in Grant Park in the early days, hence the misleading name.

CHICAGO THEATRE   THEATER

Map p286 (⌨312-462-6300; www.thechicago theatre.com; 175 N State St; MBrown, Orange, Green, Purple, Pink Line to State/Lake) Take a gander at the six-story sign out front. It's an official landmark (and an excellent photo op). Everyone from Duke Ellington to Frank Sinatra to Prince has taken the stage here over the years (and left their signature on the famous backstage walls). The real show-stopper, though, is the opulent French baroque architecture, including the lobby modeled on the Palace of Versailles.

Opened in 1921, the theater originally screened silent movies with a full orchestra and white-gloved ushers leading patrons to their seats. Tickets cost just 50 cents, so rich and poor alike could revel in the splendor. Today it's a concert venue. One-hour tours ($15) are available most days at noon.

GOODMAN THEATRE   THEATER

Map p286 (⌨312-443-3800; www.goodman theatre.org; 170 N Dearborn St; MBrown, Orange, Green, Purple, Pink, Blue Line to Clark/ Lake) The Goodman is one of Chicago's premier drama houses, and its Theater District facility is gorgeous. It specializes in new and classic American productions and has been cited several times as one of the USA's best regional theaters. At 10am, Goodman puts unsold tickets for the current day's performance on sale for half-price online. They're also available at the box office from noon.

Goodman's annual production of *A Christmas Carol* has become a local family tradition.

CHICAGO SYMPHONY ORCHESTRA   CLASSICAL MUSIC

Map p286 (⌨312-294-3000; www.cso.org; 220 S Michigan Ave; MBrown, Orange, Green, Purple, Pink Line to Adams) Riccardo Muti leads the CSO, one of America's best symphonies, known for fervent subscribers and an untouchable brass section. Cellist Yo-Yo Ma is the group's creative consultant and a

> ℹ️ **DISCOUNT TICKETS**
>
> Swing by the Hot Tix (p66) office, which sells same-week theater tickets for half price (plus a service charge of $5 to $10). Drama, comedy and performing-arts venues citywide have seats on offer. You can also look and book online. The earlier in the week you visit, the better the selection.

frequent soloist. The season runs from September to May at Symphony Center; Daniel Burnham designed the Orchestra Hall.

The group also plays summer shows at the outdoor Ravinia Festival in suburban Highland Park.

LYRIC OPERA OF CHICAGO   OPERA

Map p286 (⌨312-332-2244; www.lyricopera.org; 20 N Wacker Dr; MBrown, Orange, Purple, Pink Line to Washington) Tickets are hard to come by for this bold modern opera company, which fills the chandeliered Civic Opera House with a shrewd mix of common classics and daring premieres from September to March. If your Italian isn't up to much, don't be put off; much to the horror of purists, the company projects English 'supertitles' above the proscenium.

HUBBARD STREET DANCE CHICAGO   DANCE

Map p286 (⌨312-850-9744; www.hubbardstreet dance.com; 205 E Randolph St; MBrown, Orange, Green, Purple, Pink Line to Randolph) Hubbard Street is the preeminent dance company in the city, with a well-deserved international reputation to match. The group is known for energetic and technically virtuoso performances under the direction of some of the best choreographers in the world. It leaps at the Harris Theater in Millennium Park.

GENE SISKEL FILM CENTER   CINEMA

Map p286 (⌨312-846-2800; www.siskelfilm center.org; 164 N State St; MBrown, Orange, Green, Purple, Pink Line to State/Lake) The former Film Center of the School of the Art Institute was renamed for the late *Chicago Tribune* film critic Gene Siskel. It shows everything from amateurish stuff by students to wonderful but unsung gems by Estonian directors. The monthly schedule includes theme nights of forgotten American classics.

THEATER DISTRICT PALACES

Chicago boasts several dreamboat old theaters that have been renovated and reopened in recent years as part of the Loop's Theater District. Signs are posted in front of each palatial property, detailing the zaniness that went on during its 1920s heyday. The theaters now host touring shows, everything from Cuban ballet companies to Disney musicals. **Broadway in Chicago** (☑800-775-2000; www.broadwayinchicago.com) handles tickets for most of them. The venues cluster at State and Randolph Sts; try to walk by at night when they're at their festive, neon-lit best.

➙ Auditorium Theatre
➙ PrivateBank Theatre
➙ Cadillac Palace Theatre
➙ Chicago Theatre (p63)
➙ Oriental Theatre

JOFFREY BALLET
DANCE

Map p286 (☑312-386-8905; www.joffrey.com; 10 E Randolph St; ⓜBrown, Orange, Green, Purple, Pink Line to Randolph) The famed Joffrey has flourished since it relocated from New York in 1995. Noted for its energetic work, the company frequently travels the world and boasts an impressive storehouse of regularly performed repertoire. Joffrey practices and instructs in the swanky Joffrey Tower on Randolph St in the Theater District, though it typically performs at the Auditorium Theatre.

The annual run of *The Nutcracker* draws big crowds.

HARRIS THEATER
FOR MUSIC AND DANCE
THEATER

Map p286 (☑312-334-7777; www.harristheaterchicago.org; 205 E Randolph St; ⓜBrown, Orange, Green, Purple, Pink Line to Randolph) This avant-garde theater in Millennium Park hosts a huge slate of performing-arts groups, including Hubbard Street Dance Chicago, Music of the Baroque, Chicago Opera Theater and 35 others.

CIVIC ORCHESTRA
OF CHICAGO
CLASSICAL MUSIC

Map p286 (☑312-294-3420; www.cso.org/civic; 220 S Michigan Ave; ⓜBrown, Orange, Green, Purple, Pink Line to Adams) Founded in 1919, this orchestra is something of the kid sibling to the Chicago Symphony Orchestra, made up of young players who often graduate to the big-time professional symphonic institutions around the world. It's the only training orchestra of its kind in the world and tickets to performances at Symphony Center are free (or $5 per ticket if you reserve in advance).

CHICAGO SINFONIETTA
CLASSICAL MUSIC

Map p286 (☑312-284-1554; www.chicagosinfonietta.org; 220 S Michigan Ave; ⓜBrown, Orange, Green, Purple, Pink Line to Adams) This beloved organization is all about knocking down the cultural walls that surround traditional classical ensembles. Expect broad-minded premieres and wide-ranging guest artists, including jazz luminaries and ethnic folk musicians. Many of its concerts are at the Chicago Symphony Orchestra's center.

MUSIC OF THE BAROQUE
CLASSICAL MUSIC

Map p286 (MoB; ☑312-551-1415; www.baroque.org; 205 E Randolph St; ⓜBrown, Orange, Green, Purple, Pink Line to Randolph) One of the largest choral and orchestral groups of its kind in the USA, MoB brings the music of the Middle Ages and the Renaissance to vibrant life. Its Christmas brass and choral concerts are huge successes. It performs at the Harris Theater, as well as at various churches around town.

INTERNATIONAL
SCREENINGS PROGRAM
CINEMA

Map p286 (☑312-744-6630; www.chicagofilmfestival.com; 78 E Washington St; ⊙6:30pm Wed Jun-Sep; ⓜBrown, Orange, Green, Purple, Pink Line to Randolph) The same group that puts on the Chicago International Film Festival hosts a free program from June through September showing foreign films in the Chicago Cultural Center's Claudia Cassidy Theater (2nd floor). Seating is first come, first served.

CHICAGO OPERA THEATER OPERA

Map p286 (☑312-704-8414; www.chicagoopera theater.org; 205 E Randolph St; ⓜBrown, Orange, Green, Purple, Pink Line to Randolph) Philip Glass's *The Perfect American* and Henry Purcell's *The Fairy Queen* are recent schedule headliners – indications of the innovative group's broad range. Performances usually take place at the Harris Theater to great critical acclaim.

CHICAGO CHAMBER MUSICIANS CLASSICAL MUSIC

Map p286 (☑847-521-8506; www.chicagocham bermusiciansensemble.org; 78 E Washington St; ⓜBrown, Orange, Green, Purple, Pink Line to Randolph) This 15-member ensemble is comprised of world-class soloists and Chicago Symphony Orchestra section leaders. The best place to hear them is at the Chicago Cultural Center during free shows the first Monday of each month, from 12:15pm to 1pm in Preston Bradley Hall. They also play at halls and theaters around town.

AUDITORIUM THEATRE THEATER

Map p286 (☑312-341-2300; www.auditorium theatre.org; 50 E Congress Pkwy; ⓜBrown, Orange, Purple, Pink Line to Library) Famed architects Louis Sullivan and Dankmar Adler designed this 1889 beauty, an example of the Chicago School style that used thick bases to support the towering walls above. Today it hosts lots of dance productions and jazz and world-music shows.

ORIENTAL THEATRE THEATER

Map p286 (☑312-977-1700; www.broadwayin chicago.com; 24 W Randolph St; ⓜBrown, Orange, Green, Purple, Pink Line to State/Lake) The Oriental, known for its stunning Far East architectural elements, was built in 1926. It now hosts touring Broadway shows.

CADILLAC PALACE THEATRE THEATER

Map p286 (☑312-977-1700; www.broadwayin chicago.com; 151 W Randolph St; ⓜBrown, Orange, Purple, Pink Line to Washington) Neon-lit 1926 theater with interior elements based on the Palace of Versailles; hosts touring Broadway productions.

PRIVATEBANK THEATRE THEATER

Map p286 (☑312-977-1700; www.broadwayinchi cago.com; 18 W Monroe St; ⓜBlue, Red Line to Monroe) Glittering, century-old landmark theater that hosts big touring shows.

🛍 SHOPPING

CHICAGO ARCHITECTURE FOUNDATION SHOP GIFTS & SOUVENIRS

Map p286 (☑312-322-1132; www.architecture. org/shop; 224 S Michigan Ave; ⊙9am-9pm, reduced hours in winter; ⓜBrown, Orange, Green, Purple, Pink Line to Adams) Skyline posters, Frank Lloyd Wright note cards, skyscraper models and heaps of books celebrate local architecture at this haven for anyone with an edifice complex. The items make excellent only-in-Chicago-type souvenirs.

OPTIMO HATS ACCESSORIES

Map p286 (☑312-922-2999; www.optimo.com; 320 S Dearborn St; ⊙10am-5pm Mon-Sat; ⓜBlue Line to Jackson) Optimo is a Chicago institution, the last custom hat-maker for men in town. Want a lid like Capone? Get one here, made with serious, old-school craftsmanship. Clients include Johnny Depp, Jack White and a slew of local bluesmen. The shop is located in the landmark Monadnock Building.

TARGET DEPARTMENT STORE

Map p286 (www.target.com; 1 S State St; ⊙7am-10pm Mon-Fri, 9am-6pm Sat & Sun; ⓜBrown, Orange, Green, Purple, Pink Line to Madison) The big-box retailer's downtown store sits in the landmark Sullivan Center building. It's a bit more upscale than the usual Target and it's a prime place to pick up picnicking items (basket, blanket, paper plates, drinks, snacks) and other Chicago necessities (umbrella, warm hat, souvenirs). Upscale sandwich chain Pret A Manger is inside, too.

AFTER SCHOOL MATTERS STORE ART

Map p286 (☑312-702-8975; 66 E Randolph St; ⊙10am-6pm Mon-Fri, 11am-4pm Sat; ⓜBrown, Orange, Green, Purple, Pink Line to Randolph) At

---

> **LOCAL KNOWLEDGE**
>
> ## ARCHITECTURE BOOKS
>
> For DIY explorations of Chicago's steely structures, staff at the Chicago Architecture Foundation Shop recommend using the *Pocket Guide to Chicago Architecture* by Judith Paine McBrien or *A View from the River*, the foundation's book that highlights buildings along its popular tour-boat routes. The shop sells both paperbacks.

this nonprofit entity painters, sculptors and other artists get paid for creating their wares while teaching inner-city teens – who serve as apprentices – to do the same. Their artworks, including paintings, mosaic tables, puppets and carved-wood walking sticks, are sold in the gallery here. Profits return to the organization.

BLOCK 37 MALL

Map p286 (☎312-261-4700; www.block37.com; 108 N State St; ◎10am-8pm Mon-Sat, 11am-6pm Sun; ⓂBlue Line to Washington) The stretch of State St between W Randolph and W Washington Sts is known as Block 37, a retail corridor that has been a city boondoggle for years. National retailers such as the Disney Store and Zara are there now, but much of the space remains empty. There is a fancy movie theater inside, and a Hot Tix desk on the 1st floor.

5 S WABASH AVE JEWELRY

Map p286 (☎312-424-2664; www.jewelerscenter. com; 5 S Wabash Ave; ◎9am-5pm Mon-Sat; ⓂBrown, Orange, Green, Purple, Pink Line to Randolph) This historic building, on a block commonly referred to as 'Jewelers Row,' is the center of Chicago's family-jeweler trade. Hundreds of shops in here sell every kind of watch, ring, gemstone and bauble imaginable. Most are quick to promise, 'I can get it for you wholesale!'

CENTRAL CAMERA ELECTRONICS

Map p286 (☎312-427-5580; www.centralcamera. com; 230 S Wabash Ave; ◎8:30am-5:30pm Mon-Fri, to 5pm Sat; ⓂBrown, Orange, Green, Purple, Pink Line to Adams) Whatever your photo needs, Central Camera has the answer. Once shutterbugs step inside the long, narrow store, it will be days before they surface again.

🏃 SPORTS & ACTIVITIES

BIKE CHICAGO CYCLING

Map p286 (☎312-729-1000; www.bikechicago. com; 239 E Randolph St; bikes per hour/day from $9/30; ◎6:30am-10pm Mon-Fri, 8am-10pm Sat & Sun Jun-Aug, reduced hours rest of year; ⓂBrown, Orange, Green, Purple, Pink Line to Randolph) Rent a bike to explore DIY-style, or go on a guided tour. Tours cover themes such as lakefront parks and attractions, pizza and hot-dog munching, or downtown's sights and fireworks at night (highly recommended). Prices include lock, helmet and map. This main branch operates out of the McDonald's Cycle Center in Millennium Park; there's another branch on Navy Pier.

MCCORMICK TRIBUNE ICE RINK SKATING

Map p286 (www.millenniumpark.org; 55 N Michigan Ave; ◎late Nov-late Feb; ⓂBrown, Orange, Green, Purple, Pink Line to Randolph) Millennium Park's busy rink is the city's most scenic, tucked between the Bean sculpture and the twinkling lights of Michigan Ave. Admission on the ice is free; skate rental costs $12.

MILLENNIUM PARK WORKOUTS HEALTH & FITNESS

Map p286 (www.millenniumpark.org; 201 E Randolph St; ◎7-11am Sat early Jun-early Sep; ⓂBrown, Orange, Green, Purple, Pink Line to Randolph) FREE Each Saturday in summer, Millennium Park offers free exercise classes with instructors and live music on the Great Lawn. The lineup: tai chi at 7am, yoga at 8am, Pilates at 9am and Zumba dance at 10am. There's an additional yoga class on Wednesdays at 7:30am.

URBAN KAYAKS KAYAKING

Map p286 (☎312-965-0035; www.urbankayaks. com; 435 E Riverwalk S; per hour $30, tours $65-80; ◎10am-6pm Mon-Fri, 9am-6pm Sat & Sun May-early Oct; ⓂBrown, Orange, Green, Purple, Pink Line to State/Lake) Located on the Riverwalk, this outfitter rents kayaks for Chicago River explorations; experience is required to head out on your own. The company also offers guided tours that glide past downtown's skyscrapers and historic sites. The nighttime fireworks jaunt is a sweet one. Beginners are welcome on tours; each begins with a 20-minute training session.

For extra skills help, the company offers an hour-long 'intro to paddling' class ($45).

Near North & Navy Pier

Neighborhood Top Five

1 **Navy Pier** (p69) Walking on this boat-bedecked wharf and taking in the views – especially from the stomach-churning 196ft Ferris wheel.

2 **Giordano's** (p75) Hefting a gooey slice of pizza that's even mightier than deep-dish.

3 **Magnificent Mile** (p70) Shopping with the frenzied masses along this busy stretch of road jam-packed with retailers from Burberry to Nike to Uniqlo.

4 **Tribune Tower** (p70) Examining the neo-Gothic building for its inlaid stones from the Taj Mahal, Parthe-

non, Great Wall of China and other global structures.

5 **Billy Goat Tavern** (p74) Submerging beneath Michigan Ave to eat burgers and knock back Schlitz beer with local journalists while getting the lowdown on famed local stories.

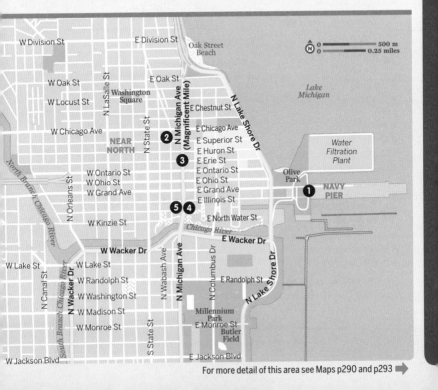

For more detail of this area see Maps p290 and p293 ➡

Lonely Planet's Top Tip

Navy Pier is about a mile from the El station and the pier itself is a half-mile long. Prepare for lots of walking. The free trolley can help in summer. It picks up at the Red Line Grand station, then makes several stops along Illinois St heading east toward the pier. It then runs the length of the pier, before looping back along Grand Ave to the El station.

 Best Places to Eat

➡ Topolobampo/Frontera Grill (p77)

➡ Giordano's (p75)

➡ Purple Pig (p75)

➡ Billy Goat Tavern (p74)

➡ Kitchen Chicago (p75)

➡ Xoco (p74)

For reviews, see p74 ➡

 Best Places to Drink

➡ Watershed (p78)

➡ Clark Street Ale House (p78)

➡ Henry's (p78)

➡ Brehon Pub (p78)

➡ Dollop (p78)

For reviews, see p78 ➡

 Best Places to Shop

➡ Garrett Popcorn (p79)

➡ Nike Chicago (p79)

➡ Burberry (p80)

For reviews, see p79 ➡

Explore Near North & Navy Pier

The Loop may be where Chicago fortunes are made, but the Near North is where those fortunes are spent. Shops, restaurants and amusements abound. This is also where the majority of hotels roll out their welcome mats.

The epicenter is the upscale shopping haven of N Michigan Ave, aka the Magnificent Mile (Mag Mile). Stretching north from the Chicago River to Oak St, the road is silly with multistory malls, high-end department stores and outlets of big-name national chains. More than 450 shops ka-ching in the tidy span.

In the River North area, west of State St, art is the big business. What was formerly a grimy, noisy assortment of warehouses and factories is now Chicago's high-end gallery district.

Jutting off Near North's eastern end is Navy Pier, which attracts more visitors than any other sight in Chicago. It's a cavalcade of kid-oriented shops, carnival rides and a freakin' big Ferris wheel, though adults will appreciate the opportunity for romantic, windswept strolling. Several boat tours depart from here, and renovations are adding an ice rink and more amusements to the mix.

The Mag Mile and Navy Pier are busy day and night. Most visitors spend quite a bit of time in the neighborhood eating, if nothing else. A multitude of pizza parlors, Italian beef shacks and eclectic bistros ensures no one goes hungry during their visit.

Local Life

➡ **Speakeasy entertainment** After munching a burger alongside locals at Green Door Tavern (p75), head down to the basement bar for jugglers, tarot card readings and burlesque shows.

➡ **Happy hour** Clark Street Ale House (p78) and Brehon Pub (p78) are neighborhood favorites for kicking back after work with a Midwest microbrew.

➡ **Big swim** The city's triathletes dive in for swim practice in the shallow water at Ohio St Beach (p80).

Getting There & Away

➡ **El** Red Line to Grand for the Magnificent Mile's southern end; Red Line to Chicago for the Mag Mile's northern end; Brown, Purple Line to Chicago for River North.

➡ **Trolley** A free trolley runs from the Red Line Grand stop to Navy Pier from late May to early September.

➡ **Bus** Number 151 runs along N Michigan Ave; 65 heads to Navy Pier.

➡ **Car** The further you get away from the Mag Mile, the more common the metered parking ($4 per hour). Navy Pier's garage costs around $28 per day.

Navy Pier was once the city's municipal wharf. Today it's Chicago's most visited attraction, with eight million people per year flooding its half-mile length. Locals may groan about its commercialization, but even they can't refute the brilliant lakefront views, cool breezes and whopping fireworks displays in summer. Kids go gaga over the high-tech rides, fast-food restaurants and trinket vendors.

No visit to the pier is complete without a stomach-curdling turn on the gigantic **Ferris wheel** (adult/child $15/12) – recently pumped up from 150ft to 196ft – which unfurls great views. The **carousel** (per ride $5) is a beloved kiddie classic, with bobbing carved horses and organ music. There's also a **giant swing** that spins you out over the pier. Each attraction costs $5 to $15. For young ones in need of further amusements, the Chicago Children's Museum (p70) is on the pier near the main entrance.

An **IMAX Theater** (☑312-595-5629; www.imax.com/chicago; tickets $12-18) and the Chicago Shakespeare Theater (p79) also call the pier home. Keep an eye on the glistening white-canopied 'tent': the Shakespeare Theater is converting it into an additional venue for its populist takes on the Bard. Competing tour boats depart from the pier's south side, where you can set sail in everything from a tall-masted schooner (p263) to thrill-ride speedboat (p263). In summer the Shoreline water taxi (adult/child $8/4) glides from here to the Museum Campus, offering a fun alternative to land-based transport.

Crowds amass for the summer fireworks shows on Wednesdays at 9:30pm and Saturdays at 10:15pm. Vendors sell beer and alcohol from walk-up windows, so you can stroll and drink on the pier. A multi-million-dollar renovation is bringing an ice rink, upgraded eating and drinking options, a hotel and more through 2018.

DON'T MISS

➡ Fireworks
➡ Ferris wheel
➡ Lakefront views
➡ Boat rides
➡ Shakespeare Theater

PRACTICALITIES

➡ Map p293
➡ ☑312-595-7437
➡ www.navypier.com
➡ 600 E Grand Ave
➡ admission free
➡ ⊙10am-10pm Sun-Thu, to midnight Fri & Sat Jun-Aug, 10am-8pm Sun-Thu, to 10pm Fri & Sat Sep-May
➡ 👪
➡ Ⓜ Red Line to Grand, then trolley

◉ SIGHTS

NAVY PIER WATERFRONT
See p69.

MAGNIFICENT MILE AREA
Map p290 (www.themagnificentmile.com; N
Michigan Ave; MRed Line to Grand) Spanning
Michigan Ave between the river and Oak
St, the Mag Mile is Chicago's much-touted
upscale shopping strip, where Bloomingdale's, Apple, Burberry and many more will
lighten your wallet. The retailers are mostly
high-end chains that have stores nationwide. Granted, they're more slicked up than
usual and their vacuum-packed proximity
on Michigan Ave is handy. The road goes
all out in December with a festive spread of
tree lights and holiday adornments.

TRIBUNE TOWER ARCHITECTURE
Map p290 (435 N Michigan Ave; MRed Line to
Grand) Take a close look when passing by
this 1925 neo-Gothic edifice. Colonel Robert
McCormick, eccentric owner of the *Chicago
Tribune* in the early 1900s, collected – and
asked his reporters to send – rocks from
famous buildings and monuments around
the world. He stockpiled pieces of the Taj
Mahal, Westminster Abbey, the Great Pyramid and more than 140 others, which are
now embedded around the tower's base.

The unusual 'bricks' are all marked and
viewable from street level. And the tradition continues: a twisted piece from the
World Trade Center wreckage is one of the
more recent additions.

WRIGLEY BUILDING ARCHITECTURE
Map p290 (400 N Michigan Ave; MRed Line to
Grand) The Wrigley Building glows as white
as the Doublemint Twins' teeth, day or
night. Chewing-gum guy William Wrigley
built it that way on purpose, because he
wanted it to be attention-grabbing like a
billboard. More than 250,000 glazed terra-
cotta tiles make up the facade; a computer
database tracks each one and indicates
when it needs to be cleaned and polished.

Banks of megawatt lamps on the river's
south side light up the tiles each night.

MARINA CITY ARCHITECTURE
Map p290 (300 N State St; MBrown, Orange,
Green, Purple, Pink Line to State/Lake) For post-
modern fun, check out the twin corncob
towers of the 1964 Marina City. Bertrand
Goldberg designed the futuristic high-rise,
and it has become an iconic part of the
Chicago skyline (check out the cover of the
Wilco CD *Yankee Hotel Foxtrot*). And yes,
there is a marina at the towers' base.

DRIEHAUS MUSEUM MUSEUM
Map p290 (☎312-482-8933; www.driehaus
museum.org; 40 E Erie St; adult/child $20/10;
◷10am-5pm Tue-Sun; MRed Line to Chicago)
Set in the exquisite Nickerson Mansion, the
Driehaus immerses visitors in Gilded Age
decorative arts and architecture. You'll feel
like a *Great Gatsby* character as you wander three floors stuffed with sumptuous ob-
jets d'art and stained glass. Recommended
guided tours ($5 extra) are available four
times daily. The price seems steep, but the
museum is a prize for those intrigued by
opulent interiors.

CHICAGO CHILDREN'S MUSEUM MUSEUM
Map p293 (☎312-527-1000; www.chicagochild
rensmuseum.org; 700 E Grand Ave; $14; ◷10am-
5pm Mon-Wed, to 8pm Thu, to 6pm Fri, to 7pm
Sat & Sun; ♿; MRed Line to Grand, then trolley)
Designed to challenge the imaginations
of toddlers to 10-year-olds, this colorful
museum near Navy Pier's main entrance
gives young visitors enough hands-on exhibits to keep them climbing and creating
for hours. Among the favorites, Dinosaur
Expedition explores the world of paleon-

THE DOWNWARD SPIRE

The 2000ft **Chicago Spire** (Map p290; 400 N Lake Shore Dr), designed by uberarchitect
Santiago Calatrava, was supposed to become the nation's tallest building back in 2007.
Excitement was high (pun!), and nicknames for the twisting design abounded – The
Twizzler, The Drill Bit, The Vibrator among them. But construction screeched to a halt
in 2008 when the economy went limp and funds dried up. Now there's a dormant 76ft-
deep, 110ft-wide hole in the ground at downtown's pricey edge. You can see it from high
rises, but not easily at street level, as a landscaped berm hides it. Residents remain
miffed that it's there, and refer to it by its less savory nickname, 'The Big Screw.'

LOCAL KNOWLEDGE

NEAR NORTH ART GALLERIES

The River North district is the most established of Chicago's five gallery-rich zones (West Loop, Pilsen, Bridgeport and Wicker Park/Bucktown are the others), with art from top international names. Several venues hover within a few-block radius. Franklin and Superior Sts are the bull's-eye. Most galleries have a map you can take covering the scene. Local favorites:

Richard Norton Gallery (Map p290; ☏312-644-8855; www.richardnortongallery.com; 222 W Merchandise Mart Plaza, Suite 612; ☺9am-5pm Mon-Fri; ⓂBrown, Purple Line to Merchandise Mart) Specializes in impressionist and modernist works, as well as historic Chicago-focused art. Check out the early beach and street scenes of the city.

Carl Hammer Gallery (Map p290; ☏312-266-8512; www.carlhammergallery.com; 740 N Wells St; ☺11am-6pm Tue-Fri, to 5pm Sat; ⓂBrown, Purple Line to Chicago) Focuses on eye-popping folk and outsider art from the US and abroad, and is known for its excellent exhibitions.

Ann Nathan Gallery (Map p290; ☏312-664-6622; www.annnathangallery.com; 212 W Superior St; ☺10am-5:30pm Tue-Fri, 11am-5pm Sat; ⓂBrown, Purple Line to Chicago) Displays cool contemporary art in various media (paintings, photography, sculpture, furniture) from established and emerging artists.

---

tology and lets kids excavate 'bones'. They can also climb a ropey schooner and bowl in a faux alley.

Waterways lets them get wet (and learn about hydroelectric power). And they can use real tools to build things in the Invention Lab. The museum is free for all ages on Thursdays from 5pm to 8pm; it's free for kids aged 15 and under on the first Sunday of the month.

HOLY NAME CATHEDRAL
CHURCH
Map p290 (www.holynamecathedral.org; 735 N State St; ⓂRed Line to Chicago) Holy Name Cathedral is the seat of Chicago's Catholic Church and where its powerful cardinals do their preaching. It provides a quiet place for contemplation, unless the excellent choirs are practicing, in which case it's an entertaining respite. Check out the sanctuary's ceiling while you're inside. The hanging red hats are for Holy Name's deceased cardinals; the hats remain until they turn to dust.

Built in 1875 to a design by the unheralded Patrick Keely, the neo-Gothic cathedral has been remodeled several times, most recently after a fire in 2009. Thus the bullet holes from a Capone-era hit outside the church are no longer visible. Actually, a couple of gangland killings took place near here. In 1924, North Side boss Dion O'Banion was gunned down in his florist shop (738 N State St) after he crossed Al Capone. In 1926, his successor, Hymie

Weiss, died en route to the cathedral in a hail of bullets that came from the window at 740 N State St.

The cathedral is open most of the day and holds frequent services.

MERCHANDISE MART
NOTABLE BUILDING
Map p290 (☏800-677-6278; www.themart.com; 222 Merchandise Mart Plaza; ☺9am-6pm Mon-Fri, 10am-3pm Sat; ⓂBrown, Purple Line to Merchandise Mart) The Merchandise Mart is the world's largest commercial building and largest LEED-certified building (Leadership in Energy and Environmental Design; silver status, thanks in part to a hefty thermal storage facility). Spanning two city blocks, the 1931 behemoth has its own zip code and gives most of its copious space to wholesale showrooms for home furnishing and design professionals. The first two floors are mall-like and open to the public.

To go beyond these you must be escorted by an interior designer, architect or other industry professional. The Mart also hosts occasional design shows that are open to the public; check the 'events' section of the website for details.

Outdoors on the Mart's river side, a collection of heads on poles rises up like giant Pez dispensers. This is the Merchant's Hall of Fame; the creepy busts depict famous local retailers such as Marshall Field and Frank Woolworth.

Near North & Navy Pier – on the Waterfront

Chicago has a nautical side, and Navy Pier is the place to experience it. Boats galore still tie up at the old municipal wharf, from powerboats to tall-masted schooners to water taxis that ply green-glinting Lake Michigan. The Chicago River slices through the neighborhood, too, adding more tour boats to the mix.

1. Marina City (p70)
Flash back to *The Jetsons* at these mod 'corn cob' towers.

2. Ohio St Beach (p80)
A conveniently located beach for a dip.

3. Fireworks at Navy Pier (p69)
Spectacular, twice-weekly shows light up the sky during summer.

4. Navy Pier (p69)
The half-mile long pier is Chicago's most visited attraction.

POETRY FOUNDATION
LIBRARY

Map p290 (☎312-787-7070; www.poetryfounda
tion.org; 61 W Superior St; ☺11am-4pm Mon-
Fri; ⓜRed Line to Chicago) **FREE** This odd,
mod building is where *Poetry* magazine
is published. The reading room makes a
nice refuge from inclement weather. Pop
in and grab a book or journal to read on
the low-slung couches. Well-known poets
do readings here. The website offers a free
downloadable audio tour of iconic city sites
matched with the poetry they inspired.

TRUMP TOWER
ARCHITECTURE

Map p290 (401 N Wabash Ave; ⓜRed Line to
Grand) The Donald's 1360ft tower is now
Chicago's second-tallest building, though
architecture critics have mocked its 'tooth-
pick' look.

CENTENNIAL FOUNTAIN
FOUNTAIN

Map p290 Centennial Fountain shoots a massive arc of water across the Chicago River. It
spurts for five minutes straight every hour
on the hour, from 10am to midnight. The exercise is meant to commemorate the labor-
intensive reversal of the Chicago River in
1900, which tidily began sending all of the
city's waste downriver rather than into the
lake. (Chicago's neighbors downstate, as you
can imagine, do not go out of their way to
celebrate this feat of civil engineering).

MUSEUM OF BROADCAST
COMMUNICATIONS
MUSEUM

Map p290 (☎312-245-8200; www.museum.tv;
360 N State St; adult/child $12/6; ☺10am-5pm
Tue-Sat; ⓜRed Line to Grand) This museum of
radio and TV nostalgia is pretty sparsely
populated considering the admission price.
But if you have a hankering to see old Bozo
the Clown clips, or the camera that taped
the famous Nixon-Kennedy debate, or the
salvaged door from Oprah's studio, it might
be for you.

✕ EATING

BILLY GOAT TAVERN
BURGERS $

Map p290 (☎312-222-1525; www.billygoattavern.
com; lower level, 430 N Michigan Ave; burgers
$4-6; ☺6am-2am Mon-Fri, 10am-2am Sat & Sun;
ⓜRed Line to Grand) *Tribune* and *Sun-Times*
reporters have guzzled in the subterranean
Billy Goat for decades. Order a 'cheezborger' and Schlitz beer, then look around at the
newspapered walls to get the scoop on infamous local stories, such as the Cubs Curse.

The place is a tourist magnet, but a deserv-
ing one. Follow the tavern signs that lead
below Michigan Ave to get here. Cash only.

If the cantankerous Greeks manning the
grill sound familiar, it's because they've enjoyed the fame of John Belushi's *Saturday
Night Live* skit ('Cheezborger! Cheezborger!
No fries! Cheeps!'). The Billy Goat is also a
fine spot for cheap, late-night boozing. And
ignore the other outlets around town; this
is the original and the one with the most
personality.

XOCO
MEXICAN $

Map p290 (www.rickbayless.com; 449 N Clark St;
mains $10-14; ☺8am-9pm Tue-Thu, to 10pm Fri
& Sat; ⓜRed Line to Grand) 🍃 At celeb-chef
Rick Bayless' Mexican street-food restaurant (pronounced '*show*-co') everything is
sourced from local small farms. Crunch
into warm churros (spiraled dough fritters)
with chili-spiked hot chocolate for breakfast, crusty *tortas* (sandwiches, such as the
succulent ham and Wisconsin cheddar) for
lunch and *caldos* (meal-in-a-bowl soups) for
dinner. Queues can be long; breakfast is the
least crowded time.

DOUGHNUT VAULT
BAKERY $

Map p290 (☎312-285-2830; www.doughnut
vault.com; 401 N Franklin St; doughnuts $2.25-
3; ☺8am-3pm Mon-Fri, 9:30am-3pm Sat & Sun;
ⓜBrown, Purple Line to Merchandise Mart) This
teensy, chandelier-clad shop is indeed in a
vault – an old bank vault – with room for
only a handful of people. The glazed doughnuts (vanilla or chestnut) are the beauties here, giant and fluffy as a pillow. The
shop usually sells out before closing time,
so check Twitter (@doughnutvault) before
embarking. Don't be put off by the queue;
it moves fast.

LOU MALNATI'S
PIZZA $

Map p290 (☎312-828-9800; www.loumalnatis.
com; 439 N Wells St; small pizzas from $12.25;
☺11am-11pm Sun-Thu, to midnight Fri & Sat;
ⓜBrown, Purple Line to Merchandise Mart) It's a
matter of dispute, but some say Malnati is the
innovator of Chicago's deep-dish pizza (Lou's
father Rudy was a cook at Pizzeria Uno,
which also lays claim to the title). Malnati's
certainly concocted the unique 'buttercrust'
and the 'sausage crust' (it's literally just meat,
no dough) to cradle its tangy toppings.

MR BEEF
SANDWICHES $

Map p290 (☎312-337-8500; 666 N Orleans St;
sandwiches $6-9; ☺10am-6pm Mon-Thu, to 5am

THE DEEP-DISH DEBATE

Everyone agrees the Near North neighborhood is where deep-dish pizza originated. But as to who invented it? That's where the consensus ends.

What we do know is that pizza first bulked up in 1943. That's when a chef who thought big arrived. He rolled out the mighty dough that cradled the first deep-dish pie – with a full inch of red sauce, chopped plum tomatoes and shredded American-style mozzarella cheese – and the city went gaga.

So who is this genius? The nod usually goes to Ike Sewell, who owned a restaurant called Pizzeria Uno (p76). But Ike's cook Rudy Malnati – father of Lou – claimed he created the gooey-cheesed behemoth. The war over who's first, and best, continues today.

Fri & Sat; ⓂBrown, Purple Line to Chicago) It's a classic for the local Italian beef-sandwich specialty. The signature item arrives on a long, spongy white bun that begins dribbling (that's a good thing!) after a load of the spicy meat and cooking juices has been ladled on. The *giardiniera* (spicy pickled vegetables) adds heat. Don't be afraid of the dumpy decor. Cash only.

Weekends bring in a boozed-up late-night crowd.

GREEN DOOR TAVERN
PUB FOOD **$**

Map p290 (☑312-664-5496; www.greendoor chicago.com; 678 N Orleans St; mains $10-14; ⏰11:30am-2am Mon-Fri, 10am-2am Sat & Sun; 🛜; ⓂBrown, Purple Line to Chicago) The Green Door, tucked in an 1872 building, is your place to mingle with locals over a beer and well-made burger amid old photos and memorabilia. During Prohibition years, a door painted green meant there was a speakeasy in the basement. It's still there and now holds a small cocktail bar with jazz singers, burlesque shows, jugglers and other quirky entertainment.

PORTILLO'S
AMERICAN **$**

Map p290 (☑312-587-8910; www.portillos.com; 100 W Ontario St; mains $4-7; ⏰10am-11pm Sun-Thu, to midnight Fri & Sat; ⓂRed Line to Grand) Die-hard hot-dog purists might bemoan the lack of true Chicago dogs in the vicinity of tourist hot spots, but this outpost of the local Portillo's chain – gussied up in a *nearly* corny 1930s gangster theme – is the place to get one. Try one of its famous dogs and a slice of the heavenly chocolate cake.

EGGSPERIENCE
AMERICAN **$**

Map p290 (☑312-870-6773; www.eggsperience cafe.com; 35 W Ontario St; mains $7-13; ⏰6am-3pm Sun-Thu, 6am-3pm & 10pm-6am Fri & Sat; ⓂRed Line to Grand) It's 4am and you're starving? This bright, clean, sprawling diner – open late night over the weekend – will fix the problem with its big portions of pancakes, omelets, club sandwiches and other staples, plus your very own pot of coffee.

★GIORDANO'S
PIZZA **$$**

Map p290 (☑312-951-0747; www.giordanos.com; 730 N Rush St; small pizzas from $15.50; ⏰11am-11pm Sun-Thu, to midnight Fri & Sat; ⓂRed Line to Chicago) Giordano's makes 'stuffed' pizza, a bigger, doughier version of deep dish. It's awesome. If you want a slice of heaven, order the 'special,' a stuffed pie containing sausage, mushroom, green pepper and onions. Each pizza takes 45 minutes to bake.

Giordano's has loads of branches around town, but this one is particularly festive (and crowded) and has an open area where you can see pizza makers throwing dough around.

PURPLE PIG
MEDITERRANEAN **$$**

Map p290 (☑312-464-1744; www.thepurplepigchi cago.com; 500 N Michigan Ave; small plates $9-19; ⏰11:30am-midnight Sun-Thu, to 1am Fri & Sat; 🍴; ⓂRed Line to Grand) The Pig's Magnificent Mile location, wide-ranging meat and veggie menu, and late-night serving hours make it a crowd-pleaser. Milk-braised pork shoulder is the hamtastic specialty. Dishes are meant to be shared, and the long list of affordable vinos gets the good times rolling at communal tables both indoors and out. Alas, there are no reservations to help beat the crowds.

KITCHEN CHICAGO
MODERN AMERICAN **$$**

Map p290 (☑312-836-1300; www.thekitchen. com; 316 N Clark St; mains $18-34; ⏰11am-10pm; ⓂBlue, Brown, Orange, Green, Purple, Pink Line to Clark/Lake) 🍴 The space right on the river is a knockout: an airy room of exposed concrete, glittery chandeliers and chunky wood tables with water views. The motto is

FAMILY-FRIENDLY SIGHTS & ACTIVITIES

Near North and Navy Pier have a lot for families to do.

Chicago Children's Museum (p70) Tots can climb, dig and splash their way through the educational playground.

Navy Pier (p69) The carnival-like wharf spins a Ferris wheel, carousel and other rides.

Bobby's Bike Hike (p80) The cycling company offers a guided two-hour, 4.5-mile 'tike hike' for families.

Gino's East Everyone gets to scribble on the walls while waiting for their deep-dish pizza.

'community through food,' which translates into an upscale hippie-type ambience where you can watch the chefs create your sustainably sourced fava-bean bruschetta, lemon-sauced chicken and smoked mussels in the open kitchen

GINO'S EAST   PIZZA $$

Map p290 (☑312-266-3337; www.ginoseast.com; 162 E Superior St; small pizzas from $15; ⊙11am-9pm Sun-Thu, to 10pm Fri & Sat; Ⓜ Red Line to Chicago) In the great deep-dish pizza wars, Gino's is easily one of the top-five heavies. And it encourages customers to do something wacky: cover every available surface – walls, chairs, staircases – with graffiti. The classic cheese-and-sausage pie oozes countless pounds of gooey goodness over a crispy golden crust. Prepare to wait for the pleasure (reservations not accepted).

This is the original Gino's location and the most atmospheric. The company also has other branches around town.

EATALY   ITALIAN $$

Map p290 (☑312-521-8700; www.eataly.com; 43 E Ohio St; snack items $3-13, mains $14-25; ⊙11am-10pm; Ⓜ Red Line to Grand) This two-story food emporium overwhelms when you step inside. The winners among the many restaurants and cafe stations strewn throughout include La Focaccia (warm, bread-y goodness), Nutella (spread thick on bread or in crepes) and the Birreria (suds brewed on-site). Can't decide? Hit the wine bar (2nd floor) for a takeaway glass, then sip as you wander the premises to choose.

PIZZERIA UNO   PIZZA $$

Map p290 (☑312-321-1000; www.unos.com; 29 E Ohio St; small pizzas from $13; ⊙11am-1am Mon-Fri, to 2am Sat, to 11pm Sun; Ⓜ Red Line to Grand) Ike Sewell supposedly invented Chicago-style pizza here on December 3, 1943, although his claim to fame is hotly contested.

A light, flaky crust holds piles of cheese and a herb-laced tomato sauce. The pizzas take a while, but stick to the pitchers of beer and cheap red wine to kill time and avoid the salad and other distractions to save room for the main event.

Sister outlet Pizzeria Due is one block north; it's marginally less packed than Uno.

GIORDANO'S NAVY PIER   PIZZA $$

Map p293 (☑312-288-8783; www.giordanos. com; 700 E Grand Ave; small pizzas from $15.50; ⊙10am-midnight; Ⓜ Red Line to Grand, then trolley) The city's top purveyor of stuffed pizza – a bigger, gooier riff on deep dish – has an outpost on Navy Pier.

BEATRIX   MODERN AMERICAN $$

Map p290 (☑312-284-1377; www.beatrixchicago. com; 519 N Clark St; mains $17-25; ⊙7am-10pm Mon-Thu, to 11pm Fri, 8am-11pm Sat, to 9pm Sun; 🛜☑; Ⓜ Red Line to Grand) Beatrix buzzes with business types, ladies who lunch and tourists staying at the attached hotel. Light wood tables and mason jars full of seeds form the rustic decor. The all-encompassing menu spans *shakshuka* (poached eggs in tomato sauce) to pot-roast sandwiches to chili-and-chocolate-glazed salmon. With lots of gluten-free and vegetarian options to boot, Beatrix is a real crowd-pleaser.

CAFE IBERICO   SPANISH $$

Map p290 (☑312-573-1510; www.cafeiberico. com; 739 N LaSalle St; tapas $6-13; ⊙11am-midnight Sun-Thu, to 1:30am Fri & Sat; Ⓜ Brown, Purple Line to Chicago) Iberico's creative tapas burst with flavor. Among the standouts: *salpicon de marisco* (seafood salad with shrimp, octopus and squid), *croquetas de pollo* (chicken and ham puffs with garlic sauce) and *vieiras a la plancha* (grilled scallops with saffron). The cafe's heady sangria draws wearied Loop workers by the dozens in the summer.

★TOPOLOBAMPO/
FRONTERA GRILL   MEXICAN $$$

Map p290 (📞312-661-1434; www.rickbayless.com; 445 N Clark St; Topolo 5-course set menu $90, Frontera mains $24-35; ⏱11:30am-10pm Tue-Thu, to 11pm Fri, 10:30am-11pm Sat; Ⓜ Red Line to Grand) 🥢 You've probably seen chef-owner Rick Bayless on TV, stirring up pepper sauces and other jump-off-the-tongue Mexican creations. His isn't your typical taco menu: Bayless uses seasonal, sustainable ingredients for his wood-grilled meats, flavor-packed mole sauces, chili-thickened braises and signature margaritas. Though they share space, Topolobampo and Frontera Grill are actually two separate restaurants: Topolo is sleeker and pricier, while Frontera is more informal.

Both places are always packed. Frontera takes some reservations but mostly seats on a first-come basis. Reserve in advance for Topolobampo (eight to 10 weeks beforehand is recommended). Its menu is based around DIY tasting menus with five or seven courses. Note the restaurants close between 2:30pm and 5:30pm (in which case you might want to try Bayless' lower-priced Xoco (p74) eatery next door). Frontera is open Saturday mornings for brunch, but Topolo is closed.

NOMI   MODERN AMERICAN $$$

Map p290 (📞312-239-4030; www.nomirestaurant.com; 800 N Michigan Ave; mains $28-45; ⏱6:30am-10pm; Ⓜ Red Line to Chicago) NoMi is perched on the 7th floor of the Park Hyatt hotel, offering a sleek, art-filled interior and spectacular views over the Magnificent Mile. The seasonally driven menu changes regularly. There's an open kitchen, so you can watch your lamb stew with turnip puree or Maine lobster with fava beans being cooked. Reserve a window table around sunset for a true romantic experience.

SHAW'S CRAB HOUSE   SEAFOOD $$$

Map p290 (📞312-527-2722; www.shawscrabhouse.com; 21 E Hubbard St; mains $25-50; ⏱11:30am-10pm Mon-Thu, to 11pm Fri, 10am-11pm Sat, to 10pm Sun; Ⓜ Red Line to Grand) Shaw's beautiful old dining room and adjoining lounge have an elegant, historic feel, complemented by dark woods and sea-worn nautical decor. The efficient servers know what selections are freshest; they can also provide a sustainable seafood menu. A crab-cake appetizer and key-lime-pie dessert make faultless bookends to any meal.

Blues bands play for free in the lounge Sunday through Thursday.

CHICAGO CHOP HOUSE   STEAK $$$

Map p290 (📞312-787-7100; www.chicagochophouse.com; 60 W Ontario St; mains $50-75; ⏱5-10:30pm Mon-Fri, 4:30-11pm Sat, to 10pm Sun; Ⓜ Red Line to Grand) This comfortable, upscale steakhouse does Chicago proud. Expect perfectly cured meats hand-cut on-site and an atmosphere befitting the city's famous politicos and mob bosses – many of whom look down from framed portraits lining the walls. If you're not up for a slab of meat, you can always pop in to the piano bar and sample the 600-strong wine list.

BANDERA   AMERICAN $$$

Map p290 (📞312-644-3524; www.banderarestaurants.com; 535 N Michigan Ave; mains $19-36; ⏱11am-10pm Sun-Thu, to 11pm Fri & Sat; Ⓜ Red Line to Grand) Looking up at the entry to this 2nd-story restaurant on Michigan Ave, you'd have no idea of the gem that waits inside. The red-bedecked Bandera has the comfortable retro feel of an expensive supper club, without the snooty waiters. American classics – grilled fish, rotisserie chicken and ice-cream sandwiches – predominate here.

When you've shopped till you've dropped, this is the place to come to pick yourself back up again. There's live jazz nightly.

GENE & GEORGETTI   STEAK $$$

Map p290 (📞312-527-3718; www.geneandgeorgetti.com; 500 N Franklin St; mains $30-50; ⏱11am-11pm Mon-Thu, to midnight Fri & Sat; Ⓜ Brown, Purple Line to Merchandise Mart) For once, a place touting itself as one of Frank Sinatra's favorite restaurants can back it up – a fact evidenced in the framed pic of Ol' Blue Eyes by the door. Old-timers, politicos and crusty regulars are seated downstairs. New-timers, conventioneers and tourists are seated upstairs. The steaks are the same on both levels: thick, well aged and well priced.

TRU   MODERN FRENCH $$$

Map p290 (📞312-202-0001; www.trurestaurant.com; 676 N St Clair St; set menus $125-158; ⏱6-9pm Tue-Thu, to 10pm Fri, 5-10pm Sat; Ⓜ Red Line to Chicago) Considered one of the city's best, Tru's prix fixe menu (from seven to 13 courses) is artful and capricious, with highly seasonal offerings and brilliant desserts. As you might expect by the price, the service is ace and a jacket is required for men. Paintings by Warhol and other modern stars adorn the walls. If you don't feel like indulging in the full course load, try snagging a reservation for the four-course dessert menu (around $40); bookings are available after the evening's last dinner times.

SUNDA
ASIAN $$$

Map p290 (☑312-644-0500; www.sundachicago.com; 110 W Illinois St; mains $26-38; ⊙11:30am-11pm Mon-Wed, to midnight Thu & Fri, 10:30am-midnight Sat, to 11pm Sun; Ⓜ Red Line to Grand) Scenesters and the occasional celebrity glam it up while swirling specialty cocktails and forking into pan-Asian dishes and sushi, set against a backdrop of black-lacquered wood and travertine marble. Make reservations a week in advance for prime-time weekend dinner.

🍷 DRINKING & NIGHTLIFE

★ WATERSHED
BAR

Map p290 (☑312-266-4932; www.watershedbar.com; 601 N State St; ⊙5pm-2am; Ⓜ Red Line to Grand) This cozy basement bar has a speakeasy-meets-ski-lodge vibe. All of the beer and spirits hail from the Great Lakes region (hence the name) and staff procure several hard-to-find gems. Watershed sits beneath Pop's for Champagne, the long-standing wine bar where a mature crowd sips from a list of nearly 200 sparkling vintages.

CLARK STREET ALE HOUSE
BAR

Map p290 (www.clarkstreetalehouse.com; 742 N Clark St; ⊙4pm-4am Mon-Fri, 11am-4am Sat & Sun; 🛜; Ⓜ Red Line to Chicago) Do as the retro sign advises and 'Stop & Drink.' Midwestern microbrews are the main draw. Work up a thirst on the free pretzels, order a three-beer sampler for $7 and cool off in the beer garden out back.

HENRY'S
BAR

Map p290 (☑312-955-8018; www.henrys-chicago.com; 18 W Hubbard St; ⊙5pm-2am Tue-Fri & Sun, to 3am Sat; Ⓜ Red Line to Grand) Many bars in this neighborhood are annoyingly trendy and uppity. Henry's is refreshing because it's the opposite: welcoming, laid-back and relatively cheap. Hang out on one of the couches, play pool or cards, and swill a craft cocktail or small-batch beer (six on tap, but many more by the bottle). Henry's serves its famed sliders (aka mini-burgers) until late at night.

BREHON PUB
PUB

Map p290 (☑312-642-1071; www.brehonpub.com; 731 N Wells St; ⊙11am-2am Mon-Fri, to 3am Sat, noon-2am Sun; Ⓜ Brown, Purple Line to Chicago) This Irish stalwart is a fine example of the corner saloons that once dotted the city. The ample selection of reasonably priced draft beer is served to neighborhood crowds perched on the high stools. Damn good tater tots add to Brehon's high marks.

DOLLOP
COFFEE

Map p290 (www.dollopcoffee.com; 345 E Ohio St; ⊙7am-7pm; 🛜; Ⓜ Red Line to Grand) Modern, sunny coffee-slinger Dollop fires up a mean espresso among its caffeinated arsenal. Local baked treats such as Hoosier Mama pies provide the sugar. Dollop has groovy branches all over the city.

SOUND-BAR
CLUB

Map p290 (☑312-787-4480; www.sound-bar.com; 226 W Ontario St; ⊙10pm-4am Fri & Sun, to 5am Sat; Ⓜ Brown, Purple Line to Chicago) This enormous nightspot rises above the city's other megaclubs by way of big-name touring trance and house DJs, as well as a sturdy lineup of resident DJs. There's an amazing sound system and a dramatic setting of futuristic neon and steely, minimalist decor.

HARRY CARAY'S TAVERN
BAR

Map p293 (www.harrycaraystavern.com; 700 E Grand Ave; ⊙11am-10pm Sun-Thu, to midnight Fri & Sat; Ⓜ Red Line to Grand, then trolley) Order a brewski at this bar named after the Cubs' famed announcer, then sip while perusing the photos and memorabilia of local sports heroes that are strewn throughout. The tavern is located on Navy Pier, near the entrance. It's touristy, but not bad by Pier standards.

BEER GARDEN
BAR

Map p293 (⊙11am-10pm daily late May-Sep, Fri-Sun only Oct; Ⓜ Red Line to Grand, then trolley) If you're dying for an alfresco drink while on Navy Pier, the beer garden pours them. Rock cover bands add to the semi-cheesy vibe.

TERRACE AT TRUMP TOWER
LOUNGE

Map p290 (☑312-588-8600; 401 N Wabash Ave; ⊙2pm-midnight May-Oct; Ⓜ Brown, Orange, Green, Purple, Pink Line to State/Lake) Trump's small, view-a-riffic, 16th-floor alfresco lounge is for when you want to live large, with a glass of champagne in hand, looking at the Wrigley Building and the river from a bird's-eye vantage point. No reservations, unless you opt for the $100 per person 'premium' tables.

⭐ ENTERTAINMENT

CHICAGO
SHAKESPEARE THEATER   THEATER
Map p293 (☑312-595-5600; www.chicagoshakes.com; 800 E Grand Ave; Ⓜ Red Line to Grand, then trolley) Snuggled into a beautiful glass home on Navy Pier, this company is at the top of its game, presenting works from the Bard that are fresh, inventive and timeless. In summer the group puts on Shakespeare in the Parks – free performances of one of Will's classics that travel to more than a dozen neighborhoods.

The theater is expanding and adding a new high-tech performance space that will join its current one on the pier by late 2017.

ANDY'S   JAZZ
Map p290 (☑312-642-6805; www.andysjazzclub.com; 11 E Hubbard St; cover charge $10-15; ☺4pm-1:30am; Ⓜ Red Line to Grand) This comfy jazz club programs a far-ranging lineup of local traditional, swing, bop, Latin, fusion and Afro-pop acts, along with the occasional big-name performer. It has been on the scene for several years and its downtown location makes it a popular spot for postwork boppers.

BLUE CHICAGO   BLUES
Map p290 (☑312-661-0100; www.bluechicago.com; 536 N Clark St; cover charge $10-12; ☺8pm-2am Sun-Fri, to 3am Sat; Ⓜ Red Line to Grand) If you're staying in the neighborhood and don't feel like hitting the road, you won't go wrong at this mainstream blues club. Commanding local acts wither the mics nightly.

HOUSE OF BLUES   LIVE MUSIC
Map p290 (☑312-923-2000; www.houseofblues.com/chicago; 329 N Dearborn St; Ⓜ Brown, Orange, Green, Purple, Pink Line to State/Lake) House of Blues has multiple stages and, despite the name, not all play in the minor-key groove. The one that does is the Back Porch Stage, with live blues nightly. The bands aren't necessarily big names, but they're always high quality.

Show times vary; they're typically around 6:30pm and 9pm on weekends, an hour or so earlier on weekdays. There's usu-

ally no cover charge until after 8pm, when it costs $10. If you come early and dine in the restaurant, you avoid the fee.

UNDERGROUND WONDER BAR   LIVE MUSIC
Map p290 (☑312-266-7761; www.undergroundwonderbar.com; 710 N Clark St; cover charge $8-15; ☺5pm-4am; Ⓜ Red Line to Chicago) This live-music venue run by musician Lonie Walker features little-known jazz and blues performers, along with the occasional rock or reggae player. The club is tiny and Lonie herself takes the stage with her 'big bad-ass company band' several nights a week.

HOWL AT THE MOON   LIVE MUSIC
Map p290 (☑312-863-7427; www.howlatthemoon.com; 26 W Hubbard St; ☺5pm-2am Mon-Sat, 7pm-2am Sun; Ⓜ Red Line to Grand) The Guns N' Roses covers, happy-hour specials and flirty singles scene here could turn nearly anyone into a piano-bar convert. Billy Joel? Sorry, how about AC/DC? Lots of bachelorette parties sing along at Howl (which is part of a national chain).

🔒 SHOPPING

⭐GARRETT POPCORN   FOOD
Map p290 (☑312-944-2630; www.garrettpopcorn.com; 625 N Michigan Ave; ☺10am-8pm Mon-Thu, to 10pm Fri & Sat, to 7pm Sun; Ⓜ Red Line to Grand) Like lemmings drawn to a cliff, people form long lines outside this store on the Mag Mile. Granted, the caramel corn is heavenly and the cheese popcorn decadent, but is it worth waiting in the whipping snow for a chance to buy some? Actually, it is. Buy the Garrett Mix, which combines the two flavors. The entrance is on Ontario St.

Several other Garrett branches waft their tempting aroma around town. Resistance is futile.

NIKE CHICAGO   SPORTS
Map p290 (☑312-642-6363; www.nike.com/chicago; 669 N Michigan Ave; ☺10am-9pm Mon-Sat, to 7pm Sun; Ⓜ Red Line to Chicago) This flashy Nike outpost is fun to meander. The 1st floor is a temple to Chicago Bulls legend Michael Jordan; there's more Jordan-brand merchandise here than in any store worldwide. The 2nd floor is loaded with football and soccer gear. The 3rd floor has treadmills where runners can try out shoes. The 4th floor has an area to design your own swooshed kicks.

BURBERRY
FASHION & ACCESSORIES

Map p290 (312-787-2500; www.burberry.com; 633 N Michigan Ave; 10am-7pm Mon-Thu, to 8pm Fri & Sat, noon-6pm Sun; Red Line to Grand) What is the bizarre, five-story building on Michigan Ave that has an exterior covered in plaid? It's the British luxury fashion house Burberry, of course. The iconic company is known for its plaid designs and its trench coats, both of which are here in abundance. The plaid exterior lights up at night, by the way.

CRATE & BARREL
HOMEWARES

Map p290 (312-787-5900; www.crateandbarrel.com; 646 N Michigan Ave; 10am-8pm Mon-Sat, 11am-6pm Sun; Red Line to Grand) The handsome housewares purveyor started right here in Chicago and this glassy, sassy uberstore is the flagship. Inside, suburban soccer moms shop for hip but functional lamps, wine goblets, casserole dishes and brass beds, same as the downtown loft-nesters alongside them.

APPLE STORE
ELECTRONICS

Map p290 (312-529-9500; www.apple.com; 679 N Michigan Ave; 10am-8pm Mon-Sat, to 7pm Sun; Red Line to Chicago) This bright, airy store offers iPads, iPods and everything else for Mac enthusiasts splayed across butcher-block tables. The user-friendly setup comes with plenty of clued-up staff to answer product questions, a 'genius bar' on the 2nd floor to sort out equipment issues, and free internet access on machines throughout the store.

The store plans to move a half-mile south to bigger, glossier digs on the riverfront. Who knows: it might already be at 401 N Michigan Ave by the time you're reading this.

SHOPS AT NORTH BRIDGE
MALL

Map p290 (312-327-2300; www.theshopsatnorthbridge.com; 520 N Michigan Ave; 10am-9pm Mon-Sat, 11am-7pm Sun; Red Line to Grand) Shops at North Bridge appeals to a less hoity-toity demographic than some of the other Mag Mile malls, with stores such as Swatch and True Religion. The multilevel mall connects anchor department store Nordstrom to Michigan Ave via a gracefully curving, shop-lined atrium.

ZARA
CLOTHING

Map p290 (312-255-8123; www.zara.com; 700 N Michigan Ave; 10am-8pm Mon-Sat, 11am-7pm Sun; Red Line to Chicago) New products arrive weekly and inventory changes bi-weekly at Spanish fashion house Zara. It's sort of Gap meets H&M, with youthful, off-the-runway styles at low prices in women's, men's and kids' clothing. The three-story building is Zara's biggest US store.

 ## SPORTS & ACTIVITIES

BOBBY'S BIKE HIKE
CYCLING

Map p290 (312 245-9300; www.bobbysbikehike.com; 540 N Lake Shore Dr; per hour/day from $10/34; 8:30am-8pm Mon-Fri, 8am-8pm Sat & Sun Jun-Aug, 9am-7pm Mar-May & Sep-Nov; Red Line to Grand) Locally based Bobby's earns rave reviews from riders. It rents bikes and has easy access to the Lakefront Trail. It also offers cool tours ($35 to $65) of South Side gangster sites, the lakefront, nighttime vistas, and venues to indulge in pizza and beer. The Tike Hike caters to kids. Enter through the covered driveway to reach the shop.

BIKE CHICAGO NAVY PIER
CYCLING

Map p293 (312-729-1000; www.bikechicago.com; 600 E Grand Ave; bikes per hour/day from $9/30; 8am-10pm Jun-Aug, 9am-7pm Apr, May, Sep & Oct; Red Line to Grand, then trolley) Rents bikes (and offers tours) from a seasonal booth on Dock St. Bike Chicago's main, year-round shop is in Millennium Park.

OHIO ST BEACH
BEACH

Map p293 (www.cpdbeaches.com; 600 N Lake Shore Dr; Red Line to Grand, then trolley) Just a few minutes' walk from Navy Pier, this small beach is convenient for those who want a quick dip. The water's shallowness makes it the preferred spot for triathletes practicing open-water swims. A cafe pours beer and wine and serves sandwiches.

Gold Coast

Neighborhood Top Five

❶ Signature Lounge (p91) Getting high by taking the 20mph elevator to this 96th-floor lounge for a tall drink and sparkling views.

❷ Museum of Contemporary Art (p84) Perusing the avant-garde paintings, sculptures and videos by day, then seeing an experimental performance in the museum's theater at night.

❸ Astor Street (p86) Ogling the genteel mansions where Chicago's rich and powerful have lived since the 1880s.

❹ International Museum of Surgical Science (p85) Examining the eerie gallstones and cadaver murals at this hair-raising museum set in a spooky old mansion.

❺ Rush Street Wandering between flashy bars and restaurants during the see-and-be-seen weekend nights.

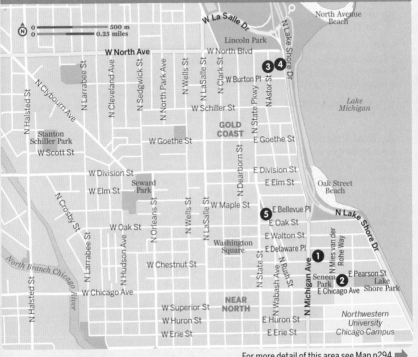

For more detail of this area see Map p294 →

Lonely Planet's Top Tip

The Gold Coast may be one of Chicago's most moneyed neighborhoods, but it offers several freebies to take advantage of: the International Museum of Surgical Science (p85) and Charnley-Persky House (p86) are free on Tuesday and Wednesday respectively, while the Newberry Library (p85) and City Gallery (p85) at the Water Tower are always free.

 Best Places to Eat

➡ Le Colonial (p87)

➡ Gibson's (p87)

➡ Hendrickx Belgian Bread Crafter (p87)

➡ Pizano's (p87)

For reviews, see p87 ➡

Best Places to Drink

➡ Signature Lounge (p91)

➡ Coq d'Or (p92)

➡ 3 Arts Club Cafe (p92)

➡ Pump Room (p92)

For reviews, see p91 ➡

Best Places to Shop

➡ American Girl Place (p93)

➡ Hershey's (p93)

➡ Lego Store (p93)

➡ Uniqlo (p93)

For reviews, see p93 ➡

Explore the Gold Coast

The Gold Coast has been the address of Chicago's crème de la crème for more than 125 years. When you stroll through the neighborhood, especially the Astor St area, you'll take in some of the most beautiful old mansions in Chicago. One of them belonged to Hugh Hefner and was the Original Playboy Mansion (p85).

Beyond the sky-high 360° Chicago (p83) observatory and the underappreciated Museum of Contemporary Art (p84), the Gold Coast offers several small, quirky sights, such as the hair-raising surgery museum (p85), and memorabilia-filled sports museum (p85). The best way to get a feel for the neighborhood's moneyed present is to spend an afternoon browsing luxuriant designer wares around Oak and Rush Sts, or an evening among the glittering high heels and good cheekbones of the neighborhood's nightlife. On Friday evening, see-and-be-seen crowds glide through bars and restaurants at Rush and State Sts, where businessmen carve porterhouses while downing martinis and ogling the action – no wonder locals call the area the 'Viagra Triangle.' It's quite a spectacle.

East along Michigan Ave the shopping gives way to high-rise malls that will be likely destinations for anyone with kids. American Girl Place (p93), Hershey's (p93) and the Lego Store (p93) send out their siren call from here. Oak Street Beach (p94) is a stone's throw away, offering a bit of breathing room from the high-rise jungle and a fine place to dip your toes in the lake.

Local Life

➡ **Hidden treats** Only neighborhood folks know that Hendrickx Belgian Bread Crafter (p87), purveyor of top-notch chocolate croissants, hides inside the bland apartment building on Walton St.

➡ **Low-key drinks** Locals looking for a well-made cocktail without the usual Gold Coast sceney vibe head upstairs to the relaxed bar at Le Colonial (p87).

➡ **Late-night munchies** When the bars and clubs close, everyone heads to Tempo Cafe (p87), open 24/7 for skillet-fried replenishment.

Getting There & Away

➡ **El** Red Line to Clark/Division for the neighborhood's northern reaches; Red Line to Chicago for the southern areas.

➡ **Bus** Number 151 runs along Michigan Ave, handy for further-flung sights.

➡ **Car** Resident-only streets stymie street parking. Try LaSalle St, much of which is unmetered.

TOP SIGHT
360° CHICAGO

In the John Hancock Center, the city's fourth-tallest skyscraper, 360° Chicago is a dandy place to get high. In many ways the view here surpasses the one at Willis Tower, as the Hancock is closer to the lake and provides unfettered panoramic vistas. If that's not enough, the observatory offers a couple of lofty thrill features as well.

The 94th-floor observatory offers informative displays that tell you the names of the surrounding buildings. It has the **Skywalk**, a sort of screened-in porch that lets you feel the wind and hear the city sounds. The biggest draw is **TILT**, aka floor-to-ceiling windows that you stand in as they move and tip out over the ground; it costs $7 extra and is actually less spine-tingling than it sounds. The observatory is probably your best bet if you have kids or if you're a newbie and want to beef up your Chicago knowledge, but there are other options.

Not interested in frivolities? Shoot straight up to the 96th-floor Signature Lounge (p91), where the view is free if you buy a drink ($8 to $16). That's right, here you'll get a glass of wine and a comfy seat while staring out at almost identical views from a few floors higher than the observatory. The elevators for the lounge (and its companion restaurant on the 95th floor) are separate from the observatory. Look for signs that say 'Signature 95th/96th' one floor up from the observatory entrance.

The Hancock Center was completed in 1969. Fazlur Khan and Bruce Graham were the chief architects, and they designed the structure to sway 5in to 8in in Chicago's windy conditions. They went on to build the Willis Tower four years later.

DON'T MISS

→ Skywalk
→ TILT feature
→ Nighttime views, including Wednesday and Saturday fireworks in summer

PRACTICALITIES

→ Map p294
→ ☎888-875-8439
→ www.360chicago.com
→ 875 N Michigan Ave, John Hancock Center, 94th fl
→ adult/child $20/13
→ ⊗9am-11pm
→ Ⓜ Red Line to Chicago

TOP SIGHT
MUSEUM OF CONTEMPORARY ART

Consider it the Art Institute's brash, rebellious sibling, with especially strong minimalist, surrealist and conceptual photography collections. Covering art from 1945 onward, the MCA's collection spans the gamut, with displays arranged to blur the boundaries between painting, sculpture, video and other media. Exhibits change regularly so you never know what you'll see, but count on it being offbeat and provocative.

The Museum of Contemporary Art mounts themed exhibitions that typically focus on underappreciated or up-and-coming artists that curators are introducing to American audiences. For example, you might see a three-decade retrospective of German artist Isa Genzken's sculpture, or Turner Prize winner Simon Starling's mixed-media works made of recycled materials. Shows last three months or so before the galleries morph into something new.

The terraced sculpture garden at the back of the museum makes for a nifty browse. In summer a jazz band plays amid the greenery every Tuesday at 5:30pm. Patrons bring blankets and sip drinks from the bar. The museum's front plaza also sees lots of action, especially on Tuesday mornings when a farmers market with veggies, cheeses and baked goods sets up from 7am to 2pm. Both events are big local to-dos.

The Museum of Contemporary Art's theater regularly hosts dance, music and film events by contemporary A-listers. Much of it is pretty far out, for example an Inuit throat singer performing to a silent-film backdrop. Bonus: a theater ticket stub provides free museum admission any time during the week after the show.

Other MCA tips: Docents lead free, 45-minute tours through the galleries daily at 1pm. Meet at the 2nd-floor visitor service desk. And the museum's shop wins big points for its cool books, gifts and children's toys.

DON'T MISS

➡ Free tours at 1pm
➡ Groovy shop
➡ Sculpture garden
➡ Terrace with lake views

PRACTICALITIES

➡ Map p294
➡ ☎312-280-2660
➡ www.mcachicago.org
➡ 220 E Chicago Ave
➡ adult/student $12/7
➡ ⏱10am-8pm Tue, to 5pm Wed-Sun
➡ Ⓜ Red Line to Chicago

◉ SIGHTS

360° CHICAGO
OBSERVATORY

See p83.

MUSEUM OF
CONTEMPORARY ART
MUSEUM

See p84.

NEWBERRY LIBRARY
LIBRARY

Map p294 (☑312-943-9090; www.newberry.org;
60 W Walton St; ⊘galleries 8:15am-5pm Mon, Fri
& Sat, to 7:30pm Tue-Thu; Ⓜ Red Line to Chicago)
FREE The Newberry's public galleries are
for bibliophiles: those who swoon over original Thomas Paine pamphlets about the
French Revolution, or get weak-kneed seeing Thomas Jefferson's copy of the *History
of the Expedition under Captains Lewis
and Clark* (with margin notes!). Intriguing
exhibits rotate yellowed manuscripts and
tattered first editions from the library's extensive collection. The on-site bookstore is
tops for Chicago-themed tomes.

On the upper floors is the library itself
(open 9am to 5pm Tuesday to Friday, and to
1pm Saturday), stacked with books, maps,
photographs and other humanities-related
materials. Those trying to research far-
flung branches of their family tree will have
a field day here. Entry requires a library
card, but one-day passes are available for
curious browsers. Once inside, you can pes-
ter the patient librarians with requests for
help in tracking down all manner of historical ephemera. Free tours of the impressive
building take place at 3pm Thursday and
10:30am Saturday.

WATER TOWER
LANDMARK

Map p294 (108 N Michigan Ave; Ⓜ Red Line to
Chicago) The 154ft-tall, turreted tower is a
defining city icon: it was the sole downtown city survivor of the 1871 Great Chicago
Fire, thanks to its yellow limestone bricks,
which withstood the flames. Today the
tower houses the free **City Gallery** (Map
p294; ☑312-742-0808; 108 N Michigan Ave;
⊘10am-6:30pm; Ⓜ Red Line to Chicago) **FREE**,
showcasing Chicago-themed works by local photographers and artists and well
worth a peek.

Built in 1869, the tower and its companion
Water Works Pumping Station (p86) were
constructed in a Gothic style popular at the
time. They were the great hope of Chicago
when they first opened, part of a technologi-
cal breakthrough that was going to provide

fresh, clean water for the city. Alas, the plan
ultimately was a failure. By 1906 the Water
Tower was obsolete and only public outcry
saved it from demolition three times. Restoration in 1962 ensured its survival.

INTERNATIONAL MUSEUM
OF SURGICAL SCIENCE
MUSEUM

Map p294 (☑312-642-6502; www.imss.org; 1524
N Lake Shore Dr; adult/child $15/7, Tue free;
⊘10am-4pm Tue-Fri, to 5pm Sat & Sun; ⬚151)
Amputation saws, iron lungs and other early tools of the trade are strewn throughout
a creaky, Gold Coast mansion. The ancient
Roman vaginal speculum leaves a lasting
impression, while the pointy-ended hem-
orrhoid surgery instruments serve as a reminder to eat lots of fiber. The collection of
'stones' (as in 'kidney' and 'gall-') and blood-
letting displays look equally painful.

Medical art gets its due here, too, from a
life-size, toga-clad sculpture of Hippocrates
to a roomful of cadaver murals (available as
postcards in the gift shop).

CHICAGO SPORTS MUSEUM
MUSEUM

Map p294 (☑312-202-0500; http://harrycarays.
com/chicago-sports-museum; 835 N Michigan
Ave, 7th fl; $6; ⊘11:30am-8:30pm Mon-Sat, to
6pm Sun; Ⓜ Red Line to Chicago) To understand
Chicago's tortured sports psyche, check out
the memorabilia-filled cases at this gallery
beside Harry Caray's 7th Inning Stretch
tavern. Shake your head in sadness at the
last-out ball from the 1945 World Series
(the last time the Cubs were in the baseball
championship). Examine Sammy Sosa's
corked bat and the infamous Bartman ball.
The museum also enshrines relics for Da
Bears, Bulls, Blackhawks and White Sox.
Admission is free if you eat or drink at the
attached restaurant.

It's located atop Water Tower Place (p93)
mall.

ORIGINAL
PLAYBOY MANSION
NOTABLE BUILDING

Map p294 (1340 N State Pkwy; Ⓜ Red Line to
Clark/Division) The sexual revolution started in the basement 'grotto' of this 1899
manor. Hugh Hefner bought the manor in
1959 and hung a brass plate over the door
warning 'If You Don't Swing, Don't Ring.'
Heavy partying ensued. In the mid 1970s,
Hef decamped to LA. The building contains condos now, but a visit still allows
you to boast 'I've been to the Playboy Mansion.' Hef's company, Playboy Enterprises,

ASTOR STREET RICHES

In 1882, Bertha and Potter Palmer were the power couple of Chicago. Potter's web of businesses included the city's best hotel and a huge general merchandise store that he later sold to a clerk named Marshall Field. When the Palmers decided to move north from Prairie Ave to a manor at what is now 1350 N Lake Shore Dr, they set off a lemminglike rush of Chicago's wealthy to the neighborhood around them. The mansions sitting along Astor St, especially the 1300 to 1500 blocks, reflect the grandeur of that heady period. Here are the highlights, from south to north:

Charnley-Persky House (Map p294; ☎312-573-1365; www.charnleyhouse.org; 1365 N Astor St; tours Wed free, Sat $10; ☉noon Wed, 10am & noon Sat Apr-Oct; ⓂRed Line to Clark/Division) While he was still working for Louis Sullivan, Frank Lloyd Wright (who was 19 at the time) designed the 11-room Charnley-Persky House, which sparked a new era in architectural design. Why? Because it did away with Victorian gaudiness in favor of plain, abstract forms that went on to become the modern style. It was completed in 1892 and now houses the Society of Architectural Historians. Guided tours are offered Wednesdays; they're first come, first served, up to 15 people. Tours are also offered on Saturdays, for which you can make reservations.

Cyrus McCormick Mansion (Map p294; 1500 N Astor St; ⓠ151) The industrialist's 1893 neoclassical home, designed by New York architect Stanford White, is one of the neighborhood standouts. McCormick and his family had the whole place to themselves, but it's now divided up into condos. It's still the high-rent district – a three-bedroom, three-bathroom unit goes for $1.75 million (washer and dryer included).

Archbishop's Residence (Map p294; 1555 N State Pkwy; ⓠ151) The 1885 mansion, complete with 19 chimneys, is where seven of Chicago's past archbishops lived. World leaders from Franklin D Roosevelt to Pope John Paul II crashed here while in town. Alas, the current archbishop does not live on-site. He opted for humbler digs at Holy Name Cathedral's rectory, but the diocese still owns the building.

stayed headquartered in Chicago until 2012, and then it too moved west. The last vestige is 'Honorary Hugh M Hefner Way,' which is what the city renamed Walton St (at Michigan Ave) in an official tip of the hat to Hef.

WASHINGTON SQUARE PARK
Map p294 (901 N Clark St; ⓂRed Line to Chicago) This plain-looking park across from the Newberry Library (p85) has quite a history. In the 1920s it was known as 'Bughouse Square,' where communists, socialists, anarchists and other -ists congregated and gave soapbox orations. (Many supposedly lived in nearby 'bughouses' – cheap hotels – hence the nickname.) Clarence Darrow and Carl Sandburg are among the respected speakers who climbed up and shouted.

In the 1970s, when Washington Sq was a gathering place for young male prostitutes, it gained tragic infamy as the preferred pick-up spot of mass murderer John Wayne Gacy. Gacy took his victims back to his suburban home, where he killed them and

buried their bodies in the basement. Convicted on 33 counts of murder (although the actual tally may be higher), he was executed in 1994.

Today the square bears little trace of its past lives – except for one weekend a year in late July. That's when the **Bughouse Debates** occur and orators return to holler at each other.

WATER WORKS
PUMPING STATION NOTABLE BUILDING
Map p294 (163 E Pearson St; ☉9am-7pm Mon-Thu, 9am-6pm Fri & Sat, 11am-5pm Sun; ⓂRed Line to Chicago) Built in 1869, the Pumping Station and Water Tower (p85), its companion building across the street, were constructed in Gothic style with yellow limestone. It's this stone that saved them when the Great Fire roared through town in 1871. Today the building holds Lookingglass Theatre Company (p92), a Hot Tix (p92) discount ticket outlet and a branch of the Chicago Public Library.

EATING

HENDRICKX BELGIAN BREAD CRAFTER
BAKERY **$**

Map p294 (☑312-649-6717; www.hendrickx bakery.com; 100 E Walton St; mains $5-12.50; ☉8am-7pm Tue-Sat, 9am-3pm Sun; ⓜRed Line to Chicago) Hiding in a nondescript apartment building, Hendrickx is a local secret. Push open the bright-orange door and behold the waffles, white-chocolate bread and dark-chocolate croissants among the flaky, buttery, Belgian treats. The place is tiny, with just a few indoor seats, but in warm weather it sets up tables on the sidewalk. Soups and sandwiches are also available.

TEMPO CAFE
AMERICAN **$**

Map p294 (☑312-943-3929; 6 E Chestnut St; mains $8-15; ☉24hr; ⓜRed Line to Chicago) Bright and cheery, this diner brings most of its meals to the table the way they're meant to be served – in a skillet. The omelet-centric menu includes all manner of fresh veggies and meat, as well as sandwiches. It's nothing fancy, but it is open round the clock and makes for a relatively cheap meal in the pricey Gold Coast. Cash only.

FOODLIFE
INTERNATIONAL **$**

Map p294 (☑312-787-7100; www.foodlifechicago. com; 835 N Michigan Ave; mains $8-14; ☉8am-8pm Mon-Thu, to 8:30pm Fri & Sat, to 7pm Sun; ⓜRed Line to Chicago) It bills itself as an 'urban food hall,' which translates to an upscale food court with more than a dozen different globally themed kitchens featuring gourmet à la carte options in a sleek atmosphere. Sushi, stir-fries, pizza, pasta, burritos and barbecue are among the offerings. It's situated inside Water Tower Place (p93) mall on the mezzanine level.

PIZANO'S
PIZZA **$$**

Map p294 (☑312-751-1766; www.pizanoschi cago.com; 864 N State St; 10in pizzas from $16; ☉11am-2am Sun-Fri, to 3am Sat; ⓜRed Line to Chicago) Congenial Pizano's gets lost amid Chicago's pizza places, which is a shame since it's one of the best and has an illustrious pedigree (founded by Rudy Malnati Jr, whose dad created the deep-dish pizza, so the legend goes). The buttery crust impresses, even more so in its thin-crust incarnation. There's another Pizano's in the Loop (p60).

FRANCESCA'S ON CHESTNUT
ITALIAN **$$**

Map p294 (☑312-482-8800; www.miafrancesca. com; 200 E Chestnut St; mains $16-28; ☉11am-10pm Mon-Thu, to 11pm Fri & Sat, to 9pm Sun; ⓜRed Line to Chicago) Part of a well-loved local chain, Francesca's buzzes with regulars who come for the trattoria's rustic standards, such as seafood linguine, spinach ravioli and mushroom-sauced veal medallions, all prepared with simple flair. It's a sweet, unpretentious spot for the neighborhood. It's located in the Seneca building.

★LE COLONIAL
FRENCH, VIETNAMESE **$$$**

Map p294 (☑312-255-0088; www.lecolonialchica go.com; 937 N Rush St; mains $20-29; ☉11:30am-3pm & 5-11pm Mon-Fri, to midnight Sat, to 10pm Sun; ☑; ⓜRed Line to Chicago) Step into the dark-wood, candlelit room, where ceiling fans swirl lazily and big-leafed palms sway in the breeze, and you'd swear you were in 1920s Saigon. Staff can arrange vegetarian and gluten-free substitutions among the curries and banana-leaf-wrapped fish dishes. If you want spicy, be specific; everything typically comes out mild.

Le Colonial is perfect for a romantic date. You'll need reservations for a table, though walk-ins can head upstairs to the bar and eat there.

GIBSON'S
STEAK **$$$**

Map p294 (☑312-266-8999; www.gibsons steakhouse.com; 1028 N Rush St; mains $40-55; ☉11am-midnight; ⓜRed Line to Clark/Division) There is a scene nightly at this local original. Politicians, movers, shakers and the shaken-down swirl the famed martinis and compete for prime table space in the buzzing dining room. The rich and beautiful mingle at the bar. As for the meat on the plates, the steaks are as good as they come and ditto for the ginormous lobsters.

LOCAL KNOWLEDGE

CUPCAKE ATM

The cupcake craze may be losing its pizzazz, but the novelty of getting a thick-icing'ed chocolate marshmallow or triple cinnamon confection at 2am from an automated teller machine is hard to resist. The Cupcake ATM dispenses 24 hours a day in front of **Sprinkles Cupcakes** (Map p294; www. sprinkles.com; 50 E Walton St; cupcakes $3.25-4.25; ☉9am-9pm Mon-Sat, 10am-8pm Sun; ⓜRed Line to Chicago). The machine even stocks one for dogs (sugar-free, of course).

Gold Coast – Magnificent Mansions

Astor St has been the address of Chicago's elite for more than 125 years. Several spectacular pieces of real estate went up back then, with well-heeled families trying to outdo each other in grandeur. Everyone from Frank Lloyd Wright to Hugh Hefner has passed through the neighborhood's distinguished doors.

1

GREGOBAGEL/GETTY IMAGES ©

CHICAGOPHOTO/GETTY IMAGES ©

1. Gold Coast (p82)
Stroll past extravagant mansions, many of which date back to the 19th century.

2. Original Playboy Mansion (p85)
In 1959, Hugh Hefner and his sexual revolution rolled into the area.

3. Charnley-Persky House (p86)
Frank Lloyd Wright proclaimed this as the 'first modern building.'

4. Architectural details
Get up close to admire the elegant structures in this moneyed neighborhood.

BRUCE LEIGHTY/GETTY IMAGES ©

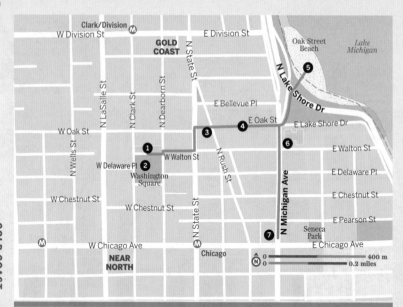

Local Life
Gold Coast Saunter

Chicago's wealthiest residents have lived in the Gold Coast since the late 1800s. Bentleys park in mansion driveways. Women in fur coats hobnob in posh cafes. But it's not all so chichi. Plenty of, er, less gilded locals live here and have their hot spots, too.

❶ Newberry Library

Let's say you need a prehistoric map of Kentucky's Cumberland River Valley. Or a map of Saxon Britain c AD 1000. The Newberry Library (p85) has it! You don't need to be a research egghead to stop by, though. The on-site bookstore is known as one of the best places to find Chicago-themed tomes, such as a photo-filled treatise on local hot dogs.

❷ Washington Square

The park across from Newberry Library is officially called Washington Square (p86), famed for its history of soapbox orators. Many of them supposedly lived in nearby 'bughouses' (cheap hotels), hence the park's nickname, 'Bughouse Square.' Today residents walking their dogs, workers eating lunch, and crusty, arguing old-timers hang out around the fountain. The park was added to the National Register of Historic Places in 1991.

❸ High Society at Barneys

The neighborhood society ladies know where to go to have it all: Barneys New York (p93). The luxe department store offers six floors of high-fashion clothing and accessories. When they tire of shopping, the ladies then ascend to the penthouse restaurant – Fred's – for lobster bisque and a soothing glass of Chardonnay (best sipped on the terrace overlooking the lake).

❹ Oak Street Boutiques

Oak Street is where moneyed locals come to find that hand-folded Hermès tie, a Harry Winston diamond or the perfect pair of Jimmy Choo pumps. The designer boutiques line up in a pretty row along the street, between Michigan Ave and Rush St. Non-moneyed locals window shop and sigh.

❺ Oak Street Beach

Oak Street Beach (p94) has been the lay-out spot for downtowners for more than a

Oak Street Beach (p94)

century. Records show that area mansion owners were making complaints as early as 1910 that too many bathers were recreating on the prized stretch of sand. On sunny summer days, the beach still fills with families and body-beautiful types vying for a place to unfurl a towel.

⑥ Coq d'Or Drinks

The Coq d'Or (p92) is in the Drake Hotel, which means plenty of out-of-towners are sitting at the bar. But residents from the neighborhood high-rises are the regulars. See the dapper older gentleman carving into a steak? Or the fur-coat-clad woman clutching her martini? They're here more nights than not, enjoying dinner, drinks and the jazzy crooners who entertain on weekends.

⑦ Water Tower

If the Water Tower (p85) had a disco theme song, it would be 'I Will Survive.' That's because the 154ft-tall, turreted structure was the only thing left standing downtown after the 1871 Great Chicago Fire, thanks to its flameproof limestone. Step inside to see the cool, free gallery of works by local photographers and other artists.

SIGNATURE ROOM
AT THE 95TH
AMERICAN **$$$**

Map p294 (⌨312-787-9596; www.signatureroom.com; 875 N Michigan Ave, John Hancock Center, 95th fl; mains $30-50; ⊘11am-10pm Mon-Thu, to 11pm Fri & Sat, 10am-10pm Sun; 🍴; Ⓜ Red Line to Chicago) Given that diners spend most of the meal view-gaping, you'd think the kitchen atop the Hancock wouldn't trouble itself over the food, but the chef does a fine job with the fish, steak and pasta dishes. Vegetarians will find a fair number of dishes available. Dress for dinner is business casual; no jeans or tennis shoes allowed.

Cheapskates should note they can get the same vista for the price of a (costly) beer, one floor up in the Signature Lounge.

MORTON'S
STEAK **$$$**

Map p294 (⌨312-266-4820; www.mortons.com/statestreet; 1050 N State St; mains $35-75; ⊘5-11pm Mon-Sat, to 10pm Sun; Ⓜ Red Line to Clark/Division) Morton's is a chain now, but Chicago is where it all began. The meat here is aged to perfection and displayed tableside before cooking. See that half a cow? It's the 48oz double porterhouse. Smaller – but still quite dangerous if dropped on your toe – are the fillets, strip steaks and other cuts. The immense baked potatoes could prop up church foundations.

Or you could try the hash browns, a superb version of a side dish all too often ignored. Expensive reds anchor the wine list.

MIKE DITKA'S RESTAURANT
AMERICAN **$$$**

Map p294 (⌨312-587-8989; www.ditkasrestaurants.com; 100 E Chestnut St; mains $20-45; ⊘11am-10pm Mon-Thu, 11am-11pm Fri & Sat, 10am-10pm Sun; Ⓜ Red Line to Chicago) When it's too cold for a tailgate party, come to this spot in the Tremont Hotel (p225) owned by the famously cantankerous former coach of the Chicago Bears (who often pops in). The menu is as meaty as you'd expect, with steaks galore and heaps of oysters, crab legs and other seafood. Fans will love the memorabilia-filled display cases.

🍷 DRINKING & NIGHTLIFE

★ SIGNATURE LOUNGE
LOUNGE

Map p294 (www.signatureroom.com; 875 N Michigan Ave, John Hancock Center, 96th fl; ⊘11am-12:30am Sun-Thu, to 1:30am Fri & Sat; Ⓜ Red Line to Chicago) Grab the elevator to the 96th

ℹ DISCOUNT TICKETS

One of the city's three Hot Tix booths is in the Water Works building (p86; the other two are in the Loop). Stop by to purchase half-price theater tickets. Drama, comedy and performing-arts venues citywide have seats on offer for shows throughout the week. The earlier in the week you visit, the better the selection.

floor of the John Hancock Center and order a beverage while looking out over the city from some 1000ft up in the sky. It's particularly gape-worthy at night. Ladies: don't miss the bathroom view. Note that children aren't allowed in the lounge after 7pm.

The lounge and restaurant have a separate elevator from the Hancock's observatory. Look for signs that say 'Signature 95th/96th.'

COQ D'OR
LOUNGE

Map p294 (☑312-787-2200; 140 E Walton St; ☺11am-1am Sun-Thu, to 2am Fri & Sat; Ⓜ Red Line to Chicago) This classy joint in the Drake Hotel (p225) opened the day after Prohibition was repealed. It offers a taste of old Chicago: burgundy-colored leather booths, snazzy bartenders and bejeweled women in furs sipping Manhattans. A piano player starts tinkling the ivories around 9pm on weekends.

3 ARTS CLUB CAFE
CAFE

Map p294 (☑312-475-9116; www.3artscafe.com; 1300 N Dearborn St; ☺10am-8pm Mon-Sat, 11am-6pm Sun; Ⓜ Red Line to Clark/Division) Chandeliers dangle from the high ceiling, fountains gurgle, and sleek couches offer respite under leafy trees. This elegant cafe sits inside a five-floor Restoration Hardware home-decor store. See the host for seats in the gorgeous main room, or walk onward to the coffee bar and order a glass of wine that you can take with you to other floors.

The cafe serves casual comfort food by the chef behind Doughnut Vault and Small Cheval. The 3 Arts Club, which long occupied the century-old building, was a home for women in the 'three arts' of music, painting and drama.

PUMP ROOM
BAR

Map p294 (☑312-601-2970; www.pumproom. com; 1301 N State Pkwy; ☺5-10pm Sun-Thu, to midnight Fri & Sat; Ⓜ Red Line to Clark/Division) Frank Sinatra and Bette Davis were among the movie stars who used to swirl martinis in the old Pump Room. It recently got a makeover that recaptures the glamour of yesteryear, and once again pretty people are drinking under the romantic paper-globe lights. Be sure to head downstairs by the bathrooms and check out the photos of the famous people who've dined here.

LODGE
BAR

Map p294 (☑312-642-4406; http://lodgetavern. com; 21 W Division St; ☺2pm-4am Mon-Thu, from noon Fri-Sun; Ⓜ Red Line to Clark/Division) Dressed up like a misplaced hunting cabin, the Lodge has a bit more polish than most of its neighbors on Division St. A Wurlitzer jukebox spins oldies and the bowls of salty peanuts complement the abundance of beers on tap. The crowd of mostly 40-somethings drink like they mean it, sometimes until dawn.

 ENTERTAINMENT

CHICAGO CHILDREN'S THEATRE
THEATER

Map p294 (CCT; ☑773-227-0180; www.chicago childrenstheatre.org; 1016 N Dearborn St; Ⓜ Red Line to Clark/Division) CCT is dedicated exclusively to putting on quality productions for young audiences. Many plays are adapted from children's books, and many use puppets or music. The group is building a swanky new theater in the West Loop to be completed in 2020. Until then, performances take place at the Ruth Page Center for Arts in the Gold Coast.

LOOKINGGLASS
THEATRE COMPANY
THEATER

Map p294 (☑312-337-0665; www.looking glasstheatre.org; 821 N Michigan Ave; Ⓜ Red Line to Chicago) This well-regarded troupe works in a nifty theater hewn from the old Water Works (p86) building. The ensemble cast – which includes cofounder David Schwimmer of TV's *Friends* – often uses physical stunts and acrobatics to enhance its dreamy, magical, literary productions.

ZEBRA LOUNGE
LIVE MUSIC

Map p294 (☑312-642-5140; www.thezebra lounge.net; 1220 N State St; ☺5pm-2am Mon-Fri, from 7:30pm Sat & Sun; Ⓜ Red Line to Clark/Division) The piano in this tiny, dark and mirrored room can get as scratchy as the voices of the crowd, which consists mainly of older folks who like to sing along. The ivory strokers here are veterans who know their stuff.

 SHOPPING

★AMERICAN GIRL PLACE — CHILDREN

Map p294 (www.americangirl.com; 835 N Michigan Ave, Water Tower Place; ⊙10am-8pm Mon-Thu, 9am-9pm Fri & Sat, 9am-6pm Sun; 👶; Ⓜ Red Line to Chicago) This is not your mother's doll shop; it's an *experience*. Here, dolls are treated as real people: the 'hospital' carts them away in wheelchairs for repairs, and the cafe seats the dolls as part of the family during tea service. While there are American Girl stores in many cities, this flagship remains the largest and busiest.

HERSHEY'S — FOOD

Map p294 (📞312-337-7711; www.hersheyschocolateworldchicago.com; 822 N Michigan Ave; ⊙10am-10pm; 📶👶; Ⓜ Red Line to Chicago) How about a personalized chocolate bar with your photo on the wrapper? Hershey's has a handful of flashy retail stores around the globe and one is right here on the Mag Mile. Seasonal sweets and hard-to-find flavors of Kisses and other chocolates fill the shelves and there are usually samples to be scoffed.

LEGO STORE — CHILDREN

Map p294 (www.lego.com; 835 N Michigan Ave, Water Tower Place, 2nd fl; ⊙10am-9pm Mon-Sat, 11am-6pm Sun; 👶; Ⓜ Red Line to Chicago) After ooohhing and aaahhing at the cool models of rockets, castles and dinosaurs scattered throughout the store, kids can build their own designs at pint-sized tables equipped with bins of the signature little bricks. It's located in Water Tower Place.

UNIQLO — CLOTHING

Map p294 (📞877-486-4756; https://m.uniqlo.com/us; 830 N Michigan Ave; ⊙10am-9pm Mon-Sat, 11am-8pm Sun; Ⓜ Red Line to Chicago) Take the escalators up from street level to the rainbow array of affordable, clean-lined jeans, T-shirts, jackets and other clothing staples. Japanese fashion retailer Uniqlo puts on a spread that draws men and women of all ages. If you tire of flipping through racks, hit the 6th-floor Starbucks for a drink and great views out over Michigan Ave.

BURTON SNOWBOARDS — SPORTS

Map p294 (📞312-202-7900; www.burton.com; 56 E Walton St; ⊙11am-8pm Mon-Sat, to 6pm Sun; Ⓜ Red Line to Chicago) Midwesterners shred the slopes too, and this is where air dogs come to get their gear. Burton, of course, is the biggest brand in the business. Its multistory Chicago shop carries a sweet selection of boards, jackets, watches and other accessories. There's a chill-out lounge on the top floor where you can check email and watch snowboarding films.

WATER TOWER PLACE — MALL

Map p294 (www.shopwatertower.com; 835 N Michigan Ave; ⊙10am-9pm Mon-Sat, 11am-6pm Sun; Ⓜ Red Line to Chicago) Water Tower Place launched the city's love affair with vertical shopping centers. Many locals swear this first one remains the best. The mall houses 100 stores on seven levels, including Abercrombie & Fitch, Macy's, Aritzia (the mod Canadian chain), Akira (the hip local clothing vendor), Lego and American Girl Place.

BARNEYS NEW YORK — CLOTHING

Map p294 (📞312-587-1700; 15 E Oak St; ⊙10am-7pm Mon-Sat, 11am-6pm Sun; Ⓜ Red Line to Chicago) Barneys provides the quintessential Gold Coast shopping experience. Its six floors sparkle with mega-high-end designer goods, while the penthouse holds a posh restaurant with a toasty fireplace.

JIMMY CHOO — SHOES

Map p294 (📞312-255-1170; www.jimmychoo.com; 114 E Oak St; ⊙10am-6pm Mon-Sat, noon-5pm Sun; Ⓜ Red Line to Chicago) The prices are almost as high as the stiletto heels at Jimmy Choo, revered foot stylist to the rich and famous. Oh, go ahead – be like J Lo and Beyoncé. All it takes is a toss of the head, the willingness to drop $800 on a pair of shoes and the attitude that footwear doesn't make the outfit – it *is* the outfit.

BEST BUY — ELECTRONICS

Map p294 (📞312-397-2146; www.bestbuy.com; 875 N Michigan Ave; ⊙10am-9pm Mon-Sat, to 8pm Sun; Ⓜ Red Line to Chicago) A convenient store for those looking to pick up laptop or cellphone supplies, Best Buy offers good prices on things like SIM cards, flash drives, handheld computing devices and more. Come with a clear idea of what you want, as it can be difficult to flag down staff for help. The store is in the Hancock Center.

GOLD COAST SHOPPING

900 N MICHIGAN
MALL

Map p294 (☏312-915-3916; www.shop900.com; 900 N Michigan Ave; ⊙10am-7pm Mon-Sat, noon-6pm Sun; ⓂRed Line to Chicago) This huge mall is home to an upscale collection of stores including Diesel, Gucci and J Crew among many others. Water Tower Place (p93) is under the same management and they simply placed all the really expensive stores over here.

JIL SANDER
CLOTHING

Map p294 (☏312-335-0006; www.jilsander.com; 48 E Oak St; ⊙10am-6pm Mon-Sat; ⓂRed Line to Chicago) Jil Sander's minimalist colors and simple designs somehow manage to remain fashionable long after other trendsetters have disappeared from the scene.

H&M
CLOTHING

Map p294 (☏312-640-0060; www.hm.com/us; 840 N Michigan Ave; ⊙10am-9pm Mon-Sat, to 8pm Sun; ⓂRed Line to Chicago) This Swedish-based purveyor of trendy togs is usually packed with customers clawing the racks for high fashion at low prices. Men and women will find a variety of European-cut styles ranging from business suits to bathing suits. There's another outlet at 22 N State St, but this one is bigger.

TOPSHOP
CLOTHING

Map p294 (☏312-280-6834; http://us.topshop.com; 830 N Michigan Ave; ⊙10am-9pm Mon-Sat, 11am-8pm Sun; ⓂRed Line to Chicago) The popular British purveyor of youthful, urban-cool style recently opened this big store on the Magnificent Mile.

SPORTS & ACTIVITIES

OAK STREET BEACH
BEACH

Map p294 (www.cpdbeaches.com; 1000 N Lake Shore Dr; ⓂRed Line to Chicago) This beach packs in bodies beautiful at the edge of downtown in the shadow of skyscrapers. Lifeguards are on duty in summer. You can rent umbrellas and lounge chairs. The island-y, yellow-umbrella-dotted cafe provides drinks and DJs.

Though the hulking Lake Shore Dr condos cast shadows in the afternoon, the beach remains busy.

WATERIDERS
KAYAKING

(☏312-953-9287; www.wateriders.com; 950 N Kingsbury St; per hour single/double $20/30; ⓂBrown/Purple Line to Chicago) Wateriders rents kayaks for paddles on the Chicago River. It also offers excellent tours, including the daily 2½-hour 'Ghost and Gangster' trip ($65) that glides by notorious downtown sites. The dock is at Kingsbury Yacht Club, where Oak St meets the river. It's about a half-mile northwest of the Brown/Purple Line El station at Chicago.

Lincoln Park & Old Town

Neighborhood Top Five

1 **Lincoln Park** (p97) Meandering the park's byways and hearing lions roar in the zoo, smelling exotic flowers in the conservatory and finding the calm of the hidden lily pool.

2 **Second City** (p105) Laughing and drinking and shouting out plot sugges-tions during an improv show at this legendary comedy venue.

3 **Alinea** (p103) Digging into space-age, Jetsons-like cuisine in one of the world's best restaurants.

4 **North Avenue Beach** (p108) Joining the fun in the sun with a kayak, stand-up paddleboard, beach yoga class, volleyball game or frosty margarita.

5 **Steppenwolf Theatre** (p105) Seeing a provocative play from the Pulitzer Prize–winning, movie-star-filled ensemble.

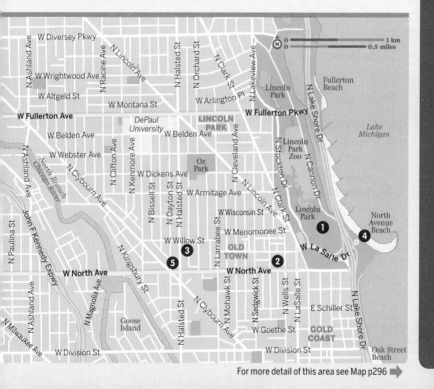

For more detail of this area see Map p296 ➡

Lonely Planet's Top Tip

While you have to pay admission to see a show at Second City (p105), there's free improv afterward. You heard right: show up at the Mainstage or ETC stage after the last show of the evening (Friday and Saturday excluded) and you can watch the performers riff through a half-hour of improv. The freebie begins around 10pm. Arrive 15 minutes prior.

Best Places to Eat

➡ Alinea (p103)
➡ La Fournette (p104)
➡ Pequod's Pizza (p99)
➡ Balena (p103)
➡ Twin Anchors (p104)

For reviews, see p99 ➡

Best Places to Drink

➡ Old Town Ale House (p104)
➡ Delilah's (p104)
➡ Eva's Cafe (p105)
➡ J Parker (p105)

For reviews, see p104 ➡

☆ Best Entertainment

➡ Steppenwolf Theatre (p105)
➡ Second City (p105)
➡ BLUES (p106)
➡ Kingston Mines (p106)
➡ Lincoln Hall (p106)

For reviews, see p105 ➡

(sidebar, rotated) LINCOLN PARK & OLD TOWN

Explore Lincoln Park & Old Town

Lincoln Park is the city's premier playground. Almost 50% larger than Central Park in New York, Lincoln Park is where Chicagoans flock when the weather warms up to savor the lakefront oasis of ponds, paths and exotic creatures in the free zoo.

Lincoln Park is also the name for the abutting neighborhood, which is home to the city's yuppie population mixed with DePaul University's large student body. The area is alive day and night with people walking dogs, riding bikes, pushing strollers and looking for a place to park so they can shop in the swanky boutiques and eat in the excellent restaurants. Add in several theaters (led by world-renowned Steppenwolf) and lively live-music clubs, and you've got a day's worth of action here.

Old Town was the epicenter of Chicago's hippie culture in the 1960s. A few trippy holdovers from the old days remain, but now stylish stores and eateries stuff the neighborhood, which joins Lincoln Park to the south. Wells St is in the main vein and most visitors make a pilgrimage here at some point – it's the home of the comedy club and improv stronghold, Second City.

Local Life

➡ **Funny bar** Performers from Second City often duck into the Old Town Ale House (p104) for a beverage after the show.
➡ **Blues jam** Musicians aged 17 to 70 tune up for the free blues jam at Kingston Mines (p106) every Sunday.
➡ **Farmers market** Chicagoans flock to the park to stock up on farm fare at Green City Market (p98) on Wednesday and Saturday mornings.

Getting There & Away

➡ **El** Brown, Purple, Red Line to Fullerton for Lincoln Park; Brown, Purple Line to Sedgwick for Old Town.
➡ **Bus** Number 151 from downtown (along Michigan Ave) for zoo and park sites.
➡ **Car** Parking is difficult. In Lincoln Park, try the meters along Diversey Harbor. In Old Town, try the pay garage at Piper's Alley, at North Ave and Wells St.

TOP SIGHT
LINCOLN PARK

The neighborhood gets its name from this park, Chicago's largest. Its 1200 acres stretch for 6 miles, from North Ave north to Diversey Pkwy, where it narrows and continues until the end of Lake Shore Dr. On sunny days locals come out to play in droves, taking advantage of the ponds, paths and playing fields or visiting the zoo and beaches.

Opened in 1868, the free Lincoln Park Zoo (p98) has entertained generations of Chicagoans. Families swarm the grounds, which are smack in the park's midst. The leafy conservatory (p98) and hidden **lily garden** are also nearby and free.

At the park's southern edge, sculptor Augustus Saint-Gaudens' **Standing Lincoln** (🚋22) shows the 16th president deep in contemplation before giving a speech. Saint-Gaudens based the work on casts made of Lincoln's face and hands while Lincoln was alive. The statue stands behind the Chicago History Museum (p98).

Nearby, at the corner of LaSalle Dr and Clark St, take a gander at the **Couch Mausoleum** (🚋22). It's the sole reminder of the land's pre-1864 use, when it was a municipal cemetery. Many graves contained dead soldiers from Camp Douglas, a horrific prisoner-of-war stockade on the city's South Side during the Civil War. The city eventually relocated the bodies.

There's more beyond the zoo, gardens and monuments. Head north and there are sailboat harbors, golf courses, bird sanctuaries and rowing clubs gliding on the lagoons. Walk east from anywhere in the park and you'll come to the **Lakefront Trail** that connects several beaches along the way.

Convenient Divvy stations to grab a bike for a short ride are at the corner of Lake Shore Dr and North Blvd, and at the Theater on the Lake building (near the intersection of Lake Shore Dr and W Fullerton Pkwy). Markets and takeaway joints pop up along Clark St and Diversey Pkwy, prime for picnic provisions.

DON'T MISS
→ Zoo
→ Conservatory
→ *Standing Lincoln* statue
→ Couch Mausoleum
→ Alfred Caldwell Lily Pool

PRACTICALITIES
→ Map p296
→ ⏲ 6am-11pm
→ 🚶
→ 🚌 151

⊙ SIGHTS

LINCOLN PARK   PARK
See p97.

LINCOLN PARK ZOO   ZOO
Map p296 (⌨312-742-2000; www.lpzoo.org; 2200 N Cannon Dr; ⊙10am-5pm Mon-Fri, to 6:30pm Sat & Sun Jun-Aug, 10am-5pm Apr, May, Sep & Oct, 10am-4:30pm Nov-Mar; ⓘ; ⌑151) **FREE** The zoo has been around since 1868 and is a local freebie favorite, filled with lions, snow monkeys and other exotic creatures in the shadow of downtown. Check out the Regenstein African Journey and dragonfly-dappled Nature Boardwalk for the cream of the crop. The Gateway Pavilion (on Cannon Dr) is the main entrance; pick up a map and schedule of feedings and training sessions.

Families swarm the grounds. Kids beeline for the African exhibit, which puts them close to pygmy hippos and dwarf crocodiles. The Ape House pleases with its swingin' gorillas and chimps. Snow monkeys chill in the Macaque Forest. **Farm-in-the-Zoo** features a full range of barnyard animals and offers frequent demonstrations of cow milking, horse grooming and other chores. The half-mile-long **Nature Boardwalk** circles the adjacent South Pond and teaches about wetlands ecology; keep an eye out for endangered birds such as the black-crowned night heron. Kids can also climb aboard the vintage train and carousel ($3 per ride).

As well as the Gateway Pavilion, the zoo has multiple entrances around its perimeter. Drivers be warned: parking here is among the city's worst. If you do find a spot in the Cannon Dr lot, it can cost up to $35 for four hours.

LOCAL KNOWLEDGE

SIGHTSEEING FROM THE EL

The El (short for 'elevated') provides a great cheap sightseeing tour of the city. For the best views, hop on the Brown Line and ride into the Loop. Get on in Lincoln Park at either the Fullerton or Armitage stops, take a seat by the window and watch as the train clatters downtown, swinging past skyscrapers so close you can almost touch them. Stay aboard as the El loops the Loop and get off at the Clark stop if you want to remain downtown.

CHICAGO HISTORY MUSEUM   MUSEUM
Map p296 (⌨312-642-4600; www.chicagohistory.org; 1601 N Clark St; adult/child $16/free; ⊙9:30am-4:30pm Mon-Sat, noon-5pm Sun; ⓘ; ⌑22) Curious about Chicago's storied past? Multimedia displays at this museum cover it all, from the Great Fire to the 1968 Democratic Convention. President Lincoln's deathbed is here; the bell from Mrs O'Leary's cow is here. So is the chance to 'become' a Chicago hot dog covered in condiments (in the kids' area, but adults are welcome for the photo op).

The Diorama Hall is nifty, especially the model that shows the 1893 World's Fair set up. When you pay your entrance fee, ask for the free audio tour to enhance your visit. The on-site bookstore stocks a good assortment of local history tomes.

LINCOLN PARK CONSERVATORY   GARDENS
Map p296 (⌨312-742-7736; www.lincolnparkconservancy.org; 2391 N Stockton Dr; ⊙9am-5pm; ⌑151) **FREE** Walking through the conservatory's 3 acres of desert palms, jungle ferns and tropical orchids is like taking a trip around the world in 30 minutes. The glass-bedecked hothouse remains a sultry, 75°F escape even in winter.

**PEGGY NOTEBAERT
NATURE MUSEUM**   MUSEUM
Map p296 (⌨773-755-5100; www.naturemuseum.org; 2430 N Cannon Dr; adult/child $9/6; ⊙9am-5pm Mon-Fri, 10am-5pm Sat & Sun; ⓘ; ⌑151) This hands-on museum has turtles and croaking frogs in its 1st-floor marsh, fluttering insects in its 2nd-floor butterfly haven and a bird boardwalk meandering through its rooftop garden. It's geared mostly to kids. Check the schedule for daily creature feedings.

In winter, the Green City Market sets up inside on Saturdays.

GREEN CITY MARKET   MARKET
Map p296 (⌨773-880-1266; www.greencitymarket.org; 1790 N Clark St; ⊙8am-1pm Wed & Sat May-Oct; ⌑22) Stands of purple cabbages, red radishes, green asparagus and other bright-hued produce sprawl through Lincoln Park at Chicago's biggest farmers market. Follow your nose to the demonstration tent, where local cooks such as *Top Chef*-winner Stephanie Izard prepare dishes – say rice crepes with a mushroom *gastrique* – using market ingredients. In winter the market moves

into the Peggy Notebaert Nature Museum and is held from 8:30am to 1pm on Saturdays only.

BIOGRAPH THEATER HISTORIC SITE

Map p296 (2433 N Lincoln Ave; M Brown, Purple, Red Line to Fullerton) In 1934 the 'lady in red' betrayed gangster John Dillinger at this theater, which used to show movies. FBI agents shot him in the alley beside the building.

The whole thing started out as a date: Dillinger took new girlfriend Polly Hamilton to the show and Polly's roommate Anna Sage tagged along, wearing a red dress. Alas, Dillinger was a notorious bank robber and the FBI's very first 'Public Enemy Number One'. Sage also had troubles with the law and was about to be deported. To avoid it, she agreed to set up Dillinger. The venue now hosts plays by the Victory Gardens Theater.

ALFRED CALDWELL LILY POOL GARDENS

Map p296 (www.lincolnparkconservancy.org; 2391 N Stockton Dr; ⊙7:30am-dusk mid-Apr–mid-Nov; ☐151) **FREE** The enchanting Lily Pool hides in a plot northeast of the Lincoln Park Conservatory, at the corner of Fullerton and Cannon Drs. Built in 1938 by landscape architect Jens Jenson, the garden is designated a National Historic Landmark for its Prairie School style, native plant use and stonework that resembles the stratified canyons of the Wisconsin Dells.

The pool has become an important stopover for migrating birds and also welcomes turtles and dragonflies. It's a lovely escape from the Lincoln Park crowds. Docents lead free, half-hour tours on various weekends.

DEPAUL ART MUSEUM MUSEUM

Map p296 (☎773-325-7506; http://museums.depaul.edu; 935 W Fullerton Ave; ⊙11am-7pm Wed & Thu, to 5pm Fri, noon-5pm Sat & Sun; M Brown, Purple, Red Line to Fullerton) **FREE** DePaul University's compact art museum hosts changing exhibits of 20th-century works. Pieces from the permanent collection – by sculptor Claes Oldenburg, cartoonist Chris Ware, architect Daniel Burnham and more – hang on the 2nd floor. It's definitely worth swinging through if you're in the neighborhood; you can see everything in less than 30 minutes.

**ST VALENTINE'S DAY
MASSACRE SITE** HISTORIC SITE

Map p296 (2122 N Clark St; ☐22) At this infamous spot on February 14, 1929, Al Capone's henchmen, dressed as cops, lined up seven members of Bugs Moran's gang against the garage wall that used to stand here and sprayed them with bullets. After that, Moran cut his losses and Al Capone gained control of Chicago's North Side vice. The garage was torn down in 1967 to make way for a retirement home and its parking lot (which is what you see at the site now).

A house (2119 N Clark St) used as a lookout by the killers stands across the street.

EATING

✗ Lincoln Park

PEQUOD'S PIZZA PIZZA $

Map p296 (☎731-327-1512; www.pequodspizza.com; 2207 N Clybourn Ave; small pizzas from $12; ⊙11am-2am Mon-Sat, to midnight Sun; ☐9 to Webster) Like the ship in *Moby Dick,* from which this neighborhood restaurant takes its name, Pequod's pan-style (akin to deep dish) pizza is a thing of legend – head and shoulders above chain competitors because of its caramelized cheese, generous toppings and sweetly flavored sauce. The atmosphere is affably rugged, too, with surly waitstaff and graffiti-covered walls.

BOURGEOIS PIG CAFE $

Map p296 (☎773-883-5282; www.thebourgeoispigcafe.com; 738 W Fullerton Ave; mains $7-10; ⊙9am-9:30pm; ☎✑; M Brown, Purple, Red Line to Fullerton) An old-style cafe with big, creaking wooden tables and chairs, the Pig serves strong java and whopping sandwiches. It's a convivial place to grab a bite while working through the newspaper or chatting with friends. Tea drinkers and vegetarians will find many options on offer.

SULTAN'S MARKET MIDDLE EASTERN $

Map p296 (☎312-638-9151; www.chicagofalafel.com; 2521 N Clark St; mains $4-7; ⊙10am-10pm Mon-Sat, to 9pm Sun; M Brown, Purple, Red Line to Fullerton) Neighborhood folks dig the falafel sandwiches, spinach pies and other quality Middle Eastern fare at family-run

Lincoln Park – Park Life

Chicago's largest park is where locals come out to play. They swim and spike volleyballs at North Ave Beach. They ogle the lions, gorillas and other creatures in the zoo and nature museum. They browse for veggies and homemade pie at the Green City farmers market. But mostly they just hang out, kick a soccer ball or jog the leafy pathways.

JAMESTUNG/GETTY IMAGES ©

PETER PTSCHELINZEW/GETTY IMAGES ©

1. North Avenue Beach (p108)
Enjoy sun and sports at Chicago's most popular beach.

2. Polar bear, Lincoln Park Zoo (p98)
Talk to the animals for free at this family-favorite zoo.

3. Peggy Notebaert Nature Museum (p98)
Keep your eyes peeled in the butterfly room on the 2nd floor of this museum.

4. Lincoln Park (p97)
The 1200-acre park offers many lakes, trails and paths.

5. Green City Market (p98)
Gather picnic supplies at Chicago's biggest farmers market.

LONELY PLANET/GETTY IMAGES ©

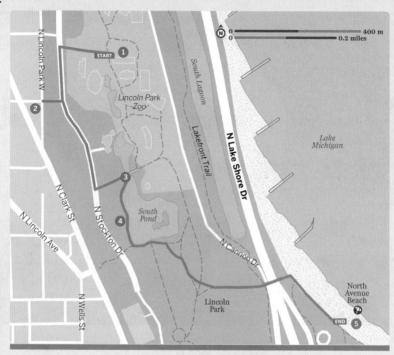

Neighborhood Walk
The Zoo & Beyond

START LINCOLN PARK ZOO
END NORTH AVENUE BEACH
LENGTH 2 MILES; FOUR TO FIVE HOURS

Looking to entertain the little ones? A day in Lincoln Park will keep you busy without breaking the bank. Generations of Chicagoans have been coming here, to what's now one of the last free zoos in the country.

Stroll through re-created regions in the Regenstein African Journey and watch Ape House monkeys play at the two best exhibits at the ❶ **Lincoln Park Zoo** (p98). Can your kids identify the smallest member of the bear family? The big beast prized for its horns? The panda of a different color?

Moving fast, you can hit the highlights of the zoo in two hours or so, before heading to ❷ **RJ Grunts** (p103) for lunch. The hostess will store your stroller while you order a chocolate-peanut-butter-banana milkshake and burgers. The menu, and the hubbub, are entirely kid friendly.

Head back into the park and hop on the ❸ **Nature Boardwalk**, a half-mile path around the South Pond's wetlands ecosystem. Placards explain about the marshy environment and the critters that live there. The mod-looking arch you pass on the east side is the Education Pavilion. Local starchitect Jeanne Gang (of Aqua Tower fame) designed it and it's meant to resemble a turtle shell.

Next it's the big ol' barn and the ❹ **Farm-in-the-Zoo** (p98). Little ones seem to love petting sheep, watching chicks hatch and learning how to milk a cow. Parents like that this, too, is free. By now you've spent more than four hours in the park. If you have enough energy to continue...

Walk south along the pond and turn east past ball fields before you cross the bridge to ❺ **North Avenue Beach** (p108). Grab a refreshment, rent a beach chair and watch the kids construct castles in the sand. Walk out on the curving breakwater for one of the city's best skyline views. It's the ideal background for a keepsake family photo.

Sultan's Market. The small, homey space doesn't have many tables, but Lincoln Park is nearby for picnicking.

PATIO AT CAFE BRAUER
CAFE $

Map p296 (☏312-507-9053; 2021 N Stockton Dr; mains $9-13; ☺11am-9pm Mon-Fri, 8:30am-9pm Sat & Sun; 👶) Take a break from zoo explorations at pretty Cafe Brauer. It's perfect for an ice-cream cone, flatbread pizza or glass of wine refresher while sitting by the pond.

FLORIOLE CAFE
BAKERY $

Map p296 (☏773-883-1313; www.floriole.com; 1220 W Webster Ave; items $3-10; ☺7am-5:30pm Tue-Fri, 8:30am-5:30pm Sat-Mon; 🛜; Ⓜ Brown, Purple, Red Line to Fullerton) The chef got her start selling lemon tarts, twice-baked croissants and rum-tinged *caneles* (a pastry with a custard center and caramelized crust) at the Green Market. She now sells her French-influenced baked goods and sandwiches – which use Midwest-sourced meats, cheeses and produce – in an airy, loft-like space punctuated by a big wooden farm table.

ALOHA EATS
HAWAIIAN $

Map p296 (☏773-935-6828; www.alohaeats. com; 2534 N Clark St; mains $9-14; ☺11am-10pm Tue-Sun; Ⓜ Brown, Purple, Red Line to Fullerton) From *musubis* (rice rolls wrapped in seaweed) to *saimin* (egg noodle soup) to *katsus* (breaded cutlets), it's all about whopping portions of Hawaiian food here. Spam, aka 'the Hawaiian steak,' is the main ingredient in many dishes, including the popular Loco Moco (meat, fried eggs and brown gravy atop rice). Macaroni or fries always arrive on the side.

The massive menu includes several tofu and fish options for those watching their girlish figures. The bright-yellow interior and island dishes soothe especially well in winter.

WIENERS CIRCLE
AMERICAN $

Map p296 (☏773-477-7444; 2622 N Clark St; hot dogs $3-7; ☺11am-4am Sun-Thu, to 5am Fri & Sat; Ⓜ Brown, Purple Line to Diversey) As famous for its unruly, foul-mouthed ambience as its charred hot dogs and cheddar fries, the Wieners Circle is a scene for late-night munchies. During the day and on weeknights it's a normal hot-dog stand – with damn good food. The wild show is on weekend eves, around 2am, when the nearby bars close and everyone starts yelling.

The f-bombs fly and it can get raucous between staff and customers.

RJ GRUNTS
BURGERS $

Map p296 (☏773-929-5363; www.rjgruntschi cago.com; 2056 N Lincoln Park W; mains $10-18; ☺11:30am-11pm Mon-Fri, 10am-11pm Sat, 10am-9pm Sun; 👶; ☐22) The very first of the now-ubiquitous Lettuce Entertain You stable of restaurants, RJ Grunts came on to the scene in the 1970s, when Lincoln Park emerged as the young singles' neighborhood of choice. Now, as then, the huge salad bar, burgers and beer are the mainstays.

This is a fun post-zoo lunch spot; even the pickiest of kids will find something to love. The awesome milkshakes can be spiked with booze for the adults in the crowd.

BALENA
ITALIAN $$

Map p296 (☏312-867-3888; www.balenachicago. com; 1633 N Halsted St; mains $18-26; ☺5-9pm Mon, to 10pm Tue-Thu, to 11pm Fri & Sat, 11am-9pm Sun; Ⓜ Red Line to North/Clybourn) 'Mamma mia!,' you want to shout after forking into the fat, creamy, roasted mushrooms atop grilled bread. Balena tastes like an Italian grandmother whipped up the wood-fired pizzas, house-cured *salumi* and saucy pastas. But don't let the rusticness fool you: complex, finessed flavors are at work here. The cavernous, exposed-brick and wood-beam room echoes with chatter and clattering plates.

A huge list of European wines and prosecco flow by the bottleful. Balena sits across from Steppenwolf Theatre and makes a terrific stop pre- or post-show. Reserve ahead.

CAFE BA-BA-REEBA!
SPANISH $$

Map p296 (☏773-935-5000; www.cafebaba reeba.com; 2024 N Halsted St; tapas $5-12; ☺4-10pm Mon-Thu, 11:30am-midnight Fri, 9am-midnight Sat, 9am-10pm Sun; Ⓜ Brown, Purple Line to Armitage) At this long-standing, delightfully ersatz tapas joint, the garlic-laced menu changes often but always includes some spicy meats, marinated fish and heaps of hot or cold small plates. For a main event, order one of the paellas ($12 to $17 per person, minimum two people) as soon as you get seated – they take a while to prepare.

★ALINEA
MODERN AMERICAN $$$

Map p296 (☏312-867-0110; www.alinearestau rant.com; 1723 N Halsted St; 10-/16-course menu from $175/285; ☺5-9:30pm Wed-Sun; Ⓜ Red Line to North/Clybourn) One of the world's best restaurants, Alinea brings on multiple courses of mind-bending molecular gastronomy. Dishes may emanate from a centrifuge or be pressed into a capsule, a la duck served with a 'pillow of lavender air.' There are no reservations. Instead Alinea sells tickets two to three months in advance via its website. Check the Twitter feed (@Alinea) for last-minute seats.

Chef Grant Achatz gutted and renovated the restaurant in early 2016, so it feels a bit less mod and more classic. Vegetarians need to call in advance to see if the ever-changing menu can be modified. Note that there's no sign on the restaurant's door, so look for the street number.

BOKA   MODERN AMERICAN $$$

Map p296 (☎312-337-6070; www.bokachicago.com; 1729 N Halsted St; mains $28-41, 7-course menu $115; ☺5-10pm Sun-Thu, to 11pm Fri & Sat; ⓂRed Line to North/Clybourn) A Michelin-starred restaurant-lounge hybrid with a seafood-leaning menu, Boka is a pre- and post-theater stomping ground for younger Steppenwolf patrons. Order a cocktail at the bar or slip into one of the booths for small-plate dishes such as mango-laced tabbouleh salad or veal sweetbreads with Moroccan barbecue sauce.

✕ Old Town

LA FOURNETTE   FRENCH $

Map p296 (☎312-624-9430; www.lafournette.com; 1547 N Wells St; items $3-7; ☺7am-6:30pm Mon-Sat, to 5:30pm Sun; ⓂBrown, Purple Line to Sedgwick) The chef hails from Alsace in France and he fills his narrow, rustic-wood bakery with bright-hued macarons (purple passionfruit, green pistachio, red raspberry-chocolate), cheese-infused breads, crust-crackling baguettes and buttery croissants. They all beg to be devoured on the spot with a cup of locally roasted Intelligentsia coffee. Staff make delicious soups, crepes, quiches and sandwiches with equal French love.

OLD JERUSALEM   MIDDLE EASTERN $

Map p296 (☎312-944-0459; www.oldjerusalemrestaurant.net; 1411 N Wells St; mains $9-15; ☺11am-10:30pm Sun-Thu, to 11pm Fri & Sat; ☒; ⓂBrown, Purple Line to Sedgwick) A humble, hidden gem in Old Town, this mom-and-pop Middle Eastern spot has been serving falafel and pita sandwiches, kabobs and baked *kefta* (spiced lamb) for more than 40 years. Vegetarians will find lots of options. If the weather's good, get your food to go and feast in nearby Lincoln Park.

TWIN ANCHORS   BARBECUE $$

Map p296 (☎312-266-1616; www.twinanchorsribs.com; 1655 N Sedgwick St; mains $17-27; ☺5-11pm Mon-Thu, to midnight Fri, noon-midnight Sat, to 10.30pm Sun; ⓂBrown, Purple Line to Sedgwick) Twin Anchors is synonymous with ribs – smoky, tangy-sauced baby backs in this case. The meat drops from the ribs as soon as you lift them. The restaurant doesn't take reservations, so you'll have to wait outside or around the neon-lit 1950s bar, which sets the tone for the place. An almost-all-Sinatra jukebox completes the supper-club ambience.

SALPICON   MEXICAN $$$

Map p296 (☎312-988-7811; www.salpicon.com; 1252 N Wells St; mains $22-32; ☺5-10pm Mon-Thu, to 11pm Fri & Sat, 11am-9pm Sun; ⓂRed Line to Clark/Division) Priscila Satkoff's high-end Mexican place has elevated *ceviche* (seafood marinated in lemon or lime juice, garlic and seasonings) and *chiles rellenos* (stuffed poblano peppers that are batter-fried) to an art. Many other items come slathered in heavenly *mole* (chili and chocolate sauce). The festive interior features high ceilings and bold colors.

Create bright colors in your head by trying some of the 60 tequilas, including some rare, oak-barrel-aged numbers.

🍷 DRINKING & NIGHTLIFE

★OLD TOWN ALE HOUSE   BAR

Map p296 (☎312-944-7020; www.theoldtownalehouse.com; 219 W North Ave; ☺3pm-4am Mon-Fri, noon-4am Sat & Sun; ⓂBrown, Purple Line to Sedgwick) Located near the Second City comedy club and the scene of late-night musings since the 1960s, this unpretentious neighborhood favorite lets you mingle with beautiful people and grizzled regulars, seated pint by pint under the nude-politician paintings. Classic jazz on the jukebox provides the soundtrack for the jovial goings-on. Cash only.

DELILAH'S   BAR

Map p296 (☎773-472-2771; www.delilahschicago.com; 2771 N Lincoln Ave; ☺4pm-2am Sun-Fri, to 3am Sat; ⓂBrown Line to Diversey) A bartender rightfully referred to this bad-ass black sheep of the neighborhood as the 'pride of Lincoln Ave' – a title earned for the heavy pours and the best whiskey selection in the city. Staff know their way around a beer list, too, tapping unusual domestic and international suds (though cheap Pabst longnecks are always behind the bar as well).

EVA'S CAFE   CAFE

Map p296 (312-280-8900; www.evasoldtown. com; 1447 N Sedgwick St; 7am-8pm Mon-Fri, 8am-8pm Sat & Sun; ; Brown, Purple Line to Sedgwick) The long room charms, with a fireplace, brick floor and antique wood tables and chairs. Coffee and tea steam out of mismatched ceramic cups. The young and bookish crowd tap-tap-taps on laptops, while the occasional writers group convenes to discuss plot. It's about as writerly as a cafe can be.

J PARKER   LOUNGE

Map p296 (312-254-4747; www.jparkerchicago. com; 1816 N Clark St; 5pm-1am Mon-Thu, 4pm-1am Fri, 11:30am-1pm Sat & Sun; 22) It's all about the view from the Hotel Lincoln's 13th-floor rooftop bar. And it delivers, sweeping over the park, the lake and downtown skyline. Prepare to jostle with the young and preppy crowd, especially if it's a warm night.

WEEDS   BAR

Map p296 (312-943-7815; www.weedstavern. com; 1555 N Dayton St; 4pm-2am Mon-Fri, to 3am Sat, noon-2am Sun; Red Line to North/Clybourn) Weeds has the tenacity of its namesake flora, sticking to its beatnik-meets-bohemia roots for years while the neighborhood gentrified around it. If the walls could talk, you'd hear some strange yarns from the crew who work and drink here. Weeds hosts open-mic poetry (Monday; p106) and sometimes live music, and you can quaff in the laid-back beer garden.

ROSE'S LOUNGE   BAR

Map p296 (773-327-4000; 2656 N Lincoln Ave; 2pm-2am; Brown, Purple Line to Diversey) Once your eyes adjust to the dark of Rose's, the eclectic bric-a-brac, drop ceiling and groovy jukebox make it an odd duck among Lincoln Park's cocktail and sports bars. The ultracheap beers and free pretzels are the big draw, bringing in a motley set of spendthrift regulars. Late night the young and drunk flock in.

ALIVE ONE   BAR

Map p296 (773-348-9800; www.aliveone.com; 2683 N Halsted St; 5pm-2am Sun-Fri, to 3am Sat; Brown, Purple Line to Diversey) The jukebox is stuffed with hundreds of bootlegged, all-live (get the name?) recordings by The Clash, The Who, Hendrix, Phish and more. The atmosphere converts from jam-absorbing to lounge-like on weekends. A good selection of microbrews flows from the taps.

GOOSE ISLAND BREWPUB   BREWERY

Map p296 (312-915-0071; www.gooseisland brewpubs.com; 1800 N Clybourn Ave; 11am-10pm Sun-Wed, to 11pm Thu & Fri, to midnight Sat; ; Red Line to North/Clybourn) Goose Island's popular beers are served in bars and restaurants around Chicago, and much of it is brewed right here. The pub pours the flagship Honker's Ale and 14 or so other potent brews. Four-beer flights are available. Decent grub complements the suds; special kudos to the Stilton burger and chips ($14).

☆ ENTERTAINMENT

★ SECOND CITY   COMEDY

Map p296 (312-337-3992; www.secondcity. com; 1616 N Wells St; tickets $23-29; Brown, Purple Line to Sedgwick) Bill Murray, Stephen Colbert, Tina Fey and more honed their wit at this slick venue. Shows take place nightly. The Mainstage and ETC stage host sketch revues (with an improv scene thrown in); they're similar in price and quality. Donny's Skybox is for incubating shows. Bargain: turn up around 10pm (Friday and Saturday excluded) and watch the comics improv a set for free. Weekend shows sell out fast; buy tickets a few weeks in advance.

★ IO THEATER   COMEDY

Map p296 (312-929-2401; www.ioimprov.com/chicago; 1501 N Kingsbury St; tickets $5-16; Red Line to North/Clybourn) One of Chicago's top-tier improv houses, iO is a bit edgier (and cheaper) than its competition, with four stages hosting bawdy shows nightly. Two bars and a beer garden add to the fun. The Improvised Shakespeare Company is awesome; catch them if you can.

★ STEPPENWOLF THEATRE   THEATER

Map p296 (312-335-1650; www.steppenwolf. org; 1650 N Halsted St; Red Line to North/Clybourn) Steppenwolf is Chicago's top stage for

WEEDS POETRY NIGHT

Verse comes in all shapes and sizes at **Weeds Poetry Night** (Map p296; ☑312-943-7815; 1555 N Dayton St; Ⓜ Red Line to North/Clybourn). Every Monday at 10pm a cast of delightfully eccentric poets gets on the tavern's mic to vent about love, sex, war, booze, urban living and pretty much everything in between. Some of it rhymes, some of it rambles, but the proportions make for a pretty cool scene.

quality, provocative theater productions. The Hollywood-heavy ensemble includes Gary Sinise, John Malkovich, Martha Plimpton, Gary Cole, Joan Allen and Tracy Letts. A money-saving tip: the box office releases 20 tickets for $20 for each day's shows. They go on sale at 11am Monday to Saturday and at 1pm Sunday, and are available by phone.

The Downstairs Theatre is the main performance space, the Upstairs Theatre is more intimate, and the Garage hosts emerging actors and playwrights. Recent additions include a new cafe, bar and small black box theater for experimental works.

LINCOLN HALL
LIVE MUSIC

Map p296 (☑773-525-2501; www.lh-st.com; 2424 N Lincoln Ave; 🛜; Ⓜ Brown, Purple, Red Line to Fullerton) Hyped national indie bands are the main players at this ubercool, midsized venue with acoustically perfect sound. The front room has a kitchen that offers small plates and sandwiches until 10pm.

BLUES
BLUES

Map p296 (☑773-528-1012; www.chicagoblues bar.com; 2519 N Halsted St; cover charge $7-10; ⊙8pm-2am Wed-Sun; Ⓜ Brown, Purple, Red Line to Fullerton) Long, narrow and high volume, this veteran blues club draws a slightly older crowd that soaks up every crackling, electrified moment. As one local musician put it, 'The audience here comes out to *understand* the blues.' Big local names grace the small stage.

KINGSTON MINES
BLUES

Map p296 (☑773-477-4646; www.kingstonmines. com; 2548 N Halsted St; cover charge $12-15; ⊙8pm-4am Mon-Thu, 7pm-4am Fri & Sat, 6pm-4am Sun; Ⓜ Brown, Purple, Red Line to Fullerton)

Popular enough to draw big names on the blues circuit, Kingston Mines is so noisy, hot and sweaty that blues neophytes will feel as though they're having a genuine experience – sort of like a gritty Delta theme park. Two stages, seven nights a week, ensure somebody's always on. The blues jam session from 6pm to 8:30pm on Sundays is free.

UP COMEDY CLUB
COMEDY

Map p296 (☑312-662-4562; www.upcomedyclub. com; 230 W North Ave; tickets $20-41; Ⓜ Brown, Purple Line to Sedgwick) UP is part of the Second City family and shares the same building, though it has a different entrance. It's a smaller space that hosts more experimental shows. It also adds stand-up acts by well-known touring comedians to its roster.

VICTORY GARDENS THEATER
THEATER

Map p296 (☑773-871-3000; www.victorygar dens.org; 2433 N Lincoln Ave; Ⓜ Brown, Purple, Red Line to Fullerton) Long established and playwright-friendly, Victory Gardens specializes in world premieres of plays by Chicago authors. It's located in the historic Biograph Theater, where bank robber John Dillinger – aka Public Enemy Number One – was shot in 1934.

FACETS MULTIMEDIA
CINEMA

Map p296 (☑773-281-4114; www.facets.org; 1517 W Fullerton Ave; Ⓜ Brown, Purple, Red Line to Fullerton) Facets' main business is as the country's largest distributor of foreign and cult films, so it follows that its 'cinematheque' movie house shows interesting, obscure films that would never get booked elsewhere.

ZANIES
COMEDY

Map p296 (☑312-337-4027; www.chicago.zanies. com; 1548 N Wells St; tickets $25; Ⓜ Brown, Purple Line to Sedgwick) This comedy shack has been booking well-known jokesters for more than three decades. The shows last around two hours and usually include the efforts of a couple of up-and-comers before the main act. The ceiling is low and the seating is cramped, which only adds to the good cheer.

ROYAL GEORGE THEATRE
THEATER

Map p296 (☑312-988-9000; www.theroyalgeor getheatre.com; 1641 N Halsted St; Ⓜ Red Line to North/Clybourn) The Royal George is actually four theaters in one building. The cabaret venue stages long-running mainstream productions such as *Late Nite Catechism,* a nun-centered comedy. The main stage presents works with big-name stars, and the galleries host various improv and small-troupe works.

APOLLO THEATER · THEATER

Map p296 (☎773-935-6100; www.apollochicago. com; 2540 N Lincoln Ave; ⒨Red, Brown, Purple Line to Fullerton) This midsize theater hosts a variety of productions and improv shows. It's also a frequent host to Emerald City Theatre Company, which stages children's plays.

THEATER ON THE LAKE · THEATER

Map p296 (www.chicagoparkdistrict.com/events/ theater-on-the-lake; 2401 N Lake Shore Dr; ⓑ151) Set under a canopy of trees in Lincoln Park, with Lake Michigan sparkling in front, the open-air Theater on the Lake brings to edgy, off-Loop companies to put on eight plays in eight weeks – basically a new show every week of the mid-June to mid-August season. While the theater is being renovated through 2017, performances take place at other venues citywide.

 # SHOPPING

DAVE'S RECORDS · MUSIC

Map p296 (☎773-929-6325; www.davesrecords chicago.com; 2604 N Clark St; ⓗ11am-8pm Mon-Sat, noon-7pm Sun; ⒨Brown, Purple Line to Diversey) *Rolling Stone* magazine picked Dave's as one of the nation's best record stores. It has an 'all vinyl, all the time' mantra, meaning crate diggers will be in their glory flipping through the stacks of rock, jazz, blues, folk and house. Dave himself usually mans the counter, where you'll find a slew of 25-cent cheapie records for sale.

SPICE HOUSE · FOOD

Map p296 (☎312-274-0378; www.thespicehouse. com; 1512 N Wells St; ⓗ10am-7pm Mon-Sat, to 5pm Sun; ⒨Brown, Purple Line to Sedgwick) A bombardment of fragrance socks you in the nose at this exotic spice house in Old Town, offering delicacies such as black and red volcanic salt from Hawaii and pomegranate molasses among the tidy jars. Best, though, are the housemade herb blends themed after Chicago neighborhoods, such as the Bronzeville Rib Rub, allowing you to take home a taste of the city.

ROTOFUGI · TOYS

Map p296 (☎773-868-3308; www.rotofugi.com; 2780 N Lincoln Ave; ⓗ11am-7pm; ⒨Brown, Purple Line to Diversey) Rotofugi has an unusual niche: urban designer toys. The spacey, robot-y, odd vinyl and plush items will certainly distinguish you from the other kids on the block. It's also a gallery showcasing artists in the fields of modern pop and illustration art. You can usually find locally designed Shawnimals here.

GREENHEART SHOP · ARTS & CRAFTS

Map p296 (☎312-264-1625; www.greenheart shop.org; 1714 N Wells St; ⓗ11am-7pm Mon-Fri, 10am-6pm Sat, to 5pm Sun; ⒨Brown, Purple Line to Sedgwick) 🌿 This nonprofit, eco-friendly, fair-trade store stocks chocolate from Ghana, banana-fiber stationery from Uganda, rubber soccer balls from Pakistan and organic cotton baby clothes from, well, Chicago. There's much more, all part of the Center for Cultural Interchange's project that ensures fair wages to artisans.

VOSGES HAUT-CHOCOLAT · FOOD & DRINKS

Map p296 (☎773-296-9866; www.vosgeschoco late.com; 951 W Armitage Ave; ⓗ10am-8pm Mon-Thu, to 9pm Fri & Sat, 11am-6pm Sun; ⒨Brown, Purple Line to Armitage) Owner-chocolatier Katrina Markoff has earned a national reputation for her brand by blending exotic ingredients such as curry powder, chilies and wasabi into her truffles, ice cream and candy bars. They sound weird but taste great, as the samples lurking around prove.

The dark-chocolate blends are the sweets to beat, dressed up with sea salt, 'enchanted mushrooms' and bacon. Wine, beer and coffee are available at the back counter in the chichi boutique.

CROSSROADS TRADING CO · CLOTHING

Map p296 (☎773-296-1000; www.crossroads trading.com; 2711 N Clark St; ⓗ10am-8pm Mon-Sat, 11am-7pm Sun; ⒨Brown, Purple Line to Diversey) Crossroads sells funky, name-brand used clothing for men and women that you can count on being in good condition. Lots of jeans usually hang on the racks, including labels such as Seven for all Mankind, Citizens of Humanity and Miss Sixty. Shoes, coats and handbags are also abundant. You can sell or trade items, too.

BARKER & MEOWSKY · ACCESSORIES

Map p296 (☎773-868-0200; www.barkerand meowsky.com; 1003 W Armitage Ave; ⓗ10am-7pm Mon-Fri, to 6pm Sat, noon-5pm Sun; ⒨Brown Line to Armitage) Fido and Fluffy get their due here. Sales staff welcome four-legged visitors with a treat from the all-natural pet-food stash and then the critters are allowed to commence sniffing up and over the fun apparel, beds and carriers. Top wags go to the Chewy Vuitton purse-shaped squeaky toys and Cubs ball caps, the shop's best sellers.

GRAMAPHONE RECORDS   MUSIC

Map p296 (☑773-472-3683; www.gramaphone records.com; 2843 N Clark St; ☺noon-9pm Mon-Fri, 11am-8:30pm Sat, noon-6pm Sun; ⓂBrown, Purple Line to Diversey) Gramaphone is one of the hippest record stores in Chicago – you'd have to either be a DJ or be dating a DJ to have heard of most of the hip-hop and electronic music sold here. Along with its collection of trendsetting sounds, Gramaphone offers record needles and DJ supplies, as well as a host of info on upcoming parties.

APPLE STORE   ELECTRONICS

Map p296 (☑312-777-4200; www.apple.com; 801 W North Ave; ☺9am-9pm Mon-Sat, 10am-7pm Sun; ⓢ; ⓂNorth/Clybourn) Here's another Apple branch to help with all of your iPhone, iPad and other iNeeds. It's fronted by a plaza with a fountain, and tables and chairs where locals hang out and mooch off the free wi-fi.

LORI'S   SHOES

Map p296 (☑773-281-5655; www.lorisshoes.com; 824 W Armitage Ave; ☺11am-7pm Mon-Fri, 10am-6pm Sat, noon-5pm Sun; ⓂBrown, Purple Line to Armitage) Lori's caters to shoe junkies, who tear through boxes and tissue paper to get at Franco Sarto, Apepazza and other European brands. The general frenzy morphs into a true gorge-fest during season-ending

sales in July/August and January/February; lines can form out the door during these sales.

SPORTS & ACTIVITIES

NORTH AVENUE BEACH   BEACH

Map p296 (www.cpdbeaches.com; 1600 N Lake Shore Dr; ⓢⓗ; ☐151) Chicago's most popular strand of sand wafts a southern California vibe. Buff teams spike volleyballs, kids build sandcastles and everyone jumps in for a swim when the weather heats up. Bands and DJs rock the steamboat-shaped beach house, which serves ice cream and margaritas in equal measure. Kayaks, Jet Skis, stand-up paddleboards and lounge chairs are available to rent, and there are daily beach yoga classes.

A short walk on the curving breakwater yields postcard skyline views. Lifeguards are on duty throughout summer.

DIVERSEY DRIVING RANGE   GOLF

Map p296 (☑312-742-7929; www.cpdgolf.com; 141 W Diversey Pkwy; ☺7am-11pm; ☐151) If you want to knock a bucket of balls around, this driving range in Lincoln Park will let you whack away to your heart's content. Rental clubs are available and a bucket of balls costs $10 to $16. You can also play an 18-hole round of mini-golf for $10; the scenic course is adjacent to the driving range.

FULLERTON BEACH   BEACH

Map p296 It's technically part of North Avenue Beach, so it doesn't have many amenities of its own. But it did grow recently: the city added about 6 acres of shore as part of a stabilization project in 2015.

Lake View & Wrigleyville

Neighborhood Top Five

1 Wrigley Field (p111) Spending an afternoon in the bleachers, hot dog and beer in hand, hoping for a win at the ivy-clad home of the Cubs.

2 Lincoln Square (p116) Making a beer-and-bratwurst detour to this German enclave.

3 Metro (p120) Hearing a soon-to-be-famous band at Chicago's premier loud-rock venue, a tastemaker for more than three decades.

4 Boystown (p113) Joining the thumping nightlife amid the rainbow flags in the city's main gay neighborhood.

5 Sluggers (p120) Practicing your home-run swing in the batting cages at this bar and grill a stone's throw from Wrigley Field.

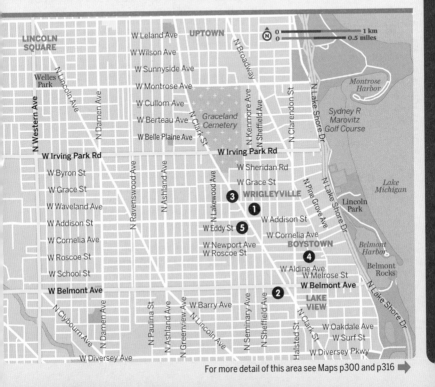

For more detail of this area see Maps p300 and p316

Lonely Planet's Top Tip

If there's a Cubs game at Wrigley Field, plan on around 30,000 extra people joining you for a visit to the neighborhood. The trains and buses will be stuffed to capacity, traffic will be snarled, and bars and restaurants will be jam-packed. It can be fun...if that's your scene. If not, you might want to visit on a non-game day for a bit more elbow room.

Best Places to Eat

➜ Home Bistro (p116)

➜ Crisp (p113)

➜ mfk (p118)

➜ Andy's Thai Kitchen (p113)

For reviews, see p113 ➜

Best Places to Drink

➜ Half Acre Tap Room (p118)

➜ Smart Bar (p119)

➜ Hungry Brain (p119)

➜ Begyle Brewing (p119)

➜ Bar Pastoral (p119)

For reviews, see p118 ➜

☆ Best Live Music

➜ Metro (p120)

➜ Schubas (p121)

➜ Martyrs' (p121)

➜ Constellation (p121)

➜ Vic Theatre (p122)

For reviews, see p120 ➜

Explore Lake View & Wrigleyville

Lake View is the overarching name of this good-time neighborhood, inhabited mostly by 20- and 30-somethings. Wrigleyville is the pocket that surrounds star attraction Wrigley Field. It's usually well mannered by day, with an impish dose of carousing in the bars along Clark St by night.

Either the rainbow flags or the abundance of bars and dance clubs will let you know you've arrived in Boystown, just east of the ballpark. The well-heeled hub of Chicago's gay community, Boystown bustles on Broadway St during the day and gets hedonistic on Halsted St at night. Head west and you'll run into a funky shopping district centered on Belmont Ave and Clark St. The stores here cater to the lifestyle whims of local goths, rockers and kitschy hipsters. Whether you need a bong, Fender Telecaster or vintage Morrissey T-shirt, you can count on the area's shops to come through for you. The Southport Corridor, along Southport Ave between Belmont Ave and Irving Park Rd, is another rich shopping and entertainment district, but one for those who outgrew their goth lifestyle and now seek designer wares.

For all its copious energy, Lake View has little in the way of historic sights or cultural attractions beyond the ballpark. Just bring your credit cards, your walking shoes and a festive attitude, and you'll be set for an afternoon or evening of fun.

Those wishing to explore further can travel northwest to Lincoln Square, the historic heart of Chicago's German community, rich in cafes and beer gardens.

Local Life

➜ **Hometown bands** Beat Kitchen (p122) is a popular venue for local bands to play.

➜ **Hangouts** In a tourist-heavy neighborhood, the Hungry Brain (p119) and Ten Cat Tavern (p119) stand out as off-the-beaten-path bars where locals go for a relaxing beverage.

➜ **Good beer** Neighborhood types kick back at Begyle Brewing (p119) for ales and board games.

➜ **Brunch time** Even carnivores line up for the French toast and other vegetarian dishes at Victory's Banner (p113), a 'hood hot spot on weekend mornings.

Getting There & Away

➜ **El** Red Line to Addison for Wrigleyville and around; Red, Brown, Purple Line to Belmont for much of Boystown. Brown Line to Western for Lincoln Square.

➜ **Bus** Number 77 plies Belmont Ave.

➜ **Car** Parking is a nightmare, especially in Wrigleyville, where side streets are resident-only. Take the El!

TOP SIGHT
WRIGLEY FIELD

Built in 1914, Wrigley Field – aka the Friendly Confines – is the second-oldest baseball park in the major leagues. It's filled with legendary traditions and curses, and has a home team that suffers from the longest dry spell in US sports history. The hapless Cubbies haven't won a championship since 1908, a sad record unmatched in pro football, hockey or basketball.

The Environs
The ballpark provides an old-school slice of Americana, with a hand-turned scoreboard, ivy-covered outfield walls and an iconic neon sign over the front entrance. The field is uniquely situated smack in the middle of a neighborhood, surrounded on all sides by houses, bars and restaurants. Modern elements have been incorporated recently, including a jumbo-sized video board in left field. The owners continue to develop the area around the park, and a hotel and more amenities are forthcoming.

The Curse
It started with Billy Sianis, owner of the Billy Goat Tavern. The year was 1945 and the Cubs were in the World Series against the Detroit Tigers. When Sianis tried to enter Wrigley Field with his pet goat to see the game, ballpark staff refused, saying the goat stank. Sianis threw up his arms and called down a mighty hex, saying that the Cubs would never win another World Series. And they haven't.

The Traditions
When the middle of the seventh inning arrives, it's time for the seventh inning stretch. You then stand up for the group sing-along of 'Take Me Out to the Ballgame,' typically led by a guest celebrity along the lines of Mr T, Ozzy Osbourne or the local weather reporter.

DON'T MISS

➡ Taking a photo under the neon entrance sign
➡ Harry Caray statue
➡ The 'knothole'
➡ Ballpark tour

PRACTICALITIES

➡ Map p300
➡ www.cubs.com
➡ 1060 W Addison St
➡ Ⓜ Red Line to Addison

BABE'S 'CALLED SHOT'

Babe Ruth's famous 'called shot' happened at Wrigley. During the 1932 World Series, Ruth pointed to center field to show where he was going to homer the next ball. And he did. It's still debated as to whether he called it or was just pointing at the pitcher.

If a ball gets lost in the ivy, it's considered a ground-rule double as long as the outfielder raises his hands to indicate that the ball is lost. If he doesn't, it's considered fair play.

THE WIND

Wrigley Field is known for its havoc-wreaking wind patterns caused by nearby Lake Michigan. If the wind is blowing in, it's a pitcher's paradise. If it's blowing out, expect a big day for home runs.

The Bears played at Wrigley from 1921 to 1970. They were called the Staleys for the first season but then renamed themselves to be in sync with the Cubs.

Here's another tradition: if you catch a home run slugged by the competition, you're honor-bound to throw it back onto the field. After every game the ballpark hoists a flag atop the scoreboard. A white flag with a blue 'W' indicates a victory; a blue flag with a white 'L' means a loss.

The Statues

Statues of Cubs heroes ring the stadium. Ernie Banks, aka 'Mr Cub,' stands near the main entrance on Clark St; the shortstop/first baseman was the team's first African American player. Billy 'Sweet-Swinging' Williams wields his mighty bat by the Captain Morgan Club bar on Addison St. Adored third baseman Ron Santo makes a smooth catch beside him. And mythic TV sportscaster Harry Caray dons his barrel-sized eyeglasses in front of the bleacher entrance on Waveland Ave. Caray was known for broadcasting among the raucous bleacher fans while downing a few Budweisers himself. It's said the sculptors mixed a dash of his favorite beer in with the white bronze used for the statue.

Food & Drink

It's a pre-game ritual to beer up at Murphy's Bleachers (p120), only steps away from the ballpark.

Inside Wrigley Field, bite into a gourmet hot dog at the Hot Doug's food stand at Platform 14 (behind the bleachers, though you need a bleacher ticket to get there).

Top Tips

➡ Buy tickets at the Cubs' website or Wrigley box office. Online ticket broker StubHub (www.stubhub.com) is also reliable.

➡ The Upper Reserved Infield seats are usually pretty cheap. They're high up, but have decent views.

➡ No tickets? Peep through the 'knothole,' a garage-door-sized opening on Sheffield Ave, to watch the action for free on game days.

➡ Ninety-minute stadium tours ($25) are available most days April through September. Try going on a non-game day, as you'll see more.

⊙ SIGHTS

WRIGLEY FIELD   STADIUM

See p111.

BOYSTOWN   AREA

Map p300 (btwn Halsted St & Broadway, Belmont Ave & Addison St; Ⓜ Red Line to Addison) What the Castro is to San Francisco, Boystown is to the Windy City. The mecca of queer Chicago (especially for men), the streets of Boystown are full of rainbow flags and packed with bars, shops and restaurants catering to residents of the gay neighborhood.

CENTER ON HALSTED   CULTURAL CENTER

Map p300 (☎773-472-6469; www.centeronhal sted.org; 3656 N Halsted St; ☺8am-9pm; 🛜; Ⓜ Red Line to Addison) The mod, glassy Center on Halsted is the Midwest's largest LGBT community center. It's mostly a social service organization for locals, but visitors can use the free wi-fi and reading library, plus there's a Whole Foods grocery store inside.

ROSEHILL CEMETERY   CEMETERY

(☎773-561-5940; 5800 N Ravenswood Ave; ☺8am-4pm; 🚌84) The entrance gate to Chicago's largest cemetery is worth the trip alone. Designed by WW Boyington the architect who created the Water Tower on Michigan Ave), the entry looks like a cross between high Gothic and low Disney. Inside you'll see the graves of plenty of Chicago bigwigs, from Chicago mayors and a US vice president to meat-man Oscar Mayer.

You'll also find some of the weirdest grave monuments in the city, including a postal train and a huge carved boulder from a Civil War battlefield in Georgia. More than one ghost story started here; keep an eye out for vapors as night falls.

ALTA VISTA TERRACE   AREA

Map p300 (btwn Byron & Grace Sts; Ⓜ Red Line to Sheridan) Chicago's first designated historic district is worthy of the honor. Developer Samuel Eberly Gross re-created a block of London row houses on Alta Vista Terrace in 1904. The 20 exquisitely detailed homes on either side of the street mirror each other diagonally and the owners have worked hard at maintaining the spirit of the block.

Individuality isn't dead, however – head to the back of the west row and you'll notice that the back of every house has grown in a dramatically different fashion.

✕ EATING

CRISP   KOREAN $

Map p300 (www.crisponline.com; 2940 N Broadway; mains $9-13; ☺11:30am-9pm; Ⓜ Brown, Purple Line to Wellington) Music pours from the stereo, while delicious Korean fusions arrive from the kitchen at this cheerful cafe. The 'Bad Boy Buddha' bowl, a variation on *bi bim bop* (mixed vegetables with rice), is one of the best healthy lunches in town. Crisp's fried chicken (especially the 'Seoul Sassy' with its savory soy-ginger sauce) also wows the casual crowd.

ANDY'S THAI KITCHEN   THAI $

Map p300 (www.andysthaikitchen.com; 946 W Wellington Ave; mains $9-14; ☺11am-9:30pm Mon-Fri, noon-9:30pm Sat & Sun; Ⓜ Brown, Purple Line to Wellington) Little 11-table Andy's earns big praise from foodies who swoon over the authentic Thai menu. Andy is not afraid to use organ parts in his dishes, or to atomically spice them. Standouts include the fish maw salad, basil preserved egg, and boat noodles swimming with beef brisket and pork skin. BYO; cash only. Note the restaurant closes between 4pm and 5pm each day.

VICTORY'S BANNER   VEGETARIAN $

Map p300 (☎733-665-0227; www.victorys banner.com; 2100 W Roscoe St; mains $8-11; ☺8am-3pm, closed Tue; 🖉; Ⓜ Brown Line to Paulina) The tough decision at this revered breakfast house is between the fresh, free-range-egg omelets and the legendary French toast, cooked in rich cream batter and served with peach butter. New Age tunes and muted colors give the room a soothing vibe, even when the place is mobbed on weekend mornings. The staff are all followers of global meditation master Sri Chinmoy.

BANG BANG PIE & BISCUITS   AMERICAN $

Map p316 (☎773-530-9020; www.bangbangpie. com; 4947 N Damen Ave; slices $5; ☺8am-7pm Mon & Wed-Fri, to 4pm Sat & Sun; Ⓜ Brown Line to Damen) The cozy new outpost of the adored Logan Square bakery lets you fork into flaky pie slices and biscuit sandwiches under the skylight or in front of the fireplace.

CHICAGO DINER   VEGETARIAN $

Map p300 (☎773-935-6696; www.veggiediner. com; 3411 N Halsted St; mains $10-14; ☺11am-10pm Mon-Thu, 11am-11pm Fri, 10am-11pm Sat, 10am-10pm Sun; 🖉; Ⓜ Red Line to Addison) The

Wrigley Field

You'll experience more than just a game at Wrigley Field. A tangible sense of history comes alive at the 100-plus-year-old baseball park, thanks to the hand-turned scoreboard, iconic neon entrance sign and time-honored traditions that infuse each inning. Plus the streets around it erupt into one big party during games.

KENT WEAKLEY/SHUTTERSTOCK ©

1. The park (p111)
Score tickets for a Cubs game at this legendary ball park, known as the 'Friendly Confines.'

2. Sign for the Chicago Cubs (p124)
Spend an afternoon or evening cheering on Wrigley Field's home team.

3. Sluggers (p120)
Enjoy a pre-game beer, and even a whack in the batting cages, at this sports bar.

4. Statue of Ron Santo (p112)
Pay tribute to this much-loved Cubs third baseman and radio broadcaster.

STATUE OF RON SANTO BY ARTIST LOU CELLA OF ROTBLATT AMRANY STUDIO/CHARLES COOK/GETTY IMAGES ©

CHARLES COOK/GETTY IMAGES ©

gold standard for Chicago vegetarians, this place has been serving shepherd's pie (made with tempeh) and lentil casserole for decades. The tattooed staff will guide you to the best stuff, including the peanut butter 'supershakes' and the 'Radical Ruben.' Anything on the menu can be made vegan-style, and there are lots of gluten-free options as well.

VILLAGE TAP
BURGERS $

Map p300 (☏773-883-0817; www.thevillagetap. com; 2055 W Roscoe St; mains $10-13; ⊙5-10pm Mon-Thu, 3pm-midnight Fri, noon-midnight Sat, noon-10pm Sun; ⊛Brown Line to Paulina) Even though it can get packed on weekends, this neighborhood tavern does everything well: food, drink and atmosphere. The friendly bartenders give out samples of the ever-changing and carefully chosen Midwestern microbrews. The kitchen turns out great burgers, veggie burgers and meatloaf. The picnic-table-dotted beer garden buzzes in warm weather. Inside, the tables enjoy good views of the TVs for ball games.

FALAFILL
MIDDLE EASTERN $

Map p300 (☏773-525-0052; www.eatfalafill. com; 3202 N Broadway; mains $6.50-11; ⊙11am-10pm; ☏; ⊛Red, Brown, Purple Line to Belmont) Buy a falafel sandwich or falafel salad at the counter, then customize it at the topping bar with cilantro chutney, Moroccan olives, *zhug* (hot jalapeño sauce), tabbouleh, pickled ginger and 15 other fresh items. Soup, hummus and sweet-potato fries sum up the side dishes.

CLARK STREET DOG
AMERICAN $

Map p300 (☏773-281-6690; www.clarkstdog. com; 3040 N Clark St; mains $3.50-8; ⊙9am-3am Sun-Thu, to 4am Fri & Sat; ⊛Brown, Purple Line to Wellington) Apart from signature hot dogs, carnivorous delights include the Italian sausage combo – which marries Italian beef *and* Italian sausage on a single soggy bun – and the chili cheese fries. If all the salty meats make you thirsty, head to the adjoining divey Clark Street Bar for some cheap cold ones.

★HOME BISTRO
MODERN AMERICAN $$

Map p300 (☏773-661-0299; www.homebistro chicago.com; 3404 N Halsted St; mains $20-25; ⊙5:30-10pm Tue-Thu, 5-10:30pm Fri & Sat, 11am-9pm Sun; ⊛Red Line to Addison) Home Bistro (aka 'HB') feels as cozy as the nouveau comfort food it serves. Cider-soaked

🏃 Local Life
Lincoln Square Toddle

Once a neighborhood of German immigrants, Lincoln Square has morphed into a hot spot for local eating, drinking and shopping. This walk starts just a hint southwest of the area and moseys into Lincoln Square proper along Lincoln Ave, the community's main vein. Beer, bratwursts, books and beef bourguignon are all on tap.

❶ Half Acre Tap Room
Half Acre was one of Chicago's craft-brewing leaders. The beer earned a cult following and the guys opened the Half Acre Tap Room (p118) at the source. Local beer fanatics hunker down in the rustic space, knocking back the lineup of mega-strong brews.

❷ Bistro Campagne
Chicago has a lot of French bistros, but not many perfect the balance of fine but unfussy dining the way **Bistro Campagne** (Map p316; ☏773-271-6100; www.bistrocampagne.com; 4518 N Lincoln Ave; mains $21-28; ⊙5:30-9pm Mon-Thu, to 10pm Fri, 5-10:30pm Sat, 11am-9pm Sun; ⊛Brown Line to Western) does. The neighborhood favorite plates classics such as beef bourguignon, mussels and chocolate soufflé alongside a robust wine list.

❸ Old Town School of Folk Music
The Old Town School of Folk Music (p121) gets street cred for moving to the neighborhood before it gentrified. Swing into the music shop to blow a harmonica or strum a mandolin. The little cafe whips up healthy, kid-friendly snacks. The first Friday of each month local musicians and families gather for an open jam session (admission $5), no experience necessary.

❹ Merz Apothecary
Merz Apothecary (Map p316; ☏773-989-0900; www.merzapothecary.com; 4716 N Lincoln Ave; ⊙9am-6pm Mon-Sat; ⊛Brown Line to Western) has been around since 1875. Antique pharmacy jars contain herbs, homeopathic remedies, vitamins and supplements, and the shelves are

stacked high with skin care, bath and aromatherapy products from around the world.

❺ Huettenbar

Pay homage to the neighborhood's old German roots at the stalwart **Huettenbar** (Map p316; ☎773-561-2507; www.huettenbar.com; 4721 N Lincoln Ave; ☺2pm-2am Mon-Fri, noon-2am Sat & Sun; Ⓜ Brown Line to Western). The kitschy, wood-paneled ambience is straight out of the Black Forest. So are the beers flowing from the taps. A crisp *kölsch* from Frankfurt and a seat by the big open windows, and you're stylin'.

❻ Book Cellar

The independent **Book Cellar** (Map p316; ☎773-293-2665; www.bookcellar inc.com; 4736 N Lincoln Ave; ☺10am-10pm Mon & Wed-Sat, noon-6pm Tue & Sun; Ⓜ Brown Line to Western) is an integral part of the neighborhood. Local book groups hold their meetings here, and authors do readings several nights per week, while the cafe pours wine and beer to add to the festivities.

❼ Gene's Sausage Shop

As if the hanging sausages and ripe cheeses lining the shelves at this European market weren't enough, **Gene's** (Map p316; ☎773-728-7243; www.genessausage.com; 4750 N Lincoln Ave; ☺9am-8pm Mon-Sat, to 4pm Sun; Ⓜ Brown Line to Western) rocks a rooftop summer beer garden. Sit at communal picnic tables and munch hot-off-the-grill bratwursts while sipping worldly brews. It's sort of a local secret.

❽ Timeless Toys

Charming **Timeless Toys** (Map p316; ☎773-334-4445; www.timelesstoyschi cago.com; 4749 N Lincoln Ave; ☺10am-6pm Mon-Wed & Sat, to 7pm Thu & Fri, to 6pm Sun; Ⓜ Brown Line to Western) carries high-quality, old-fashioned wares, many made in Germany or other European countries. Have fun playing with the bug magnifiers, microscopes, glitter balls and wooden spinning tops.

PETER PTSCHELINZEW/GETTY IMAGES ©

Entrance to Lincoln Square

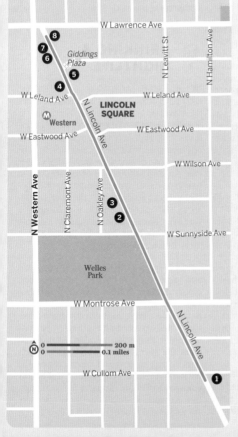

mussels, duck meatball gnocchi, and buttermilk fried chicken hit the tables in the wood-and-tile-lined space. Try to snag a seat by the front window, which entertains with Boystown people-watching. You can bring your own wine or beer, which is a nice money saver.

MFK   SPANISH $$

(☎773-857-2540; www.mfkrestaurant.com; 432 W Diversey Pkwy; small plates $10-18; ☺5-10pm Mon, noon-10pm Tue-Thu, noon-midnight Fri & Sat, 10am-10pm Sun; ☒22) In mfk's teeny space it feels like you're having a romantic meal in Spain, with the sea lapping just outside the door. Dig into crunchy prawn heads, garlicky octopus and veal meatballs amid the whitewashed walls and decorative tiles. Sunny cocktails and a wine list dominated by whites and rosés add to the goodness.

The restaurant is named after food writer MFK Fisher, a foodie well before her time.

MIA FRANCESCA   ITALIAN $$

Map p300 (☎773-281-3310; www.miafrancesca. com; 3311 N Clark St; mains $16-29; ☺5-10pm Mon-Thu, 5-11pm Fri, 11:30am-11pm Sat, 11am-9pm Sun; ⓂRed, Brown, Purple Line to Belmont) Diners quickly fill up the room at this family-run Italian bistro (part of a local chain) and energy swirls among the closely spaced tables, topped with white tablecloths and fresh flowers. The handwritten menu features earthy standards – seafood linguine, spinach ravioli, veal medallions – with aggressive seasoning from southern Italy. Other treats include wafer-thin pizzas and flavor-packed polenta.

CHILAM BALAM   MEXICAN $$

Map p300 (☎773-296-6901; www.chilambalam chicago.com; 3023 N Broadway; small plates $9-15; ☺5-10pm Tue-Thu, to 11pm Fri & Sat; ⓂBrown, Purple Line to Wellington) The chef is only in her 20s, but she has already apprenticed under Rick Bayless and brought his 'farm to table' philosophy to this vibrant brick-and-Spanish-tile eatery, which sits below street level. The close-set tables pulse with a young crowd ripping into fiery seviche, mushroom empanadas, chocolate-chili mousse and other imaginative fare. It's BYOB. Cash only.

TANGO SUR   STEAK $$

Map p300 (☎773-477-5466; www.folklorechica go.com/tangosur; 3763 N Southport Ave; mains $17-30; ☺5-10:30pm Mon-Thu, 5-11:30pm Fri, 3-11pm Sat, noon-10:30pm Sun; ⓂBrown Line to Southport) This candlelit BYO Argentine steakhouse makes an idyllic date location, serving classic skirt steaks and other tender grass-fed options. In addition to the traditional cuts, the chef's special is 'Bife Vesuvio,' a prime strip stuffed with garlic, spinach and cheese – it's a triumph. In summer, tables outside expand the seating from the small and spare interior.

YOSHI'S CAFE   FUSION $$$

Map p300 (☎773-248-6160; www.yoshiscafe.com; 3257 N Halsted St; mains $20-33; ☺5-10:30pm Tue-Sat, 11am-9:30pm Sun; ⓂRed, Brown, Purple Line to Belmont) Yoshi's is one of the most innovative casual places in town, known for its changing Japanese- and French-flared menu and its gracious standards during the past three decades. The chefs treat all ingredients with the utmost respect, from the salmon to the tofu to the Kobe beef. Service in the low-lit, well-spaced room is every bit as snappy as the food.

🍷 DRINKING & NIGHTLIFE

★HALF ACRE TAP ROOM   BREWERY

(☎773-248-4038; www.halfacrebeer.com; 4257 N Lincoln Ave; ☺11am-11pm Tue, Wed & Sun, to midnight Thu, to 1am Fri & Sat; 🛜; ⓂBrown Line to Montrose) Half Acre was one of the leaders of Chicago's craft brewing movement, concocting the deliciously hoppy Daisy Cutter Pale Ale and selling it in cans. An upscale pub-grub menu (with an emphasis on eclectic burritos) accompanies the beer lineup. Tours ($10) take place at 11am on Saturdays. Half Acre opened another outpost a couple of miles north at 2050 W Balmoral Ave (near Rosehill Cemetery).

GINGERMAN TAVERN   BAR

Map p300 (☎773-549-2050; www.facebook. com/gmantavern; 3740 N Clark St; ☺3pm-2am Sun-Fri, to 3am Sat; ⓂRed Line to Addison) The pool tables, large and eclectic beer selection, and pierced-and-tattooed patrons make the Gingerman wonderfully different from the surrounding Wrigleyville sports bars. Singer-songwriters often play on the back-room stage. The name technically changed to 'GMan Tavern' a few years ago, but everyone still calls it the Gingerman. It's a splendid spot to pass an evening.

HUNGRY BRAIN
BAR

(📞773-935-2118; www.hungrybrainchicago. com; 2319 W Belmont Ave; ⊘7pm-2am, closed Tue; 🚋77) The owner of nearby music club Constellation (p121) also owns this off-the-beaten-path little bar. It charms with its kind bartenders and well-worn, thrift-store decor. It's a hub of the underground jazz scene; Sunday nights are the mainstay (suggested donation $10), though there are shows and literary readings other nights of the week, too. Cash only.

BEGYLE BREWING
MICROBREWERY

Map p300 (📞773-661-6963; www.begylebrewing. com; 1800 W Cuyler St, 1E; ⊘noon-9pm Mon-Thu, noon-10pm Fri, 11am-10pm Sat, noon-8pm Sun; Ⓜ Brown Line to Irving Park) Begyle is a terrific little brewery tucked away in an old warehouse by the train track. The no-frills tap room has board games and skee ball to play while sucking down the 10 beers on tap (the blonde ale and wheat ale are big sellers). They come in 5oz pours and pints, and you can bring in your own food to eat alongside them.

Brewery tours ($10) take place at noon on Saturday and include generous samples.

BAR PASTORAL
WINE BAR

Map p300 (www.barpastoral.com; 2947 N Broadway; ⊘5-10pm Mon-Wed, 5-11pm Thu, 5pm-midnight Fri, 11am-midnight Sat, 11am-10pm Sun; Ⓜ Brown, Purple Line to Wellington) Popular deli minichain Pastoral has added a wine bar to its Lake View shop. Half-glasses are available for $5, which means you can sample widely. The deli's awesome breads and cheeses help soak it up (stick to these rather than the dishes listed on the menu).

SMART BAR
CLUB

Map p300 (📞773-549-4140; www.smartbarchicago.com; 3730 N Clark St; ⊘10pm-4am Thu-Sun; Ⓜ Red Line to Addison) Smart Bar is a long-standing, unpretentious favorite for dancing, located in the basement of the Metro (p120) rock club. The DJs are often more renowned than you'd expect the intimate space to accommodate. House and techno dominate the turntables. Ticket prices range from $5 to $15.

TEN CAT TAVERN
PUB

Map p300 (📞773-935-5377; 3931 N Ashland Ave; ⊘3pm-2am; Ⓜ Brown Line to Irving Park) Pool is serious business on the two vintage tables that the pub refelts regularly with material

from Belgium. The ever-changing, eye-catching art comes courtesy of neighborhood artists and the furniture is a garage saler's dream. Regulars (most in their 30s) down leisurely drinks at the bar or, in warm weather, head to the beer garden.

GLOBE PUB
PUB

Map p300 (📞773-871-3757; www.theglobe pub.com; 1934 W Irving Park Rd; ⊘11am-2am; Ⓜ Brown Line to Irving Park) This warm, dark-oak pub is ground zero for English soccer and rugby fanatics, since it shows all the international league games on satellite TV. It even opens at 6am for big matches so patrons can watch the action live. The kitchen cooks up a traditional English breakfast daily and the taps flow with ales from the homeland.

DUKE OF PERTH
PUB

Map p300 (📞773-477-1741; www.dukeofperth. com; 2913 N Clark St; ⊘5pm-2am Mon, from noon Tue-Sun; Ⓜ Brown, Purple Line to Wellington) The UK beers and more than 80 bottles of single-malt scotch are nearly overwhelming at this cozy, laid-back pub. After enough of them, try the fish and chips, which is all-you-can-eat for lunch and dinner for $13.50 on Wednesday and Friday.

GUTHRIE'S
PUB

Map p300 (📞773-477-2900; www.guthriestavern.com; 1300 W Addison St; ⊘5pm-2am Mon-Thu, from 4pm Fri, from 2pm Sat & Sun; Ⓜ Red Line to Addison) A local institution and the perfect neighborhood hangout, Guthrie's remains true to its mellow roots even as the Cubs-fueled neighborhood goes manic around it. The glassed-in back porch is fittingly furnished with patio chairs and filled with 30- and 40-somethings, and board games abound.

SOUTHPORT LANES
BAR

Map p300 (📞773-472-6600; www.southport lanes.com; 3325 N Southport Ave; ⊘4pm-2am Mon-Thu, from noon Fri-Sun; Ⓜ Brown Line to Southport) An old-fashioned, four-lane bowling alley with hand-set pins hides inside this busy neighborhood bar and grill. Those who prefer to shoot stick can chalk up at the six regulation pool tables. The main bar features an inspirational mural of cavorting nymphs, and tables sprawl onto the sidewalk in summer. A fine selection of regional beers flows from the taps.

LAKE VIEW & WRIGLEYVILLE DRINKING & NIGHTLIFE

MURPHY'S BLEACHERS SPORTS BAR

Map p300 (☎773-281-5356; www.murphys bleachers.com; 3655 N Sheffield Ave; ☺11am-2am; ⓜRed Line to Addison) It's a Cubs game prerequisite to beer up at this well-loved, historic watering hole, only steps away from the entrance to Wrigley Field's bleacher seats. Fans jam into this place like sardines on game day.

SLUGGERS SPORTS BAR

Map p300 (☎773-472-9696; www.sluggersbar. com; 3540 N Clark St; ☺3pm-2am Mon-Thu, from 11am Fri-Sun; ⓜRed Line to Addison) Practice your home-run swing at Sluggers, a cheesy but popular bar and grill across from Wrigley Field. Sidestep the schnockered Cubs fans and giant-screen TVs and head to the 2nd floor, where there are four batting cages. Ten pitches cost $2.

BERLIN CLUB

Map p300 (☎773-348-4975; www.berlinchicago. com; 954 W Belmont Ave; ☺10pm-4am Tue, from 5pm Wed-Sun; ⓜRed, Brown, Purple Line to Belmont) Looking for a packed, sweaty dance floor? Berlin caters to a mostly gay crowd midweek, though partiers of all stripes jam the place on weekends. Monitors flicker through the latest video dispatches from cult pop and electronic acts, while DJs take the dance floor on trancey detours.

CHICAGO BRAUHAUS BAR

Map p316 (☎773-784-4444; www.chicagobrau haus.com; 4732 N Lincoln Ave; ☺11am-10pm Mon, Wed & Thu, to midnight Fri-Sun; ⓜBrown Line to Western) Unlikely as it may seem for a bar, the oompah soundtrack, rosy-cheeked staff and early last call give this spacious Bavarian-themed joint the all-ages appeal of a Disney ride. Dinnertime is best, when the 'world-famous' lederhosen-clad Brauhaus Trio starts bumping, and steaming plates of schnitzel seem heaven-sent. Bring your dancing shoes, too – there's polka action nightly.

SIDETRACK CLUB

Map p300 (☎773-477-9189; www.sidetrackchica go.com; 3349 N Halsted St; ☺3pm-2am Mon-Fri, from 1pm Sat & Sun; ⓜRed, Brown, Purple Line to Belmont) Massive Sidetrack thumps dance music for a gay and straight crowd alike. Get ready to belt out your Broadway best at the good-time 'show-tune nights' on Sunday and Monday. If the indoor action gets too much, the huge outdoor courtyard beckons.

SPYNER'S LESBIAN

Map p316 (☎773-784-8719; www.spyners.com; 4623 N Western Ave; ☺11am-2am; ⓜBrown Line to Western) Lesbian karaoke! Perhaps you didn't know the niche existed. But it does. And it's here, in Lincoln Square. Friday and Saturday nights are the main party. It's a fun scene regardless of your sexual orientation.

CLOSET GAY & LESBIAN

Map p300 (☎773-477-8533; www.thecloset chicago.com; 3325 N Broadway; ☺4pm-4am Mon-Fri, from noon Sat & Sun; ☎; ⓜRed, Brown, Purple Line to Belmont) One of the few lesbian-centric bars in Chicago, the Closet changes mood and tempo at 2am, when the crowd becomes more mixed (male and female), the music gets louder and things get a little rowdier. Cash only.

HYDRATE CLUB

Map p300 (☎773-975-9244; www.hydratechi cago.com; 3458 N Halsted St; ☺8pm-4am Mon, Wed & Thu, from 6pm Fri & Sat, from 2pm Sun; ⓜRed Line to Addison) A wild night on the Boystown club circuit requires a visit to this frenzied spot, which boasts an open-air feel (thanks to retractable windows) and a chatty pickup scene (thanks to cheap mixed drinks). It's not all roses: the service gets rude and the crowds unruly (also thanks to the cheap mixed drinks).

L&L TAVERN BAR

Map p300 (☎773-528-1303; 3207 N Clark St; ☺2pm-2am Mon-Fri, from noon Sat & Sun; ⓜRed, Brown, Purple Line to Belmont) The dimly lit L&L is an unapologetic dive bar, complete with curt, seen-it-all staff. It's a great place to duck the Wrigleyville madness. Relax with cheap Pabst beer or a sip from the impressive assortment of Irish whiskey. Cash only.

★ ENTERTAINMENT

★ METRO LIVE MUSIC

Map p300 (☎773-549-4140; www.metrochicago. com; 3730 N Clark St; ☺box office noon-6pm Mon, to 8pm Tue-Sat; ⓜRed Line to Addison) For more than three decades the Metro has been synonymous with loud rock. Sonic Youth and the Ramones in the '80s. Nirvana and Jane's Addiction in the '90s. White Stripes and the Killers in the new millennium. Each night prepare to hear noise by three or four bands who may well be teetering on the verge of stardom.

SCHUBAS
LIVE MUSIC

Map p300 (773-525-2508; www.lh-st.com; 3159 N Southport Ave; 11:30am-2am Sun-Fri, to 3am Sat; Brown Line to Southport) Set in an old Schlitz brewery building, Schubas presents twangy acoustic artists, plus indie rock acts on their way up (like the National and Janelle Monáe in their early days). Bands play most nights in the cozy back-room club, which is noted for its great sound, thanks to the all-wood construction. A boisterous bar pours microbrews in the front room.

CONSTELLATION
LIVE MUSIC

(www.constellation-chicago.com; 3111 N Western Ave; 6pm-midnight Mon & Tue, 7pm-2am Wed, Thu & Sun, 6pm-2am Fri & Sat; 77) The producer of Pitchfork Music Festival opened this intimate club, which actually breaks down into two small venues inside. The city's hepcats come out of the woodwork for the progressive jazz and improvisational music. Many acts are free, most cost $10 to $15, and none cost more than $25.

ANNOYANCE THEATRE
COMEDY

Map p300 (773-697-9693; www.theannoyance. com; 851 W Belmont Ave; Red, Brown, Purple Line to Belmont) The Annoyance masterminds naughty and absurd shows, often musicals, such as *Tiny Fascists: A Boy Scout Musical*. Both the shows and the theater itself are of surprisingly high quality. Susan Messing's $5 Thursday-night session always provides good yuks.

OLD TOWN SCHOOL
OF FOLK MUSIC
LIVE MUSIC

Map p316 (773-728-6000; www.oldtownschool. org; 4544 N Lincoln Ave; ; Brown Line to Western) You can hear the call of the banjos from the street outside this venerable institution, where major national and international acts such as Richard Thompson and Joan Baez play when they come to town. Old Town also hosts superb world-music shows, including every Wednesday at 8:30pm when they're free (or a $10 donation if you've got it). Do-it-yourselfers can take guitar and other musical classes here. Note some concerts take place in Szold Hall, located across the street.

EMERALD CITY
THEATRE COMPANY
THEATER

Map p300 (773-529-2690; www.emeraldcity theatre.com; 2936 N Southport Ave; Brown Line to Southport) Presenting some of the most innovative plays for children in the country, from blockbusters such as *School House Rock Live* to lesser-known works like *Three Little Kittens* and *How I Became a Pirate*. Performances are at the group's on-site Little Theatre, as well as the Apollo Theater (p107) in Lincoln Park and other places around town.

MUSIC BOX THEATRE
CINEMA

Map p300 (773-871-6604; www.musicboxthea tre.com; 3733 N Southport Ave; Brown Line to Southport) It hardly matters what's playing here; the Music Box itself is worth the visit. The perfectly restored theater dates from 1929 and looks like a Moorish palace, with clouds floating across the ceiling under twinkling stars. The art-house films are always first-rate and there's a midnight roster of cult hits such as *The Big Lebowski*. A second, smaller theater shows held-over films.

MARTYRS'
LIVE MUSIC

Map p300 (773-404-9494; www.martyrslive. com; 3855 N Lincoln Ave; 6pm-2am Sun-Fri, to 3am Sat; Brown Line to Irving Park) Martyrs' is a small, catch-all venue where pretty much anything goes musically: Frank Zappa's former band, a Tom Petty tribute band, a Mexican folk-music group. It's also the home of the popular Moth Story Slam: participants get on stage and tell a true story; the best story (and storytelling prowess) wins. The slam is held the last Tuesday of the month. There's mighty fine pub grub to boot.

CSZ THEATER
COMEDY

Map p300 (773-549-8080; www.cszchicago. com; 929 W Belmont Ave; shows from 8pm Mon & Wed-Fri, from 6pm Sat, from 7pm Sun; Red, Brown, Purple Line to Belmont) The signature show here is ComedySportz. The gimmick? Two teams compete to make you laugh. The

---

LOCAL KNOWLEDGE

JAZZ HOT SPOTS

Sports bars you expect in the neighborhood. Cutting-edge jazz music? Not so much. But it's here:

Hungry Brain (p119) Sunday evenings bring in the young and avant-garde.

Constellation Improvised music fills the air.

show is totally improvised, with the audience dictating the action. A referee moderates and the wittiest team 'wins' at the end. The comedy is profanity- and vulgarity-free, so all ages are welcome. Adults can bring in alcohol from the lobby bar. Prime-time weekend shows are $25.

The theater hosts other improv and sketch comedy shows as well, and they're generally cheaper (tickets $5 to $15). There are no shows on Tuesdays.

AMERICAN THEATER COMPANY THEATER

Map p300 (ATC; ☑773-409-4125; www.atcweb. org; 1909 W Byron St; Ⓜ Brown Line to Irving Park) The ATC has been around for more than three decades, putting on both new and established works by American playwrights. Its productions usually garner great acclaim and subsequently travel onward to other cities.

VIC THEATRE LIVE MUSIC

Map p300 (☑773-472-0449; www.jamusa.com/the-vic; 3145 N Sheffield Ave; Ⓜ Red, Brown, Purple Line to Belmont) The Vic – a vintage 1912 vaudeville theater – now hosts big-name bands several nights a week, and second-run Hollywood and cult films on the off nights. Music fans dig the Vic's smallish (1300 capacity) size and great sight lines. Movie fans like the venue's Brew & View program, with pizzas and pitchers of beer on offer, and tickets for $5.

BEAT KITCHEN LIVE MUSIC

Map p300 (☑773-281-4444; www.beatkitchen. com; 2100 W Belmont Ave; ⊘4pm-2am Mon-Fri, 11:30am-3am Sat, 11:30am-2am Sun; ☒77) Everything you need to know is in the name – entertaining beats traverse a spectrum of sounds and the kitchen turns out better-than-average dinners. Dine early in the front of the house, since service is un-hurried. Music in the homely back room can be funky or jammy, but a crop of Chicago's smart, broadly appealing songwriters dominates the calendar.

LAUGH FACTORY CHICAGO COMEDY

Map p300 (☑773-327-3175; www.laughfactory. com; 3175 N Broadway; Ⓜ Red, Brown, Purple Line to Belmont) Newbie comics line up hours in advance for Wednesday's open mike at the Laugh Factory. Such is the cachet of its parent LA club, where everyone from Richard Pryor to Sarah Silverman has tried out

jokes. Expect lots of seasoned local stand-up acts the rest of the week.

CORN PRODUCTIONS COMEDY

(☑312-409-6435; www.cornservatory.org; 4210 N Lincoln Ave; Ⓜ Brown Line to Irving Park) Though Corn occasionally stages something serious, most of its productions are kitschy and inexpensive. One of its recent draws was *Drink!*, lampooning college drinking games. The theater is just west of Lake View in the North Center neighborhood. Cash only at the box office.

SHOPPING

STRANGE CARGO CLOTHING

Map p300 (www.strangecargo.com; 3448 N Clark St; ⊘11am-6:45pm Mon-Sat, to 5:30pm Sun; Ⓜ Red Line to Addison) This retro store stocks hipster wear, platform shoes, wigs and a mind-blowing array of kitschy T-shirts. Staff will iron on decals of Harry Caray, Mike Ditka, the Hancock Center or other local touchstones, as well as Obama, Smurfs and more – all supreme souvenirs.

CHICAGO COMICS BOOKS

Map p300 (☑773-528-1983; www.chicagocom ics.com; 3244 N Clark St; ⊘noon-8pm Mon-Fri, 11am-8pm Sat, noon-7pm Sun; Ⓜ Red, Brown, Purple Line to Belmont) This emporium is frequently cited as one of the nation's best comic-book stores. Old Marvel *Superman* back issues share shelf space with hand-drawn works by cutting-edge local artists such as Chris Ware, Ivan Brunetti and Dan Clowes (who lived here during his early *Eightball* days). *Simpsons* fanatics will 'd'oh!' with joy at the huge toy selection.

ARCHITECTURAL ARTIFACTS ANTIQUES

(☑773-348-0622; www.architecturalartifacts. com; 4325 N Ravenswood Ave; ⊘10am-5pm; Ⓜ Brown Line to Montrose) This mammoth, 80,000-sq-ft salvage warehouse is a treasure trove that prompts continual mutterings of 'Where on earth did they find *that*?'. Italian marionettes, 1920s French mannequins and Argentinian cast-iron mail-boxes rest alongside decorative doors, tiles, stained-glass windows, fireplace mantels and garden furnishings. There are several museum-quality pieces worth an ogle, such as doors designed by famed local architect Louis Sullivan.

UNABRIDGED BOOKSTORE BOOKS

Map p300 (☏773-883-9119; www.unabridged bookstore.com; 3251 N Broadway; ◷10am-9pm Mon-Fri, to 7pm Sat & Sun; ⓂRed, Brown, Purple Line to Belmont) This indie shop is known for its stellar gay and lesbian section (including gay fiction, gay parenting and queer spirituality), as well as travel, sci-fi and children's sections. Staff tape up notes on the shelves next to their recommendations.

BELMONT ARMY SURPLUS CLOTHING

Map p300 (☏773-549-1038; 855 W Belmont Ave; ◷11am-8pm Mon-Sat, noon-6pm Sun; ⓂRed, Brown, Purple Line to Belmont) Don't be fooled by the name – the goods at this sprawling, five-story shop go well beyond combat gear. Fashion-of-the-moment clothes hang from the 1st floor's racks. A rainbow array of Converse, Vans, Adidas, Dr Martens, Red Wing and sky-high goth shoes fills the 2nd floor's shelves. The 3rd floor is where you finally get to the peacoats and other military wares. Skateboard gear and vintage/ thrift clothes also get a floor apiece.

SPORTS WORLD GIFTS & SOUVENIRS

Map p300 (☏844-462-4422; www.sportsworld chicago.com; 3555 N Clark St; ◷9am-6pm; ⓂRed Line to Addison) This store across from Wrigley Field overflows with – that's right, Sherlock – Cubs sportswear. It carries all shapes and sizes of jerseys, T-shirts, sweatshirts and ballcaps, plus baby clothes and drink flasks. Surprisingly, the prices aren't bad given the location.

CHOPPING BLOCK FOOD & DRINKS

Map p316 (☏773-472-6700; www.thechopping block.com; 4747 N Lincoln Ave; ◷9:30am-7:30pm Mon-Sat, to 5:30pm Sun; ⓂBrown Line to Western) Let's say your recipe calls for Hungarian cinnamon, gray sea salt and Balinese long pepper. Instead of throwing up your hands in despair after searching the local grocery store and then calling for a pizza delivery, stop in here for specialty foods, high-end cookware and hard-to-find utensils. Chopping Block also offers cooking classes.

EGOIST UNDERWEAR CLOTHING

Map p300 (☏773-281-5121; www.egoistunder wear.com; 3526 N Halsted St; ◷11am-8pm Mon-Sat, to 7pm Sun; ⓂRed Line to Addison) This boutique in the heart of Boystown specializes in men's designer underwear. Peruse

---

LOCAL KNOWLEDGE

SOUVENIRS

Lake View is a swell neighborhood to pick up unique Chicago souvenirs. Try the following:

Strange Cargo For a T-shirt with a diagram of what's on a Chicago-style hot dog.

Sports World For a sweatshirt, coffee cup or anything with a Cubs logo.

Chicago Comics For a hand-drawn magazine made by a local artist.

---

briefs, boxers, G-strings, swimming shorts, v-neck T-shirts and tank tops. Brands include AussieBum and Cocksox.

BROWN ELEPHANT RESALE SHOP HOMEWARES

Map p300 (☏773-549-5943; 3020 N Lincoln Ave; ◷10am-6pm; ⓂBrown, Purple Line to Wellington) Proceeds benefit the Howard Brown Health Center, which specializes in health care for the LGBT communities. The shop has a consistently good selection of books, vintage furniture and kitchen items.

UNCLE DAN'S SPORTS & OUTDOORS

Map p300 (☏773-348-5800; www.udans.com; 3551 N Southport Ave; ◷10am-7pm Mon-Sat, 11am-6pm Sun; ⓂBrown Line to Southport) This store offers top travel and outdoor gear for those looking to escape the concrete jungle, or at least get some abrasion-reinforced fleece to protect them from the elements. It's a relaxed place to buy hiking boots, camping supplies, backpacks and whatnot without the macho posturing that gear stores sometimes give off.

WINDWARD SPORTS SPORTS

Map p300 (☏773-472-6868; www.windward boardshop.com; 3317 N Clark St; ◷11am-8pm Mon-Sat, noon-6pm Sun; ⓂRed, Brown, Purple Line to Belmont) One-stop shopping for sporty board gear, whether you're into surfing, windsurfing, kiteboarding, snowboarding or skateboarding. Windward carries the requisite apparel labels, too (Quiksilver, Billabong, Split etc). Staff members are clued in to local boarding hot spots. Ask about various beach rentals of windsurfing equipment during the summer.

LAKE VIEW & WRIGLEYVILLE SHOPPING

MIDWEST PRO SOUND ELECTRONICS

Map p300 (☎773-975-4250; 1613 W Belmont Ave; ⊗11am-7pm Mon-Fri, to 6pm Sat; Ⓜ Brown Line to Paulina) This is a hub for DJ gear, both used and new. If you're looking for a basic mixer or a Technics turntable (or a PA system that will quickly make you the talk of your neighborhood), this is your store.

YESTERDAY SPORTS

Map p300 (☎773-248-8087; 1143 W Addison St; ⊗4-7pm Mon-Fri, 1-7pm Sat, 2-6pm Sun; Ⓜ Red Line to Addison) If you've ever actually lived through the classic 'Mom's thrown out all of my baseball cards' tale, you can come here to find out what a fortune you've lost. Old sports memorabilia is the specialty of this shop, which is even older and mustier than some of the goods on sale. Hours can be erratic.

 # SPORTS & ACTIVITIES

★**CHICAGO CUBS** BASEBALL

Map p300 (☎800-843-2827; www.cubs.com; 1060 W Addison St; Ⓜ Red Line to Addison) The beloved, beleaguered Cubs plays at Wrigley Field. It has been more than a century since the team won the World Series, but that doesn't stop fans from coming out to see the games. Ticket prices vary, but in general you'll be hard-pressed to get in for under $35. The popular bleacher seats cost around $55.

SYDNEY R MAROVITZ GOLF COURSE GOLF

Map p300 (☎312-742-7930; www.cpdgolf.com; 3600 N Recreation Dr/Lake Shore Dr; ⊟151) The nine-hole course enjoys sweeping views of the lake and skyline. It is very popular and in order to secure a tee time golfers cheerfully arrive at 5:30am. You can avoid that sort of lunacy by reserving in advance (either online or by phone; no extra fee). Fees are $26 to $29 in summer. You can also rent clubs here.

DIVERSEY-RIVER BOWL BOWLING

(☎773-227-5800; www.drbowl.com; 2211 W Diversey Ave; lanes per hour $21-36; ⊟76) It's nicknamed the 'rock 'n' bowl' for its late-night light show, fog machines and loud music.

WAVELAND BOWL BOWLING

(☎773-472-5900; www.wavelandbowl.com; 3700 N Western Ave; per person per game $1-6; ⊗9am-1am Sun-Thu, to 3am Fri & Sat; Ⓜ Brown Line to Addison, then bus 152) Waveland fires up the fog machines, trippy lights and rock music most evenings. It's called 'cosmic bowling.'

Andersonville & Uptown

Neighborhood Top Five

① Clark Street Ambling along this busy thoroughfare, popping into funky shops by day and drinking and dining in gastronome taverns at night.

② Green Mill (p133) Listening to jazz and sipping martinis with Al Capone's ghost in velvet booths amid candlelit, art-deco decor.

③ Argyle Street (p127) Slurping pho and bubble tea in the steamy-windowed shops of 'Little Saigon.'

④ Neo-Futurists (p133) Watching 30 plays in 60 minutes at this offbeat theater, where a dice throw determines your admission cost.

⑤ Montrose Beach (p134) Exploring the dunes and bird-filled 'magic hedge,' or lounging at the bar while watching sailboats float in the harbor.

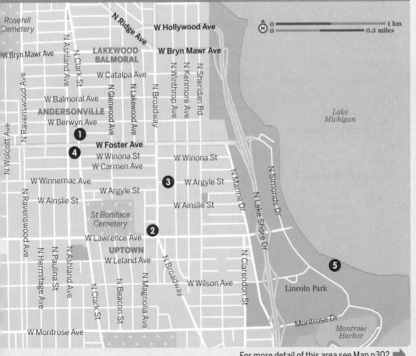

For more detail of this area see Map p302 ➡

Lonely Planet's Top Tip

In addition to serving some of the neighborhood's best food, Hopleaf (p129) and Acre (p132) are fantastic beer bars. Stop in before dinner and enjoy a strong Trappist ale or an unusual microbrew. At Acre you can supplement with $1.50 oysters.

Best Places to Eat

➡ Hopleaf (p129)

➡ Big Jones (p129)

➡ Tiztal Cafe (p127)

➡ Hot G Dog (p128)

➡ Swedish Bakery (p128)

For reviews, see p127 ➡

Best Places to Drink

➡ Simon's (p132)

➡ Hamburger Mary's (p132)

➡ Big Chicks (p132)

➡ Crew (p132)

➡ SoFo Tap (p132)

For reviews, see p132 ➡

☆ Best Entertainment

➡ Green Mill (p133)

➡ Neo-Futurists (p133)

➡ Paper Machete (p133)

➡ Black Ensemble Theater (p133)

For reviews, see p133 ➡

Explore Andersonville & Uptown

These northern neighborhoods are good for a delicious browse. Andersonville is an old Swedish enclave centered on Clark St, where timeworn European-tinged businesses and bakeries mix with new foodie restaurants, funky boutiques, vintage shops and gay and lesbian bars. Places like the butter-lovin' Swedish Bakery carry on the legacy of the original inhabitants, but the residential streets are now home mostly to creative types, young professionals and folks who fly the rainbow flag.

Around the corner to the south, Uptown is a whole different scene. Argyle St runs through the heart of 'Little Saigon,' filled with pho-serving restaurants and clattering shops selling exotic goods from the homeland. Several historic theaters cluster at N Broadway and Lawrence Ave, including Al Capone's favorite speakeasy, the Green Mill. It's still a timeless venue to hear jazz and to tipple.

Traditional sights are in short supply. You're in the neighborhoods to stroll and window-shop, eat and drink and maybe see a show. Begin in the afternoon and linger on through the night. Or make a full day of it by starting at Montrose Beach for surf and sand in the morning. Further north, Devon Ave – a wild mash-up of Indian, Pakistani, Russian and Jewish shops and restaurants – offers a worthy detour for those with more time.

Local Life

➡ **Solstice party** In mid-June Andersonville harks back to its Swedish roots, and everyone gets together to dance around the maypole and eat lingonberries for Midsommarfest.

➡ **Saturday salon** Local artists and journalists gather to discuss life on the Green Mill's stage for the Paper Machete (p133) every Saturday.

➡ **Dog beach** When locals need to let Fido roam and splash, they unleash at Montrose Beach (p134). It is *the* four-legged scene.

Getting There & Away

➡ **El** Red Line to Berwyn (six blocks east of Clark St) for Andersonville. Red Line to Argyle for Argyle St; Red Line to Lawrence for Green Mill and around.

➡ **Bus** Number 22 travels along Clark St.

➡ **Car** Meter and on-street parking are available in Andersonville and Uptown, though it gets congested on weekends.

⊙ SIGHTS

ARGYLE STREET — AREA

Map p302 (btwn N Broadway & Sheridan Rd; Ⓜ Red Line to Argyle) It's also known as 'Little Saigon.' Many residents came here as refugees from the Vietnam War and subsequently filled the storefronts with pho-serving lunch spots, bubble-tea-pouring bakeries and shops with exotic goods from the homeland. The pagoda-shaped Argyle El station, painted in the auspicious colors of green and red, puts you in the fishy-smelling heart of it.

The area is great for a wander (even if it looks a little scruffy). The businesses spill out onto N Broadway as well.

GRACELAND CEMETERY — CEMETERY

Map p302 (🖉773-525-1105; www.gracelandcem etery.org; 4001 N Clark St; ⊙8am-4:30pm; Ⓜ Red Line to Sheridan) Graceland Cemetery is the final resting place for some of the biggest names in Chicago history, including architects Louis Sullivan and Ludwig Mies van der Rohe and retail magnate Marshall Field. Most of the notable tombs lie around the lake, in the northern half of the 121 acres. Pick up a map at the entrance to navigate the swirl of streets.

Many of the memorials relate to the lives of the dead in symbolic and touching ways. National League founder William Hulbert lies under a baseball. Daniel Burnham, who did so much to design Chicago, gets his own island. George Pullman, the railroad car magnate who sparked so much labor unrest, lies under a hidden fortress designed to prevent angry union members from digging him up. Power couple Potter and Bertha Palmer also have a doozy memorial.

SWEDISH AMERICAN MUSEUM CENTER — MUSEUM

Map p302 (🖉773-728-8111; www.swedishameri canmuseum.org; 5211 N Clark St; adult/child $4/3; ⊙10am-4pm Mon-Fri, 11am-4pm Sat & Sun; Ⓜ Red Line to Berwyn) The permanent collection at this small storefront museum focuses on the lives of the Swedes who originally settled Chicago. Check out the items people felt were important to bring with them on their journey to America; butter churns, traditional bedroom furniture, religious relics and more are included. The children's section lets kids climb around on a steamship and milk fake cows.

THE MAGIC HEDGE

The Montrose Point Bird Sanctuary – more commonly known as 'the Magic Hedge' – lies at the southeast edge of Montrose Beach (p134). The bushy area is an important stopover point for migratory birds. More than 300 species have been spotted here, everything from white-crowned sparrows to roosting owls and red-throated loons.

To find the feathery oasis, follow Montrose Ave toward the beach. Take a right at the street by the bait shop, then follow the 'hedge' signs.

ESSANAY STUDIOS — FILM LOCATION

Map p302 (1333-1345 W Argyle St; Ⓜ Red Line to Argyle) Back before the talkies made silent film obsolete, Chicago reigned supreme as the number one producer of movie magic in the USA. Essanay churned out silent films with soon-to-be household names like WC Fields and Charlie Chaplin. Filming took place at the big studio that was here. Essanay's terra-cotta Indian head logo remains above the door at 1345 Argyle.

These days, the building belongs to a local college. Essanay folded in 1917, about the time that many of its actors were being lured to the bright lights of a still-nascent Hollywood.

HUTCHINSON STREET DISTRICT — ARCHITECTURE

(Ⓜ Red Line to Sheridan) Homes here were built in the early 1900s and represent some of the best examples of Prairie School architecture in Chicago. Many residences – including the one at 839 Hutchinson St – are the work of George W Maher, a famous student of Frank Lloyd Wright. Also of note are 817 Hutchinson St and 4243 Hazel St.

In marked contrast to some of Uptown's seedier areas, the district is well maintained and perfect for a genteel promenade.

✗ EATING

TIZTAL CAFE — BREAKFAST $

Map p302 (🖉773-271-4631; 4631 N Clark St; mains $7-10; ⊙8am-4pm Mon-Sat, to 3pm Sun; 🖳22) Everyone from hipsters nursing hangovers to moms nursing babies piles in to

WORTH A DETOUR

DEVON AVENUE

Known as Chicago's 'International Marketplace,' Devon Ave is where worlds collide. Indian, Pakistani, Georgian, Russian, Cuban, Israeli – you name the ethnicity and someone from the group has set up a shop or eatery along the street. It's a fun destination for browsing.

Devon at Western Ave is the main intersection. Indian sari and jewelry shops start near 2600 W Devon; to the west they give way to Jewish and Islamic goods stores, while to the east they trickle out into a gaggle of electronics and dollar stores. It's a good place to stock up on low-cost cell-phone necessities, luggage and other travel goods. Or just buy an armful of jangly bangles.

While you're here, you've got to stay for a meal. The best curry in the city simmers in Devon's aromatic restaurants. Vegetarians will find scads of options. Local favorites include the following:

Udupi Palace (☑773-338-2152; www.udupipalacechicago.net; 2543 W Devon Ave; mains $9-16; ⏰11:30am-9:30pm; ☑; ☐155) This bustling all-vegetarian South Indian restaurant serves toasty, kite-sized *dosas* (crepes made with rice and lentil flour) stuffed with all manner of vegetables and spices, along with an array of curries. The room gets loud once it packs with 20-something Anglo hipsters and a young Indian crowd.

Mysore Woodlands (☑773-338-8160; www.mysorewoodlands.info; 2548 W Devon Ave; mains $10-17; ⏰11am-9:30pm Mon-Thu, 11am-10:30pm Fri & Sat, noon-9:30pm Sun; ☑; ☐155) Another South Indian all-veg favorite, where friendly servers deliver well-spiced curries, *dosas* and *iddlies* (steamed rice-lentil patties) in the spacious low-lit room.

Sabri Nihari (☑773-465-3272; www.sabrinihari.com; 2502 W Devon Ave; mains $12-20; ⏰noon-11:30pm; ☐155) Fresh, fresh meat and vegetable dishes, distinctly seasoned, set this Pakistani place apart from its competitors on Devon. Try the 'frontier' chicken, which comes with a plate of freshly cut onions, tomatoes, cucumber and lemon, and enough perfectly cooked chicken for two. For dessert, check out the *kheer*, a creamy rice pudding.

Devon's epicenter is about 2.5 miles northwest of Andersonville. Take the Red Line to Loyola and transfer to bus 155, or take the Brown Line to Western and then transfer to bus 49B.

family-run Tiztal for brunch. The chorizo scrambles, gravy-slathered biscuits and country-fried steak are house favorites, along with oatmeal shakes and fresh fruit juices. There are only a dozen tables or so, but they turn over fast.

HOT G DOG
AMERICAN **$**

Map p302 (☑773-209-3360; www.hotgdog.com; 5009 N Clark St; hot dogs $2.50-4; ⏰10:30am-8pm Mon-Sat, to 4pm Sun; Ⓜ Red Line to Argyle) The Garcia brothers (hence the 'G') learned the gourmet sausage trade working at Hot Doug's famed shop. This is the place to bite into, say, a chicken, apple and cranberry hot dog with whiskey cheese and pecans. It's also a fine place to try a regular Chicago-style dog. Cash only.

SWEDISH BAKERY
BAKERY **$**

Map p302 (☑773-561-8919; www.swedishbakery.com; 5348 N Clark St; pastries $1.50-4; ⏰6:30am-6:30pm Mon-Fri, to 5pm Sat; ☑; Ⓜ Red Line to Berwyn) Locals have been getting in line for custard-plumped éclairs, French silk tortes, chocolate-chip streusels and chocolate-drop butter cookies for more than 80 years. Free samples and coffee help ease the wait. Take a number from the ticket dispenser and scope out what you want before you're called to make the difficult final decision.

FIRST SLICE
CAFE **$**

Map p302 (☑773-275-4297; www.firstslice.org; 5357 N Ashland Ave; mains $5-10; ⏰10am-9pm Mon-Thu, 10am-10pm Fri, 9am-10pm Sat, 10am-8pm Sun; ☐50) First Slice not only serves made-from-scratch soups, salads, quiches, sandwiches and eight different flaky-crusted pies daily, but proceeds help supply needy families with fresh, healthy meals. So you're doing good by eating well.

TWEET

AMERICAN $

Map p302 (☏773-728-5576; www.tweet.biz; 5020 N Sheridan Rd; mains $8-16; ⊗8:30am-3pm; ☏☏; Ⓜ Red Line to Argyle) ✿ Reimagined breakfast standards hit the tables at this cozy morning spot. The Havarti omelet folds in green apple slices and the namesake cheese. The 'Country Benedict' adds two poached eggs and a thick slab of sausage alongside biscuits and gravy for a decadent opening meal. Most ingredients are organic, and there's lots for gluten-free and vegetarian eaters, too. Cash only.

Tweet has the same owners as the next-door gay bar Big Chicks.

NHA HANG VIET NAM

VIETNAMESE $

Map p302 (☏773-878-8895; 1032 W Argyle St; mains $7-13; ⊗7am-10pm; Ⓜ Red Line to Argyle) Little Nha Hang may not look like much from the outside, but it offers a huge menu of authentic, well-made dishes from the homeland. It's terrific for slurping pho and clay-pot catfish. Staff give out free vanilla ice cream at meal's end, which is a nice digestive.

KOPI, A TRAVELER'S CAFE

CAFE $

Map p302 (☏773-989-5674; 5317 N Clark St; mains $7-11; ⊗8am-11pm Mon-Thu, 8am-midnight Fri & Sat, 9am-11pm Sun; ☏; Ⓜ Red Line to Berwyn) Kopi wafts an Asian trekker-lodge vibe, from the pile of pillows to sit on by the front window to the bean-sprouty sandwiches, bohemian clientele and flyer-filled community bulletin board. The little shop in back sells travel books and fair-trade global gifts. Wine and beer are also available, along with all kinds of coffee drinks.

BA LE BAKERY

VIETNAMESE $

Map p302 (☏773-561-4424; www.balesandwich. com; 5014 N Broadway; sandwiches $6-9; ⊗7am-9pm; Ⓜ Red Line to Argyle) Ba Le serves Saigon-style *banh mi* sandwiches, with steamed pork, shrimp cakes or meatballs on fresh baguettes made right here. The futuristic digs offer several tables to eat at.

★HOPLEAF

EUROPEAN $$

Map p302 (☏773-334-9851; www.hopleaf.com; 5148 N Clark St; mains $12-27; ⊗noon-11pm Mon-Thu, to midnight Fri & Sat, to 10pm Sun; Ⓜ Red Line to Berwyn) A cozy, European-like tavern, Hopleaf draws crowds for its Montreal-style smoked brisket, cashew-butter-and-fig-jam sandwich, uber-creamy macaroni and Stilton cheese, and the house-specialty *frites* (fries) and ale-soaked mussels. It also pours 200 types of brew (around 60 are on tap), emphasizing craft and Belgian suds.

In winter, a fireplace warms the jam-packed tables full of chattering locals. In summer, everyone heads to the umbrella-shaded patio in the back garden.

BIG JONES

AMERICAN $$

Map p302 (☏773-275-5725; www.bigjoneschi cago.com; 5347 N Clark St; mains $17-25; ⊗11am-9pm Mon-Thu, to 10pm Fri, from 9am Sat & Sun; Ⓜ Red Line to Berwyn) Warm, sunny Big Jones puts sustainable 'Southern heirloom cooking' on the menu, mixing dishes from New Orleans, the Carolina Lowcountry and Appalachia. Locals flock in for chicken and dumplings, crawfish étouffée, and shrimp and grits (though the menu changes with the seasons). The decadent, biscuit-laden brunch draws the biggest crowds. It's best to reserve in advance.

TANK NOODLE

VIETNAMESE $$

Map p302 (☏773-878-2253; www.tank-noodle. com; 4953 N Broadway; mains $11-21; ⊗8:30am-10pm Mon, Tue & Thu-Sat, to 9pm Sun; Ⓜ Red Line to Argyle) The crowds come to this spacious utilitarian eatery for *banh mi*, served on crunchy fresh baguette rolls, and the pho, which is widely regarded as the city's best. The 200-plus-item menu sprawls on from there and includes *banh xeo* (crispy pancakes), catfish and squid dishes, and a rainbow array of bubble teas.

JIN JU

KOREAN $$

Map p302 (☏773-334-6377; www.jinjurestaurant. com; 5203 N Clark St; mains $12-22; ⊗5-9:30pm Sun, Tue & Wed, to 10pm Thu, to 11pm Fri & Sat; Ⓜ Red Line to Berwyn) One of only a handful of nouveau Korean restaurants in town, Jin Ju throws a culinary curveball by tempering Korean food to Western tastes. The minimalist candlelit interior of Jin Ju echoes softly with downbeat techno, and the stylish 30-something clientele enjoys mains like *haemul pajon* (a fried pancake stuffed with seafood) and *kalbi* (beef short ribs).

The drinks menu must is the 'soju-tini,' a cocktail made with *soju*, a Korean spirit distilled from sweet potatoes.

KEN ILIO/GETTY IMAGES ©

1. Montrose Beach (p134)
Watch kitesurfers glide across the ocean at one of Chicago's best beaches.

2. Swedish pastries (p128)
Enjoy a slice of Scandinavia in Andersonville, a former Swedish enclave.

3. Green Mill (p133)
Swill a cocktail and take in smooth jazz sounds at this former haunt of Al Capone.

LONELY PLANET/GETTY IMAGES ©

ACRE
AMERICAN $$

Map p302 (☎773-334-7600; www.acrerestau rant.com; 5308 N Clark St; mains $14-23; ⊙5-10pm Mon-Thu, 5-11pm Fri, 11am-11pm Sat, 11am-9pm Sun; Ⓜ Red Line to Berwyn) 🍴 Acre isn't doing anything unique with its farm-to-table pretzel-crusted trout and broccolini, pork burger with house-cured bacon, and flaky chicken pot pie. But it does it well enough to be a neighborhood favorite. A terrific beer selection flows from 25 taps. And the $1.50 oysters may well be the best deal in town.

HAI YEN
VIETNAMESE $$

Map p302 (☎773-561-4077; www.haiyenres taurant.com; 1055 W Argyle St; mains $9-15; ⊙10:30am-10pm Mon, Tue, Thu & Fri, from 9:30am Sat & Sun; Ⓜ Red Line to Argyle) Many of the dishes at this warm Argyle St eatery require some assembly, pairing shrimp, beef or squid with rice crepes, mint, Thai basil and lettuce. For an appetizer, try the *goi cuon,* fresh rolls of vermicelli rice noodles along with shrimp, pork and carrots. The *bo bay mon* consists of seven (yes, seven) different kinds of beef.

Order sparingly, or ask for some help from your server – like the *bo bay mon,* many of the dishes are large enough to feed an army.

THAI PASTRY
THAI $$

Map p302 (☎773-784-5399; www.thaipastry. com; 4925 N Broadway; mains $9-15; ⊙11am-10pm Sun-Thu, to 11pm Fri & Sat; Ⓜ Red Line to Argyle) A lunchtime favorite with workers from both Uptown and Andersonville, this Thai restaurant has a window filled with accolades and awards, and the food to back it up. The pad Thai is excellent, and the spot-on curries arrive still simmering in a clay pot. For a quick, cheap snack, visit the counter for a baked pastry.

ANDIE'S
MEDITERRANEAN $$

Map p302 (☎773-784-8616; www.andieschicago. com; 5253 N Clark St; mains $13-19; ⊙11am-10pm Sun-Thu, to 11pm Sat & Sun; 🖕🎫; Ⓜ Red Line to Berwyn) Reliable Andie's has anchored Andersonville's restaurant row from the get-go, and it still draws crowds for smooth hummus, dill rice and much more in the cool Mediterranean interior. Gluten-free pita bread arrives in place of regular pita if you ask. There's also a kids menu.

🍷 DRINKING & NIGHTLIFE

★ SIMON'S
BAR

Map p302 (☎773-878-0894; 5210 N Clark St; ⊙11am-2am; Ⓜ Red Line to Berwyn) An Andersonville mainstay that has been around since 1934, Simon's is a dimly lit musicians' watering hole. The jukebox rocks an eclectic menu ranging from Robert Gordon to Elastica to Television to the Clash. In winter, in homage to its Swedish roots, Simon's serves *glogg* (spiced wine punch). A giant neon fish holding a martini glass marks the spot. Cash only.

HAMBURGER MARY'S
BAR

Map p302 (☎773-784-6969; www.hamburger marys.com/chicago; 5400 N Clark St; ⊙11:30am-midnight Sun-Wed, to 1:30am Thu & Fri, to 2:30am Sat; Ⓜ Red Line to Berwyn) This is Chicago's outpost of the campy San Francisco–based chain that bills itself as an 'open-air bar and grill for open-minded people.' Yes, it serves well-regarded burgers and weekend brunch in the downstairs restaurant, but the action's on the rowdy, booze-soaked patio. Andersonville Brewing Company is attached; it makes its own beer and turns on the HDTVs for sports fans.

The Attic lounge upstairs hosts cabaret, karaoke and DJs.

BIG CHICKS
GAY & LESBIAN

Map p302 (☎773-728-5511; www.bigchicks.com; 5024 N Sheridan Rd; ⊙4pm-2am Mon-Fri, from 11am Sat & Sun; 🛜; Ⓜ Red Line to Argyle) Despite the name, both men and women frequent Big Chicks, with its weekend DJs, fun dance floor, art displays and next-door organic restaurant Tweet, where weekend brunch packs 'em in. Cash only.

CREW
GAY

Map p302 (☎773-784-2739; www.crewbarchica go.com; 4804 N Broadway; ⊙4pm-midnight Mon-Wed, 4pm-2am Thu & Fri, 11am-2am Sat, 11am-midnight Sun; Ⓜ Red Line to Lawrence) Sporty Crew offers a change from the usual scene, with good microbrews and 21 hi-def TVs tuned to all the big games. Weekly trivia and karaoke nights slip into the schedule, as does the occasional underwear contest.

SOFO TAP
GAY

Map p302 (☎773-784-7636; www.thesofotap. com; 4923 N Clark St; ⊙5pm-2am Mon-Thu, from 3pm Fri, from noon Sat & Sun; Ⓜ Red Line to Argyle) SoFo is a normal neighborhood bar with a sweet dog-friendly patio. Then again, there are also raucous live game shows and rock and soul karaoke. And if you happen in on Friday night, the vast majority of the male crowd will be shirtless for 'bear' night.

@MOSPHERE
GAY

Map p302 (☏773-784-1100; www.atmospherebar. com; 5355 N Clark St; ☺6pm-2am Tue-Sun; Ⓜ Red Line to Berwyn) The good-looking boys have a lot of action to choose from at @mosphere: Bored Gaymes on Tuesday (cards, Scrabble) and especially the male go-go dancers Thursday through Sunday. DJs and drag revues also entertain, and there's never a cover charge.

⭐ ENTERTAINMENT

★ GREEN MILL
JAZZ

Map p302 (☏773-878-5552; www.greenmilljazz. com; 4802 N Broadway; ☺noon-4am Mon-Sat, 11am-4am Sun; Ⓜ Red Line to Lawrence) The timeless Green Mill earned its notoriety as Al Capone's favorite speakeasy (the tunnels where he hid the booze are still underneath the bar). Sit in one of the curved velvet booths and feel his ghost urging you on to another martini. Local and national jazz artists perform nightly; Sundays also host the nationally acclaimed poetry slam. Cash only. FYI, Capone's designated booth is the one at the end of the bar, on the north side – the only seat in the house that has a view of both doors.

NEO-FUTURISTS
THEATER

Map p302 (☏773-878-4557; www.neofuturists. org; 5153 N Ashland Ave; Ⓜ Red Line to Berwyn) The theater is best known for its long-running *Too Much Light Makes the Baby Go Blind,* in which the hyper troupe makes a manic attempt to perform 30 plays in 60 minutes. It runs Friday and Saturday at 11:30pm and Sunday at 7pm. Admission cost is $10 to $15; what you pay within that range is based on a dice throw.

The group puts on plenty of other original works that'll make you ponder and laugh simultaneously. Well worth the northward trek, but prepare to wait in line.

PAPER MACHETE
LIVE PERFORMANCE

Map p302 (☏773-227-4433; 4802 N Broadway; ☺3-5pm Sat; Ⓜ Brown Line to Western) FREE Poets, musicians, journalists, playwrights,

comedians and the occasional trash-talking puppet get together for this witty 'live magazine' discussing culture and politics. It's always free and held at the Green Mill jazz club on Saturday afternoons.

BLACK ENSEMBLE THEATER
THEATER

Map p302 (☏773-769-4451; www.blackensem bletheater.org; 4450 N Clark St; Ⓜ Brown Line to Montrose) This well-established group saw its fledgling production of *The Jackie Wilson Story* attract wide attention and national tours. The focus here has long been on original productions about the African American experience through mostly historical, biographical scripts.

CAROL'S PUB
LIVE MUSIC

Map p302 (☏773-334-2402; 4659 N Clark St; ☺11am-4am; 🚌22) The closest thing Chicago has to a honky-tonk, divey Carol's offers (at times ironic) boot-stompin', Bud-drinkin' good times to patrons, who come out on weekends to dance like crazy to the house country band.

🛍 SHOPPING

WOOLLY MAMMOTH
ANTIQUES & ODDITIES
ANTIQUES

Map p302 (☏773-989-3294; www.woollymam mothchicago.com; 1513 W Foster Ave; ☺1-7pm Mon, from 3pm Tue, from noon Wed-Sun; Ⓜ Red Line to Berwyn) Woolly Mammoth Antiques & Oddities is part morbid curiosity shop, part art installation. Creepy doll heads, a stuffed wallaby, a jar of old dentures, the record book from an insane asylum – all here, and then some. Set designers often come here for props.

WOMEN & CHILDREN FIRST BOOKS

Map p302 (☎773-769-9299; www.womenandchildrenfirst.com; 5233 N Clark St; ⊙11am-7pm Mon & Tue, 11am-9pm Wed-Fri, 10am-7pm Sat, 11am-6pm Sun; 👪; Ⓜ Red Line to Berwyn) A feminist mainstay, this independent bookstore has been around for more than 35 years. Book signings and author events happen most weeks at the welcoming shop, which features fiction and nonfiction by and about women, a big selection of gay and lesbian titles, and scads of children's books.

EARLY TO BED ACCESSORIES

Map p302 (☎773-271-1219; www.early2bed.com; 5044 N Clark St; ⊙noon-7pm Mon & Tue, to 8pm Wed-Sat, to 6pm Sun; Ⓜ Red Line to Argyle) This low-key, women-owned sex shop is good for novices: it provides explanatory pages and customer reviews throughout the store, so you'll be able to know your anal beads from cock rings from bullet vibes. Also on hand are fishnet stockings, bondage tapes and vegan condoms (made with casein-free latex; casein is a milk-derived product usually used in latex production).

An excellent selection of resource books rounds out the offerings, including sex manuals for rape survivors and people with mobility issues.

SCOUT HOMEWARES

Map p302 (☎773-275-5700; www.scoutchicago.com; 5221 N Clark St; ⊙11am-6pm Tue, Wed & Sat, noon-7pm Thu & Fri, noon-5pm Sun; Ⓜ Red Line to Berwyn) With groovy displays of retro tables, chairs, dishware and outdoor gear set up in little scenes throughout the rooms, the owners of this 'urban antique shop' make it difficult to keep your money in your wallet. The classic pieces are all in good repair.

ANDERSONVILLE GALLERIA ART

Map p302 (☎773-878-8570; www.andersonvillegalleria.com; 5247 N Clark St; ⊙11am-7pm Mon-Sat, to 6pm Sun; Ⓜ Red Line to Berwyn) Ninety indie vendors sell their fair-trade and locally made artisan wares in mini-boutiques spread over three floors. Sweets, coffee, clothing, handbags, paintings, photography, jewelry – it's a smorgasbord of cool, crafty goods in a community-oriented marketplace. Support the little guy!

ALAMO SHOES SHOES

Map p302 (☎773-784-8936; www.alamoshoes.com; 5321 N Clark St; ⊙9am-8pm Mon-Fri, to 6pm Sat, 10am-6pm Sun; Ⓜ Red Line to Berwyn) This throwback to the 1960s focuses on hip, comfortable shoes for men, women and children. Brands include Dansko, Ecco, Naot, Birkenstock, Keen and Dr Martens, all at good prices. The enthusiastic staffers hop off to the back room and emerge with stacks of boxes until you either find what you want or are entirely walled in by the possibilities.

SPORTS & ACTIVITIES

MONTROSE BEACH BEACH

(www.cpdbeaches.com; 4400 N Lake Shore Dr; 🚌146) Montrose is one of the city's best beaches. You can rent kayaks, stand-up paddleboards and Jet Skis. Sometimes you'll see surfers and kitesurfers, and anglers frequently cast here. Sailboats glide in the harbor. The Dock bar and grill provides waterside snacks. A wide, dog-friendly beach with a curving breakwater abuts the main beach to the north.

KAYAK CHICAGO KAYAKING

(☎312-852-9258; www.kayakchicago.com; 4400 N Lake Shore Dr; ⊙10am-7pm Wed-Sun Jun-Aug; 🚌146) This group rents kayaks and stand-up paddleboards for $20 per hour or $80 per day. Staff also provide lessons. Located in the southeast corner of Montrose Beach.

WILSON SKATE PARK OUTDOORS

(cnr W Wilson Ave & N Lake Shore Dr; 🚌146) FREE Watch the kids kick-turn and heel-flip at this free facility by Montrose Beach's northern edge.

Wicker Park, Bucktown & Ukrainian Village

Neighborhood Top Five

① Milwaukee Ave (p149) Trawling for treasures – an old Devo record, a vintage pillbox hat, steel-toed boots, a mustache disguise kit – in the shops along the half-mile stretch between Damen and Ashland Aves.

② Hideout (p148) Hearing an alt-country band, watch-ing a local politics talk show, or singing along with a Meatloaf tribute band in one of Chicago's coolest venues.

③ Matchbox (p147) Squeezing into the teeny bar for a gimlet, sidecar or other retro cocktail.

④ 606 (p137) Strolling on high through the neighbor-hood past hip restaurants, clackety El trains and locals' backyards via this elevated trail.

⑤ Quimby's (p149) Perus-ing the zines and getting the lowdown on the city's underground culture.

For more detail of this area see Map p304 ➡

Lonely Planet's Top Tip

In summer the neighborhood throws excellent street festivals with big-name bands. Watch for Do Division (www.do-divisionstreetfest.com) in early June; Green Music Fest (www.greenmusicfestchicago.com) in late June; West Fest (www.westfestchicago.com) in mid-July; and the Hideout Block Party (www.hideoutchicago.com) – the best of the bunch – in early September.

Best Places to Eat

➡ Dove's Luncheonette (p141)

➡ Irazu (p138)

➡ Ruxbin (p145)

➡ Mana Food Bar (p141)

➡ Pub Royale (p138)

➡ Small Cheval (p139)

For reviews, see p138 ➡

Best Places to Drink

➡ Matchbox (p147)

➡ Danny's (p146)

➡ Map Room (p146)

➡ Violet Hour (p146)

➡ Forbidden Root (p147)

➡ Happy Village (p147)

For reviews, see p146 ➡

Best Places to Shop

➡ Reckless Records (p149)

➡ Quimby's (p149)

➡ Dusty Groove (p149)

➡ Una Mae's (p149)

➡ Wicker Park Secret Agent Supply Co (p149)

For reviews, see p149 ➡

Explore Wicker Park, Bucktown & Ukrainian Village

For a taste of trendy young Chicago, wander up Milwaukee Ave near Damen Ave in Wicker Park on a Friday night. You'll pass booming bars, packed restaurants and stages hosting indie rock on one side of the street and shushed underground author readings on the other. By Saturday morning the scene shifts to the dozens of cool vintage stores, in-the-know record shops and buzzing brunch spots. Buttressed by the slightly fancier Bucktown and slightly scruffier Ukrainian Village, this neighborhood has a lot happening, so strap on some comfortable (hip) sneakers and take it block by block.

Working-class Central and Eastern European immigrants arrived in the late 1800s to work in the factories and breweries that used to be prevalent in the area. Although signs of the community's past are fading fast, there are plenty of traces of the immigrants who founded it, especially in the western reaches of Ukrainian Village. A stroll here will take you past Ukrainian scrawl on shop windows, Orthodox churches and proud corner taverns.

Milwaukee, North and Damen Aves are the main veins through the neighborhood. Division St is also chockablock. Once a polka-bar-lined thoroughfare known as the 'Polish Broadway,' it's now full of burger bars and boutiques.

The neighborhood holds very few sights, but you could easily while away the day shopping and the night eating and drinking. And it's definitely Chicago's best 'hood for rock clubs, with the Hideout and Empty Bottle leading the cool-cat pack.

Local Life

➡ **Group soup** Crowds gather at the Hideout (p148) on Wednesdays in winter for Soup and Bread, a hobnobbing dinner series where local foodies, musicians and artists take turns making, well, soup and bread.

➡ **Bar crafts** The Handmade Market (p150) brings out the crafting community to the Empty Bottle each month.

➡ **Vinyl freaks** Crate diggers find their bliss near the corner of Milwaukee and Ashland Aves, where Reckless Records (p149), Shuga Records (p150) and Dusty Groove (p149) all hover.

Getting There & Away

➡ **El** Blue Line to Damen for Bucktown and northern Wicker Park; Blue Line to Division for southern Wicker Park; Blue Line to Chicago for Ukrainian Village.

➡ **Bus** Bus 72 runs along North Ave; bus 70 along Division St; bus 66 along Chicago Ave.

➡ **Car** Meter and free on-street parking are at a premium in Wicker Park and Bucktown; they're more available in Ukrainian Village.

⊙ SIGHTS

⊙ Wicker Park & Bucktown

FLAT IRON BUILDING ARTS CENTER

Map p304 (www.flatironchicago.com; 1579 N Milwaukee Ave; Ⓜ Blue Line to Damen) Galleries, studios and workshops fill the landmark Flat Iron Building, with contemporary painters, realist photographers, digital animators, pop-art printmakers, experimental videographers and metal sculptors all doing their thing here. There's an open house on the first Friday of every month (suggested donation $5), as well as group shows around the winter holidays. You can usually walk inside and see what's going on any day.

NELSON ALGREN'S HOUSE HISTORIC SITE

Map p304 (1958 W Evergreen Ave; Ⓜ Blue Line to Damen) You can't go inside, but on the 3rd floor of this apartment building writer Nelson Algren created some of his greatest works about life in the once down-and-out neighborhood. A plaque marks the spot. Algren won the 1950 National Book Award for his novel *The Man with the Golden Arm,* about a drug addict hustling on Division St near Milwaukee Ave (a half-mile southeast).

Other insights Algren picked up in the 'hood: 'Never play cards with a man called Doc. Never eat at a place called Mom's. Never sleep with a woman whose troubles are worse than your own' – classic advice he relayed in *A Walk on the Wild Side.* His short *Chicago: City on the Make* summarizes 120 years of thorny local history and is the definitive read on the city's character.

WICKER PARK PARK

Map p304 (1425 N Damen Ave; Ⓜ Blue Line to Damen) The neighborhood's favorite green space is home to softball fields, a children's water playground, a winter ice rink, an active dog park, and indoor and outdoor movies.

Try to see a 16-Inch Softball game in action here. Chicago invented the game a century ago. It uses the same rules as normal softball, but with shorter games, a bigger, squishier ball and no gloves or mitts on the fielders. There's a league that plays in the park.

POLISH MUSEUM OF AMERICA MUSEUM

Map p304 (✆773-384-3352; www.polishmuseofamerica.org; 984 N Milwaukee Ave; adult/child $7/6; ⊙11am-4pm Mon, Tue & Fri-Sun, to 7pm Wed; Ⓜ Blue Line to Division) If you don't know Pulaski from a pierogi, this is the place to get the scoop on Polish culture. It's one of the oldest ethnic museums in the country, crammed with traditional Polish costumes, WWII artifacts, ship models and folk-art pieces. Head up to the 2nd floor and ring the doorbell to get buzzed

LOCAL KNOWLEDGE

THE 606 TRAIL

Like NYC's High Line, Chicago's **606** (Map p304; www.the606.org; ⊙6am-11pm; Ⓜ Blue Line to Damen) is a similar urban-cool elevated path along an old train track. Cycle or stroll past factories, smokestacks, clattering El trains and locals' backyard affairs for 2.7 miles between Wicker Park and Logan Square. It's a fascinating trek through Chicago's socioeconomic strata: moneyed at the east, becoming more industrial and immigrant to the west. The trail parallels Bloomingdale Ave, with access points every quarter mile.

The entrance at Churchill Field (1825 N Damen Ave) is a handy, sculpture-laden place to ascend. For those wanting to cycle, there's a Divvy bike-share station a few blocks from the trail's eastern end at the corner of N Marshfield Ave and W Cortland St.

Top spots to take a break along the way (from east to west) include the following:

Mindy's Hot Chocolate (p141); exit at Damen.

Small Cheval (p139); exit at Leavitt.

Donut Delight (p156); exit at California.

Parson's Chicken & Fish (p156); exit at Humboldt.

WICKER PARK & UKRAINIAN VILLAGE GALLERIES

These neighborhoods are great places to seek out emerging talent. Several artists live and work in the landmark Flat Iron Building and host a monthly First Friday open house, which also offers reasonably priced art for purchase. Keep an eye on telephone poles around the area for fliers detailing the latest shows and open-houses in the 'hood. Other good art galleries:

Intuit: The Center for Intuitive and Outsider Art (Map p304; ☑312-243-9088; www.art.org; 756 N Milwaukee Ave; suggested donation $5; ☺11am-6pm Tue, Wed, Fri & Sat, to 7:30pm Thu, noon-5pm Sun; ⓂBlue Line to Chicago) Behold the museum-like collection of folk art, including watercolors by famed local Henry Darger. In fact, Intuit has re-created his awesomely cluttered studio, complete with balls of twine, teetering stacks of old magazines and a Victrola.

Monique Meloche Gallery (Map p304; ☑773-252-0299; www.moniquemeloche.com; 2154 W Division St; ☺11am-6pm Tue-Sat; ⓂBlue Line to Division) One of Chicago's taste-makers, this gallery features provocative paintings, neon and mixed media. If nothing else, have a look at the 'wall' that shows works through huge windows to engage passersby on Division St.

in. The curator can give you a personalized tour, since you'll likely be the only one here. It's a fine opportunity to learn about the Poles who helped shape Chicago, which has one of the world's largest Polish communities. (Casimir Pulaski, by the way, was a Polish hero in the American Revolution who was known as the 'father of the American cavalry' and the guy who saved George Washington's life at the Battle of Brandywine; a pierogi, meanwhile, is a Polish dumpling.)

⊙ Ukrainian Village

UKRAINIAN INSTITUTE OF MODERN ART　　　MUSEUM

Map p304 (☑773-227-5522; www.uima-chicago.org; 2320 W Chicago Ave; ☺noon-4pm Wed-Sun; ▣66) **FREE** Step into the bright white storefront and make a choice. To the right is the permanent collection of mod, colorful paintings and sculpture (which rotates a few times per year). To the left are the playful and provocative temporary exhibits, done in various media. While most artists are Ukrainian, plenty of other locals get shelf space, too.

The small galleries make for a quick and easy browse. Afterward, keep the Ukrainian theme going by checking out the resplendent churches nearby.

EATING

✖ Wicker Park & Bucktown

★IRAZU　　　LATIN AMERICAN $

Map p304 (☑773-252-5687; www.irazuchicago.com; 1865 N Milwaukee Ave; mains $11-15; ☺11:30am-9:30pm Mon-Sat; ⓂBlue Line to Western) Chicago's unassuming lone Costa Rican eatery turns out burritos bursting with chicken, black beans and fresh avocado, and sandwiches dressed in a heavenly, spicy-sweet vegetable sauce. Wash them down with an *avena* (a slurpable oatmeal milkshake). For breakfast, the *arroz con huevos* (peppery eggs scrambled into rice) relieves hangovers. Irazu is BYOB with no corkage fee. Cash only.

PUB ROYALE　　　INDIAN $

Map p304 (☑773-661-6874; www.pubroyale.com; 2049 W Division St; mains $12-17; ☺5pm-midnight Mon-Fri, 11am-midnight Sat & Sun; ⓂBlue Line to Damen) Loud and fun with brightly painted wood cutouts of Indian gods on the walls, Royale serves distinctive Anglo-Indian pub grub. Sit at a booth or one of the communal tables and tear into lamb dumplings, hot-spiced chicken or cashew coconut eggplant curry, washed down with great beers, ciders and Pimm's Cup–inspired cocktails (Pimm's is a British fruit liqueur).

SMALL CHEVAL
BURGERS $

Map p304 (www.smallcheval.com; 1732 N Milwaukee Ave; mains $9-12; ⊙11am-midnight Mon-Sat, to 10pm Sun; ⓂBlue Line to Damen) Maybe you've heard of Au Cheval, the foodie-adored West Loop burger joint with standard two-hour waits for the famed burgers (after national press crowned it best burger in the nation)? Small Cheval is its pared-down little sibling, a festive burger shack serving, er, burgers. And milkshakes, cocktails and beer. Wait time is minimal. It's located near the 606 trail.

STAN'S DONUTS
BAKERY $

Map p304 (☑773-360-7386; www.stansdonuts chicago.com; 1560 N Damen Ave; donuts $2-3.50; ⊙6:30am-9pm Sun-Wed, to 10pm Thu, to 10:30pm Fri & Sat; ⓂBlue Line to Damen) In a field rich with contenders, Stan's may have Chicago's best doughnuts. Staff are always super nice, the retro vibe rocks, and the Biscoff pockets (that's cookie butter inside a frosted square doughnut) and lemon pistachio old-fashioned doughnuts are glorious. There are around 30 flavors, including a couple of gluten-free options. Other Stan's branches send out their siren song in the South Loop, Near North and Lake View.

BIG STAR TAQUERIA
MEXICAN $

Map p304 (☑773-235-4039; www.bigstarchi cago.com; 1531 N Damen Ave; tacos $3-4; ⊙11:30am-1:30am Sun-Thu, to 2:30am Fri & Sat; ⓂBlue Line to Damen) Once a filling station, now a taco-serving honky-tonk bar helmed by a big-name Chicago chef (Paul Kahan). So goes gentrification in Wicker Park. The place gets packed, but damn, those tacos are worth the wait – pork belly in tomato-*guajillo* chili sauce and mole-spiced carrots drizzled with date-infused yogurt accompany the specialty whiskey list.

If the table-studded patio is too crowded, order from the walk-up window.

MARGIE'S
DESSERTS $

Map p304 (☑773-384-1035; www.margiesfine candies.com; 1960 N Western Ave; sundaes from $6; ⊙9am-midnight; ⸱; ⓂBlue Line to Western) Margie's has held court at Bucktown's edge for more than 90 years, dipping ice-cream sundaes for everyone from Al Capone to the Beatles (check the wall photos). Sure, you can admire the marble soda fountain and the booths with mini-jukeboxes. But the star is the hot fudge, unbelievably thick, rich and bountiful, served in its own silver pot.

Burgers and sandwiches are just clumsy foreplay to the 50 massive sundaes on offer. Margie's makes its own chocolates, too, encasing a huge variety of nuts, fruits and creams.

HANDLEBAR
INTERNATIONAL $

Map p304 (☑773-384-9546; www.handlebar chicago.com; 2311 W North Ave; mains $11-15; ⊙10am-midnight Mon-Fri, 9am-midnight Sat

WICKER PARK, BUCKTOWN & UKRAINIAN VILLAGE EATING

CHURCHES OF UKRAINIAN VILLAGE

Take a minute to wander by these beauties, the majestic domes of which pop out over the neighborhood's treetops:

St Nicholas Ukrainian Catholic Cathedral (Map p304; ☑773-276-4537; www.stnicho laschicago.org; 2238 W Rice St; ▣66) The less traditional of the main churches. Its 13 domes represent Christ and the Apostles. The intricate mosaics – added to the 1915 building in 1988 – owe their inspiration to the Cathedral of St Sophia in Kiev.

Saints Volodymyr & Olha Church (Map p304; ☑312-829-5209; www.stsvo.org; 739 N Oakley Blvd; ▣66) This church was founded by traditionalists from nearby St Nicholas, who broke away over liturgical differences and built this showy church in 1975. It makes up for its paucity of domes (only five) with a massive mosaic of the conversion of Grand Duke Vladimir of Kiev to Christianity in AD 988.

Holy Trinity Russian Orthodox Cathedral (Map p304; ☑773-486-6064; www. holytrinitycathedral.net; 1121 N Leavitt St; ▣70) This creamy structure looks like it was scooped straight out of the Russian countryside and deposited here. But famed Chicago architect Louis Sullivan actually designed the 1903 stunner and its octagonal dome, front bell tower, and stucco and wood-framed exterior. Czar Nicholas II helped fund the church, which is now a city landmark. Cathedral staff give tours of the gilded interior by appointment on weekdays.

LOCAL KNOWLEDGE

THE SWEETEST TREATS

The neighborhood is rich in sugar. The best places to spike your insulin:

Hoosier Mama Pie Company (p144) Sniff out what's cooling on the racks.

Stan's Donuts (p139) Sink your teeth into a Biscoff pocket.

Mindy's Hot Chocolate Sip the ridiculously rich namesake beverage.

Margie's (p139) Ladle on the thick hot fudge.

Alliance Bakery Pray it has the doughnuts made of croissant dough (aka cronuts).

Black Dog Gelato (p144) Lick a Whiskey Gelato Bar.

& Sun; ☑; ⓜBlue Line to Damen) The cult of the bike messenger runs strong in Chicago, and this clamorous restaurant-bar is a way station for tattooed couriers and locals who come for the strong, microbrew-centric beer list, vegetarian-friendly food (including West African groundnut stew and fried avocado tacos) and festive back beer garden.

VIENNA BEEF FACTORY STORE & CAFE　　　　　　　AMERICAN $

(☏773-435-2277; www.viennabeef.com; 2501 N Damen Ave; mains $3-6; ◷6am-4pm Mon-Fri, 10am-3pm Sat; ▣50) A true Chicago hot dog uses a Vienna Beef weenie, and this factory is where they're made. There's no better place to indulge than right at the source, in the employee cafeteria. Grab a tray, go through the line, then join hair-netted workers at the tables. The shop in front sells well-priced cases of franks and superb meaty T-shirts, posters and condiments.

Alas, the factory will be moving to Bridgeport on the South Side at some point. Try to get here before it goes.

SULTAN'S MARKET　　　　　MIDDLE EASTERN $

Map p304 (☏773-235-3072; www.chicagofalafel. com; 2057 W North Ave; mains $4-9; ◷10am-10pm Mon-Sat, to 9pm Sun; ☑; ⓜBlue Line to Damen) Steps from the Blue Line, this Middle Eastern spot is a neighborhood favorite with meat-free delights such as falafel sandwiches, spinach pies and a sizable sal-

ad bar. Carnivores can come in, too; many swear by the chicken shawarma. Cash only.

BELLY SHACK　　　　　　　　　　FUSION $

Map p304 (www.bellyshack.com; 1912 N Western Ave; mains $9-13; ◷11:30am-9pm Tue-Thu & Sun, to 10pm Fri & Sat; ⓜBlue Line to Western) It may have a wee menu and an impersonal, industrial-metallic ambience, but that hasn't stopped Belly Shack from receiving Michelin Bib Gourmand awards (bestowed upon great food for great value) year after year. The chefs meld their Korean and Puerto Rican heritages in fat-flavored dishes such as the Belly Bowl, with lentils, fried egg and hoisin barbecue pork and a side of tostones (fried plantains).

LETIZIA'S NATURAL BAKERY　　　BAKERY $

Map p304 (☏773-342-1011; www.superyummy. com; 2144 W Division St; sandwiches $6-8, pizzas from $20; ◷6am-7pm Mon-Sat, 7am-7pm Sun; ☎; ⓜBlue Line to Division) Early risers can get their fix of fantastic baked goods here starting at 6am, and everyone else can swing by at a more reasonable hour for Letizia's crunchy, toasty panini, slices of gourmet pizza and cups of mind-expanding coffee. The patio with plush seats wins kudos in summer.

LA PASADITA　　　　　　　　　MEXICAN $

Map p304 (☏773-278-2130; www.pasadita.com; 1140 N Ashland Ave; mains $3-9; ◷10am-1am Sun-Thu, to 3am Fri & Sat; ⓜBlue Line to Division) The national press crowned La Pasadita's burrito as one of America's 10 best. They are absolutely behemoth and delicious. But cheapos prefer the tacos; you can make a meal on two fat ones, plus get a drink and basket of nacho chips for around $6.

It explains why 20-something hipsters, TV repair guys, and Latino families with kids all pile in here. It gets especially busy late at night.

ALLIANCE BAKERY　　　　　　　BAKERY $

Map p304 (☏773-278-0366; www.alliance-bak ery.com; 1736 W Division St; items $2-5; ◷6am-9pm Mon-Sat, 7am-9pm Sun; ☎; ⓜBlue Line to Division) Order your macaroons, red velvet cupcakes and other creamy-frosted goodies in the bakery, then take them to the 'lounge' next door (or out to the sidewalk tables) and make like a local by hanging out, reading or tap-tap-tapping on your laptop using the free wi-fi.

PODHALANKA
POLISH **$**

Map p304 (☏773-486-6655; 1549 W Division St; mains $8-15; ☺9am-8pm Mon-Sat, 10am-7pm Sun; Ⓜ Blue Line to Division) Since you're in the middle of the old 'Polish Broadway' area, why not eat like they did in the old days? This hole-in-the-wall holdover from the era serves up massive portions of potato pancakes, pierogi, dill-flecked borscht and other Polish fare on red vinyl seats as Pope JP2 stares from the wall. Cash only.

MILK & HONEY
CAFE **$**

Map p304 (☏773-395-9434; www.milkand honeycafe.com; 1920 W Division St; mains $7-9; ☺7am-4pm Mon-Fri, 8am-4pm Sat & Sun; Ⓜ Blue Line to Division) A bright, stylish cafe, Milk & Honey has become the hangout du jour for discerning neighborhood socialites. The orange brioche French toast rocks the breakfast menu, while the thick-cut bacon, lettuce and tomato sandwich and crab-cake baguette please the lunch crowd. The fireplace and small list of beer and wine soothe when the weather blows.

LAZO'S TACOS
MEXICAN **$**

Map p304 (☏773-486-3303; www.lazostacos. com; 2009 N Western Ave; tacos $2.50-3.50, mains $8-14; ☺24hr; Ⓜ Blue Line to Western) The quintessential taco stop after a long night of drinking.

★DOVE'S LUNCHEONETTE
TEX-MEX **$$**

Map p304 (☏773-645-4060; www.doveschicago. com; 1545 N Damen Ave; mains $13-19; ☺9am-10pm Sun-Thu, to 11pm Fri & Sat; Ⓜ Blue Line to Damen) Grab a seat at the retro counter for Tex-Mex plates of pork-shoulder posole and shrimp-stuffed sweet-corn tamales. Dessert? It's pie, of course, maybe lemon cream or peach jalapeno, depending on what staff have baked that day. Soul music spins on a record player, tequila flows from the 70 bottles rattling behind the bar, and presto: all is right in the world.

MANA FOOD BAR
VEGETARIAN **$$**

Map p304 (☏773-342-1742; www.manafood bar.com; 1742 W Division St; small plates $7-16; ☺4-10pm Mon-Thu, to 11pm Fri, noon-11pm Sat, 3-9pm Sun; ☝; Ⓜ Blue Line to Division) What's unique here is the focus on creating global dishes without using fake meats. So you won't find soy chorizo or tempeh reubens, but rather multiethnic veggie dishes from the likes of Japan, Korea, Italy and the American southwest. Beer, smoothies and sake cocktails help wash it down. The small, sleek eatery buzzes, so reserve ahead or prepare to wait.

MINDY'S HOT CHOCOLATE
AMERICAN **$$**

Map p304 (☏773-489-1747; www.hotchocolate chicago.com; 1747 N Damen Ave; mains $18-24; ☺5:30-10pm Tue, 11:30am-2pm & 5:30-10pm Wed & Thu, to midnight Fri, 10am-2pm & 5:30pm-midnight Sat, to 10pm Sun; Ⓜ Blue Line to Damen) ✐ 'Come for dessert, stay for dinner' might be the motto at this mod restaurant helmed by renowned pastry chef Mindy Segal. With nine kinds of hot chocolate available (they're like dipping your mug into Willy Wonka's chocolate river), along with cakes, cookies and mini brioche doughnuts, you may forget to order the caramel-roasted chicken, crab spaghetti and other seasonally changing mains on offer.

It's a great date night or girls' night out place.

ENOTECA ROMA
ITALIAN **$$**

Map p304 (☏773-772-7700; www.facebook.com/ enotecaroma; 2146 W Division St; mains $15-19; ☺5-10pm Mon-Thu, to 11pm Fri & Sat, 2:30-9pm Sun; Ⓜ Blue Line to Damen) Candlelit and cozy, family-run Enoteca Roma feels like an old country ristorante. Bruschetta flights and handmade pastas steal the show, best consumed on the starry back patio in summer. During the day, sibling eatery Letizia's Natural Bakery wafts toasty panini, lemon tarts and lattes next door.

PIECE
PIZZA **$$**

Map p304 (☏773-772-4422; www.piecechicago. com; 1927 W North Ave; small pizzas from $12.50; ☺11am-10:30pm Mon-Thu, to 12:30am Fri & Sat, to 10pm Sun; Ⓜ Blue Line to Damen) The thin flour-dusted crust of 'New Haven–style' pizza at this spacious Wicker Park microbrewery offers a welcome reprieve from the city's omnipresent deep-dish version. The best is the white variety – a sauceless pie dressed simply in olive oil, garlic and mozzarella – which makes a clean pairing with brewer Jon Cutler's award-winning beer.

The easygoing, sky-lit ambience changes after dark, when ball games beam down from ubiquitous flat screens, an occasional band plugs in, and the 30-something patrons get a bit more boisterous.

142

CHARLES COOK/GETTY IMAGES ©

1. Myopic Books (p150)
Trawl three floors of used books, and get inspired at a Saturday-night poetry reading.

2. St Nicholas Ukrainian Catholic Cathedral (p139)
Enjoy sweeping views from this majestic, 13-domed cathedral.

3. Stan's Donuts (p139)
With around 30 types of doughnut to sample here, sweet tooths will rejoice.

4. Ukrainian Village (p138)
Wander this atmospheric area and explore its Eastern European immigrant history.

KENDALL COLLEGE DINING ROOM
MODERN AMERICAN $$

Map p304 (☎312-752-2328; www.kendall.edu; 900 N North Branch St; 3-course menu lunch/dinner $18/29; ☺hours vary; ☐8, Ⓜ Blue Line to Grand) The School of Culinary Arts at Kendall College has turned out a host of local cooking luminaries and this classy space with river and skyline views is where they honed their chops. Students prepare and serve inventive contemporary American dishes, with forays into French and international fusion styles, all of which come with white-glove service at fantastic value.

Call ahead for reservations (and note the hours vary depending on the school term schedule). It's located on Goose Island, west of the Gold Coast.

SCHWA
MODERN AMERICAN $$$

Map p304 (☎773-252-1466; www.schwarestaurant.com; 1466 N Ashland Ave; 9-course menu $130; ☺5:30-9:30pm Tue-Sat; Ⓜ Blue Line to Division) The fact that chef Michael Carlson worked at Alinea is apparent in his avant-garde, nine-course menu that redefines American comfort food via such dishes as apple-pie soup. The setup is progressive, too, with chefs also acting as servers. The intimate room is bookended by black wood floors and has a mirrored ceiling. Make reservations well in advance.

TRENCHERMEN
MODERN AMERICAN $$$

Map p304 (☎773-661-1540; www.trenchermen.com; 2039 W North Ave; mains $20-33; ☺5pm-midnight Mon-Thu, to 1am Fri, 10am-1am Sat, to 10:30pm Sun; Ⓜ Blue Line to Damen) Trenchermen defies easy description. Imagine steam-punk decor set in an old Turkish bathhouse. Imagine unconventional flavor mash-ups such as chocolate-cured ham, chai tofu ice cream and pickle tots (the tangy love child of fried pickles and tater tots). It's bizarre, playful, exotic, inspired – you'll think of more adjectives after tipping back one (or two) of the divine cocktails.

MIRAI SUSHI
JAPANESE $$$

Map p304 (☎773-862-8500; www.miraisushi.com; 2020 W Division St; maki $6-12, small plates $8-17; ☺5-10pm Sun-Thu, to 11pm Fri & Sat; Ⓜ Blue Line to Damen) This high-energy restaurant has a higher-energy saki lounge upstairs; both are packed with young locals enjoying some of the freshest sushi in the area. From the trance-hop electronic music to the young, black-clad staff, Mirai is where connoisseurs of sashimi and *maki* (rolled sushi) gather to throw back cocktails between savory morsels of yellowtail and shiitake tempura lightly fried to perfection.

✗ Ukrainian Village

HOOSIER MAMA PIE COMPANY
AMERICAN $

Map p304 (☎312-243-4846; www.hoosiermama-pie.com; 1618 ½ Chicago Ave; slices $5-6.25; ☺8am-7pm Tue-Fri, 9am-5pm Sat, 10am-4pm Sun; Ⓜ Blue Line to Chicago) There's a statistic that states one out of five people has eaten an entire pie solo. Hoosier Mama is your place to do it. Pastry chef Paula Haney hand rolls and crimps her dough, then plumps it with fruit or creamy fillings. Favorites include the banana cream, chocolate chess (aka 'brownie pie') and classic apple. A handful of meat and veg savory pies tempt, too.

On Fridays the shop offers a pie 'flight' (three small slices) for eat-in diners. Seating is limited in the itty-bitty storefront.

FLO
MEXICAN $

Map p304 (☎312-243-0477; www.flochicago.com; 1434 W Chicago Ave; mains $12-16; ☺8:30am-10pm Tue-Thu, to 11pm Fri & Sat, 9am-3pm Sun; Ⓜ Blue Line to Chicago) Think you've had a good breakfast burrito before? Not until you've eaten here. The Southwestern-bent dishes and jovial staff draw hordes of late-rising neighborhood hipsters on the weekend. Tart, potent margaritas and fish tacos take over after dark, but the breakfast foods are the main draw.

BARI FOODS
DELI $

Map p304 (☎312-666-0730; www.bariitaliansubs.com; 1120 W Grand Ave; sandwiches $5-9; ☺8am-6:30pm Mon-Fri, to 6pm Sat, to 2pm Sun; Ⓜ Blue Line to Grand) This Italian grocery store and butcher cuts a mean salami. If you're planning a picnic, drop by and pick up a 9in sub sandwich or two (the Italian meatball is particularly scrumptious) and a nice bottle of earthy red wine.

BLACK DOG GELATO
GELATERIA $

Map p304 (www.blackdogchicago.com; 859 N Damen Ave; gelato from $3.50; ☺noon-11pm Tue-Sun mid-Apr–Oct; Ⓜ Blue Line to Division) All hail the oddball masterpieces that come forth from this little shop. Will it be the goat's cheese cashew caramel flavor or the sesame fig chocolate chip? What about the bacon-studded, booze-tinged, chocolate Whiskey Gelato Bar? Black Dog has an outpost that's open year-round in the French Market. You can also find the gelato at big-name restaurants around town.

BITE CAFE
INTERNATIONAL $

Map p304 (☏773-395-2483; www.bitecafechicago.com; 1039 N Western Ave; mains $10-16; ⏲9am-midnight Mon-Thu, to 1am Fri, 8am-1am Sat, to midnight Sun; ✐; 🚌49) Join the shaggy rockers reading graphic novels and eating challah-bread French toast for breakfast, grilled Gruyere-cheese sandwiches for lunch or gnocchi and braised oxtail for dinner. The small room is industrial-chic, with sky-blue chairs around plain wood tables, and funky artwork peppering exposed-brick walls.

Up until 8:30pm, you can bring booze over from the Empty Bottle (p148) bar/music venue next door to accompany meals (or BYOB with no corkage fee).

TWISTED SPOKE
AMERICAN $

Map p304 (☏312-666-1500; 501 N Ogden Ave; mains $9-14; ⏲11am-2am Mon-Fri, 9am-2am Sat & Sun; Ⓜ Blue Line to Chicago) Don't let the motorcycle theme, burly burgers and steel finishing intimidate you: behind the macho facade at this popular brunch spot are artful dishes better calibrated for nesting yuppies than hardscrabble Hell's Angels. If the smoky-sweet BBQ Kobe Brisket isn't tough enough for you, order the 'Road Rash' Bloody Mary extra spicy, and chomp your way through its array of harpooned veggies.

TECALITLAN
MEXICAN $

Map p304 (☏773-384-4285; 1814 W Chicago Ave; mains $7-16; ⏲10am-midnight Sun-Thu, to 3am Fri & Sat; 🚌66, Ⓜ Blue Line to Chicago) Weighing in at more than a pound, the carne asada (steak) burrito with cheese is not just one of the city's best food values, it's one of the city's best foods. Add the optional avocado and you'll have a full day's worth of food groups wrapped in a huge flour tortilla.

The creamy *horchata* (a rice-based beverage made with water, sugar, cinnamon, vanilla and lime) refreshes as you plow through the main course.

MR BROWN'S LOUNGE
JAMAICAN $$

Map p304 (☏773-278-4445; www.mrbrownslounge.com; 2301 W Chicago Ave; mains $11-20; ⏲4pm-2am Tue-Thu, noon-3am Fri & Sat, to 2am Sun; 🚌66) Named after a Jamaican folklore tale that Bob Marley adapted into a song, this bar-restaurant cooks up such Jamaican staples as jerk chicken and stewed oxtail along with American riffs such as 'island-style' macaroni and cheese. Wash it down with a spicy rum punch. DJs spin reggae and dance-hall tunes on weekends. Ya, mon.

★RUXBIN
MODERN AMERICAN $$$

Map p304 (☏312-624-8509; www.ruxbinchicago.com; 851 N Ashland Ave; 5-dish menu $65; ⏲6-10pm Tue-Fri, 5:30-10pm Sat, to 9pm Sun; Ⓜ Blue Line to Division) ✐ The passion of the Kim family, who run Ruxbin, is evident in everything from the decor made of found items, such as antique theater seats and church pews, to the artfully prepared flavors on the small, ever-changing, hyper-local menu. Pick five dishes from the week's list; they're shared by the table. Ruxbin is a wee place of just 32 seats, and BYOB.

BOEUFHAUS
STEAK $$$

Map p304 (☏773-661-2116; www.boeufhaus.com; 1012 N Western Ave; mains $30-60; ⏲11am-3:30pm & 5:30-11pm Tue-Sat, 5:30-10pm Sun; 🚌49) Chicago has heaps of steakhouses, but none like European-style Boeufhaus. Sit in a snug banquette or at the copper-topped bar and carve into dry-aged steaks and appetizers such as the beloved short-rib beignets or *cavatelli* (small pasta shells) with *merguez* sausage. It seats less than 40, so reserve well ahead. Need more meat? Take some to go from the rustic butcher and deli counter.

Boeufhaus is located in Ukrainian Village near the Empty Bottle music club, if you want to make a night of it.

GREEN ZEBRA
VEGETARIAN $$$

Map p304 (☏312-243-7100; www.greenzebrachicago.com; 1460 W Chicago Ave; small plates $8-13; ⏲5:30-9:30pm Tue-Thu, 5-10pm Fri & Sat, 5-9pm Sun; ✐; Ⓜ Blue Line to Chicago) ✐ Chicago doesn't offer many opportunities for chic vegetarian fare, which may explain why Beard-award-winning chef Shawn McClain's slick restaurant has been so successful for the past decade-plus. The menu focuses on creative seasonal odes to meatless fare. Rich broths, unconventional curries and dumplings all make appearances. It's a small-plate setup, so you'll have to order three or four to make a meal.

⚇ DRINKING & ⚐ NIGHTLIFE

⚑ Wicker Park & Bucktown

DANNY'S   BAR
Map p304 (☎773-489-6457; 1951 W Dickens Ave; ⊙7pm-2am; Ⓜ Blue Line to Damen) Danny's comfortably dim and dog-eared ambience is perfect for conversations over a pint early on, then DJs arrive to stoke the dance party as the evening progresses. The groovy spot is more like a house than a bar, filled with 20- and 30-somethings getting their moves on. Cash only.

MAP ROOM   BAR
Map p304 (☎773-252-7636; www.maproom. com; 1949 N Hoyne Ave; ⊙6:30am-2am Mon-Fri, 7:30am-3am Sat, 11am-2am Sun; ☎; Ⓜ Blue Line to Western) At this map- and globe-filled 'travelers' tavern,' artsy types sip coffee by day and suds from the 200-strong beer list by night. Board games and old issues of *National Geographic* are within reach for entertainment.

VIOLET HOUR   COCKTAIL BAR
Map p304 (☎773-252-1500; www.theviolethour. com; 1520 N Damen Ave; ⊙6pm-2am Sun-Fri, to 3am Sat; Ⓜ Blue Line to Damen) This nouveau speakeasy isn't marked, so look for the mural-slathered, wood-panel building and the door topped by a yellow lightbulb. Inside, high-backed booths, chandeliers and long velvet drapes provide the backdrop to elaborately engineered cocktails that the Beard Awards deemed best in the US. The Armageddon (lemon-and-cinnamon-tinged whiskey) shows why. As highbrow as it sounds, Violet Hour is welcoming and accessible.

GOLD STAR BAR   BAR
Map p304 (☎773-227-8700; 1755 W Division St; ⊙4pm-2am Sun-Fri, to 3am Sat; Ⓜ Blue Line to Division) A vestige from the days when Division St was 'Polish Broadway,' the Gold Star remains a divey winner, drawing a posse of bike messengers – and people who dress like them – for cheapie libations and a great metal-and-punk jukebox.

QUENCHERS SALOON   BAR
Map p308 (☎773-276-9730; www.quenchers. com; 2401 N Western Ave; ⊙noon-2am Sun-Fri, to 3am Sat; ☎; 🚌74) At the Logan Square/ Bucktown border, Quenchers peddles a global selection of nearly 300 beers from more than 40 nations. Locals, artisans, laborers and visiting brewmasters enjoy the bar's hospitality (and tater-tot pizza or beef chili). There's entertainment nightly, with rock bands, literary readings and improv comedy all on the agenda.

RAINBO CLUB   BAR
Map p304 (☎773-489-5999; 1150 N Damen Ave; ⊙4pm-2am Sun-Fri, to 3am Sat; Ⓜ Blue Line to Damen) The center for Chicago's indie elite during the week, the boxy, dark-wood Rainbo Club has an impressive semicircular bar and one of the city's best photo booths. The service is slow and the place goes a little suburban on weekends, but otherwise it's a fun place to hang out with artsy locals. Cash only.

WORMHOLE COFFEE   COFFEE
Map p304 (☎773-661-2468; www.thewormhole. us; 1462 N Milwaukee Ave; ⊙7am-11pm; ☎; Ⓜ Blue Line to Damen) The Wormhole is pretentious in an endearing way. Take the seasonal drinks such as autumn's Everything Nice (Indian sarsaparilla, wintergreen and milk) and winter's Peanut Butter Koopa Troopa (peanut mousse, chocolate and coffee): pompous, but also cutely delicious. Students and hipsters caffeinate while staring at their laptops amid movie kitsch (yes, that is a Delorean car in front).

ED & JEAN'S   BAR
Map p304 (☎773-276-9383; www.edandjeans tavern.com; 2032 W Armitage Ave; ⊙5pm-2am Sun-Fri, to 3am Sat; ☎; Ⓜ Blue Line to Damen) It's one of the city's classic dive bars, where the wood paneling, kitschy knickknacks and 'shot-ana-beer' orders impart authentic Chicago character bathed in a neon glow. Can't decide what shot to order? Spin the wheel behind the bar and let fate decide. The pool table is free to play. Cash only for booze.

FILTER   CAFE
Map p304 (☎773-904-7819; 1373 N Milwaukee Ave; ⊙7am-10pm Mon-Thu, to 8pm Fri & Sat, 8am-9pm Sun; ☎; Ⓜ Blue Line to Damen) Linger over good coffee at thrift-store tables and couches along with all the laptop-toting writers tapping out their screenplays. The in-house roasting system uses oil from the coffee beans to run the machine. Cash only.

INNERTOWN PUB
BAR

Map p304 (☏773-235-9795; 1935 W Thomas St; ☺3pm-2am Sun-Fri, to 3am Sat; Ⓜ Blue Line to Division) A cigar-smoking moose and a bronze bust of Elvis overlook the crowd of artsy regulars playing pool and drinking cheap at this lovably divey watering hole. Order a Christmas Morning, a delightful shot of hot espresso and chilled Rumple Minze liqueur.

DEBONAIR SOCIAL CLUB
CLUB

Map p304 (☏773-227-7990; www.debonair socialclub.com; 1575 N Milwaukee Ave; ☺9pm-2am Wed, 8pm-2am Thu & Fri, to 3am Sat; Ⓜ Blue Line to Damen) It's mostly a younger, hipster crowd dancing their asses off at Debonair to oldies mash-ups, hard rock and new electro. The main action takes place on the upstairs floor. The downstairs floor is less hot and packed, though still grooving with rock or whatnot. Reggae and burlesque shows entertain on other nights.

🍷 Ukrainian Village

★ MATCHBOX
BAR

Map p304 (☏312-666-9292; 770 N Milwaukee Ave; ☺4pm-2am Mon-Fri, 3pm-2am Sat & Sun; Ⓜ Blue Line to Chicago) Lawyers, artists and bums all squeeze in for retro cocktails. It's as small as – you got it – a matchbox, with about 10 bar stools; everyone else stands against the back wall. Barkeeps make the drinks from scratch. Favorites include the pisco sour and the ginger gimlet, ladled from an amber vat of homemade ginger-infused vodka.

FORBIDDEN ROOT
MICROBREWERY

Map p304 (☏312-929-2202; www.forbidden root.com; 1746 W Chicago Ave; ☺4pm-midnight Mon-Sat; 🚌66, Ⓜ Blue Line to Chicago) Forbidden Root is a 'botanical brewery' that uses roots, bark, spices and flowers to make eclectic beers such as Wildflower Pale Ale (with marigold and elder) and Sublime Ginger (a ginger lime wheat beer). The weird mash-ups are delicious. The cool space is done up with farm-industrial decor (think tractor parts as lamps), and punk music plays softly in the background.

HAPPY VILLAGE
BAR

Map p304 (☏773-486-1512; www.happyvil lagebar.com; 1059 N Wolcott Ave; ☺4pm-2am Mon-Fri, noon-2am Sat & Sun; Ⓜ Blue Line to Division) Happy Village may well be the jolliest bar in the neighborhood. Unapologetically divey, with cheap, non-craft beer, it earns smiles for its fierce table-tennis matches, starry vine-covered patio and strolling tamale vendor who seems to appear just when you need him most. Cash only.

LUSH WINE AND SPIRITS
WINE BAR

Map p304 (☏312-666-6900; www.lushwineand spirits.com; 1412 W Chicago Ave; ☺noon-10pm Sun-Thu, to 11pm Fri & Sat; Ⓜ Blue Line to Chicago) Lush is a local mini-chain that is part wine shop and part wine bar. Buy a bottle on the one side, then take it over to the other and sit at the butcher-block tables in a decibel-friendly, Euro-style ambience. It's all very economical, especially during the free tastings on Sundays from 2pm to 5pm.

RICHARD'S BAR
BAR

Map p304 (☏312-733-2251; 491 N Milwaukee Ave; ☺7am-2am Mon-Fri, 9am-3am Sat, noon-2am Sun; Ⓜ Blue Line to Grand) Richard's is a timeless dive complete with lingering cigarette-smoke aroma. The bar – with its tall, humming refrigerated coolers for to-go orders and a strange mix of Rat Pack and *Saturday Night Fever* on the jukebox – feels like something out of a Jim Jarmusch movie. The only food option is hard-boiled eggs served in a shot glass. Cash only.

BEAUTY BAR
CLUB

Map p304 (☏312-226-8828; www.thebeautybar. com; 1444 W Chicago Ave; ☺7pm-2am Sun-Fri, to 3am Sat; Ⓜ Blue Line to Chicago) The interior is an imported and restored late-1960s beauty salon from New Jersey. 'Martinis and manicures' are the shtick, and you can get the latter anytime for $10 (Sunday through Thursday) or $15 (Friday and Saturday). Genre-spanning DJs spin nightly. If the Beauty Bar sounds familiar, it's because it's part of a chain with outposts in several US cities.

OLA'S LIQUOR
BAR

Map p304 (☏773-384-7259; 947 N Damen Ave; ☺7am-2am Mon-Sat, 11am-2am Sun; 🚌50) This classic 'slashie' – the term for a bar/liquor-store combo, where the bar is stashed in the back room – has hours catering to third-shift locals and the most indomitable night owls. Order the advertised *zimne piwo* (Polish for 'cold beer') and blast some tunes on the juke in the same language.

☆ ENTERTAINMENT

★ HIDEOUT
LIVE MUSIC

Map p304 (☎773-227-4433; www.hideoutchi cago.com; 1354 W Wabansia Ave; ⏰7pm-2am Tue, 4pm-2am Wed-Fri, 7pm-3am Sat, hours vary Sun & Mon; 🚌72) Hidden behind a factory at the edge of Bucktown, this two-room lodge of indie rock and alt-country is well worth seeking out. The owners have nursed an outsider, underground vibe, and the place feels like your grandma's rumpus room. Music and other events (bingo, literary readings etc) take place nightly. Tickets cost between $5 and $15.

EMPTY BOTTLE
LIVE MUSIC

Map p304 (☎773-276-3600; www.emptybottle. com; 1035 N Western Ave; ⏰5pm-2am Mon-Thu, 3pm-2am Fri, 11am-2am Sat & Sun; 🚌49) Chicago's music insiders fawn over the Empty Bottle, the city's scruffy, go-to club for edgy indie rock, jazz and other beats. Monday's show is often a freebie by a couple of up-and-coming bands. Cheap beer, a photo booth and good graffiti-reading in the bathrooms add to the dive-bar fun.

HOUSE THEATRE
THEATER

Map p304 (☎773-769-3832; www.thehousethea tre.com; 1543 W Division St; Ⓜ️Blue Line to Division) By throwing out the rule book, this exhilarating company presents a mix of quirky, funny, touching shows written by newbie playwrights. Magic, music and good old-fashioned storytelling usually tie in

---

LOCAL KNOWLEDGE

SOUP & BREAD DINNERS

The Hideout (p148) hosts a groovy dinner series at 5:30pm Wednesdays. From January to early April, Soup and Bread (www.soupandbread.net) offers a free meal of – yes – homemade soup and bread. Local foodies, musicians and artists take turns making the wares. Donations are collected and go to local food banks.

From late June until early September, the action morphs into a cookout and Veggie Bingo. You pay a few bucks to play, and winners receive organic produce as prizes. Proceeds support community gardens.

The jolly shindigs attract a big crowd, so don't be late.

---

somehow. House typically performs at the Chopin Theatre, but sometimes it turns up in offbeat locations (such as a hotel room), as well.

CHOPIN THEATRE
THEATER

Map p304 (☎773-278-1500; www.chopintheatre. com; 1543 W Division St; Ⓜ️Blue Line to Division) Looking for a tasty slice of Chicago fringe theater? Maybe something oddball, thought provoking or just plain silly? Chopin is the place. The city's best itinerant companies, such as House Theatre and Theater Oo-bleck, often turn up here.

PHYLLIS' MUSICAL INN
LIVE MUSIC

Map p304 (☎773-486-9862; 1800 W Division St; ⏰4pm-2am Mon-Fri, 3pm-2am Sat, 2pm-2am Sun; Ⓜ️Blue Line to Division) One of the all-time great dives, this former Polish polka bar features scrappy up-and-coming bands nightly. It's hit or miss for quality, but you've got to applaud them for taking a chance. If you don't like the sound you can always slip outside to the bar's basketball court for relief. Cheap brewskis, to boot.

SUBTERRANEAN
LIVE MUSIC

Map p304 (☎773-278-6600; www.subt.net; 2011 W North Ave; ⏰7pm-2am Sun-Thu, 6pm-3am Fri & Sat; Ⓜ️Blue Line to Damen) A trendy crowd comes to Subterranean, which looks slick inside and out. The main room upstairs draws good indie rock, funk and hip-hop bands. The downstairs lounge hosts smaller shows, DJ dance parties and popular open-mic events.

TRAP DOOR THEATRE
THEATER

Map p304 (☎773-384-0494; www.trapdoorthea tre.com; 1655 W Cortland St; 🚌9) This ragtag operation once had to hold a fundraiser to purchase a bathroom for its tiny theater (located in a converted garage), but it is now drawing bigger audiences for its consistently great productions of European avant-garde plays and originals.

CHICAGO DRAMATISTS THEATRE
THEATER

Map p304 (☎312-633-0630; www.chicagodram atists.org; 1105 W Chicago Ave; Ⓜ️Blue Line to Chicago) For a visit to the heart of Chicago's dramatic scene, step into this small, functional theater space, a testing ground for Chicago's new playwrights and plays. The embracing spot has sent more than a few works on to Broadway (such as Keith Huff's *A Steady Rain*).

DAVENPORT'S
PIANO BAR & CABARET   LIVE MUSIC

Map p304 (☑773-278-1830; www.davenports
pianobar.com; 1383 N Milwaukee Ave; ☺7pm-
midnight Mon, Wed & Thu, to 2am Fri & Sat, to
11pm Sun; ⓜBlue Line to Damen) Old standards
get new interpretations and new songs are
heard for the first time at swanky Daven-
port's. The front room is a fun, inclusive
(read: sing-along) place, while the back
is reserved for more fancy-pants cabaret
events (where singing along will get you
thrown out). There's a two-drink minimum.

SHOPPING

⭐ **RECKLESS RECORDS**   MUSIC

Map p304 (☑773-235-3727; www.reckless.com;
1379 N Milwaukee Ave; ☺10am-10pm Mon-Sat, to
8pm Sun; ⓜBlue Line to Damen) Chicago's best
indie-rock record and CD emporium allows
you to listen to everything before you buy.
It's certainly the place to get your finger on
the pulse of the local, au courant underground scene. There's plenty of elbow room
in the big, sunny space, which makes for
happy hunting through the new and used
bins. Reasonable prices, too.

QUIMBY'S   BOOKS

Map p304 (www.quimbys.com; 1854 W North
Ave; ☺noon-9pm Mon-Thu, to 10pm Fri & Sat, to
7pm Sun; ⓜBlue Line to Damen) The epicenter
of Chicago's comic and zine worlds, Quimby's is one of the linchpins of underground
culture in the city. Here you can find everything from crayon-powered punk-rock
manifestos to slickly produced graphic novels. It's a groovy place for cheeky literary
souvenirs and bizarro readings.

DUSTY GROOVE   MUSIC

Map p304 (☑773-342-5800; www.dustygroove.
com; 1120 N Ashland Ave; ☺10am-8pm; ⓜBlue
Line to Division) Old-school soul, Brazilian
beats, Hungarian disco, bass-stabbing hip-
hop – if it's funky, Dusty Groove (which
also has its own record label) stocks it. Flip
through stacks of vinyl, or get lost amid the
tidy shop's CDs. Be sure to check out the
dollar bin.

UNA MAE'S   CLOTHING

Map p304 (☑773-276-7002; www.unamaeschica
go.com; 1528 N Milwaukee Ave; ☺noon-8pm Mon-
Fri, 11am-8pm Sat, noon-7pm Sun; ⓜBlue Line to

LOCAL KNOWLEDGE

VINTAGE & THRIFT SHOPS

The stretch of Milwaukee Ave heading southeast from North Ave holds
the mother lode of vintage and thrift
shops, with some funky shoe stores
thrown in for good measure. Within a
half-mile you'll pass around eight hot
spots, including US #1 (p151), Una
Mae's (p149), Kokorokoko and Buffalo
Exchange (p150), where, as long as
you have some suitably fashionable
threads of your own to trade, you don't
even need cash.

Damen) It's a fine spot to browse for a pillbox
hat or velvet-and-lace dress. Along with its
vintage wares, Una Mae's has a collection of
new, cool-cat designer duds and accessories
for both men and women.

WICKER PARK SECRET
AGENT SUPPLY CO   GIFTS & SOUVENIRS

Map p304 (☑773-772-8108; www.826chi.org;
1276 N Milwaukee Ave; ☺noon-5pm Mon & Sun,
11am-6pm Tue-Sat; ⊞; ⓜBlue Line to Division)
This place sells 'espionagical wares' (aka
crazy spy gear). Mustache disguise kits, un-
derwater voice amplifiers, banana-shaped
cases to hide your cell phone in – it's genius. Loads of creative books and games
for children also fill shelves. Better yet:
profits from sales go toward supporting
the after-school writing and tutoring programs that take place on-site at nonprofit
group 826CHI.

PERMANENT RECORDS   MUSIC

Map p304 (☑773-278-1744; www.permanent
recordschicago.com; 1914 W Chicago Ave;
☺noon-8pm; ⓜBlue Line to Chicago) Flip
through new and used vinyl, CDs and cas-
settes in Permanent's long, narrow space.
Maybe you'll find a Rectal Hygienics LP or
something by a Krautrock band or Simon
and Garfunkel. It's not the cheapest place
in town, but prices are generally fair.

Permanent also has its own record label
that puts out music by old punk bands and
current garage pop bands.

KOKOROKOKO   VINTAGE

Map p304 (☑773-252-6996; www.kokorokoko
vintage.com; 1323 N Milwaukee Ave; ☺noon-7pm
Mon-Sat, to 6pm Sun; ⓜBlue Line to Division)
The smell of incense greets you as you walk

in to peruse the array of Bionic Woman lunchboxes, Backstreet Boys trading cards, yo-yos, and racks of vintage men's and women's clothing (average price per shirt or jacket around $20). The shop is a neighborhood favorite.

BUFFALO EXCHANGE CLOTHING

Map p304 (☎773-227-9558; www.buffaloexchange.com; 1478 N Milwaukee Ave; ⊙11am-8pm; MBlue Line to Damen) You can 'Buy, Sell, Trade,' as the sign flashes in the front window of this secondhand clothing shop for men and women. Part of a national chain, the Wicker Park outpost has a good selection of designer wares mixed in with the everyday shirts, jackets and jeans on the packed racks.

MYOPIC BOOKS BOOKS

Map p304 (☎773-862-4882; www.myopicbookstore.com; 1564 N Milwaukee Ave; ⊙9am-11pm; MBlue Line to Damen) Myopic is one of the city's oldest and largest used bookstores, with stacks upon stacks of tomes. It rambles through three floors and hosts poetry readings (on occasional Saturday evenings) and experimental music (most Monday evenings). Staff is hard-core about the rules here – no picture taking, no phones etc – so mind your manners.

AKIRA CLOTHING

Map p304 (☎773-227-9401; www.shopakira.com; 1814 W North Ave; ⊙11am-9pm Mon-Thu, 10am-9pm Fri & Sat, 11am-7pm Sun; MBlue Line to Damen) Several design students work at this local fashion house, which stocks up-and-coming and newly popular lines of women's clothing. The stylish jeans, dresses, skirts and accessories are usually quite affordable. A companion Akira footwear shop is a block west at 1910 W North Ave.

SHUGA RECORDS MUSIC

Map p304 (☎773-278-4085; www.shugarecords.com; 1272 N Milwaukee Ave; ⊙10am-10pm Mon-Sat, to 8pm Sun; MBlue Line to Division) The smallish shop carries lots of soul and funk vinyl, plus a bit of everything else, from stoner doom to Native American ballads. Shuga focuses on harder-to-find music. Prices typically hover around $20 per record.

T-SHIRT DELI CLOTHING

Map p304 (☎773-276-6266; www.tshirtdeli.com; 1739 N Damen Ave; ⊙11am-7pm Mon-Fri, to 6pm Sat, to 5pm Sun; MBlue Line to Damen) They take the 'deli' part seriously: after they cook (ie iron a retro design on) your T-shirt, they wrap it in butcher paper and serve it to you with potato chips. Choose from heaps of shirt styles and decals, of which Mao, Sean Connery, Patty Hearst and a red-white-and-blue bong are but the beginning.

HANDMADE MARKET ARTS & CRAFTS

Map p304 (☎773-276-3600; www.handmadechicago.com; 1035 N Western Ave; ⊙noon-4pm 2nd Sat of the month Oct-Apr; ☐49) Held the second Saturday of the month at the Empty Bottle (p148), this event showcases Chicago crafters who make funky glass pendants, knitted items, handbags, scarves, journals and greeting cards. The bar serves drinks throughout the event, for those who enjoy sipping while shopping.

PENELOPE'S CLOTHING

Map p304 (☎773-395-2351; www.shoppenelopes.com; 1913 W Division St; ⊙11am-7pm Mon-Sat, noon-6pm Sun; MBlue Line to Division) Named after the owners' ridiculously cute pug, Penelope's is a warm boutique for 20- and 30-somethings. It offers both men's and women's fashions (they're new, but look thrift-store bought) along with housewares, jewelry and nifty gifty things.

FLIGHT 001 ACCESSORIES

Map p304 (☎773-384-1001; www.flight001.com; 1616 N Damen Ave; ⊙11am-6pm Sun-Fri, to 7pm Sat; MBlue Line to Damen) The brightly colored, hard-shelled luggage and the stock of super-cool travel gadgets will get a rise out of any would-be jet-setter. The sleek store resembles the interior of an airplane. It's located on the ground floor of the IHSP Chicago hostel.

UPRISE SKATEBOARDS SPORTS

Map p304 (☎773-342-7763; www.upriseskateboards.com; 1820 N Milwaukee Ave; ⊙noon-7pm Mon-Sat, to 5pm Sun; MBlue Line to Western) Looking for a Street Sweeper or a pair of Lakais? Uprise is the city's top spot for skateboarders to pick up gear, boards and tips on the local scene. Drop in for a rad T-shirt and to find out where the action is. No attitude here: they're friendly and patient with newbies.

JOHN FLUEVOG SHOES SHOES

Map p304 (☎773-772-1983; www.fluevog.com; 1539-1541 N Milwaukee Ave; ⊙11am-7pm Mon-Fri, to 8pm Sat, noon-6pm Sun; MBlue Line to Damen)

Bold and colorful shoes by the eccentric designer are the order of the day at this footwear haven. They come as tough-girl chunky or sex-kitten pointy as you like, and there are equally hip selections for men. Shoes are pricey, but known for their longevity.

BEADNIKS ARTS & CRAFTS

Map p304 (☑773-276-2323; www.beadnikschicago.com; 1937 W Division St; ☺11am-9pm Mon-Sat, to 7pm Sun; Ⓜ Blue Line to Division) Incense envelops you at the door, and you know right away you're in for a hippie treat. Mounds of worldly baubles rise up from the tables. African trade beads and Thai silver-dipped beads? Got 'em. Bright-hued stone beads, ceramic beads, glass beads? All present. For $3 the kindly staff will help you string your choices into a necklace.

Or take a workshop (two to three hours, $10 to $60) and learn to wield the pliers yourself; they take place several evenings throughout the week. The website has the schedule.

US #1 VINTAGE

Map p304 (☑773-489-9428; 1460 N Milwaukee Ave; ☺noon-7pm; Ⓜ Blue Line to Damen) Rack after rack of '70s bowling and western-wear shirts, leather motorcycle jackets, cowboy boots and secondhand jeans (including big-name brands) cram this vintage shop. It's like someone raided a rock star's closet and put the contents up for sale. Alas, the goods don't come cheap, and the owner can be cantankerous with those who aren't serious about buying.

MILDBLEND SUPPLY CO CLOTHING

Map p304 (☑773-772-9711; www.mildblend.com; 1342 N Milwaukee Ave; ☺11am-8pm Mon-Sat, noon-6pm Sun; Ⓜ Blue Line to Division) Stacks and racks of premium denim fill this shop, which feels a bit like a country store. Staff will hem any jeans you buy at the sewing machines on-site.

RED BALLOON CO CHILDREN

Map p304 (☑773-489-9800; www.theredballoon.com; 1940 N Damen Ave; ☺10am-6pm Mon-Sat, 11am-5pm Sun; Ⓜ Blue Line to Damen) When hipsters get good jobs and start having kids, this is where they outfit the li'l pups. Adorable clothes, classic children's books and '50s-style wooden block toys prevail in the cozy space.

PAPER DOLL GIFTS & SOUVENIRS

Map p304 (☑773-227-6950; www.paperdoll chicago.com; 2027 W Division St; ☺11am-7pm Tue-Fri, to 6pm Sat, to 5pm Sun; Ⓜ Blue Line to Damen) Stationery rules the house at Paper Doll, and many a Wicker Park thriftster has ordered her wedding cards or baby announcements from the mod assortment on hand. Kitschy gifts round out the inventory.

WICKER PARK, BUCKTOWN & UKRAINIAN VILLAGE SHOPPING

Logan Square & Humboldt Park

Neighborhood Top Five

1 **Parachute** (p160) Scoring a coveted seat at this Michelin-starred eatery and forking into the Korean-meets-American fare that has made this one of America's best restaurants.

2 **Logan Hardware** (p162) Flicking through sweet vinyl, then playing Donkey Kong, Ms Pac-Man and other vintage arcade games in the back room.

3 **Humboldt Park** (p154) Strolling around the lagoon, lounging on the beach, checking out the free arts center and munching Puerto Rican snacks in the sprawling green space.

4 **Rosa's Lounge** (p162) Hearing a fret-bending set by local blues musicians in unvarnished environs.

5 **Busy Beaver Button Museum** (p154) Perusing thousands of oddball badges at this historical museum.

For more detail of this area see Map p308 ➡

Explore Logan Square & Humboldt Park

Sights are few and far between in Logan Square and Humboldt Park. No matter. You're here to eat, drink and see a show. Many of Chicago's best restaurants are tucked in along the neighborhood's tree-shaded boulevards. These aren't high-falutin' places, but rather boisterous taverns and small storefronts dishing out inventive fare (Michelin-starred, in some cases) at reasonable prices. Add in retro dive bars, sudsy brewpubs and thrifty gin lounges for sipping, plus artsy music clubs for entertainment, and you've got a stellar Chicago night out.

Logan Square is the hipster haven, home to artists and stylish types who've moved in among the Latino families. Gentrification continues its relentless push here, as all the scaffolding and emerging condo developments attest. But wild murals still splash across the area and give it an outsider's edge. Longman & Eagle, Fat Rice, Lula Cafe and several other must-eats serve during the day, but nighttime is when the action peaks.

Humboldt Park, to the south, is rougher around the edges. It's still heavily Puerto Rican, as the giant flag sculptures and island-food cafes along Division St attest. The eponymous park is the area's focal point. Morning or afternoon is the best time to visit.

Great restaurants and clubs have also popped up in Avondale. It sits next door to Logan Square, and it was only a matter of time before cool-cat spots spilled over. Kuma's and Late Bar have been here for a while, but newcomers such as Parachute and Honey Butter Fried Chicken are bringing more attention to the area.

Local Life

➜ **Free stuff** Just north of Lula Cafe (p160), there are a couple of newspaper boxes that front W Logan Blvd. Inside are free books and DVDs. Go ahead: take one or leave one.

➜ **Heavy drinking** The neighborhood hot spot is the 2300 block of N Milwaukee Ave. Joining Revolution Brewing (p161) and Cole's (p161) are a coffee roaster, a distillery, a German beer hall and several bars and cafes.

➜ **Patio party** When the weather is warm, everyone hangs out on the patio at Parson's Chicken and Fish (p156). When the weather is cold, they ice-skate on the makeshift rink.

Getting There & Away

➜ **El** Blue Line to Logan Square or California for Logan Square; Blue Line to Belmont for Avondale.

➜ **Bus** For Humboldt Park destinations, you'll need a bus. Number 70 travels along Division St, number 72 along North Ave and number 73 along Armitage Ave.

➜ **Car** Street parking isn't bad, although it can get tight around Logan Square near Lula Cafe.

Lonely Planet's Top Tip

Pack your patience for Logan Square's rich restaurant scene. Many places do not take reservations, so you'll have to wait an hour or more to fork into that goji berry pheasant sausage. Try to arrive right at opening time. Otherwise, hit the bar. At Kuma's Corner (p155) and Longman & Eagle (p160), you can order meals at the bar if you snag a seat.

 Best Places to Eat

➜ Parachute (p160)

➜ Longman & Eagle (p160)

➜ Fat Rice (p160)

➜ Kuma's Corner (p155)

➜ Lula Cafe (p160)

➜ Honey Butter Fried Chicken (p155)

For reviews, see p155 ➡

 Best Places to Drink

➜ Revolution Brewing (p161)

➜ Lost Lake (p161)

➜ Cole's (p161)

➜ Scofflaw (p161)

For reviews, see p161 ➡

 Best Entertainment

➜ Whistler (p162)

➜ Rosa's Lounge (p162)

➜ Logan Theatre (p162)

For reviews, see p162 ➡

LOGAN SQUARE & HUMBOLDT PARK

⊙ SIGHTS

HUMBOLDT PARK   PARK

Map p308 (www.chicagoparkdistrict.com; 1440 N Humboldt Dr; ⊗6am-11pm; ⊡70, 72) This 207-acre park, which lends its name to the surrounding neighborhood, comes out of nowhere and gobsmacks you with Mother Nature. A lagoon brushed by native plants takes up much of the green space, and birdsong flickers in the air. The 1907 Prairie School **boathouse** is the park's centerpiece, home to a cafe and free cultural events. The flowery Formal Garden (p154), the National Museum of Puerto Rican Arts & Culture (p154), and Chicago's only **inland beach** are other highlights.

The park was built in 1869 and named for German naturalist Alexander von Humboldt. Landscape architect Jens Jensen gave it its 'prairie style' design, using native plants and stone, in the early 1900s. The park has gone through some rough times since then, and has only come into its own again in the past decade. While it's family-filled by day, it's still pretty rough and best avoided at night (unless there's a free outdoor movie or music event happening).

Street vendors and food trucks sell fried plantains, meat dumplings and other Puerto Rican specialties around the park's edges. Many congregate on Kedzie Ave at North Ave and at Hirsch St – sniff them out for a picnic.

For more in-depth explorations, including the park's wee waterfall, wind turbine and picnic island, download the free audio tour at www.chicagoparkdistrict.com/audio-tours/humboldt-park.

LOCAL KNOWLEDGE

LOGAN SQUARE FARMERS MARKET

The **Logan Square Farmers Market** (Map p308; www.logansquarefarmers market.org; 3107 W Logan Blvd; ⊗10am-3pm Sun mid-May–Oct; ⍷Blue Line to Logan Square) is one of Chicago's best. The neighborhood operates it (versus the city), so it marches to its own progressive beat. Live music, free yoga classes and prepared foods from surrounding restaurants join the usual vendor lineup of fruits, veggies, eggs and flowers. In winter the market moves indoors at 2755 N Milwaukee Ave.

FORMAL GARDEN   GARDENS

Map p308 (⊡70) The Formal Garden sits in the park on the northwest corner of Humboldt Dr and Division St. It's rich with jelly-bean-colored flower beds and bison sculptures (by Edward Kemeys, the gent who hewed the Art Institute lions). Wander through and smell the roses.

NATIONAL MUSEUM OF PUERTO RICAN ARTS & CULTURE   MUSEUM

Map p308 (⌨773-486-8345; www.nmprac.org; 3015 W Division St; ⊗10am-4pm Tue-Fri, to 1pm Sat; ⊡70) **FREE** The institute fills the old horse stables in Humboldt Park. It's worth a stroll inside to see what free art and cultural exhibits are showing.

ILLINOIS CENTENNIAL MEMORIAL COLUMN   MONUMENT

Map p308 (Logan Blvd & Milwaukee Ave, intersection of Kedzie Blvd; ⍷Blue Line to Logan Square) What's that giant phallic thing in the middle of the road, causing traffic to swerve every which way? Excellent question. Most locals have no idea. Turns out it's a monument commemorating the 100th anniversary of Illinois' statehood, built in 1918 by a gent named Henry Bacon – the same architect who created the Lincoln Memorial in Washington DC.

The eagle atop the Doric column echoes that on the Illinois state flag. The reliefs of Native Americans, explorers, farmers and laborers represent the great changes the state experienced during its first century.

BUSY BEAVER BUTTON MUSEUM   MUSEUM

Map p308 (⌨773-645-3359; www.buttonmu seum.org; 3279 W Armitage Ave; ⊗10am-4pm Mon-Fri; ⊡73) **FREE** Even George Washington gave out campaign buttons, though in his era they were the sew-on kind. Pin-back buttons came along in 1896. Badge-making company Busy Beaver chronicles its history in displays holding thousands of the little round mementos. They tout everything from Dale Bozzio to Bozo the clown, Cabbage Patch Kids to Big Rock Point Nuclear Plant.

They're fascinating to browse (especially Washington's button), and the hipster office staff is totally gracious about letting you gawk over their desks where the framed cases hang. Ring the doorbell to enter.

GALERIE F   GALLERY
Map p308 (📞773-819-9200; www.galerief.com;
2381 N Milwaukee Ave; ⊗11am-6pm Tue-Sun;
Ⓜ Blue Line to California) Galerie F is exactly
the type of laid-back, ubercool gallery
you'd expect to find in Logan Square. It
specializes in rock-and-roll gig posters,
printmaking and street art. Walk into the
long, thin room and browse. The vibe is totally welcoming.

PASEO BORICUA   AREA
Map p308 (Division St, btwn Western Ave & Mozart
St; 📷70) Paseo Boricua, aka the Puerto Rican Passage, is a half-mile-long stretch of
Division St stuffed with Puerto Rican shops
and restaurants. It's marked at either end
by a 45-ton, steel Puerto Rican flag sculpture that arches over the road; the eastern
flag stands near Western Ave, while the
western one is at Mozart Ave.

This area has long been the epicenter
of Chicago's 103,000-strong Puerto Rican
community.

✖ EATING

KUMA'S CORNER   BURGERS $
(📞773-604-8769; www.kumascorner.com; 2900
W Belmont Ave; mains $13-15; ⊗11:30am-
midnight Mon-Wed, to 1am Thu, to 2am Fri & Sat,
noon-midnight Sun; 📷77) Ridiculously busy
and head-bangingly loud, Kuma's attracts
the tattooed set for its monster 10oz burgers, each named for a heavy-metal band
and hefted onto a pretzel-roll bun. There's
a mac 'n' cheese menu for vegetarians, and
beer and bourbon for all. Expect to queue.

Burgers include the Black Sabbath (black-
ened with chili and pepper jack cheese),
Led Zeppelin (piled with pulled pork, bacon, cheddar and pickles) and Goatsnake
(topped with herbed goat's cheese and
poblano corn relish). The prime-time wait
can reach two hours. Kuma's has a newer
outpost in Lincoln Park (at 666 W Diversey
Ave), but the original is best.

HONEY BUTTER
FRIED CHICKEN   AMERICAN $
(📞773-478-4000; www.honeybutter.com; 3361
N Elston Ave; mains $8-12; ⊗11am-9pm Tue-Thu,
to 10pm Fri, 10am-10pm Sat, to 9pm Sun; Ⓜ Blue
Line to Belmont) At this off-the-beaten-path
neighborhood spot, the namesake dish is
made up of double-buttermilk-battered

bird sprinkled with smoked paprika, onto
which the famed honey butter melts. It's
sweet and salty genius. The back patio
rocks, especially once the Ginger Mules and
other cocktails start flowing. No reservations, so expect a queue.

BANG BANG PIE & BISCUITS   AMERICAN $
Map p308 (📞773-276-8888; www.bangbangpie.
com; 2051 N California Ave; slices $5; ⊗7am-7pm
Mon-Fri, 9am-4pm Sat & Sun; 🛱; Ⓜ Blue Line to
California) Count on fruit, cream and chocolate pie variations daily. Will it be chocolate peanut butter or Kentucky bourbon
fudge you take to the sunlit, butcher-board
tables? Will it be blood orange or key lime
you fork into while sitting in the garden's
Adirondack chairs? Almost better than
pie are Bang Bang's hulking biscuits, especially after a slathering with the condiment
bar's jams.

PAPA'S CACHE SABROSO   PUERTO RICAN $
Map p308 (📞773-862-8313; 2517 W Division St;
mains $8-13; ⊗11am-9pm Mon-Thu, to 10pm Fri
& Sat; 📷70) Homey, family-run Papa's sits
in the thick of Humboldt Park's Puerto
Rican community. Specialties are roasted
chicken (as you can see from the birds slow-
turning on spits) and *jibarito* sandwiches
(garlic-mayo-slathered steak or chicken between slices of fried plantain 'bread'). The
jibarito is a Chicago invention, and Papa's
small, island-y cafe is a terrific place to try
one. BYOB.

RENO   AMERICAN $
Map p308 (📞773-697-4234; www.renochi
cago.com; 2607 N Milwaukee Ave; mains $9-16;
⊗8am-10pm Mon-Thu, to 11pm Fri, 9am-11pm
Sat, to 10pm Sun; 🛱; Ⓜ Blue Line to Logan
Square) ✿ Reno is Logan Square's de facto
community center, thanks to its reasonable prices and wood-fired bagels and
pizzas. Stylishly scruffy residents pull up
a chair at the reclaimed wood tables and
peck away at their laptops while munching

egg-and-maple-fennel-sausage sandwiches by day, and Gruyere-and-butternut-squash-topped pizzas and pastas by night. Cash only.

Reno also has a full bar and pours a good, if small, selection of beer and wine.

PARSON'S CHICKEN AND FISH AMERICAN $

Map p308 (☑773-384-3333; www.parsonschickenandfish.com; 2952 W Armitage Ave; mains $8-16; ⊙11am-1am Mon-Fri, 10am-1am Sat & Sun; ⓂBlue Line to California) Parson's fries its chicken skin hard, so the super juicy flesh underneath comes as a surprise. Everyone eats outdoors at picnic tables under striped umbrellas. This is *the* neighborhood hot spot when the weather warms, and the negroni slushies slide down with ease. The patio morphs into an ice rink come winter. No reservations.

FEED AMERICAN $

Map p308 (☑773-489-4600; www.feedrestaurantchicago.com; 2803 W Chicago Ave; mains $7-13; ⊙8am-10pm Mon-Fri, 9am-10pm Sat, 9am-9pm Sun; ☐66) With red-checked tablecloths, a free-play jukebox piled with classic rock and country, and a menu of southern home cookin', cash-only Feed has the chipper feel of a lost *Hee Haw* set. All the framed portraits of poultry allude to the house specialty – juicy, tender rotisserie chicken – but the sides, including hand-cut fries, corn pudding and mac 'n' cheese, are equally stellar. Bulging fruit pie and vanilla-wafer banana pudding follow for dessert. BYOB.

CHICAGO DINER VEGETARIAN $

Map p308 (☑773-252-3211; www.veggiediner.com; 2333 N Milwaukee Ave; mains $10-14; ⊙11am-10pm Mon-Fri, 10am-10pm Sat & Sun; ☑; ⓂBlue Line to California) Chicago's favorite, long-standing vegetarian restaurant expanded from Lake View and opened a fancier branch in Logan Square.

DONUT DELIGHT BAKERY $

Map p308 (☑773-227-2105; 1750 N California Ave; doughnuts & cake slices $2-5; ⊙6am-6pm Mon-Sat; ⓂBlue Line to California) The beauty of this little shop – besides the yummy, yeasty, perfectly sweet original glazed doughnuts – is its location right smack off the 606 trail (p137). Exit at California, head down the ramp, and you're there. Cake slices, coffee drinks, smoothies and magazine-strewn tables also await.

LOGAN SQUARE & HUMBOLDT PARK EATING

🏃 Local Life
Logan & Humboldt Boulevard Stroll

The four broad green boulevards – Logan, Kedzie, Palmer and Humboldt – that stripe the neighborhood are so impressive they're an official city landmark. Built in 1869, they roll through the heart of the community, past whimsically styled, century-old manors, modern cool-cat shops, and the lagoon-dotted park where locals go out to play.

❶ Fuel Up at Reno
Breakfast, lunch or dinner – Reno (p155) does it right. Staff make just about everything in-house with organic ingredients. Linger along with everyone else over the bottomless cups of coffee and free wi-fi (the java morphs to beer and wine as the day progresses).

❷ Rally at the Monument
Logan Square's centerpiece is the 68ft Illinois Centennial Memorial Column (p154) erected (OK, bad pun) in 1918 to mark 100 years of statehood. On sunny days folks scramble through the take-your-life-in-your-hands traffic circle to loll on the surrounding grass, people-watch and nibble goodies from the Sunday farmers market.

❸ Get Fashionable
Wolfbait & B-girls (p162) sells funky women's wear and accessories by local designers. Weren't you looking for a hand-dyed repurposed minidress made from men's boxer shorts? The name, incidentally, comes from the 1950's guidebook *Chicago Confidential* that defines 'wolfbait' as girls who moved to the city looking for success, and 'b-girls' as what they sometimes turn into.

❹ City Lit Pit Stop
City Lit (Map p308; ☑773-235-2523; www.citylitbooks.com; 2523 N Kedzie Blvd; ⊙11am-8pm Tue-Fri, 10am-7pm Sat, to 5pm Sun; ⓂBlue Line to Logan Square) is a modern, generalist bookstore that often hosts readings by local authors. A Logan resident opened the shop in 2012. Grab a novel and cozy up by the fireplace. The children's section is particularly rich.

Humboldt Park (p154)

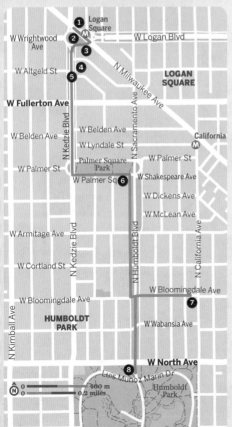

❺ Kedzie's Mansions
Meander on **Kedzie Boulevard**, a prime example of the area's wide, leafy thoroughfares. Several mansions stand sentry; the best ones are on the street's west side. European immigrants who made their fortunes in Chicago built the manors at the turn of the century. Unwelcome by the Gold Coast's old-money millionaires, the nouveau riche had to move out here.

❻ Schwinn's House
At 2128 N Humboldt Blvd (aka the southwest corner of Palmer and Humboldt) a gent named Ignaz Schwinn used to roll his two-wheeler out of the driveway. Alas, the original **Schwinn mansion** is gone now, but the neighborhood's many cyclists tip their cap when passing by, as Ignaz pretty much invented the modern bike (with 40 patents to prove it).

❼ Donut Delight
Cute little Donut Delight has perfected the art of yeasty, perfectly sweet traditional glazed doughnuts. Cake slices, coffee drinks, smoothies and magazine-strewn tables also await inside. Outside, you can hop on the 606 trail (p137) if you're feeling ambitious. The doughnut shop is mere steps from the trail ramp at California Ave.

❽ Go Fish
Humboldt Blvd runs smack into Humboldt Park (p154). Stroll around the lagoon, fish, and munch Puerto Rican snacks from the food carts. To really go native, bring a folding chair or blanket, plop it under a shade tree and lick your fresh-bought coconut popsicle.

LOGAN SQUARE & HUMBOLDT PARK

Logan Square & Humboldt Park – Hipster Haven

Whenever something new and cool opens – be it a craft whiskey maker, a pop-up sausage restaurant, a thrifty gin lounge, a record shop with an attached video-game museum – it opens here. And even though it's the hottest 'hood in town, it remains refreshingly low-key.

CHARLES COOK/GETTY IMAGES ©

CHARLES COOK/GETTY IMAGES ©

1. Wolfbait & B-girls (p162)
Check out local designers in action, then take your pick of their unique wares.

2. Dining in Logan Square (p155)
Savor delectable meals in one of Chicago's culinary hot spots.

3. Lula Cafe (p160)
Refuel at this popular eatery during your exploration of the area.

4. Neighborhood nightlife (p161)
Raucous bar-hopping or a quiet tipple – all bases are covered here.

ADAM J HORWITZ/SHUTTERSTOCK ©

WORTH A DETOUR

SMOQUE BBQ

Squeaky-clean, family-friendly **Smoque** (☎773-545-7427; www.smoquebbq.com; 3800 N Pulaski Rd; mains $10-22; ☺11am-9pm Sun-Thu, to 10pm Fri & Sat; ⓂBlue Line to Irving Park) is all about slow-cooked meats. The baby-back and St Louis–style ribs are what line 'em up: they're smoked over oak and applewood and soaked in a tangy, slightly sweet sauce. The brisket and pulled pork aren't far behind in making carnivores swoon. Brisket-flecked baked beans, cornmeal-crusted mac 'n' cheese, freshly cut fries and citrusy coleslaw round out the menu. It's BYOB, so bring a few brewskis to complement the meaty goodness. Smoque is a couple of miles northwest of Logan Square, easily reached three Blue Line stations onward at Irving Park.

★**PARACHUTE**　　　　　KOREAN **$$**

(☎773-654-1460; www.parachuterestaurant.com; 3500 N Elston Ave; mains $18-28; ☺5-10pm Tue-Thu, to 11pm Fri & Sat; ⓂBlue Line to Belmont) Michelin-starred Parachute puts an American spin on Korean street-food classics – say, mackerel and barbecued onion *bibimbap* (mixed vegetables and rice). The ambience is like a dinner party in your friend's retro-cool kitchen. There are only 40 seats, so reserve ahead; you can do so 30 days in advance. Walk-ins fare best before 6pm.

Parachute was a 2015 James Beard nominee for best new restaurant in the US, and the foodie masses are (deservedly) all over it.

LONGMAN & EAGLE　　　　AMERICAN **$$**

Map p308 (☎773-276-7110; www.longmanand eagle.com; 2657 N Kedzie Ave; mains $15-30; ☺9am-2am Sun-Fri, to 3am Sat; ⓂBlue Line to Logan Square) Hard to say whether this shabby-chic tavern is best for eating or drinking. Let's say eating, since it earned a Michelin star for its beautifully cooked comfort foods such as vanilla brioche French toast for breakfast, wild-boar sloppy joes for lunch and fried chicken and duck-fat biscuits for dinner. There's a whole menu of juicy small plates and whiskeys, too. No reservations.

Luckily, all those whiskeys ensure you can drink well while waiting. Belly up at the bar for a house-curated flight or a flight of your own making. A six-room inn fills the tavern's 2nd floor.

LULA CAFE　　　　　AMERICAN **$$**

Map p308 (☎773-489-9554; www.lulacafe.com; 2537 N Kedzie Blvd; mains $16-28; ☺9am-10pm Mon, Wed, Thu & Sun, to 11pm Fri & Sat; ⓟ; ⓂBlue Line to Logan Square) 🍃 Funky, arty Lula led the way for Logan Square's dining scene, and appreciative neighborhood folks still crowd in for the seasonal, locally sourced menu. Even the muffins here are something to drool over, and that goes double for lunch items such as pasta *yiayia* (*bucatini* pasta with Moroccan cinnamon, feta and garlic) and dinners such as steamed flounder with wild fennel and parsnips.

The six-course vegetarian tasting menu ($48) is a rare treat.

YUSHO　　　　　JAPANESE **$$**

Map p308 (☎773-904-8558; www.yusho-chi cago.com; 2853 N Kedzie Ave; mains $14-20; ☺5-10pm Mon, Wed & Thu, to 11pm Fri & Sat, noon-8pm Sun; ⓂBlue Line to Logan Square) The cook at Yusho was Charlie Trotter's executive chef for 14 years, so he knows his way around a kitchen. The focus here is *yakitori* (grilled Japanese street food). Dishes of octopus and papaya salad, eggplant-and-peanut-filled steamed buns and pork miso ramen noodles hit the unadorned wood tables and booths.

The daily draft cocktail and wildly flavored soft-serve ice cream round out the menu. Yusho is a great date place (and yes, it does take reservations). There's a prix-fixe special on Sundays: a noodle dish, drink and dessert for $25.

FAT RICE　　　　INTERNATIONAL **$$$**

Map p308 (☎773-661-9170; www.eatfatrice.com; 2957 W Diversey Ave; mains $19-36; ☺5:30-10pm Tue, 11am-2pm & 5:30-10pm Wed-Sat, 11am-3pm Sun; ⓂBlue Line to Logan Square) Queues stretch out the door at Fat Rice ever since *Bon Appétit* crowned it one of the nation's best new restaurants in 2013. It dishes the food of Macau, a whacked-out Portuguese-Indian-Chinese meld. The eponymous 'fat rice' main shows the spirit: a bowl brimming with prawns, garlicky sausage, salted duck, hard-boiled eggs, pickled chilies, jasmine rice and more. The restaurant takes limited reservations, or you can always walk in if you don't mind waiting. Fat Rice recently expanded by adding a cocktail lounge and Portuguese-Chinese bakery next door.

DRINKING & NIGHTLIFE

★ REVOLUTION BREWING   BREWERY
Map p308 (☏773-227-2739; www.revbrew.com; 2323 N Milwaukee Ave; ⏰11am-1am Mon-Fri, 10am-1am Sat & Sun; MBlue Line to California) Raise your fist to Revolution, a big, buzzy, industrial-chic brewpub that fills glasses with heady beers such as the Eugene porter and hopped-up Anti-Hero IPA. The brewmaster here led the way for Chicago's huge craft-beer scene, and his suds are top notch. The haute pub grub includes a pork belly and egg sandwich and bacon-fat popcorn with fried sage.

Revolution also has a tap room (open 2pm to 10pm Wednesday through Saturday) nearby at 3340 N Kedzie Ave. It's not usually as crowded as the brewpub, and offers a relaxed atmosphere for hop-heads to knock back pints. Free brewery tours are an added bonus. There is always one at 6pm; check the schedule for other times.

LOST LAKE   COCKTAIL BAR
Map p308 (☏773-293-6048; www.lostlaketiki. com; 3154 W Diversey Ave; ⏰4pm-2am Sun-Fri, to 3am Sat; MBlue Line to Logan Sq) Hipsters love a good tiki bar, so Lost Lake popped up in 2015 to meet the need. Take a seat under the bamboo roof by the banana-leaf wallpaper, and swirl a Mystery Gardenia or other tropical drink made from one of the 275 rums behind the bar.

COLE'S   BAR
Map p308 (☏773-276-5802; www.coleschicago. com; 2338 N Milwaukee Ave; ⏰5:30pm-2am Mon-Fri, 4pm-2am Sat & Sun; MBlue LIne to California) Cole's is a dive bar with nifty free entertainment. Young scenesters flock in to shoot pool and swill Midwest microbrews (Bell's, Two Brothers) in the front room. Then they head to the back-room stage where bands and DJs do their thing. On Wednesdays the popular comedy open-mic takes over from 9:30pm.

SCOFFLAW   COCKTAIL BAR
Map p308 (☏773-252-9700; www.scofflawchica go.com; 3201 W Armitage Ave; ⏰5pm-2am Mon-Fri, 11am-2am Sat & Sun; 🚌73) Scofflaw is a gin

joint – literally. The bar specializes in boutique, small-batch gins mixed into gimlets, martinis and other cocktails that get creative with juniper. It's mostly a 30-something crowd sipping from mismatched glassware and kicking back in vintage French armchairs by the fireplace. That may sound preciously hipster, but the cozy bar's vibe is more rebellious thrift store.

BILLY SUNDAY   COCKTAIL BAR
Map p308 (☏773-661-2485; www.billy-sunday. com; 3143 W Logan Blvd; ⏰5pm-2am Mon-Fri, 3pm-2am Sat & Sun; MBlue Line to Logan Square) Tastemakers at *Details* magazine named this cocktail haven one of the best new bars in the country. Spiced kola nut, rhubarb sherbet and pineapple bitters are among the ingredients shaken and stirred into Billy's high-end gins, bourbons and other booze. Old-timey portraits hang on the walls; sconces give the small room a warm glow. Most drinks cost around $11.

A small menu of gastronome snacks – crispy, malt-vinegar-doused pig ears or 'Things in Jars' such as whipped garbanzo beans with pickled pistachio – helps soak up the libations. Note it's easy to miss the bar's entrance, as the sign isn't very prominent.

LATE BAR   CLUB
(☏773-267-5283; www.latebarchicago.com; 3534 W Belmont Ave; ⏰10pm-4am Mon-Thu, 8pm-4am Fri & Sat; MBlue Line to Belmont) Late Bar is off the beaten path on a forlorn stretch of Belmont Ave surrounded by auto-repair shops and Polish bars, though it's easy to get to via the El. Two DJs opened the club, and its weird, new-wave vibe draws fans of all stripes: mods, hooligans, rockers, punks, goths and more. Saturday's Planet Earth alt/postpunk dance nights are popular.

CALIFORNIA CLIPPER   BAR
Map p308 (☏773-384-2547; www.californiaclip per.com; 1002 N California Ave; ⏰8pm-1:30am; 🚌52) The Clipper's retro linoleum and Naugahyde decor hasn't changed much since it opened in 1937. Guys in bowling shirts and ladies in thrift-store dresses dig the lengthy list of cocktails and nightly entertainment (jazz bands, burlesque, DJs). Duck into a booth to sip your Old Fashioned and play one of the board games if the entertainment isn't doing the trick.

SMALL BAR
BAR

Map p308 (☏773-509-9888; www.thesmallbar. com; 2956 N Albany Ave; ⏱4pm-2am Mon-Fri, noon-2am Sat & Sun; ⓂBlue Line to Belmont) Its ace jukebox, affordable food menu and kindly staff make this unpretentious gem an easygoing place to spend an evening in the neighborhood. The mirror behind the bar dates back to 1907. Alas, there's no easy public transport to get here, so you'll have to walk a half-mile or so from the El.

WHIRLAWAY LOUNGE
BAR

Map p308 (☏773-276-6809; www.whirlaway.net; 3224 W Fullerton Ave; ⏱4:30pm-2am; ⓂBlue Line to Logan Square) With threadbare couches and broken-in board games, this neighborhood fave has the homey charm of your uncle's '70s rumpus room – if your uncle had loads of young hip pals with an insatiable thirst for Pabst. Cash only.

 ## ENTERTAINMENT

★WHISTLER
LIVE MUSIC

Map p308 (☏773-227-3530; www.whistlerchicago.com; 2421 N Milwaukee Ave; ⏱6pm-2am Mon-Thu, 5pm-2am Fri-Sun; ⓂBlue Line to California) Hometown indie bands, jazz combos and DJs rock this wee, arty bar most nights. There's never a cover charge, but you'd be a shmuck if you didn't order at least one of the swanky cocktails or craft beers to keep the scene going. Whistler is also a gallery: the front window showcases local artists' work.

ROSA'S LOUNGE
BLUES

Map p308 (☏773-342-0452; www.rosaslounge. com; 3420 W Armitage Ave; tickets $7-20; ⏱8pm-2am Tue-Sat; ⎙73) Rosa's is an unadorned, real-deal blues club that brings in top local talent and dedicated fans to a somewhat derelict Logan Square block. The location is isolated from easy public transportation; a taxi or rideshare is probably the best way to get here.

LOGAN THEATRE
CINEMA

Map p308 (☏773-342-5555; www.theloganthea tre.com; 2646 N Milwaukee Ave; ⓂBlue Line to Logan Square) This 1915 deco-style movie palace has been renovated and now shows both mainstream and art-house flicks a few weeks after their initial run (so tickets are cheap). Cult classics screen late-night on weekends. Bonus: local craft beers flow from the theater's cool little bar so you can sip well while viewing.

PROP THTR
THEATER

(☏773-742-5420; www.propthtr.org; 3502 N Elston Ave; ⓂBlue Line to Belmont) This long-running storefront venue presents original plays and fresh stage adaptations of literary works by writers from Nabokov to William S Burroughs. The well-executed productions are typically provocative and dark in theme. Prop also hosts the annual fringe Rhinoceros Theater Festival.

ELASTIC ARTS FOUNDATION
PERFORMING ARTS

Map p308 (☏773-772-3616; www.elasticrevolu tion.com; 2nd fl, 3429 W Diversey Ave; ⓂBlue Line to Logan Square) The calendar at Elastic Arts is far-reaching and impossible to pin down – one day will see a funk band, the next an experimental video screening, and the next an improvised jazz performance by a cutting-edge international ensemble. Tickets rarely cost more than $10.

 ## SHOPPING

LOGAN HARDWARE
MUSIC

Map p308 (☏773-235-5030; www.logan-hard ware.com; 2532 W Fullerton Ave; ⏱noon-9pm Mon-Sat, to 7pm Sun; ⎙74) Logan Hardware is a used record store with a little something extra in its back room: the Vintage Arcade Museum. So after flicking through bins of rock, funk and Chicago band LPs – and scoring, say, a bluesy Chess Records 45 – you celebrate with a knockdown game of Donkey Kong, Ms Pac-Man, Dolly Parton pinball or several other whirring, beeping '80s games. A receipt from any purchase serves as entry to the arcade, where all games are free to play.

WOLFBAIT & B-GIRLS
CLOTHING

Map p308 (☏312-698-8685; www.wolfbaitchi cago.com; 3131 W Logan Blvd; ⏱10am-7pm Mon-Sat, to 4pm Sun; ⓂBlue Line to Logan Square) Old ironing boards serve as display tables; tape measures, scissors and other designers' tools hang from vintage hooks. You get that crafting feeling as soon as you walk in, and indeed, Wolfbait & B-girls sells the wares (dresses, handbags and jewelry) of local indie designers.

Near West Side & Pilsen

WEST LOOP | PILSEN | GREEKTOWN | LITTLE ITALY

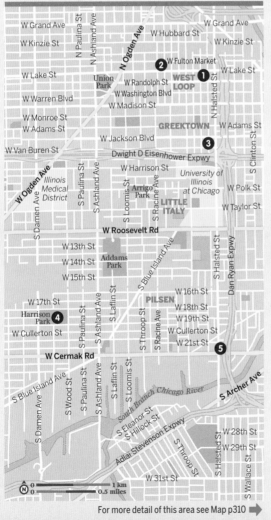

Neighborhood Top Five

1 West Loop (p166) Forking into a decadent meal by a celebrity chef at one of the mega-hot restaurants in the area.

2 Mars Gallery (p165) Wandering around forklifts and warehouses to find art hubs such as this pop-art haven.

3 Greektown (p171) Exploring the tavernas, bakeries and shops along Halsted St and indulging in flaming cheese, honeyed sweets, carafes of wine and a magical candle or three.

4 National Museum of Mexican Art (p166) Admiring psychedelic paintings, polished altars and colorful folk art at the nation's largest Latino arts institution.

5 Skylark (p175) Slouching into a booth, knocking back drinks and eating tater tots alongside Pilsen's bohemian crowd.

For more detail of this area see Map p310 ➡

Lonely Planet's Top Tip

You'll need to make reservations months in advance (at least) for hot restaurants such as Next (p172) and Girl and the Goat (p172). But if you can't get in, you can still sample the wares of chefs Grant Achatz and Stephanie Izard. Try Aviary (p174), Achatz' cocktail bar, and Little Goat (p167), Izard's diner.

 Best Places to Eat

➡ Little Goat (p167)

➡ Lou Mitchell's (p166)

➡ Publican Quality Meats (p167)

➡ Saint Lou's Assembly (p171)

➡ Sweet Maple Cafe (p172)

For reviews, see p166 ➡

 Best Places to Drink

➡ RM Champagne Salon (p174)

➡ Goose Island Brewery (p174)

➡ Skylark (p175)

➡ La Catrina Cafe (p175)

➡ Cruz Blanca (p174)

For reviews, see p174 ➡

Best Places to Shop

➡ Modern Cooperative (p175)

➡ Open Books (p175)

➡ Knee Deep Vintage (p176)

➡ Randolph Street Market (p176)

➡ Athenian Candle Co (p176)

For reviews, see p175 ➡

Explore Near West Side & Pilsen

Just west of the Loop is, well, the West Loop. It's akin to New York City's Meatpacking District, with chic restaurants, clubs and galleries poking out between meat-processing plants. The area is booming, and it seems like a new hot chef opens a restaurant (or two) here weekly. By day it's still a serious food-supply zone filled with forklifts and delivery trucks – though Google and other tech companies are joining the action with their dapper office buildings. At night the West Loop turns up the glamour. Stroll along the main veins of W Randolph St and W Fulton Market and you'll get the drift.

The Near West Side also includes the ethnic neighborhoods of Greektown (along Halsted St) and Little Italy (along Taylor St). Neither has much in the way of sights, but gustatory tourists will revel in the delicious offerings.

To the southwest lies Pilsen, the center of Chicago's Mexican community. A trip to this colorful, mural-splashed neighborhood is like stepping into a foreign country. Spend an afternoon poking around the bakeries, taquerias and the impressive art museum. Chicago's hipster underground is also here, so you'll find some great bohemian bars and restaurants if you linger into the evening.

Local Life

➡ **Vintage jackpot** Local fashionistas scour 18th St's vintage shops in Pilsen. Several pop up in the mile-long stretch between Halsted St and Ashland Ave.

➡ **Tube socks and tacos** Maxwell Street Market (p176) draws a local crowd of junk hounds and Mexican-street-food fans.

➡ **Fish for all** Pleasant House (p173) has a devoted fan base, especially during the Friday fish fry.

➡ **Pastrami for politicos** Local politicians get their sandwich fix at Manny's Deli (p167); listen in for good gossip.

Getting There & Away

➡ **El** Pink Line to 18th St for Pilsen; Green, Pink Lines to Morgan or Clinton for West Loop; Blue Line to UIC-Halsted for Greektown; Pink Line to Polk or Blue Line to Racine for Little Italy.

➡ **Bus** For United Center, buses 19 (game-day express) and 20 run along Madison St. Number 8 travels along Halsted St through Greektown and Pilsen.

➡ **Taxi** The West Loop and Greektown are only 1.25 miles west of the Loop, making them a fairly cheap ride. And cabs are easy to hail in the neighborhoods.

➡ **Car** It can be tough to find parking in the West Loop and Greektown, but valets abound. Street parking is pretty easy in Little Italy and Pilsen.

 NEAR WEST SIDE & PILSEN

⊙ SIGHTS

⊙ West Loop

UNITED CENTER   STADIUM

Map p310 (☑312-455-4650; www.unitedcenter.com; 1901 W Madison St; ☐19 or 20) The United Center arena is home to the Bulls (pro basketball team) and the Blackhawks (pro hockey team), and is a venue for big-name concerts and special events. The statue of an airborne Michael Jordan in front of the east entrance (by gate 4) pays a lively tribute to the hoops player whose talents financed the edifice. It's a popular photo op.

Expect lots of construction as the venue adds more space and a big retail store to the grounds. The area is OK by day, but gets a bit edgy and deserted at night – unless there's a game, in which case cops are everywhere to ensure public safety.

HAYMARKET SQUARE   HISTORIC SITE

Map p310 (Desplaines St, btwn Lake & Randolph Sts; ⓂGreen, Pink Line to Clinton) The odd bronze statue of guys on a wagon marks the spot where the world's labor movement began. So the next time you take a lunch break or go home after your eight-hour workday, thank Haymarket Sq, which you're now standing upon. Striking factory workers held a meeting here on May 4, 1886. Bombs, deaths, anarchists and hangings ensued.

The statue is meant to depict the speaker's platform at the rally.

BATCOLUMN   SCULPTURE

Map p310 (600 W Madison St; ⓂGreen Line to Clinton) Artist Claes Oldenburg – known for his gigantic shuttlecocks in Kansas City and oversized cherry spoon in Minneapolis – delivered this simple, controversial sculpture to Chicago in 1977. The artist mused that the 96ft bat 'seemed to connect earth and sky the way a tornado does.' Hmm... See it for yourself in front of the Harold Washington Social Security Center.

THREEWALLS   GALLERY

(www.three-walls.org) This gallery of emerging and mid-career Midwest artists is so groovy it has community-supported art (CSA), where you buy a 'share' and receive an allotment of art (maybe a handwoven placemat and ceramic dish). It sponsors lectures and performances, too.

Threewalls is in the process of relocating, so watch the website for updates.

In the interim it hosts shows at various venues around the city's northwest side.

OLD ST PATRICK'S CHURCH   CHURCH

Map p310 (☑312-648-1021; www.oldstpats.org; 700 W Adams St; ⓂBlue Line to Clinton) A Chicago fire survivor, this 1852 church is one of the city's oldest. Old St Pat's is best known for its World's Largest Block Party, a day-long bash in late June with a solid lineup of big-name rock bands on stage. The event is famed for matchmaking: more than 100 couples have met in the crowd and eventually married.

Such social programs have certainly boosted Old St Pat's membership, which has gone from four (yes, four) in 1983 to thousands three decades later. The domed steeple signifies the Eastern Church; the spire signifies the Western Church. There's a beautifully restored Celtic-patterned interior.

CHICAGO FIRE ACADEMY   HISTORIC SITE

Map p310 (☑312-747-7239; 558 W DeKoven St; ⓂBlue Line to Clinton) Rarely has a building been placed in a more appropriate location: the fire department's training school (also known as the Quinn Academy) stands on the very spot where the 1871 Great Chicago Fire began – between Clinton and Jefferson Sts. Although there's no word on whether

---

WEST LOOP GALLERIES

The West Loop art scene is arguably Chicago's most intriguing. Tucked between meatpacking plants and sought-after chefs' restaurants, galleries here are the beachhead for contemporary art in Chicago. They take bigger chances on up-and-coming and controversial artists than their more entrenched River North peers. See www.chicagogallerynews.com for listings. **Mars Gallery** (Map p310; ☑312-226-7808; www.marsgallery.com; 1139 W Fulton Market; ⊙noon-6pm Wed & Fri, to 7pm Thu, 11am-5pm Sat; ⓂGreen, Pink Line to Morgan) is a local favorite.

WORTH A DETOUR

GARFIELD PARK CONSERVATORY

Built in 1907, the **Garfield Park Conservatory** (☏312-746-5100; www.garfieldconserva tory.org; 300 N Central Park Ave; ⊙9am-5pm Thu-Tue, to 8pm Wed; MGreen Line to Con-servatory) **FREE** – 4.5 acres of gardens under glass – are the Park District's pride and joy. Designer Jens Jensen intended for the palms, ferns and other plants to re-create Chicago's prehistoric landscape. Today the effect continues – all that's missing is a rampaging stegosaurus. Newer halls contain displays of seasonal plants that are especially spectacular in the weeks before Easter.

Kids can get dirty with roots and seeds in the indoor Children's Garden. Between May and October the outdoor grounds are open, including the Demonstration Gar-den, which shows urbanites how to grow veggies, keep bees and compost in city plots; and the Monet Garden, which adapts the Impressionist painter's colorful gar-den at Giverny, France. If you drive, lock up: the neighborhood isn't the safest.

junk mail still shows up for Mrs O'Leary, the academy trains firefighters so they'll be ready the next time somebody, or some crit-ter, kicks over a lantern.

◎ Pilsen

NATIONAL MUSEUM
OF MEXICAN ART   MUSEUM
Map p310 (☏312-738-1503; www.nationalmuseu mofmexicanart.org; 1852 W 19th St; ⊙10am-5pm Tue-Sun; MPink Line to 18th St) **FREE** Founded in 1982, this vibrant museum – the largest Latino arts institution in the USA – has be-come one of the city's best. The vivid per-manent collection sums up 1000 years of Mexican art and culture through classical paintings, shining gold altars, skeleton-rich folk art, beadwork and much more.

The turbulent politics and revolution-ary leaders of Mexican history are well represented, including works about Cesar Chavez and Emiliano Zapata. Don't miss the psychedelic 'semen-acrylic' painting (that's, um, bodily fluids mixed with pig-ments). The museum also sponsors read-ings by top authors and performances by musicians and artists. October and Novem-ber are busy months with lots of festive pro-grams for Day of the Dead. The on-site store is a winner, with brightly painted Mexican crafts filling the shelves.

CHICAGO ARTS DISTRICT   AREA
Map p310 (www.chicagoartsdistrict.org; S Hal-sted & W 18th Sts; ☐8) Pilsen's art galleries are known collectively as the Chicago Arts District. There are 20 or so galleries, and they tend to be small, artist-run spaces with erratic hours. Many cluster around

18th and Halsted Sts. The best time to visit is on Second Fridays, when the galleries stay open from 6pm to 10pm on the second Friday of each month and welcome patrons with free wine, snacks, and freshly hung paintings and photos. Pick up a map at the office at 1821 S Halsted St.

COOPER DUAL
LANGUAGE ACADEMY   PUBLIC ART
Map p310 (1645 W 18th Pl; MPink Line to 18th) Check out the exterior wall of this school, the canvas for a 1990s tile mosaic that shows a diverse range of Mexican images, from a portrait of farmworker advocate Dolores Huerta to the Virgin of Guadalupe.

ST PIUS CHURCH   CHURCH
Map p310 (www.stpiusvparish.org; 1919 S Ashland Ave; MPink Line to 18th) The Romanesque revival-style church was built between 1885 and 1892 and was a hub for the city's Irish immigrants. Its smooth masonry contrasts with the rough stones of its contemporar-ies. A mural of parishioners eating corn while Jesus looks on graces the exterior.

✖ EATING

✖ West Loop & Greektown

★**LOU MITCHELL'S**   BREAKFAST **$**
Map p310 (☏312-939-3111; www.loumitchellsres taurant.com; 565 W Jackson Blvd; mains $9-14; ⊙5:30am-3pm Mon-Fri, 7am-3pm Sat & Sun; ☝; MBlue Line to Clinton) A relic of Route 66, Lou's brings in elbow-to-elbow locals and

tourists for breakfast. The old-school waitresses deliver fluffy omelets that hang off the plate and thick-cut French toast with a jug of syrup. They call you 'honey' and fill your coffee cup endlessly. There's often a queue to get in, but free doughnut holes and Milk Duds help ease the wait.

PUBLICAN QUALITY MEATS   DELI $

Map p310 (☑312-445-8977; www.publicanqualitymeats.com; 825 W Fulton Market; mains $10-14; ☺8am-6pm Mon-Fri, 9am-6pm Sat, to 5pm Sun; ⓜGreen, Pink Line to Morgan) 🍴 This butcher shop and 32-seat eatery is the casual, cheaper sibling to nearby Publican (p172). Grab a seat at the blocky tables in back and bite into a sandwich of delicately cured meat on just-baked bread. The lineup changes weekly, but might include the beefy meatball sandwich or thick-cut bacon, lettuce and tomato on sourdough. A tidy beer and wine list accompanies the fare.

Before leaving, browse the shelves of locally made condiments and spice mixes; they make great gifts for foodies.

MANNY'S DELI   DELI $

Map p310 (☑312-939-2855; www.mannysdeli.com; 1141 S Jefferson St; mains $11-16; ☺6am-8pm Mon-Sat; ⓜBlue Line to Clinton) Chicago's politicos and seen-it-all senior citizens get in the cafeteria-style line at Manny's for the towering pastrami and corned-beef sandwiches, matzo-ball soup, potato pancakes and other deli staples. Know what you want before you join the fast-moving queue.

The newspaper clippings on the wall provide a dose of city history – or you could just eavesdrop on the table next to you to hear deals being brokered that'll be tomorrow's front-page story.

MELI CAFE   BREAKFAST $

Map p310 (☑312-454-0748; www.melicafe.com; 301 S Halsted St; mains $12-15; ☺6am-3pm; ⓜBlue Line to UIC-Halsted) Meli is the Greek word for 'honey,' and it's apt for this sweet breakfast spot. Skillet dishes made from cage-free eggs (served over a bed of potatoes), goat's cheese and fig omelets, and the decadent French toast (made from challah bread dipped in vanilla-bean custard) start the day off right. Meli has a few outposts around town.

The cafe is also a juice bar, so you can also gulp beverages from wheat-grass shots to banana-maple smoothies.

WISHBONE   AMERICAN $

Map p310 (☑312-850-2663; www.wishbonechicago.com; 1001 W Washington Blvd; mains $10-17; ☺7am-3pm Mon, to 9pm Tue-Thu, to 10pm Fri, 8am-10pm Sat, to 3pm Sun; ⓜGreen, Pink Line to Morgan) They call it 'Southern reconstruction cooking,' which means items such as corn muffins, cheese grits, fried chicken, buttermilk rolls and crawfish patties top the tables. It's a folksy, down-home, gravy-laden kind of place. Wacky chicken and egg artwork splashes across the walls in the cavernous room, which was once a Goodyear Tire garage.

GLAZED AND INFUSED   BAKERY $

Map p310 (☑312-226-5556; www.goglazed.com; 813 W Fulton Market; doughnuts $2-3; ☺7am-2pm Mon-Thu, to 5pm Fri, to 3pm Sat & Sun; ⓜGreen, Pink Line to Morgan) That first bite of the vanilla crème brûlée doughnut, when you crunch into the delicate sugar crust, hooks you. If it's not available, opt for a triple-coconut bismark. Glazed and Infused has popped up in four other neighborhoods besides the West Loop.

MR GREEK GYROS   GREEK $

Map p310 (☑312-906-8731; 234 S Halsted St; mains $6-9; ☺7am-4am; ⓜBlue Line to UIC-Halsted) 'The Mr' is a classic gyros joint. While the fluorescent lighting and plastic decor may lack charm, the gyros have a beauty of their own. Carnivores: this is definitely your place in the 'hood for late-night eats, as the UIC students, club goers and occasional bum will attest.

★LITTLE GOAT   DINER $$

Map p310 (☑312-888-3455; www.littlegoatchicago.com; 820 W Randolph St; mains $10-19; ☺7am-10pm Sun-Thu, to midnight Fri & Sat; 🛜☑; ⓜGreen, Pink Line to Morgan) *Top Chef* winner Stephanie Izard opened this diner for the foodie masses across the street from her ever-booked main restaurant, Girl and the Goat. Scooch into a vintage booth and order off the all-day breakfast menu. Better yet, try lunch and dinner favorites such as the goat sloppy joe with rosemary slaw or the pork belly on scallion pancakes. Izard's flavor combinations rule.

Heavenly smelling bread baked on-site and bottomless cups of strong coffee add to the awesomeness. It's wise to reserve ahead.

Near West Side & Pilsen – Pilsen Murals

Murals are a traditional Mexican art form, and they're splashed all over Pilsen's buildings. They're on schools, on churches, on storefronts, on the El stations. Whatever the image – a sun, the Virgin of Guadalupe, Che Guevara, abstract gauchos or beady-eyed skeletons – count on it being wildly colorful.

1. Pilsen neighborhood (p166)
Color-popping murals dot this neighborhood, the center of Chicago's Mexican community.

2. Increibles las Cosas que Se Ven mural
Jeff Zimmermann's vivid 1999 mural is located at W 19th St and S Ashland Ave.

3. Spectacular street art
Get inspired by outdoor art, such as the dramatic owl mural by Brooks Blair Golden on W 16th St.

INCREIBLES
LAS COSAS QUE
SE VEN

Local Life
West Loop Wander

The West Loop has exploded in the last few years with hot-chef restaurants and condos carved from old meatpacking warehouses. Meat is still the main biz around here, and you're guaranteed to see at least one bloody-apron-clad worker as you traverse the galleries, shops and mega-stylish eateries.

❶ Cool Cat Gallery
Pop-art-filled Mars Gallery (p165) is pure fun, from the plaid-tie-wearing cat who roams the premises (he's the assistant manager, according to the sign) to the building's offbeat history (it was an egg factory, then a club where the Ramones played). Weird bonus: it sits atop an energy vortex.

❷ Meat Treat
Neighborhood dwellers come to Publican Quality Meats (p167) for its supply of smoked chorizo and maple breakfast sausage. Then they pull up a chair in the small restaurant in the back and linger over beer and artisanal sandwiches. In summer, the crowd spills out to street-side tables.

❸ Do-Good Books
Thrifty hipsters in need of a good read browse the gently used stacks at Open Books (p175). Hours slip by as they scan shelves that hold *Little House on the Prairie*

next to Gwyneth Paltrow's latest cookbook next to a 1987 guidebook to Alaska. All proceeds go toward the nonprofit shop's literacy programs for local kids.

❹ Historic Suds
Haymarket Pub & Brewery (p174) provides a nice dose of local history. It's located near where the 1886 labor riot took place in Haymarket Sq, and the brewery's suds have affiliated names, such as the Mathias Imperial IPA (named after the first police officer to die in the melee) and the Speakerswagon Pilsner.

❺ Grocery Grazing
West Loopers shop for their groceries at multilevel **Mariano's** (Map p310; ☑312-243-7657; www.marianos.com; 40 S Halsted St; ☉6am-10pm; Ⓜ Blue Line to UIC-Halsted). You can almost make a meal from all the free samples: a handful of pita chips here, a little slice of pizza in the next aisle. Pick up some-

Haymarket Memorial *sculpture by Mary Brogger, in Haymarket Square (p165)*

thing cool to drink or a gelato at the cafe to take for a picnic in the park.

❻ Park Stroll

The neighborhood's stroller-pushing families and dog-walking hipsters get their exercise in **Mary Bartelme Park** (Map p310; 115 S Sangamon St; Ⓜ Blue Line to UIC-Halsted). Five off-kilter stainless-steel arches form the gateway in; kids play in the mist that the sculptures release in summer. Grassy mounds dot the park and provide good lookout points to view the Willis Tower rising in the distance.

❼ Greek Delights

Chicago's small but busy Greektown centers on Halsted St. Residents head to **Artopolis Bakery & Cafe** (Map p310; ☎312-559-9000; www.artopolischi cago.com; 306 S Halsted St; mains $10-17; ⏱9am-midnight Mon-Thu, to 1am Fri & Sat, 10am-11pm Sun; Ⓜ Blue Line to UIC-Halsted) for classics such as baklava and spinach-and-feta pies. The cafe-bar opens onto the street, with wine-laden tables along the front.

SAINT LOU'S ASSEMBLY   CAFETERIA $$

Map p310 (☎312-600-0600; www.saintlouschi cago.com; 644 W Lake St; mains $15-25; ⏱11am-10pm; Ⓜ Green, Pink Line to Clinton) Lou's pays homage to the area's meatpacking past, when 'meat and three' cafeterias – where you'd select a meaty main dish and three sides – were popular. This is the modern version, so take a seat in a retro blue-vinyl booth and choose among meatloaf Wellington, slow-roasted duck, barbecue cauliflower, watermelon salad and other modern takes on nostalgic fare.

Cocktails, such as lavender gin lemonade, and craft beers accompany the wares. The back patio and its bocce ball court see action year-round.

DUCK DUCK GOAT   CHINESE $$

Map p310 (☎312-902-3825; www.duckduck goatchicago.com; 857 W Fulton Market; mains $17-27; ⏱4:30-11pm Sun-Thu, to midnight Fri & Sat; Ⓜ Green, Pink Line to Morgan) Star local chef Stephanie Izard recently opened her third West Loop hot spot, this one focusing on Chinese-inspired dishes. The vast menu sprawls across dim sums, soups, fried rice and main dishes. The thick, doughy, house-made noodles and Peking duck win raves. Eclectic cocktails such as the Shaoxing Redemption, made with mushroom-infused whiskey, add to the remarkable flavors.

Each of the five rooms has a different East-meets-West vibe, including family-style round tables and patterned wallpaper in one, and rich hues of red and sexy banquettes in another.

AVEC   MEDITERRANEAN $$

Map p310 (☎312-377-2002; www.avecrestau rant.com; 615 W Randolph St; mains $18-26; ⏱11:30am-2pm & 3:30pm-midnight Mon-Fri, 3:30pm-1am Sat, 10am-2pm & 3:30pm-midnight Sun; Ⓜ Green, Pink Line to Clinton) Feeling social? This happening spot gives diners a chance to rub elbows at eight-person communal tables. The mini room looks a heck of a lot like a Finnish sauna and fills with noisy chatter as stylish urbanites pile in. The bacon-wrapped dates are the menu's must. The squid-ink pasta and *salumi* plates beg for your fork, as well. No reservations.

PARTHENON   GREEK $$

Map p310 (☎312-726-2407; www.theparthenon. com; 314 S Halsted St; mains $14-25; ⏱11am-11pm; 🔖; Ⓜ Blue Line to UIC-Halsted) The Parthenon has anchored Greektown since 1968, hearing countless yells of *'opa'* to accompany the flaming *saganaki* (fried cheese), a dish that the restaurant supposedly invented. Greeks returning to the city from their suburban retreats have made the Parthenon a favorite. Vegetarians and gluten-free eaters will find lots of options. A plus for drivers: there's free valet service.

GIRL AND THE GOAT　　MODERN AMERICAN $$$
Map p310 (☎312-492-6262; www.girlandthegoat. com; 809 W Randolph St; small plates $9-16; ☺4:30-11pm Sun-Thu, to midnight Fri & Sat; ☑; Ⓜ Green, Pink Line to Morgan) ✿ Stephanie Izard's flagship restaurant rocks. The soaring ceilings, polished wood tables, and cartoony art on the walls offer a convivial atmosphere where local beer and housemade wine hit the tables, along with unique small plates such as scallops with brown butter kimchi. Reservations are difficult; try for walk-in seats before 5pm or see if anything opens up at the bar.

Goat dishes figure prominently, of course; Izard buys her signature meat from a local farm.

NEXT　　INTERNATIONAL $$$
Map p310 (☎312-226-0858; www.nextrestaurant. com; 953 W Fulton Market; multicourse menu from $125; ☺5:30-9:30pm Wed-Sun; Ⓜ Green, Pink Line to Morgan) Grant Achatz' West Loop restaurant remains one of the hottest tickets in town. And we mean it literally – you need a ticket to dine at Next, which operates like a time machine. It started by serving an eight-course French meal from 1906 Paris, but every three months the whole thing changes: new era, new country, new menu, new decor.

Sign up for tickets at the website as early as possible. Prices vary by date, time and menu (early weekdays cost less than primetime weekends), and you pay when you book. Check the Facebook feed for possible last-minute seats.

BLACKBIRD　　MODERN AMERICAN $$$
Map p310 (☎312-715-0708; www.blackbirdres taurant.com; 619 W Randolph St; mains $32-42; ☺11:30am-2pm & 5-10pm Mon-Thu, 11:30am-2pm & 5-11pm Fri, 5-11pm Sat, 5-10pm Sun; Ⓜ Green, Pink Line to Clinton) ✿ This buzzy dining destination for Chicago's young and trendy perches atop best-of lists for its exciting, notably seasonal menu. The warm-ups – such as the cauliflower soup and poached lobster with black truffles – are a perfect

introduction to the visionary mains, which pair well with the short, careful wine list. The best comes last: award-winning desserts à la coffee mascarpone and candied hazelnut crepes.

The chef offers a tasting menu (eight to 10 courses) from $115, and there's a three-course prix-fixe lunch for $25.

**GRAHAM ELLIOT
BISTRO**　　MODERN AMERICAN $$$
Map p310 (☎312-888-2258; www.gebistro.com; 841 W Randolph St; small plates $15-25; ☺5-10pm Tue-Thu, to 11pm Fri & Sat; Ⓜ Green, Pink Line to Morgan) The celebrity cook, known for his appearances on TV's *MasterChef* series, serves around 25 shareable dishes at his West Loop restaurant. They're playful creations, such as filet mignon stroganoff with toasted spaetzle and butter-dipped radishes with wildflower honey. The small, narrow room bustles with servers, loud rock music and sizzles from the open kitchen. A fine patio sprawls out back.

PUBLICAN　　AMERICAN $$$
Map p310 (☎312-733-9555; www.thepublicanres taurant.com; 837 W Fulton Market; mains $19-29; ☺3:30-10:30pm Mon-Thu, to 11:30pm Fri, 10am-11:30pm Sat, 9am-10pm Sun; Ⓜ Green, Pink Line to Morgan) ✿ Set up like a swanky beer hall with urbanites young and old sitting across from each other at long communal tables, Publican specializes in oysters, hams and fine suds – all from small family farms and microbrewers. So you'll know your pork shoulder is from Dyersville, Iowa; your orange-honey turnips from Congerville, Illinois; and your oysters from Bagaduce River, Maine.

Many locals think the weekend brunch is the best around – Publican does indeed know its bacon.

✕ Little Italy

★ SWEET MAPLE CAFE　　AMERICAN $
Map p310 (☎312-243-8908; www.sweetmaple cafe.com; 1339 W Taylor St; mains $9-13; ☺7am-2pm; Ⓜ Blue Line to Racine) The creaking floorboards, matronly staff and soulful home cookin' lend the Sweet Maple Cafe the bucolic appeal of a Southern roadside diner. The signature dishes – inch-thick banana (or, seasonally, peaches and cream) pancakes, cheddar grits and fluffy biscuits that

come smothered in spicy sausage gravy – earn the superlatives of locals.

The egg dishes, sturdy muffins and lunch sandwiches are done with equal aplomb.

AL'S #1 ITALIAN BEEF   SANDWICHES $

Map p310 (☎312-226-4017; www.alsbeef.com; 1079 W Taylor St; mains $6-10; ☺9am-11pm Mon-Thu, to midnight Fri, 10am-midnight Sat; ⓂBlue Line to Racine) Piled high with savory beef that soaks through the thick bun, Al's inexpensive sandwich is one of Chicago's culinary hallmarks. This is the original location of the local chain, which has now spread beyond the city. It might not be the place to grab lunch if you want to get off your feet – there are no tables, only a stand-up counter.

MARIO'S   DESSERTS $

Map p310 (1068 W Taylor St; items $2-4; ☺10am-midnight May-Sep; ☎; ⓂBlue Line to Racine) At this cheerful box of a shop, super Italian ice comes loaded with big chunks of fresh fruit, which keeps crowds coming in the summer. The owners have been serving the slushy goodness for a half-century. Lemon tops the list.

TUFANO'S VERNON PARK TAP   ITALIAN $$

Map p310 (☎312-733-3393; www.tufanosrestaurant.com; 1073 W Vernon Park Pl; mains $11-22; ☺11am-10pm Tue-Thu, to 11pm Fri, 4-11pm Sat, 3-9pm Sun; ⓂBlue Line to UIC-Halsted) Still family-run after three generations, Tufano's serves old-fashioned, hearty Italian fare for modest prices. The blackboards carry a long list of daily specials, which can include such wonderful items as pasta with garlic-crusted broccoli. Amid the usual celebrity photos on the wall you'll see some really nice shots of Joey DiBuono, his family and their patrons through the decades. Cash only.

CHEZ JOEL   FRENCH $$$

Map p310 (☎312-226-6479; www.chezjoelbistro.com; 1119 W Taylor St; mains $21-28; ☺11am-10pm Tue-Thu, to 11pm Fri & Sat, 3-10pm Sun; ⓂBlue Line to Racine) Whether you're dining outside under the big oak tree or tucked in a cozy corner inside, the atmosphere and exceptional French fare make Chez Joel a romantic favorite, though an odd duck among this predominantly Italian stretch of Taylor St. The menu is anchored by bistro favorites such as duck leg confit and coq au vin, complemented by an extensive wine list.

ROSEBUD   ITALIAN $$$

Map p310 (☎312-942-1117; www.rosebudrestaurants.com; 1500 W Taylor St; mains $24-36; ☺11am-10:30pm Mon-Thu, to 11:30pm Fri, noon-11:30pm Sat, to 10pm Sun; ⓂPink Line to Polk) This location in Little Italy is the first branch of an empire of quality Italian restaurants that has spread throughout the city. It is popular with politicos and old-school Taylor St Italians, who slurp down colossal piles of pasta and spinach gnocchi soaked in red sauces. Bring a big appetite.

✖ Pilsen

PLEASANT HOUSE   PUB FOOD $

Map p310 (☎773-523-7437; www.facebook.com/pleasanthousepub; 2119 S Halsted St; mains $8-10; ☺10am-10pm Tue & Wed, to midnight Thu-Sat, to 10pm Sun; ☎; ▣8) Follow your nose to Pleasant House, which bakes tall, fluffy, savory pies. Daily flavors include chicken and chutney, steak and ale, or kale and mushroom, made with produce the chefs grow themselves. The pub also serves its own beers (brewed off-site) to accompany the food. Fridays are a good day to visit, when there is a fish fry.

DON PEDRO CARNITAS   MEXICAN $

Map p310 (1113 W 18th St; tacos $1.50-2; ☺6am-6pm Mon-Fri, 5am-5pm Sat, to 3pm Sun; ⓂPink Line to 18th) At this no-frills meat den, a man with a machete salutes you at the front counter. He awaits your command to hack off pork pieces, then wraps the thick chunks with onion and cilantro in a fresh tortilla. You then devour the taco at the tables in back. Goat stew and tripe add to the carnivorous menu. Cash only.

Lines twist out the door on weekends.

CAFE JUMPING BEAN   CAFE $

Map p310 (☎312-455-0019; 1439 W 18th St; mains $5-9; ☺6am-9pm Mon-Fri, 7am-7:30pm Sat & Sun; ☎; ⓂPink Line to 18th St) This ramshackle cafe will make you feel like a regular as soon as you step through the door. It serves excellent hot focaccia sandwiches, baked goods and strong coffee to the 20- and 30-something crowd of local bohemians. Chess and domino games are always breaking out.

The comfy confines make it an excellent spot for whiling away a couple of hours with a mocha, soaking up Pilsen's colorful surrounds.

HONKY TONK BBQ
BARBECUE **$$**

Map p310 (☎312-226-7427; www.honkytonk bbqchicago.com; 1800 S Racine Ave; mains $9-18; ⊙4-11pm Tue-Sun; Ⓜ Pink Line to 18th St) Art-colored walls and a swell beer and wine list separate Honky Tonk from its Chicago barbecue brethren. It's a fun atmosphere, with live rockabilly and blues music some nights and imaginative, changing side dishes such as candied bacon and empanadas with shiitake mushrooms. That's all gravy, though, for the signature wood-roasted pork, beef and chicken.

DUSEK'S
MODERN AMERICAN **$$$**

Map p310 (☎312-526-3851; www.dusekschicago. com; 1227 W 18th St; mains $22-30; ⊙11am-1am Mon-Fri, 9am-1am Sat & Sun; Ⓜ Pink Line to 18th St) Pilsen's hipsters gather under the pressed-tin ceiling of this gastropub to fork into the ever-changing menu of beer-inspired dishes, say beer-battered soft-shell crab or dark-lager-roasted duck. The eatery shares its historic building (modeled on Prague's opera house) with an indie-band concert hall and basement cocktail bar.

🍺 DRINKING & 🍸 NIGHTLIFE

🍷 West Loop

★RM CHAMPAGNE SALON
BAR

Map p310 (☎312-243-1199; www.rmchampag nesalon.com; 116 N Green St; ⊙5pm-midnight Sun-Wed, to 2am Thu-Sat; Ⓜ Green, Pink Line to Morgan) This West Loop spot is a twinkling-light charmer for bubbles. Score a table in the cobblestoned courtyard and you'll feel transported to Paris.

GOOSE ISLAND BREWERY
BREWERY

Map p310 (www.gooseisland.com; 1800 W Fulton St; ⊙2-8pm Thu & Fri, noon-6pm Sat & Sun; Ⓜ Green, Pink Line to Ashland) Goose Island – Chicago's first craft brewer, launched in 1988 – is now owned by Anheuser-Busch InBev, so technically it's no longer a craft brewer. But it still acts like one, making excellent small-batch beers at this facility. The swanky mod-industrial tap room pours eight varieties; bring your own food to accompany them. Forty-five-minute tours ($12) are available if you reserve in advance.

CRUZ BLANCA
MICROBREWERY

Map p310 (☎312-733-1975; www.rickbayless. com; 904 W Randolph St; ⊙11am-11pm Tue-Thu, to midnight Fri & Sat, to 9pm Sun; Ⓜ Green, Pink Line to Morgan) Revered chef Rick Bayless recently opened this quirky West Loop brewery inspired by beers people were drinking in Mexico City in the 1860s. Quaff fanciful renditions of German pilsners, Vienna lagers, wheat beers and French-style Bieres de Garde. There are six house brews, six guest brews, and wine, as well as a small menu of foodie tacos.

Next door is Bayless' new restaurant Lena Brava, serving Baja-style grilled seafood.

HAYMARKET PUB & BREWERY
BREWERY

Map p310 (☎312-638-0700; www.haymarket brewing.com; 737 W Randolph St; ⊙11am-2am Sun-Fri, to 3am Sat; Ⓜ Green, Pink Line to Clinton) Fresh-from-the-tank beers and a good craft selection flow from the 24 taps at cavernous, barrel-strewn Haymarket. That's all fine and delicious, but the brewery then goes a step beyond to please hop-heads by hosting the Drinking and Writing Theater on-site. That's right: a troupe devoted entirely to exploring 'the connection between creativity and alcohol.' Check the website for the schedule.

Bands sometimes play on the weekends, and there's a monthly story slam. The brewery sits near Haymarket Sq, the historic labor riot site, hence the name.

AVIARY
COCKTAIL BAR

Map p310 (www.theaviary.com; 955 W Fulton Market; ⊙5pm-midnight Sun-Wed, to 2am Thu-Sat; Ⓜ Green, Pink Line to Morgan) The Aviary is a James Beard Award winner for best cocktails in the nation. The ethereal drinks are like nothing you've laid lips on before. Some arrive with Bunsen burners, others with a slingshot you use to break the ice. They taste terrific, whatever the science involved. It's wise to make reservations online. Drinks cost around $25 each.

The man behind the booze is Grant Achatz. Aviary sits beside his hot restaurant Next (p172), though the bar is more in spirit (pun!) with his Lincoln Park restaurant, Alinea (p103).

CITY WINERY
WINE BAR

Map p310 (☎312-733-9463; www.citywinery.com; 1200 W Randolph St; ⊙11am-midnight; Ⓜ Green, Pink Line to Morgan) City Winery pours on the grape theme, with casks and tanks of wine everywhere you look. It's very Sonoma decor-wise, with a vine-strewn, open-air patio and exposed blond brick in the airy interior rooms. The menu sprawls through 400 reds and whites, including several house-made vintages that are on tap. Can't decide? Try a flight.

The winery also has a small theater that books well-known singer-songwriter types.

BEER BISTRO BAR

Map p310 (✆312-433-0013; www.thebeerbistro. com; 1061 W Madison St; ⊙11am-2am Sun-Fri, to 3am Sat; ☐19 or 20) This bar near United Center fills with Bulls and Blackhawks fans, and it even runs a shuttle to the arena on game days. Ninety global beers (most in bottles) comprise the swill, and TVs flashing the requisite games circle the big room.

JOHNNY'S ICE HOUSE EAST SPORTS BAR

Map p310 (✆312-226-5555; www.johnnysice house.com; 1350 W Madison St; ⊙8pm-midnight; MGreen, Pink Line to Ashland) Johnny's is an ice rink, which explains why you can practically see your breath in the attached bar. The wood-paneled, neon-lit room is prime for watching Blackhawks games and knocking back Labatt's (Johnny's is supposedly the state's biggest seller of the beer). Hours can be erratic.

At Johnny's other ice house, further west at 2550 W Madison St, you can see the Blackhawks in person: they practice at the facility and it's open for free public viewing. Check the Hawks' website for the schedule.

Pilsen

SKYLARK BAR

Map p310 (✆312-948-5275; www.skylarkchicago. com; 2149 S Halsted St; ⊙4pm-2am; ☎; ☐8) The Skylark is a bastion for artsy drunkards, who slouch into big booths sipping on strong drinks and eyeing the long room. They play pinball, snap pics in the photo booth and scarf down the kitchen's awesome tater tots. It's a good stop after the Pilsen gallery hop. Cash only.

LA CATRINA CAFE CAFE

Map p310 (✆312-473-0038; www.lacatrinacafe. com; 1011 W 18th St; ⊙7am-9pm Mon-Thu, 8am-6pm Fri-Sun; ☎; MPink Line to 18th St) Activists, artists and students congregate here for the roomy window seats, bottomless cups

of coffee and funky art exhibitions. It's a come-one come-all kind of spot, prime for a Mexican hot chocolate and Frida Kahlo–face cookie. A colorful mural marks the entrance.

SIMONE'S BAR

Map p310 (✆312-666-8601; www.simonesbar. com; 960 W 18th St; ⊙11:30am-2am; ☎; MPink Line to 18th) A distinct neighborhood hot spot, Simone's packs in the young and beautiful from around Pilsen. Recycled and found materials comprise the cool decor inside; a large patio beckons outside. Bartenders shake up delicious cocktails, and the kitchen cooks well-priced worldly comfort foods.

ENTERTAINMENT

THALIA HALL LIVE MUSIC

Map p310 (✆312-526-3851; www.thaliahallchi cago.com; 1807 S Allport St; MPink Line to 18th St) This venue hosts a cool-cat slate of rock, alt-country, jazz and metal in an ornate 1892 hall patterned after Prague's opera house. A great gastropub on the 1st floor and cocktail bar in the basement invite lingering before and after shows.

UIC PAVILION CONCERT VENUE

Map p310 (✆312-413-5700; www.uicpavilion. com; 525 S Racine Ave; MBlue Line to Racine) This venue at the University of Illinois at Chicago (UIC) is used mostly for concerts and small-scale sporting events.

🛍 SHOPPING

★**MODERN COOPERATIVE** VINTAGE

Map p310 (✆312-226-8525; www.moderncoop erative.com; 1215 W 18th St; ⊙11am-7pm Wed-Fri, to 6pm Sat & Sun; MPink Line to 18th St) ModCo carries a terrific selection of mid-century modern furniture from the 1960s and '70s, as well as artworks, jewelry, pillows and bags from current local designers. It is located inside Pilsen's historic Thalia Hall building. The shop has another outpost in Hyde Park.

OPEN BOOKS BOOKS

Map p310 (✆312-475-1355; www.open-books. org; 651 W Lake St; ⊙9am-7pm Mon-Sat, noon-6pm Sun; ♿; MGreen, Pink Line to Clinton) Buy

LOCAL KNOWLEDGE

NEAR WEST SIDE MARKETS

The neighborhood hosts a couple of stellar bazaars. They're a study in contrasts.

Maxwell Street Market (Map p310; www.maxwellstreetmarket.us; 800 S Desplaines St; ☺7am-3pm Sun; Ⓜ Blue Line to Clinton) is the working man's place. Starting early in the morning, hundreds of vendors set up outdoor stalls that sell everything from Jesus statues to 10 packs of tube socks to power tools. The market draws thrifty foodies who come for the homemade churros, tamales and other Mexican noshes, but mostly it draws folks seeking cheap clothing, electronics and junk galore.

Don't be fooled by the name: the market is not on Maxwell St, though it was for decades until gentrification forced it onward. It now stretches along Desplaines St between Harrison St and Roosevelt Rd. The city runs the market and adds to the festivities with free fitness classes and the occasional band or dance group.

Randolph Street Market (Map p310; www.randolphstreetmarket.com; 1340 W Washington Blvd; $10; ☺10am-5pm Sat, to 4pm Sun, last weekend of the month Feb-Dec; Ⓜ Green, Pink Line to Ashland) is styled on London's Portobello Market and is nicknamed 'the Barneys of Vintage.' The monthly market sprawls indoors and out and has an entrance fee. Hip shoppers make a day of it, trawling the antiques and vinyl swap. Then they settle in with a snack and glass of vino to hear the live bands.

Much of the action takes place inside the beaux-arts Plumbers Hall, where more than 200 sellers hock collectibles, costume jewelry, furniture, books, Turkish rugs and pinball machines. One of the coolest facets is the Indie Designer Market, where fledgling designers sell their one-of-a-kind skirts, shawls, handbags and other pieces. A free trolley picks up patrons downtown by the Water Works Pumping Station hourly. You can save a few bucks if you buy your admission ticket online.

a used book here and you're helping to fund this volunteer-based literacy group's programs, which range from in-school reading help for grade-schoolers to book-publishing courses for teens. The jam-packed store has good-quality tomes and plenty of cushy sofas where you can sit and peruse your finds. Kids will find lots of imaginative wares. Books average around $5.

KNEE DEEP VINTAGE VINTAGE
Map p310 (☏312-850-2510; www.kneedeepvintage.com; 1425 W 18th St; ☺noon-7pm Mon-Thu, 11am-8pm Fri & Sat, noon-6pm Sun; Ⓜ Pink Line to 18th St) Knee Deep offers a trove of vintage clothing (for men and women), housewares and vinyl. There's a sale the second Friday of every month, with items slashed 25% to 50%; it's held in conjunction with the local gallery hop, starting at 6pm.

BLOMMER CHOCOLATE STORE FOOD
(☏312-492-1336; 600 W Kinzie St; ☺9am-5pm Mon-Fri, to 1pm Sat; Ⓜ Blue Line to Grand) Often in the Loop, a smell wafts through that's so enticing you'd almost shoot your own mother in the kneecaps to get to it. It comes from Blommer Chocolate Factory, which provides the sweet stuff to big-time manufacturers such as Fannie May and Nabisco. Luckily,

the wee attached store sells a line of Blommer's own goodies straight to consumers.

The dark-chocolate-covered almonds reign supreme, and there's a sweet selection of retro candies such as Zots, Pop Rocks and Zagnut bars.

ATHENIAN CANDLE CO ARTS & CRAFTS
Map p310 (☏312-332-6988; www.atheniancandle.com; 300 S Halsted St; ☺9:30am-6pm Mon, Tue, Thu & Fri, to 5pm Sat; Ⓜ Blue Line to UIC/Halsted) Whether you're hoping to get lucky at bingo, remove a jinx or fall in love, this Greektown store promises to help with its array of candles, incense, love potions and miracle oils. Though it has been making candles for Orthodox churches on-site since 1919, the owners aren't devoted to one religion: you'll find Buddha statues, Pope holograms, Turkish evil-eye stones and tarot cards.

GROOVE DISTRIBUTION MUSIC
Map p310 (☏312-997-2375; www.groovedis.com; 346 N Justine St; ☺noon-7pm Tue-Fri; Ⓜ Green, Pink Line to Ashland) Whenever you're at a club, dancing to the beat, Groove is likely the source of the music. The company provides record stores around the world with down-tempo, mash-ups, dubstep, nu jazz,

cosmic disco and lots of that Chicago specialty – house – both on vinyl and CD. You can shop right in the warehouse, which is exactly what discerning DJs do.

WORKING BIKES COOPERATIVE
SPORTS & OUTDOORS

(☎773-847-5440; www.workingbikes.org; 2434 S Western Ave; ☺noon-7pm Wed & Thu, to 5pm Fri-Sun; ⓜPink Line to Western) This nonprofit group trawls local landfills and scrap yards for junked bikes, then brings them back to its warehouse and refurbishes them. Half get sold in the storefront shop; proceeds enable the group to ship the rest to developing countries. It's a great deal – you'll get a sturdy, well-oiled machine for a bargain price (around $200) compared to regular bike shops.

SPORTS & ACTIVITIES

PILSEN MURAL TOURS
WALKING

(☎773-342-4191; 1½hr tour per group $125) Murals are a traditional Mexican art form, and they're splashed all over Pilsen's buildings.

Local artists and activists lead these highly recommended tours that take in the neighborhood's most impressive works. Call to arrange an excursion.

CHICAGO BLACKHAWKS
HOCKEY

Map p310 (☎312-455-7000; www.blackhawks. nhl.com; 1901 W Madison St; ☐19 or 20) The Hawks skate at United Center. Tickets have become difficult to get, with lots of sellouts since the team's recent Stanley Cup wins (in 2010, 2013 and 2015). Be sure to arrive in time for the national anthem at the game's start. The raucous, ear-splitting rendition is a tradition. Express bus number 19 plies Madison St on game days.

CHICAGO BULLS
BASKETBALL

Map p310 (☎312-455-4000; www.nba.com/ bulls; 1901 W Madison St; ☐19 or 20) They may not be the mythical champions of yore, but the Bulls still draw good crowds at their United Center home base. Tickets are available through the United Center box office – located at Gate 4 on the building's east side – and at Ticketmaster outlets. On game days, there's a special express bus (number 19) on Madison St that heads to the stadium.

South Loop & Near South Side

SOUTH LOOP | NEAR SOUTH SIDE | CHINATOWN

Neighborhood Top Five

1 Field Museum (p180) Sizing up Sue the T-rex, the towering totem poles and magnificent mummies at this museum of natural history, one of the world's foremost scientific research institutions.

2 Northerly Island (p181) Walking or cycling around the wild, grassy island and

checking out the animal life en route.

3 Adler Planetarium (p181) Viewing the stars and learning about asteroids inside, then taking in brilliant city skyline vistas outside.

4 Chinatown (p185) Nibbling chestnut cakes and almond cookies in the

bakeries, and shopping for trinkets and unusual food items in the shops.

5 Buddy Guy's Legends (p188) Hearing the best blues musicians in the biz bend frets.

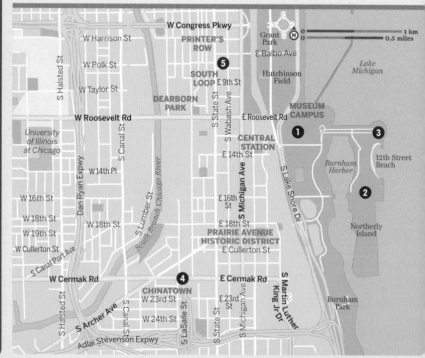

For more detail of this area see Map p314 ➡

Explore South Loop & Near South Side

What you'll see when you come to the South Loop – and come you will, as this is where the Field Museum, the Shedd Aquarium and Adler Planetarium sit side by side on the lakeshore – is a whole lot of shiny newness. The neighborhood went development crazy in recent years with high-rise condos and Columbia College's expansion, so it's also home to loads of young urbanites. The Museum Campus itself is lovely, jutting out into the blue-green lake and providing breezy skyline views. Tranquil 12th St Beach and Northerly Island, a prairie-grassed nature park, offer escapes if the crowds get to be too much.

Blues fans will want to make the pilgrimage further south to the old Chess Records site, a humble building where Muddy Waters and Howlin' Wolf plugged in their amps. History buffs will appreciate mansion-filled Prairie Ave between 16th and 20th Sts. The area around Chess, which abuts the massive McCormick Place convention center, is slated to develop into an entertainment district with restaurants and music venues. Keep an eye on this space.

To top off the wealth of offerings, the neighborhood is also home to Chicago's small but busy Chinatown, where pork buns, steaming bowls of noodles and imported wares reward an afternoon of exploring.

Local Life

→ **Global dance party** Learn to salsa, rumba or tango with Chicagoans from all over the city at SummerDance (p188).

→ **Chinatown Square** The plaza and mall are at their wonderful noisiest on weekends, when neighborhood families swarm in to eat and shop.

→ **Blues heaven** Locals stop by Willie Dixon's Blues Heaven (p184) to see who's plugging in for the free Thursday-night concerts.

Getting There & Away

→ **Bus** Numbers 130 (in summer) and 146 (year-round) go to the Museum Campus. Number 1 goes to Prairie Ave's historic homes.

→ **El** Red Line to Harrison and Red, Orange, Green Line to Roosevelt for South Loop. Red Line to Cermak-Chinatown for Chinatown. Green Line to Cermak-McCormick Pl for McCormick Place.

→ **Car** The Museum Campus boasts plenty of lot parking (from $19 per car on nonevent days). Meter parking is scarce in South Loop, but readily available in Near South Side.

Lonely Planet's Top Tip

In summer it's a good idea to buy advance tickets for the Shedd Aquarium, the most popular of the Museum Campus attractions. It's less necessary for the Field Museum unless there's an all-the-rage exhibit going on. For the Adler Planetarium and for the Shedd and Field in winter, there's no need for e-tickets. Save yourself the service charges.

 Best Places to Eat

→ Mercat a la Planxa (p187)
→ Flo & Santos (p186)
→ Yolk (p186)
→ Lou Malnati's (p186)
→ Sweet Station (p187)

For reviews, see p186 ➡

Best Places to Drink

→ Spoke & Bird (p187)
→ Vice District Brewing (p188)
→ Kasey's Tavern (p188)

For reviews, see p187 ➡

Best Places to Shop

→ Sandmeyer's Bookstore (p189)
→ ShopColumbia (p189)
→ Giftland (p189)

For reviews, see p189 ➡

 SOUTH LOOP & NEAR SOUTH SIDE

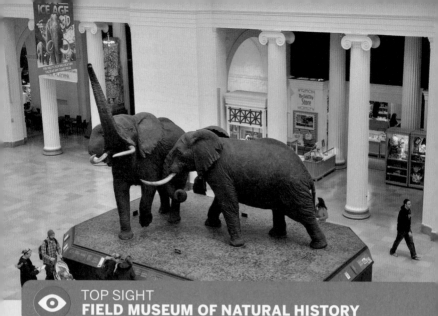

⊙ TOP SIGHT
FIELD MUSEUM OF NATURAL HISTORY

The mammoth Field Museum houses everything but the kitchen sink. The collection's rock star is Sue, the largest *Tyrannosaurus rex* yet discovered. She's 13ft tall, 41ft long, and she menaces the main floor with ferocious aplomb. The galleries beyond hold 20 million other artifacts, tended by a slew of PhD-wielding scientists, as the Field remains an active research institution.

After communing with Sue, dino lovers should head up to the 'Evolving Planet' exhibit on the 2nd floor, which has more of the big guys and gals. You can learn about the evolution of the species and watch staff paleontologists clean up fossils in the lab. There's even a mask that lets you see the world through a trilobite's eyes.

'Inside Ancient Egypt' is another good exhibit that recreates an Egyptian burial chamber on two levels. The mastaba (tomb) contains 23 actual mummies and is a reconstruction of the one built for Unis-ankh, the son of the last pharaoh of the Fifth dynasty, who died at age 21 in 2407 BC. The relic-strewn bottom level is especially worthwhile.

Other displays that merit your time include the Hall of Gems and its glittering garnets, opals, pearls and deep-blue tanzanite stones (1000 times rarer than diamonds, which you'll also see plenty of). The Northwest Coast and Arctic Peoples totem-pole collection got its start with artifacts shipped to Chicago for the 1893 World's Expo. And the largest man-eating lion ever caught is stuffed and standing sentry on the basement floor. Preserved insects and birds, and Bushman, the cantankerous ape who drew crowds at Lincoln Park Zoo for decades, are also on display in all their taxidermic glory.

Ask for the 'Basic' admission to see everything mentioned here. The 'All Access' and 'Discovery' admission tickets include extras such as the 3-D movie and special exhibits, which can be too much if you're doing lots of sightseeing.

DON'T MISS

➡ Sue the T-rex
➡ Hall of Gems
➡ Totem poles
➡ Mummies
➡ Man-eating lions of Tsavo

PRACTICALITIES

➡ Map p314
➡ ☎312-922-9410
➡ www.fieldmuseum.org
➡ 1400 S Lake Shore Dr
➡ adult/child $18/13
➡ ⊙9am-5pm
➡ 👶
➡ 🚌146, 130

◉ SIGHTS

◉ South Loop

FIELD MUSEUM OF
NATURAL HISTORY   MUSEUM
See p180.

SHEDD AQUARIUM   AQUARIUM
Map p314 (📞312-939-2438; www.sheddaquari
um.org; 1200 S Lake Shore Dr; adult/child $31/22;
⊙9am-6pm Jun-Aug, 9am-5pm Mon-Fri, to 6pm
Sat & Sun Sep-May; 🚇; 🚌146, 130) Top draws
at the kiddie-mobbed Shedd Aquarium include the Wild Reef exhibit, where there's
just 5in of Plexiglas between you and two-
dozen fierce-looking sharks, and the Oceanarium, with its rescued sea otters. Note the
Oceanarium also keeps beluga whales and
Pacific white-sided dolphins, a practice that
has become increasingly controversial in
recent years.

The Shedd Pass includes all of the
aforementioned exhibits. There is also a
little-advertised option to buy a 'general
admission' ticket for $8 ($6 for children).
This allows you to see the basic tanks of
fish, turtles and eels, but no sharks, sea otters or other more exotic creatures.

Lines can be very long at the Shedd, especially in summer. Tickets purchased in
advance online provide faster, priority entry, but they cost more (adult/child $40/31).

ADLER PLANETARIUM   MUSEUM
Map p314 (📞312-922-7827; www.adlerplanetari
um.org; 1300 S Lake Shore Dr; adult/child $12/8;
⊙9:30am-4pm Mon-Fri, to 4:30 Sat & Sun; 🚇;
🚌146, 130) Space enthusiasts will get a big
bang (pun!) out of the Adler. There are public telescopes to view the stars, 3-D lectures
to learn about supernovas, and the Planet
Explorers exhibit where kids can 'launch'
a rocket. The immersive digital films cost
extra (from $13 per ticket). The Adler's front
steps offer Chicago's best skyline view, so
get your camera ready. There's also much
to see outside the Adler, and for free. Check
out how the 1930s building has 12 sides, one
for each sign of the zodiac. Sculptor Henry
Moore's **sundial** keeps time by the main entrance, while the bronze **Copernicus statue** lords it over the front median.

NORTHERLY ISLAND   PARK
Map p314 (1521 S Linn White Dr; 🚌146, 130) This
hilly, prairie-grassed park has walking and
cycling trails, fishing, bird-watching and an

outdoor venue for big-name concerts. It's
actually a peninsula, not an island, but the
Chicago skyline views are tremendous no
matter what you call it. Stop in at the field
house, if it's open, for tour information. Bicycles are available at the Divvy bike-share
station by the Adler Planetarium.

Northerly Island was once the busy commuter airport known as Meigs Field. The
shift from runway to willowy grasses has
its root in a controversial incident that
reads a little like a municipal spy thriller,
complete with midnight operatives and
surprise bulldozings. To sum it up: Mayor
Richard M Daley wanted the land for a
park; businesses wanted to keep it for their
private planes. A standoff ensued. Then,
one dark night in March 2003, Daley fired
up the heavy machinery and razed the airfield while the city slept. His reasoning?
Terrorists could attack Chicago with tiny
planes launched from Meigs; the airfield
was a security liability. Why it couldn't be
jackhammered during daylight hours was
never answered.

MUSEUM OF CONTEMPORARY
PHOTOGRAPHY   MUSEUM
Map p314 (📞312-663-5554; www.mocp.org;
600 S Michigan Ave, Columbia College; ⊙10am-
5pm Mon-Wed, Fri & Sat, to 8pm Thu, noon-5pm
Sun; 🚇Red Line to Harrison) FREE This small
museum focuses on American and international photography from the early 20th
century onward, and is the only institution
of its kind between the coasts. The permanent collection includes the works of Henri
Cartier-Bresson, Harry Callahan, Sally
Mann, Victor Skrebneski, Catherine Wag-
ner and 500 more of the best photographers
working today. Special exhibitions (free)
augment the rotating permanent collection.

SOLDIER FIELD   STADIUM
Map p314 (📞312-235-7152; www.soldierfield.
net; 1410 S Museum Campus Dr; tours adult/
child $15/4; 🚌146, 130) Built between 1922
and 1926 to pay homage to WWI soldiers,
this oft-renovated edifice has been home
to everything from civil-rights speeches to
Martin Luther King Jr to Brazilian soccer
games. It got its latest UFO-landing-upon-
a-Greek-ruin look in a controversial 2003
makeover. The Bears now play football
here. Hour-long stadium tours are available
erratically; check the schedule online.

Before the 2003 renovation, Soldier
Field's architecture was so noteworthy it
was named a National Historic Landmark.

South Loop & Near South Side – Family-Friendly South Loop

Where to begin for family fun? The Shedd Aquarium's tropical fish? The Field Museum's hulking dinosaurs? The Adler Planetarium's lunar landscape to climb over? If the indoors gets to be too much, parkland and a beach surround the museums, so kids have space to romp and burn off steam.

CHARLES COOK/GETTY IMAGES ©

TRINA DOPP PHOTOGRAPHY/GETTY IMAGES ©

1. Adler Planetarium (p181)
Discover your inner astronaut – explore meteorites and supernovas, and even 'launch' a rocket.

2. Shedd Aquarium (p181)
Commune with creatures from the deep.

3. Field Museum of Natural History (p180)
Get up close to fossils and bones at this expansive museum that holds 20 million artifacts.

4. Views from Northerly Island (p181)
Take in vistas of Adler Planetarium and Lake Michigan from this grassy nature park.

STEVEGEER/GETTY IMAGES ©

184

LOCAL KNOWLEDGE

PRINTER'S ROW ARCHITECTURE

Chicago was a center for printing at the turn of the 20th century, and the rows of buildings on S Dearborn St from W Congress Pkwy south to W Polk St housed the heart of the city's publishing industry. By the 1970s the printers had left for more economical quarters elsewhere, and the buildings had been largely emptied out.

In the late 1970s savvy developers saw the potential in these derelicts, and one of the most successful gentrification projects in Chicago began. The following describes some of the notable buildings in the area as you travel from north to south.

Mergenthaler Lofts (Map p314; 531 S Plymouth Ct; [M]Red Line to Harrison) A snazzy renovation of this building, the 1886 headquarters for the legendary Linotype company, included the artful preservation of a diner storefront.

Pontiac Building (Map p314; 542 S Dearborn St; [M]Red Line to Harrison) A classic 1891 design by Holabird & Roche, the Pontiac features the same flowing masonry surfaces as the firm's famed Monadnock Building in the Loop.

Second Franklin Building (Map p314; 720 S Dearborn St; [M]Red Line to Harrison) A 1912 factory, it shows the history of printing on its tiled facade. The roof slopes to allow for a huge skylight over the top floor where books were hand bound (the building existed long before fluorescent lights or high-intensity lamps). The large windows on many of the other buildings in the area served the same purpose.

Dearborn Street Station (Map p314; 47 W Polk St; [M]Red Line to Harrison) Once the Chicago terminal of the Santa Fe Railroad, the 1885 building used to be the premier station for trains to and from California. Today it sees the trains of parent-propelled strollers from the Dearborn Park neighborhood, built on the site of the tracks to the south.

Unfortunately, the landmark lacked corporate skyboxes and giant bathrooms, so the city (the venue is owned by the park district) decided it was time for a change. The new look met almost unanimous derision when it was unveiled; critics quickly dubbed it 'the Mistake on the Lake.' The landmark folks agreed and removed it from their list, saying it jeopardized the National Landmark integrity.

OLMEC HEAD NO 8　　　　　SCULPTURE
Map p314 ([圖]146, 130) Staring out from the Field Museum's lawn, Olmec Head No 8 is a replica of one of many sculptures the Olmec people carved in Veracruz, Mexico, c 1300 BC. Scholars believe the colossal heads are likenesses of revered Olmec leaders. This guy's noggin weighs in at 1700lb.

◉ Near South Side

WILLIE DIXON'S
BLUES HEAVEN　　　　　HISTORIC BUILDING
Map p314 ([☎]312-808-1286; www.bluesheaven. com; 2120 S Michigan Ave; tours $10; [◷]noon-4pm Mon-Fri, to 3pm Sat; [M]Green Line to Cermak-McCormick Pl) From 1957 to 1967, this humble building was Chess Records, the seminal electric blues label. It's now named for the bassist who wrote most of Chess' hits. Staff give hour-long tours of the premises. It's pretty ramshackle, with few original artifacts on display. Still, when Willie's grandson hauls out the bluesman's well-worn stand-up bass and lets you take a pluck, it's pretty cool. Free blues concerts rock the side garden on summer Thursdays at 6pm.

The Chess brothers, two Polish Jews, ran the recording studio that saw – and heard – the likes of Muddy Waters, Bo Diddley, Koko Taylor and others. Chuck Berry recorded four top-10 singles here, and the Rolling Stones named a song '2120 South Michigan Avenue' after a recording session at this spot in 1964. (Rock trivia buffs will know that the Stones named themselves after the Muddy Waters song 'Rolling Stone.')

McCORMICK PLACE　　　NOTABLE BUILDING
Map p314 ([☎]312-791-7000; www.mccormick place.com; 2301 S Martin Luther King Jr Dr; [M]Green Line to Cermak-McCormick Pl) McCormick Place is the largest convention center in the country, spread over four halls. 'Vast' isn't big enough to describe it. And it's getting even bigger, with a new hotel and 10,000-seat event hall underway. The area around the venue is fairly bleak, but de-

velopment may at last make inroads here. Shops, microbreweries and more are starting to trickle in.

PRAIRIE AVENUE
HISTORIC DISTRICT   ARCHITECTURE

Map p314 (🖳1) In the late 1800s, Prairie Ave between 16th and 20th Sts is where Chicago's millionaires lived in their mansions. Today the district is good for a stroll. Some of the homes have been preserved as museums; others are intriguing to admire from the outside. A footbridge over the train tracks links the area to Burnham Park and the Museum Campus.

Prairie Ave was millionaire's row until the vice and industry of the nearby Levee District (four blocks west) got too close for comfort. By 1900 the crème de la crème had packed up and moved north to the Gold Coast. The neighborhood endured years of decline until the Chicago Architecture Foundation stepped in to help restore various buildings.

Nifty ones to check out include the Glessner House, Clarke House, William K Kimball House, Joseph G Coleman House and Elbridge G Keith House.

GLESSNER HOUSE MUSEUM   MUSEUM

Map p314 (☎312-326-1480; www.glessnerhouse. org; 1800 S Prairie Ave; tours adult/child $15/8, admission Wed free; ⊘tours 11:30am, 1pm & 2:30pm Wed-Sun; 🖳1) The 1887 John J Glessner House is the premier survivor of the Prairie Avenue Historic District. Much of interior is reminiscent of an English manor house, with heavy wooden beams and other English-style details. Additionally, more than 80% of the current furnishings are authentic, thanks to the Glessner family's penchant for family photos. Tours (75 minutes) take it all in.

Famed American architect Henry Hobson Richardson designed the beautiful composition of rusticated granite. The L-shaped house surrounds a sunny southern courtyard.

CLARKE HOUSE MUSEUM   MUSEUM

Map p314 (www.clarkehousemuseum.org; 1827 S Indiana Ave; ⊘tours 1pm & 3pm Wed-Fri; 🖳1) FREE The Henry B Clarke House is the oldest structure in the city. When Caroline and Henry Clarke built the imposing Greek-revival home in 1836, log cabins were still the rage in Chicago residential architecture. The interior has been restored to

the period of the Clarkes' occupation, which ended in 1872. One-hour tours delve into the family's life and times.

During the past 170-plus years the house has been moved twice to escape demolition. The present address is about as close as researchers can get to its somewhat undefined original location.

WILLIAM K KIMBALL HOUSE   HOUSE

Map p314 (1801 S Prairie Ave; 🖳1) Modeled after a 15th-century French château, the William K Kimball House dates from 1892. It now houses the US Soccer Federation, along with next-door Coleman House.

JOSEPH G COLEMAN HOUSE   HOUSE

Map p314 (1811 S Prairie Ave; 🖳1) Part of the Prairie Avenue Historic District, the Romanesque 1886 Coleman House now serves as part of the headquarters for the US Soccer Federation.

ELBRIDGE G KEITH HOUSE   HOUSE

Map p314 (www.keithhousechicago.com; 1900 S Prairie Ave; 🖳1) This 1870 limestone beauty in the Prairie Avenue Historic District combines classical and French motifs. It's now a private event space.

CHICAGO WOMEN'S PARK   PARK

Map p314 (1801 S Indiana Ave; 🖳1) Set between Indiana and Prairie Aves, with the Glessner House to the north and the Clarke House to the west, this 4-acre park has a French garden, a fountain and winding paths.

BATTLE OF FORT
DEARBORN PARK   HISTORIC SITE

Map p314 (1801 S Calumet Ave; 🖳1) The Fort Dearborn battle, in which a group of local Native Americans rebelled against the incursion of white settlers, is thought to have occurred on this spot on August 15, 1812. A plaque provides the violent details.

◉ Chinatown

Chicago's small but busy Chinatown is an easy 10-minute train ride from the Loop. Take the Red Line to the Cermak-Chinatown stop, which puts you between the neighborhood's two distinct parts: Chinatown Sq (an enormous bilevel strip mall) unfurls to the north along Archer Ave, while Old Chinatown (the traditional retail area) stretches along Wentworth Ave

CHINATOWN TOUR

The **Chicago Chinese Cultural Institute** (Map p314; ☎312-842-1988; www.chinatowntourchicago.com; tour $10; Ⓜ Red Line to Cermak-Chinatown) offers a guided, 90-minute tour taking in the neighborhood's history, architecture and cultural highlights. Departure is at 10am Friday through Sunday in summer from Chinatown Sq by the animal statues (in front of 2126 S Archer Ave). You must reserve in advance.

to the south. Either zone allows you to graze through bakeries and shop for the requisite Hello Kitty trinkets.

PING TOM MEMORIAL PARK   PARK
Map p314 (300 W 19th St; Ⓜ Red Line to Cermak-Chinatown) Ping Tom Memorial Park offers dramatic city-railroad-bridge views. In summer, Chicago Water Taxi runs a groovy boat down the Chicago River from Michigan Ave (the dock is on the bridge's northwest side, by the Wrigley Building) to the park. It costs $6 one way and takes 35 minutes.

PUI TAK CENTER   ARCHITECTURE
Map p314 (2216 S Wentworth Ave; Ⓜ Red Line to Cermak-Chinatown) Built in 1928 and originally known as the On Leong Building, this grand structure is a fantasy of Chinese architecture that makes good use of glazed terra-cotta details. Note how the lions guarding the door have twisted their heads so they don't have to risk bad luck by turning their backs to each other. The building now houses a group that provides ESL classes and other community programs.

✖ EATING

✖ South Loop

YOLK   BREAKFAST $
Map p314 (☎312-789-9655; www.eatyolk.com; 1120 S Michigan Ave; mains $10-14; ⊗6am-3pm Mon-Fri, 7am-3pm Sat & Sun; 🖶; Ⓜ Red, Orange, Green Line to Roosevelt) This cheerful diner is worth the long wait – you'll dig into the best traditional breakfast in the South Loop.

The omelets include lots of healthy options (the Iron Man is made from egg whites and comes loaded with veggies and avocado), and sweets lovers have stacks of cinnamon-roll French toast and peach-cobbler crepes to drench in syrup.

Scores of big salads and burgers are on hand for those inclined to order lunch.

LOU MALNATI'S   PIZZA $
Map p314 (☎312-786-1000; www.loumalnatis.com; 805 S State St; small pizzas from $12.25; ⊗11am-11pm Sun-Thu, to midnight Fri & Sat; Ⓜ Red Line to Harrison) Lou Malnati's is one of the city's premier deep-dish pizza makers. In fact, it claims to have invented the gooey behemoth (though that's a matter of never-ending dispute). Not in dispute: the deliciousness of Malnati's famed butter crust. Gluten-free diners can opt for the sausage crust (it's literally just meat, no dough). The restaurant has outlets citywide.

EPIC BURGER   BURGERS $
Map p314 (☎312-913-1373; www.epicburger.com; 517 S State St; mains $6-9; ⊗11am-10pm Mon-Thu, to 11pm Fri & Sat, 10am-9pm Sun; Ⓜ Brown, Orange, Purple, Pink Line to Library) 🍃 This sprawling, sunny-orange restaurant brings eco-conscious fast-food eaters the goods they crave: burgers made with all-natural beef, no hormones or antibiotics, topped with cage-free organic eggs and nitrate-free bacon; preservative-free buns; vanilla-bean-speckled milkshakes; and no petroleum-based packaging. The loud music and flat-screen TVs draw a student crowd from the surrounding college campuses in the South Loop.

FLO & SANTOS   PUB FOOD $$
Map p314 (☎312-566-9817; www.floandsantos.com; 1310 S Wabash Ave; mains $12-19; ⊗11:30am-11pm Sun-Thu, to midnight Fri & Sat; Ⓜ Red, Orange, Green Line to Roosevelt) This South Loop neighborhood pub is known for its tavern-style pizza (with wafer-thin crust and sweet sauce) and its Polish dishes (such as pierogi and potato pancakes). Eat in the warm, exposed-brick interior or in the outdoor beer garden at umbrella-shaded picnic tables under strands of winking lights.

CHICAGO CURRY HOUSE   INDIAN $$
Map p314 (☎312-362-9999; www.curryhouseonline.com; 899 S Plymouth Ct; mains $14-19; ⊗11am-10pm; 🍃; Ⓜ Red Line to Harrison) Even if it's just standard Indian food in a stand-

ard Indian-restaurant ambience, the Curry House provides a nice option for the South Loop and offers a rare bonus: Nepalese dishes. Standouts include *aloo tama bodi* (potatoes and black-eyed peas) and *khasi ko maasu* (goat meat on the bone). Sample them at the lunch buffet (weekdays/weekends $12/13). A full bar helps wash it all down.

★**MERCAT A LA PLANXA** SPANISH $$$

Map p314 (✆312-765-0524; www.mercatchicago.com; 638 S Michigan Ave; tapas $10-17, tasting menus from $65; ⏰6:30am-10pm Mon-Thu, to 11pm Fri, 7am-11pm Sat, to 10pm Sun; Ⓜ️Red Line to Harrison) This Barcelona-style tapas and seafood restaurant buzzes in an enormous, convivial room where light streams in through the floor-to-ceiling windows. Iron Chef winner Jose Garces cooks all the specialties of Catalan and stokes a festive atmosphere, enhanced by copious quantities of *cava* (sparkling wine) and sangria. It's located in the beaux-arts Blackstone Hotel.

✕ Chinatown

SWEET STATION CHINESE $

Map p314 (✆312-842-2228; www.mysweetstation.com; 2101 S China Pl; mains $5-10; ⏰8am-4am Mon-Thu, 24hr Fri & Sat, to 2am Sun; Ⓜ️Red Line to Cermak-Chinatown) Join the young, hip Asian crowd chowing at Sweet Station in Chinatown Sq. Slide into a booth, flip on the table's flat-screen TV, then settle in to examine the massive menu. It sprawls through a global medley including Portuguese pork-chop sandwiches, Hong Kong–style baked spaghetti, Szechuan hot pots, curried tofu and good ol' French toast.

When the weather blows, it's hard to beat a warm egg-custard tart and glass of almond milk for breakfast. Bonus for late-night types: Sweet Station serves into the wee hours (and all night long on Friday and Saturday).

JOY YEE'S NOODLE SHOP ASIAN $

Map p314 (✆312-328-0001; www.joyyeechicago.com; 2139 S China Pl; mains $9-15; ⏰11am-10:30pm; 🚗; Ⓜ️Red Line to Cermak-Chinatown) Folks line up for bubble teas packed with fresh fruit at this brightly colored, hip cafe in Chinatown Sq. Do yourself a favor, though, and save one of the deliciously sweet drinks for dessert after a bowl of udon, *chow fun* (rice noodles) or chow mein.

LAWRENCE'S FISHERIES SEAFOOD $

Map p314 (✆312-225-2113; www.lawrencesfisheries.com; 2120 S Canal St; mains $6-16; ⏰24hr; 🚗; Ⓜ️Red Line to Cermak-Chinatown) There's not much to look at inside this 24-hour joint, but the window at the end of the long dining room frames a stunning scene of the Willis Tower over the Chicago River. Not that you have much option but to stand agape once your order arrives – delicious treats such as popcorn shrimp, oysters and fish and chips are stalwarts.

Frog legs and scallops round out the menu of batter-crusted goodies from the sea. At night the parking lot outside of this typically family-oriented joint is a prime location for locals to sit on car hoods and shop for suspiciously current DVDs.

LAO SZE CHUAN CHINESE $$

Map p314 (✆312-326-5040; www.tonygourmetgroup.com; 2172 S Archer Ave; mains $12-20; ⏰10:30am-midnight; Ⓜ️Red Line to Cermak-Chinatown) Lao Sze Chuan is one of the most authentic options in Chinatown Sq. House specialties include the three-chili chicken, which is tender and very spicy, and *mapo* tofu, cooked in a fiery chili and fermented-bean sauce. The extensive menu also has excellent hot pots alongside other dishes from the far reaches of Szechuan province.

PHOENIX CHINESE $$

Map p314 (✆312-328-0848; www.chinatownphoenix.com; 2131 S Archer Ave; mains $14-21; ⏰9am-10pm Mon-Fri, 8am-11pm Sat & Sun; Ⓜ️Red Line to Cermak-Chinatown) Though better sit-down dinner experiences in Chinatown are abundant, the draw here is the excellent dim sum. Small plates of *char siu bao* (barbecued pork buns), shrimp-filled rice noodles, egg custards and other popular vitals roll around the dining room in a seemingly endless parade of carts. Dishes average around $4 per plate.

The language barrier can be an issue, so keep in mind that if it looks like chicken feet, it probably is.

🍷 DRINKING & NIGHTLIFE

★**SPOKE & BIRD** CAFE

Map p314 (www.spokeandbird.com; 205 E 18th St; ⏰7am-6pm; 🚗; 🚌1) The South Loop has been begging for a leafy patio like the one at Spoke & Bird. Bonus: it's surrounded by

FREE BLUES AT BUDDY GUY'S

Buddy Guy's Legends hosts free, all-ages acoustic performances from noon to 2pm Wednesday through Sunday. Listen in while having lunch (the club doubles as a Cajun restaurant) or a drink at the bar.

several cool old manors in the Prairie Avenue Historic District. Relax with a locally made brew (as in made down the street) and nifty cafe fare such as the sweet parsnip muffin or lamb barbecue sandwich.

VICE DISTRICT BREWING MICROBREWERY
Map p314 (☑312-291-9022; www.vicedistrict brewing.com; 1454 S Michigan Ave; ⊙4-11pm Tue-Thu, to 1am Fri, 2pm-1am Sat, 2-9pm Sun; MGreen, Orange, Red Line to Roosevelt) Vice opened in 2014 and has quickly become a South Loop favorite. The large, mod-industrial taproom is just right for a pint of black IPA or English-style bitter ale. Many drinkers stop in pre-Bears game. It's not far from Soldier Field, and it opens early (11am) on Sunday game days.

KASEY'S TAVERN PUB
Map p314 (☑312-427-7992; www.kaseystavern. com; 701 S Dearborn St; ⊙11am-2am; MRed Line to Harrison) Kasey's is a friendly neighborhood pub that draws a mix of artsy students from the nearby universities, local condo dwellers, and sports fans, all of whom belly up at the long wooden bar. There's something for everyone on the enormous beer list. Scads of flat-screen TVs show Chicago's teams in action.

LITTLE BRANCH CAFE CAFE
Map p314 (☑312-360-0101; www.littlebranchcafe. com; 1251 S Prairie Ave; ⊙7am-6pm Mon, Tue, Sat & Sun, to 7pm Wed-Fri; ☏; MRed, Orange, Green Line to Roosevelt) A good fortifier after the Museum Campus, Little Branch is probably more known for its food than its drinks, but it does indeed have a bar. And that bar stirs hot toddies and Irish coffees, and serves a small roster of wines and beers. The cafe hides in a residential complex.

WEATHERMARK TAVERN PUB
Map p314 (☑312-588-0230; www.weathermark tavern.com; 1503 S Michigan Ave; ⊙11:30am-2am Mon-Fri, 10:30am-3am Sat, to midnight Sun; MRed, Orange, Green Line to Roosevelt) While Weathermark is one of the least obnoxious of the South Loop's upscale pubs, it does get in your face with its nautical theme and rum-based 'sailor's rations.' Still, we forgive it because the bar also pours hard-to-find local microbrews such as Three Floyd's Zombie Dust. The place packs 'em in for Bears games and Thursday trivia night.

ENTERTAINMENT

★BUDDY GUY'S LEGENDS BLUES
Map p314 (☑312-427-1190; www.buddyguy. com; 700 S Wabash Ave; ⊙5pm-2am Mon & Tue, 11am-2am Wed-Fri, noon-3am Sat, to 2am Sun; MRed Line to Harrison) Top local and national acts wail on the stage of local icon Buddy Guy. Tickets cost $20 Friday and Saturday, $10 on other evenings. The man himself usually plugs in his axe for a series of shows in January (tickets go on sale in November). The location is a bit rough around the edges, but the acts are consistently excellent.

SUMMERDANCE WORLD MUSIC
Map p314 (www.chicagosummerdance.org; 601 S Michigan Ave; ⊙6-9:30pm Fri & Sat, 4-7pm Sun late Jun–mid-Sep; MRed Line to Harrison) To boogie with a multiethnic mash-up of locals, head to the Spirit of Music Garden in Grant Park for SummerDance. Bands play rumba, samba and other world beats preceded by fun dance lessons – all free. Ballroom-quality moves are absolutely not required.

JAZZ SHOWCASE JAZZ
Map p314 (☑312-360-0234; www.jazzshowcase. com; 806 S Plymouth Ct; tickets $20-35; MRed Line to Harrison) The Jazz Showcase, set in a gorgeous room in historic Dearborn Station, is Chicago's top club for national names. In general, local musicians take the stage Monday through Wednesday, with visiting jazz cats blowing their horns Thursday through Sunday.

REGGIES ROCK CLUB LIVE MUSIC
Map p314 (☑312-949-0121; www.reggieslive. com; 2109 S State St; ⊙11am-2am; MGreen Line to Cermak-McCormick Pl) Bring on the punk and the all-ages shows. Graffitied Reggies books mostly touring hard-core bands at the Rock Club. Next door, Reggies Music Joint is for folks 21 and older, and hosts more mainstream (we use that term

loosely) live music nightly. It also provides shuttle buses to various Bears and White Sox games and other events.

DANCE CENTER AT
COLUMBIA COLLEGE
DANCE

Map p314 (📞312-344-8300; www.colum.edu/dance-center; 1306 S Michigan Ave; Ⓜ Green, Orange Line to Roosevelt) More than an academic institution, the Dance Center is one of the most focused collegiate modern-dance programs in the country and has carved out a fine reputation. The on-site theater attracts quality performers from beyond Chicago and hosts everything from tap jams to classical Indian dance.

PAVILION AT
NORTHERLY ISLAND
CONCERT VENUE

Map p314 (📞312-540-2668; www.livenation.com; 1300 S Linn White Dr; 🚌146, 130) Northerly Island's grassy environs and skyline backdrop make a splendid place to see a touring band like Jimmy Buffet or Phish. The outdoor concert venue was supposed to be temporary when it opened more than a decade ago, but as the years roll by and the bands keep plugging in, it's clear the pavilion is here to stay.

 SHOPPING

★SANDMEYER'S BOOKSTORE
BOOKS

Map p314 (📞312-922-2104; www.sandmeyersbookstore.com; 714 S Dearborn St; ⊘11am-6:30pm Mon-Fri, to 5pm Sat, to 4pm Sun; Ⓜ Red Line to Harrison) It's not big, it's not flashy and it doesn't host many author events. Instead this small Printer's Row spot offers an old-school bookstore experience of creaking wood floors and jazz piping softly through the speakers while you browse tomes of all types.

SHOPCOLUMBIA
ART

Map p314 (📞312-369-8616; www.colum.edu/shopcolumbia; 1st fl, 623 S Wabash Ave; ⊘11am-5pm Mon-Wed & Fri, to 7pm Thu; Ⓜ Red Line to Harrison) This is Columbia College's student store, where artists and designers in training learn how to market their wares. The shop carries original pieces spanning all media and disciplines: clothes, jewelry, prints, mugs, stationery and more. Proceeds help individual students earn income, and part goes toward student scholarships. It's

attached to the college's student center and coffee-slinging cafe.

GIFTLAND
GIFTS & SOUVENIRS

Map p314 (📞312-225-0088; 2212 S Wentworth Ave; ⊘10am-7pm; Ⓜ Red Line to Cermak-Chinatown) After you see it, you'll wonder how you've lived without it: a toast-scented Hello Kitty eraser. Giftland stocks a swell supply of pens, stationery, coin purses and backpacks boasting the image of Kitty as well as Mashimaro, Pucca, Doraemon and other Asian cartoon characters.

AJI ICHIBAN
FOOD & DRINKS

Map p314 (📞312-328-9998; 2117a S China Pl; ⊘11am-8pm Mon-Fri, 10am-9pm Sat & Sun; Ⓜ Red Line to Cermak-Chinatown) The front sign at this Asian snack and candy store says 'Munchies Paradise,' and so it is. Sweet and salty treats fill the bulk bins, from dried salted plums to chocolate wafer cookies, roasted fish crisps to fruity hard candies. It's all packaged in cool, cartoony wrappers, with plenty of samples out for grabs. Located in Chinatown Sq.

HOYPOLOI
HOMEWARES

Map p314 (📞312-225-6477; www.hoypoloigallery.com; 2235 S Wentworth Ave; ⊘11am-7:30pm Thu-Mon; Ⓜ Red Line to Cermak-Chinatown) Hoypoloi is more upscale than most Chinatown stores – it's actually a gallery filled with Asian artwork, glassware, funky lamps and other interior items. The wind-chime selection wins kudos.

BUDDHIST TEMPLE
GIFT SHOP
GIFTS & SOUVENIRS

Map p314 (📞312-881-0177; www.ibfachicago.org; 2249 S Wentworth Ave; ⊘9am-6pm; Ⓜ Red Line to Cermak-Chinatown) Follow your nose into this quiet, incense-wafting storefront to contemplate charms and necklaces (for good luck and happiness), books on how to meditate, Buddha statues and other spiritual items.

 SPORTS & ACTIVITIES

CHICAGO BEARS
FOOTBALL

Map p314 (📞847-615-2327; www.chicagobears.com; 1410 S Museum Campus Dr; 🚌146, 128) Da Bears, Chicago's NFL team, tackle at Soldier Field from September through January.

Arrive early on game days and wander through the parking lots – you won't believe the elaborate tailgate feasts people cook up from the back of their cars. And for Chrissake, dress warmly. If you can't score a ticket, hit one of the South Loop bars to watch the game.

12TH STREET BEACH   BEACH

Map p314 (www.cpdbeaches.com; 1200 S Linn White Dr; ☐146, 130) A path runs south from the Adler Planetarium to this secluded crescent of sand. Despite its proximity to the visitor-mobbed Museum Campus, the small beach remains bizarrely (but happily) secluded. Bonus: if you can't get tickets to see your favorite band at the Pavilion at Northerly Island, you can sit here and still hear the tunes. There aren't many amenities besides a bathhouse, a snack shop and a couple of picnic tables.

SLEDDING HILL   SNOW SPORTS

Map p314 (☎312-235 7000; 1410 S Museum Campus Dr; ☐146, 130) The Park District operates a free, 33ft sledding hill on the southeast side of Soldier Field in winter; bring your own gear. A snow-making machine is fired up when the weather doesn't cooperate.

Hyde Park & South Side

HYDE PARK | BRIDGEPORT | BRONZEVILLE

Neighborhood Top Five

❶ **Robie House** (p194) Gawping at the eye-popping stained glass and horizontal design of Frank Lloyd Wright's Prairie-style masterpiece.

❷ **Museum of Science & Industry** (p193) Exploring the U-boat, dollhouse and mock tornado at the larg-

est science museum in the Western Hemisphere.

❸ **Stony Island Arts Bank** (p195) Seeing how creativity can reshape a downtrodden building at this one-of-a-kind cultural center.

❹ **Meyers Ace Hardware Store** (p200) Seeking out the stage where greats

like Louis Armstrong and Benny Goodman played at this unassuming, landmark building.

❺ **57th Street Books** (p204) Losing yourself in the labyrinth of low-slung rooms at this old-fashioned, basement-level bookstore.

For more detail of this area see Maps p317 and p318 ➡

Lonely Planet's Top Tip

Don't be put off by the distance of these southern neighborhoods from downtown. They're all easy to reach by public transportation, especially Hyde Park, and the sights, bookstores, bars and restaurants offer a true, exceptional slice of Chicago. Really, where else are you going to see DJ Frankie Knuckles' 5000-album vinyl trove?

✕ Best Places to Eat

➡ Duck Inn (p203)

➡ Nana (p203)

➡ Valois Cafeteria (p202)

➡ Soul Vegetarian East (p203)

➡ Medici (p202)

For reviews, see p202 ➡

Best Places to Drink

➡ Maria's Packaged Goods & Community Bar (p203)

➡ Jimmy's Woodlawn Tap (p203)

➡ Bernice's Tavern (p203)

➡ Schaller's Pump (p203)

For reviews, see p203 ➡

⊙ Best Museums

➡ Museum of Science & Industry (p193)

➡ Robie House (p194)

➡ Smart Museum of Art (p195)

➡ Oriental Institute (p195)

➡ DuSable Museum of African American History (p195)

For reviews, see p193 ➡

Explore Hyde Park & South Side

The South Side is huge, but most of the sights are concentrated in three areas: Hyde Park, home to the crowd-favorite Museum of Science & Industry (p193) and gargoyle-cluttered University of Chicago (p195); Bridgeport, a traditional Irish neighborhood that has become a pocket of cool; and Bronzeville, the historic heart of Chicago's African American arts and cultural scene.

In Hyde Park, the intersection of 57th St and S University Ave is a great place to start exploring the neighborhood. That'll put you close to the brainy bookstores, Frank Lloyd Wright's Robie House (p194) and the site (p197) where the atomic age began. You could spend a day here easily. Architecture buffs and African American–history enthusiasts should block out an afternoon for Bronzeville. Bridgeport's bars and White Sox (p204) baseball games make it ideal for an evening visit.

Beyond these areas, explorers will find neighborhoods that are slowly piecing things together in the shadow of some of the country's bleakest housing projects. Stony Island Arts Bank (p195) is a good example of positive transformation. Around 74th and 75th Sts you'll find a stretch of soul-food and barbecue spots, but you'll need a car to reach them.

Local Life

➡ **Third Fridays** The monthly open studios night that side-by-side Bridgeport Art Center (p200) and Zhou B Art Center (p200) sponsor has become one of the city's coolest soirees.

➡ **Community bars** The name doesn't lie at Maria's Packaged Goods & Community Bar (p203): it really is a communal watering hole. Schaller's Pump (p203) is the old-school version down the road.

➡ **Neighborhood news** For years neighborhood folks – including a gent named Barack Obama – have gathered to gossip while forking into Southern-style biscuits, bacon and pot pies at Valois Cafeteria (p202).

Getting There & Away

➡ **Bus** Number 6 runs from State St in the Loop to Hyde Park and beyond (express between 11th and 47th Sts). The Museum of Science & Industry has its own bus – number 10 – during museum hours (daily in summer, weekends only the rest of the year). Departs from Michigan Ave in the Loop. Bus 8 motors along Hasted St for Bridgeport.

➡ **Metra** Electric Line trains go from the Loop's Millennium Station to 51st-53rd or 55th-56th-57th stops in Hyde Park.

➡ **El** Green Line to 35th-Bronzeville-IIT for Bronzeville. Red Line to Sox-35th for the ballpark.

➡ **Car** Hyde Park can be tight for parking. Bridgeport and Bronzeville usually aren't a problem.

⊙ TOP SIGHT
MUSEUM OF SCIENCE & INDUSTRY

Geek out at the largest science museum in the Western Hemisphere. Highlights include a WWII German U-boat nestled in an underground display, the life-sized shaft of a coal mine, and the 'Science Storms' exhibit with a mock tornado and tsunami.

Level 1 holds the **U-boat**, which is pretty freaking impressive. It's given the Hollywood treatment with blue spotlights moving over it and dramatic music swelling in the background. An interactive kiosk lets you try to break codes. There's plenty more to see around the sub, but the highlight is going on board and touring the cramped quarters. Tours cost $9 extra; tickets are available at the exhibit-side kiosk (or at the main desk when you enter the museum). The **Space Center** with rockets and the **Apollo 8 lunar module**, the 'fairy castle' dollhouse, and the **Farm Tech exhibit** with huge tractors to climb are other Level 1 highlights.

Level 2 rolls out lots of trains. '**Science Storms**' lets you conjure a mock tornado and simulate a tsunami rolling toward you. Or submerge into the realistic shaft of a **coal mine** ($9 extra). The **baby chick hatchery** is also on this floor.

Level 3 hangs cool old **German dive bombers** and **English Spitfires** from the ceiling. 'You! The Experience' has a giant 3D heart to walk through and the infamous body slices (cadavers displayed in half-inch-thick pieces).

The museum's main building served as the Palace of Fine Arts at the landmark 1893 World's Expo, which was set in surrounding Jackson Park (p195). When you've had your fill at the museum, the park makes an excellent setting to recuperate.

DON'T MISS

➡ U-505 submarine
➡ Fairy castle
➡ Science Storms' tornadoes and tsunamis
➡ Body slices

PRACTICALITIES

➡ MSI
➡ Map p318
➡ ☎773-684-1414
➡ www.msichicago.org
➡ 5700 S Lake Shore Dr
➡ adult/child $18/11
➡ ⊘9:30am-5:30pm Jun-Aug, reduced hours Sep-May
➡ 🚻
➡ 🚌6 or 10, Ⓜ Metra to 55th-56th-57th

TOP SIGHT
ROBIE HOUSE

Robie House is one of the most famous dwellings in the world. Designed by Frank Lloyd Wright, it's the masterpiece of his Prairie style, and it is often listed among the most important structures in American architecture. The look is meant to reflect the Midwest's landscape – low-slung with long horizontal lines and lots of earth colors.

Frederick C Robie, a forward-thinking businessman who dealt in bicycle parts and early auto machinery, was only 28 years old when he commissioned Wright to build a mod house for his family. Wright designed it in his Oak Park studio between 1908 and 1909, but he wasn't around for the majority of the construction, as he had packed up and moved to Europe with his mistress by then. His associates finished the building, and the Robies moved into the home in 1910. Their residency was short-lived, however. After 14 months, financial and marital problems forced them to sell the house. It was threatened with demolition several times, until it became a landmark under Mayor Richard J Daley in the 1950s.

The house cost about $60,000 to build – furniture, light fixtures and 174 art glass windows included. Docents tell the story during one-hour tours, run roughly every half-hour Thursday to Monday from June through October, and hourly otherwise. They go room to room explaining Wright's design concept in each space and how he achieved it. Note how the furniture repeats the building's forms, and how the colors link to the autumnal prairie palette.

Advance tickets are highly recommended; call or go online. There's a small surcharge to make reservations. And bring the kids. The 'Wright 3' tours on Saturday are based on the same-named children's novel and use junior guides to take families through the home's mysterious spaces.

DON'T MISS

➡ Exterior view against the horizon

➡ Stained glass everywhere

➡ Cantilevered roofs

➡ Fireplace

➡ Children's tours

PRACTICALITIES

➡ Map p318

➡ ☎ 312-994-4000

➡ www.flwright.org

➡ 5757 S Woodlawn Ave

➡ adult/child $17/14

➡ ⊙10:30am-3pm Thu-Mon

➡ 🚌6, Ⓜ Metra to 55th-56th-57th

⊙ SIGHTS

⊙ Hyde Park

MUSEUM OF SCIENCE & INDUSTRY   MUSEUM
See p193.

ROBIE HOUSE   ARCHITECTURE
See p194.

STONY ISLAND ARTS BANK   GALLERY
(☑312-857-5561; www.rebuild-foundation.org; 6760 S Stony Island Ave; ⊙11am-6pm Tue-Sat; ▣6) FREE Artist Theaster Gates bought a tumbledown bank building for $1 in Chicago's neglected South Shore neighborhood, and transformed it into a fascinating African American cultural center and gallery. Staff give tours of the hodgepodge collections, including the 5000-album vinyl trove of local DJ Frankie Knuckles (the Godfather of House Music; tours at 1pm Saturdays) and a roomful of racist 'negrobilia' items.

The vintage glass lantern slides (60,000 of them, of art through the ages) and stacked-to-the-rafters library of African American art and history books are other cool sets to browse, along with the main floor exhibitions. Workshops and events take place daily. And it's all free.

UNIVERSITY OF CHICAGO   UNIVERSITY
Map p318 (www.uchicago.edu; 5801 S Ellis Ave; ▣6, Ⓜ Metra to 55th-56th-57th) Faculty and students have racked up more than 80 Nobel prizes within U of C's hallowed halls. The economics and physics departments lay claim to most of the awards. The campus is well worth a stroll, offering grand Gothic architecture and free art and antiquities museums.

The university's classes first met on October 1, 1892. John D Rockefeller was a major contributor to the institution, donating more than $35 million. The original campus was constructed in an English Gothic style. Highlights of a walkabout include the sculpture-laden Rockefeller Memorial Chapel (p197), serene Bond Chapel (p197) and Henry Moore's bronze Nuclear Energy sculpture (p197).

SMART MUSEUM OF ART   MUSEUM
Map p318 (☑773-702-0200; http://smartmuseum.uchicago.edu; 5550 S Greenwood Ave; ⊙10am-5pm Tue-Sun; ☎; ▣6, Ⓜ Metra to 55th-56th-57th) FREE Named after the founders of *Esquire* magazine, who contributed the start-up money, this is the official fine-arts museum of the University of Chicago. The collection holds 5000 years' worth of works. Twentieth-century paintings and sculptures, Central European expressionism and East Asian art are the strong suits. De Goya, Warhol and Kandinsky are just a few of the big-name artists on offer. Frank Lloyd Wright's table and chairs mix in for good measure.

It only takes a half-hour or so to see the galleries. After that, grab a drink or bite at the front cafe. From September through mid-June, the museum stays open until 8pm on Thursdays.

ORIENTAL INSTITUTE   MUSEUM
Map p318 (www.oi.uchicago.edu; 1155 E 58th St; suggested donation $10; ⊙10am-5pm Tue & Thu-Sun, to 8pm Wed; ▣6, Ⓜ Metra to 55th-56th-57th) The University of Chicago's famed archaeologists – Indiana Jones supposedly was based on one – cram their headquarters with antiquities they've unearthed from Egypt, Nubia, Persia and Mesopotamia. King Tut is the star, standing 17ft tall, weighing six tons and lording over more mummies, clay tablets and canopic jars than you can shake a papyrus scroll at.

There's no pressure for the suggested donation, so if you don't have it, don't fret.

DUSABLE MUSEUM OF AFRICAN AMERICAN HISTORY   MUSEUM
Map p318 (☑773-947-0600; www.dusablemuseum.org; 740 E 56th Pl; adult/child $10/3, Sun free; ⊙10am-5pm Tue-Sat, noon-5pm Sun; ▣6, Ⓜ Metra to 55th-56th-57th) This was the first independent museum in the country dedicated to African American art, history and culture. The collection features African American artworks and photography, permanent exhibits that illustrate African Americans' experiences from slavery through the Civil Rights movement, and rotating exhibits that cover topics such as Chicago blues music or the Black Panther movement. It's affiliated with the Smithsonian Institution.

Housed in a 1910 building, the museum takes its name from Chicago's first permanent settler, Jean Baptiste Point du Sable, a French Canadian of Haitian descent.

JACKSON PARK   PARK
Map p318 (6401 S Stony Island Ave; ▣6, Ⓜ Metra to 63rd) This 543-acre, lagoon-filled green space fringes Hyde Park to the east.

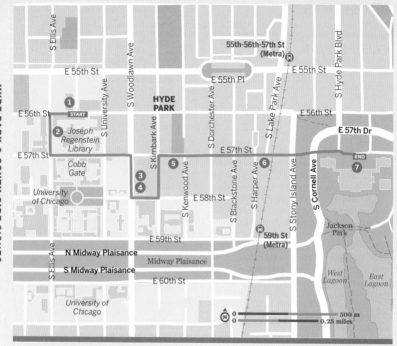

Neighborhood Walk
Higher Learning

START SMART MUSEUM OF ART
END MUSEUM OF SCIENCE & INDUSTRY
LENGTH 0.25 MILES; FIVE HOURS INCLUDING BROWSING TIME

You can learn a lot walking around the University of Chicago's Hyde Park campus and beyond. Start by brushing up on your art acumen at the **1 Smart Museum of Art** (p195). Exhibits here explore the tension between realism and abstraction. Learn about artists from Europe and the Americas, especially during the 20th century. There's also a good collection of East Asian art.

Around the corner you'll come to a real hot spot. Under the Stagg Field Stadium on the university campus, in secret, scientists initiated the first self-sustaining controlled nuclear reaction on December 2, 1942 – the precursor to the atomic bomb. Today, the spot is marked by the bronze, skull-like **2 Nuclear Energy Sculpture** (p197) flanking a tennis court.

Onward to the **3 Seminary Co-op Bookstore** (p204), an awesomely academic institution where you'll find no less than eight different versions of *War and Peace* on the shelves. Next door, Frank Lloyd Wright's **4 Robie House** (p194) rises up and provides an excellent opportunity to educate yourself on Prairie School architecture. See how all the horizontal lines resemble the Midwest's flat landscape?

All this thinking has probably made you hungry. Replenish at student-favorite **5 Medici** (p202) with an apple and blue cheese baguette. Continuing east on 57th St you'll pass more bookstores. No matter what subject you want to study – astronomy, architecture, rocket science – you're likely to find a secondhand book about it at **6 Powell's** (p204).

Finally you'll come to the **7 Museum of Science & Industry** (p193). The only German U-505 on US soil is part of a multimedia, multi-million-dollar exhibit – a fine way to improve your WWII sea-warfare knowledge. You can also explore a full-scale coal mine or manipulate the direction and speed of a tornado.

OBAMA'S HOUSE & KENWOOD HISTORIC ARCHITECTURE

Kenwood, which abuts Hyde Park to the north, earned its fame when a certain resident got elected president. Hefty security means you can't get close to **Obama's house** (Map p318; 5046 S Greenwood Ave; 🚆6, Ⓜ Metra to 51st-53rd), but you can stand across the street on Hyde Park Blvd and try to glimpse over the barricades at the redbrick Georgian-style manor. Many historic buildings are nearby. Across the street, the **KAM Synagogue** (Map p318; 1100 E Hyde Park Blvd; 🚆6, Ⓜ Metra to 51st-53rd) is a domed masterpiece in the Byzantine style with acoustics that are said to be perfect. The house at **4944 S Woodlawn Ave** (Map p318; 🚆6, Ⓜ Metra to 51st-53rd) was once home to Muhammad Ali, and Nation of Islam leader Louis Farrakhan currently lives in the 1971 **Elijah Muhammad House** (Map p318; 4855 S Woodlawn Ave; 🚆6, Ⓜ Metra to 51st-53rd). The sites are about three-quarters of a mile north of the university.

Historically, it's where the city held the 1893 World's Expo, when Chicago introduced the world to wonders such as the Ferris wheel, moving pictures and the zipper. Boat harbors, beaches, the Garden of the Phoenix (p197) and a golf course are all part of the mix today.

A long strip of land called the **Midway Plaisance** connects Jackson Park to Washington Park to the west; the Plaisance is home to an **ice rink** and college students kicking around soccer balls.

HYDE PARK ART CENTER   GALLERY

Map p318 (www.hydeparkart.org; 5020 S Cornell Ave; ⊙9am-8pm Mon-Thu, 9am-5pm Fri & Sat, noon-5pm Sun; 🚆6, Ⓜ Metra to 51st-53rd) Hyde Park Art Center shows contemporary works by Chicagoans – many of them students (current or graduated) of the center's classes. Check the schedule, as sometimes various groups offer walking or cycling tours that depart from here.

GARDEN OF THE PHOENIX   GARDENS

Map p318 (www.gardenofthephoenix.org; Jackson Park; ⊙6am-11pm; 🚆6 or 10) FREE The enchanted Garden of the Phoenix floats in Jackson Park (p195). Birds flit through the sunlight, turtles swim in the lagoons, and stone-cut lanterns dot the exotic landscape, which you'll likely have to yourself. Revitalization efforts are ongoing. Recent additions include 120 cherry trees and an art installation by Yoko Ono. It's located on Wooded Island and accessed by a bridge. From the Museum of Science & Industry (p193), walk south toward 59th St and you'll see it.

NUCLEAR ENERGY SCULPTURE   SCULPTURE

Map p318 (S Ellis Ave btwn E 56th & E 57th Sts; 🚆6, Ⓜ Metra to 55th-56th-57th) The nuclear age began at the University of Chicago: Enrico Fermi and his Manhattan Project cronies built a reactor and carried out the world's first controlled atomic reaction on December 2, 1942. The *Nuclear Energy* sculpture, by Henry Moore, marks the spot where it blew its stack.

ROCKEFELLER MEMORIAL CHAPEL   CHAPEL

Map p318 (http://rockefeller.uchicago.edu; 5850 S Woodlawn Ave; ⊙8am-5pm Mon-Sat, to 4pm Sun; 🚆6, Ⓜ Metra to 55th-56th-57th) The building's exterior will send sculpture lovers into paroxysms of joy – the facade bears 24 life-sized religious figures and 53 smaller ones, with even more inside. Check the website for times of **carillon and tower tours** ($5 donation requested).

WILLIAM RAINEY HARPER MEMORIAL LIBRARY   LIBRARY

Map p318 (1116 E 59th St; ⊙8am-4:30pm Mon-Fri; 🚆6, Ⓜ Metra to 55th-56th-57th) Once inside the building, head to the East Tower's 3rd floor, where the reading room (called the Cathey Learning Center) offers a terrific chill-out spot. The long row of arched, two-story windows bathes the space with light and an almost medieval sense of calm.

BOND CHAPEL   CHAPEL

Map p318 (1010 E 59th St; ⊙8am-4:30pm Mon-Fri; 🚆6, Ⓜ Metra to 55th-56th-57th) Built in 1926, the exquisite 150-seat chapel is worth a peek for its harmonious use of architecture, sculpture, woodcarvings and stained glass.

Hyde Park & South Side – Lofty Heights

Maybe it's the architecture that has inspired colleagues at the University of Chicago to win more than 80 Nobel prizes. It's certainly grandiose, with Gothic spires soaring into the sky and thick, turreted buildings fronting leafy quadrangles. Even Frank Lloyd Wright felt the vibe; he launched the Prairie style here.

EQROY/SHUTTERSTOCK ©

1. University of Chicago (p195)
Walk among the grand, ivy-clad buildings of this prestigious center of learning.

2. College architecture
From Gothic buildings to airy modern structures, the university is a visual feast.

3. Campus strolls
Get a taste of student life with a wander through the Earl L Neal Plaza.

4. Robie House (p194)
Don't miss Frank Lloyd Wright's Prairie School masterpiece, one of the most famous dwellings in the world.

DAVID RIUS & NURIA TUCA/GETTY IMAGES ©

BRUCE LEIGHTY/GETTY IMAGES ©

HYDE PARK HAIR SALON   NOTABLE BUILDING

Map p318 (5234 S Blackstone Ave; ⊘9am-8pm; 🚍6, Ⓜ Metra to 51st-53rd) You can visit Barack Obama's barber Zariff and the bulletproof-glass-encased presidential barber chair at the Hyde Park Hair Salon. Staff don't mind if you come in and take a look.

GREATER SALEM BAPTIST CHURCH   CHURCH

(☎773-874-2325; 215 W 71st St; 🚍29) Gospel fans can make the pilgrimage to the Greater Salem Baptist Church where gospel great Mahalia Jackson was a lifelong member.

◉ Bridgeport

A traditionally Irish, working-class neighborhood, Bridgeport has emerged as a hot spot for art centers and nifty bars and restaurants. Halsted St, from 31st St south to 43rd St, is Bridgeport's main drag. Most of the neighborhood lies west of the huge train embankment that itself is west of US Cellular Field. However, Bridgeport extends north of the park all the way to Chinatown.

PALMISANO PARK   PARK

(2700 S Halsted St; 🚍8) Opened on the site of an old limestone quarry, Palmisano Park unfurls an urban prairie landscape with great views of the Chicago skyline. Locals come here to fish for bluegill in the lagoon in summer and sled the hills in winter. The winding walkways, made of recycled construction debris, are great for a stroll anytime.

BRIDGEPORT ART CENTER   ARTS CENTER

Map p317 (☎773-247-3000; www.bridgeport art.com; 1200 W 35th St; 🚍8) FREE The old Spiegel Catalog Warehouse holds more than 50 artists' studios. The best time to come is on the third Friday of the month when the studios open to the public for a big to-do between 7pm and 10pm. Galleries on the 3rd and 4th floors are open during the week from 8am to 6pm (noon on Sundays). They offer intriguing exhibits in a variety of media. The mod sculpture garden (along Racine Ave) is also worth a peek.

ZHOU B ART CENTER   ARTS CENTER

Map p317 (☎773-523-0200; www.zhoubartcen ter.com; 1029 W 35th St; 🚍8) Like Bridgeport Art Center, which sits one block west, Zhou

---

LOCAL KNOWLEDGE

BLUES & JAZZ SHRINES

You won't find the following two spots listed on the usual tourist itinerary, but hardcore music fans will want to make the effort.

Jazz aficionados often seek out the unassuming **Meyers Ace Hardware Store** (Map p317; 315 E 35th St; ⊘9am-6pm Mon-Sat, 11am-2pm Sun; Ⓜ Green Line to 35th-Bronzeville-IIT). Why? Because in the 1920s and '30s the building was the Sunset Cafe, where all the greats gigged. Imagine Louis Armstrong blowing his trumpet over by the socket wrenches. Or Earl Hines hammering the piano, down in the plunger aisle. And that was just the house band. Benny Goodman, Jimmy Dorsey and Bix Beiderbecke all launched their careers at the Sunset.

While Chicago landmarked the building, there's no hint of its past life – no plaque marking the spot or jazz tchotchkes for sale. But if David Meyers, the store's owner, is around and not too busy, he'll take you into the back office that was once the stage, where the original red-tinged mural of jazz players splashes across the wall.

A few decades later and a few miles south, a different sound played in the night air – literally different. Guitars screamed and bass lines rolled at new decibel levels, because Muddy Waters and friends had plugged in their amps. So began the electric blues.

At **Muddy Waters' house** (4339 S Lake Park Ave), impromptu jam sessions with pals like Howlin' Wolf and Chuck Berry erupted in the front yard. Waters, of course, was Chicago's main bluesman, so everyone who was anyone came to pay homage. Waters lived here for 20 years, until 1974, but today the building stands vacant in a lonely, tumbledown lot. Preservationists have been working hard to ensure it's spared from the wrecking ball. A sign commemorates the spot.

You'll need wheels to reach Waters' home, and it's easiest if you have them for Meyers' store. Daytime is best for visits, as the 'hoods can be edgy at night.

WORTH A DETOUR

PULLMAN NATIONAL MONUMENT

Pullman (☎773-785-8901; www.nps.gov/pull; 11141 S Cottage Grove Ave; ⊙11am-3pm Tue-Sat; ⓂMetra to 111th St-Pullman) FREE got its national-park certification in 2015. Its significance? It offers a rare look at a capitalist's fallen utopia.

George Pullman was a millionaire rail-car manufacturer, and he started his namesake community in 1880 to provide his workers with homes in a wholesome environment. He built houses, apartments, stores, a hotel and churches. The town's careful design was based on French models and featured an aesthetic unknown in workers' housing then or now. But business went sour in 1893 when an economic depression hit. Pullman cut workers' pay, though he didn't lower their rent. A violent strike ensued in 1894, and things were never the same afterward. Pullman died in 1897, and the town was sold off shortly thereafter.

Pullman's design and architecture make for a fascinating walkabout. Alas, the site isn't easy to reach, as it is located on the far south side. Metra's Electric Line train makes the trip in 30 to 40 minutes from downtown's Millennium Station. The national park is still getting its legs under it. In the interim, the Historic Pullman Foundation (www.pullmanil.org) is taking the lead. It offers information and occasional walking tours; check the website for details.

B fills a massive old warehouse with galleries and studios. It also participates in the popular **Third Friday Open Studios** event from 7pm to 10pm. A trendy lounge with drinks and occasional live music operates on the 1st floor.

UNION STOCKYARDS GATE   HISTORIC SITE
Map p317 (850 W Exchange Ave; ☐8) The castle-like gate was once the main entrance to the vast stockyards where millions of cows and hogs met their ends each year. During the 1893 World's Expo the stockyards were a popular tourist draw, with nearly 10,000 people a day making the trek here to stare, awestruck, as the butchering machine took in animals and spat out blood and meat.

The value of those slaughtered in 1910 was an enormous $225 million. While sanitary conditions eventually improved from the hideous levels documented by Upton Sinclair, during the Spanish-American War American soldiers suffered more casualties because of bad cans of meat from the Chicago packing houses than because of enemy fire. The gate lies a block west of the 4100 block of S Halsted St.

⊙ Bronzeville

Once home to Louis Armstrong and other notables, Bronzeville thrived as the vibrant center of African American life in the city from 1920 to 1950, boasting an economic and cultural strength akin to New York's Harlem. Shifting populations, urban decay and the construction of a wall of public housing along State St led to Bronzeville's decline. In the last decade many young urban professionals have moved back to the neighborhood, and South Loop development stretches almost all the way here. Still, be careful at night: it's not a good place to be walking around after dark.

ILLINOIS INSTITUTE
OF TECHNOLOGY   UNIVERSITY
Map p317 (IIT; ☎312-567-7146; www.miessoci ety.org; 3201 S State St; ⓂGreen Line to 35th-Bronzeville-IIT) Famed mid-century architect Ludwig Mies van der Rohe designed many of the campus' modern buildings. Stop in at the Collens Welcome Center (at the northwest entrance of the McCormick Tribune Campus Center) to rent a 90-minute audio tour ($10) for DIY explorations. They're available from 11am to 3pm. Sometimes guided tours (same price) are also available; check the website.

SR CROWN HALL   ARCHITECTURE
Map p317 (3360 S State St; ⓂGreen Line to 35th-Bronzeville-IIT) The star of the Illinois Institute of Technology (p201) campus and Ludwig Mies van der Rohe's undisputed masterpiece is SR Crown Hall, appropriately home to the College of Architecture. The 1956 building, close to the center of campus, appears to be a transparent glass

box floating between its translucent base and suspended roof. At night it glows from within like an illuminated jewel.

STATE STREET VILLAGE ARCHITECTURE
Map p317 (cnr 33rd & State Sts; MGreen Line to 35th-Bronzeville-IIT) Helmut Jahn designed State Street Village on the Illinois Institute of Technology (p201) campus. Jahn studied at IIT in his younger days, and his strip of rounded glass-and-steel residence halls is a natural progression from the works of the modernist bigwigs he learned from while here.

SUPREME LIFE BUILDING HISTORIC BUILDING
Map p317 (3501 S Martin Luther King Jr Dr; MGreen Line to 35th-Bronzeville-IIT) The 1930s Supreme Life Building was the spot where John H Johnson Jr, the publishing mogul who founded *Ebony* magazine, got the idea for his empire, which includes *Jet* and other important titles serving African Americans. There's a little neighborhood visitors center that sells old albums and trinkets behind the bank here; enter from 35th St.

VICTORY MONUMENT MONUMENT
Map p317 (3500 S Martin Luther King Jr Dr; MGreen Line to 35th-Bronzeville-IIT) In the median at 35th St and Martin Luther King Jr Dr, the Victory Monument was erected in 1928 in honor of the African American soldiers who fought in WWI. The figures include a soldier, a mother and Columbia, the mythical figure meant to symbolize the New World.

ROBERT W ROLOSON HOUSES ARCHITECTURE
Map p317 (3213-3219 S Calumet Ave; MGreen Line to 35th-Bronzeville-IIT) Examples of stylish architecture from the past can be found throughout Bronzeville, and you can see some fine homes along two blocks of Calumet Ave between 31st and 33rd Sts, an area known as 'the Gap.' The buildings here include Frank Lloyd Wright's only row houses, the Robert W Roloson Houses.

IDA B WELLS HOUSE HOUSE
Map p317 (3624 S Martin Luther King Jr Dr; MGreen Line to 35th-Bronzeville-IIT) One of scores of Romanesque houses that date from the 1880s, the Ida B Wells House is named for its 1920s resident. Wells was a civil rights advocate who launched her ca-

reer after being forcibly removed from a train for refusing to go to the segregated car. A crusading journalist, she investigated lynchings and other racially motivated crimes. The home is a private residence and not open to the public.

PILGRIM BAPTIST CHURCH CHURCH
Map p317 (✆312-842-5830; 3301 S Indiana Ave; MGreen Line to 35th-Bronzeville-IIT) Gospel music got its start at Pilgrim Baptist Church, originally built as a synagogue by famed architects Dankmar Adler and Louis Sullivan in 1890. Unfortunately, the opulent structure was burned beyond repair in 2006 when a roof repairman lost control of his blowtorch. Only the exterior walls remain as a brooding reminder of the venue's prominence.

EATING

Hyde Park

VALOIS CAFETERIA AMERICAN $
Map p318 (✆773-667-0647; 1518 E 53rd St; mains $6-14; ⊗5:30am-10pm; 🚍6, MMetra to 51st-53rd) It's a mixed crowd at Valois. In fact, the clientele is so socioeconomically diverse that a U of C sociology professor wrote a well-known book about it, titled *Slim's Table*. It seems hot, fast, Southern-style dishes like catfish, biscuits and pot pies attract all kinds – even Barack Obama, who chowed here regularly when he lived in the neighborhood. It's a real-deal cafeteria, so know what you want before reaching the front of the fast-moving line. Cash only.

MEDICI CAFE $$
Map p318 (✆773-667-7394; www.medici57.com; 1327 E 57th St; mains $8-17; ⊗7am-10pm Mon-Fri, from 9am Sat & Sun; 🛜🍴♿; 🚍6, MMetra to 55th-56th-57th) The menu of thin-crust pizzas, sandwiches and salads draws U of C students to this colorful cafe and bakery. For breakfast, try the 'eggs espresso,' made by steaming eggs in an espresso machine. Heaps of gluten-free and vegetarian options are available.

After your meal, check the vast bulletin board out front. It's the perfect place to size up the character of the community and possibly find the complete works of John Maynard Keynes for sale, cheap.

SOUL VEGETARIAN EAST   VEGAN $$

(✆773-819-2084; www.originalsoulvegetarian.com; 203 E 75th St; mains $7-13; ⊙11am-8pm Mon-Thu, 11am-10pm Fri, from 8:30am Sat & Sun; ♪) Finding soul food that meets the tenets of the vegan diet is such a rarity that the creative barbecue sandwiches and dinner plates at this comfy South Side place have earned a national reputation. It attaches to a juice bar, so you can get your wheatgrass fix, too. You'll need wheels to get here.

LEM'S BAR-B-Q HOUSE   BARBECUE $$

(✆773-994-2428; www.lemsbarbq.com; 311 E 75th St; mains $10-15; ⊙1pm-1am Mon, Wed, Thu & Sun, to 3am Fri & Sat) Lem's is revered for its smoky-sauced rib tips, which come cushioned between a bed of fries and topping of white bread slices. You'll need a car to get here. Cash only.

✕ Bridgeport

★DUCK INN   MODERN AMERICAN $$

(✆312-724-8811; www.theduckinnchicago.com; 2701 S Eleanor St; mains $18-30; ⊙5pm-2am Tue-Fri, from noon Sat, from 10am Sun; Ⓜ Orange Line to Ashland) This superb gastropub hides on a working-class block in Bridgeport. There's much to love: the ubercool mid-century modern decor, exquisite but frugally priced cocktails, oh, and the food, especially the signature roasted duck for two and the duck-fat hot dog. It's high-quality fare in a completely non-snooty environment. A four-course tasting menu is available for $58.

NANA   MODERN AMERICAN $$

Map p317 (✆312-929-2486; www.nanaorganic.com; 3267 S Halsted St; mains $15-27; ⊙10am-2:30pm Mon & Tue, 10am-9:30pm Wed-Fri, 9am-9:30pm Sat, 9am-8:30pm Sun; ♪; 📵8) ♪ This convivial little gem received a Michelin Bib Gourmand award for great food offered at great value. It whips up yummy organic breakfasts (try the poached egg and chorizo 'nanadict') by day, and sandwiches and no-fuss dinners by candlelit night. Many dishes have a Latin twist, such as the ancho-chili-braised short ribs.

🍷 DRINKING & 🍸 NIGHTLIFE

★MARIA'S PACKAGED GOODS & COMMUNITY BAR   BAR

Map p317 (✆773-890-0588; http://community-bar.com; 960 W 31st St; ⊙3pm-2am Mon-Thu, from noon Fri-Sun; 📶; 📵8) Owner Ed works the cozy back-room bar furnished with vintage reclaimed decor, while mom Maria works the front liquor store. Both offer a fantastic craft-beer selection that Bridgeport's nouveau hipsters greedily suck down. DJs spin most nights, or there's other arty entertainment (Ed also owns a nearby gallery and 'experimental cultural center').

Maria's is Bridgeport's finest, a great stop after the neighborhood gallery hop or a White Sox game. Ed and family also opened a Korean-Polish street-food restaurant next door, and you can take the food into the bar.

SCHALLER'S PUMP   BAR

Map p317 (✆773-376-6332; 3714 S Halsted St; ⊙11am-2am Mon-Fri, 4pm-3am Sat, 4pm-midnight Sun; 📵8, Ⓜ Red Line to Sox-35th) Schaller's is Chicago's oldest continually operating tavern and is conveniently located across the street from the 11th Ward Democratic offices in Bridgeport. It's a fine place to toast the city's politicos (both Mayor Daleys have imbibed here) or the White Sox, whose ballpark is a short toss away.

Old neighborhood men sip Dewar's and soda at the bar, families order burgers and butt steak at the white-clothed tables, and there's nary a microbrew in sight. Cash only.

JIMMY'S WOODLAWN TAP   BAR

Map p318 (✆773-643-5516; 1172 E 55th St; ⊙10:30am-2am Mon-Fri, from 11am Sat & Sun; 📵6, Ⓜ Metra to 55th-56th-57th) Many of the geniuses of our age have killed brain cells right here in the Woodlawn Tap (also known as Jimmy's for the longtime owner). The place is dark and beery, and a little seedy. But for thousands of University of Chicago students craving pitchers of brew and heady conversation, it's home. Hungry? The Swissburgers are legendary. Cash only.

BERNICE'S TAVERN   BAR

Map p317 (✆312-326-9460; 3238 S Halsted St; ⊙3pm-midnight Mon, 3pm-2am Wed-Fri, 11am-3am Sat, noon-midnight Sun; 📵8, Ⓜ Red Line to

WORTH A DETOUR

CHICAGO FIRE SOCCER

The city's pro soccer team, the **Chicago Fire** (📞888-657-3473; www.chicago-fire.com; 71st St & Harlem Ave, Toyota Park, Bridgeview; tickets $20-50; 🚍Toyota Park Express), plays March through October at Toyota Park in southwest suburban Bridgeview. Tickets are fairly easy to come by. It's a long haul to reach the stadium. If you get to Midway Airport via the Orange Line, you can catch the Toyota Park Express bus, which runs on game days only. The full trip from the Loop takes at least an hour or so.

Sox-35th) A motley assemblage of local artists and neighborhood regulars haunts this workaday Bridgeport tavern, where the eclectic calendar includes wild, wacky bingo sessions on Wednesdays. Order a Starka, a honey-flavored liqueur every bit as Lithuanian as the owners. Cash only.

⭐ ENTERTAINMENT

PROMONTORY
LIVE MUSIC

Map p318 (📞312-801-2100; www.promontorychicago.com; 5311 S Lake Park Ave; 🚇6, Ⓜ Metra to 51st-53rd) The Promontory is Hyde Park's first hipster music hall. The rustic, huge-window room hosts jazz, soul and funk musicians, as well as DJs several nights a week. Even if there's no show, you can have a glass of wine at the bar and munch a wood-oven-roasted veggie sandwich.

COURT THEATRE
THEATER

Map p318 (📞773-753-4472; www.courttheatre.org; 5535 S Ellis Ave; 🚇6, Ⓜ Metra to 55th-56th-57th) A classical company hosted by the University of Chicago, the Court focuses on great works from the Greeks to Shakespeare to August Wilson, and various international plays not often performed in the USA.

🛍 SHOPPING

SEMINARY CO-OP BOOKSTORE
BOOKS

Map p318 (📞773-752-4381; www.semcoop.com; 5751 S Woodlawn Ave; ⏰8:30am-8pm Mon-Fri, 10am-6pm Sat, noon-6pm Sun; 🚇6, Ⓜ Metra to 55th-56th-57th) At awesomely academic Seminary Co-op, you might run into a Nobel laureate or three. Local scholars adore this place, where you'll find no less than eight versions of *War and Peace* on the shelves. The shop sprawls through a sunny building next

to Robie House, and provides plenty of chairs to sit and read. A busy cafe is attached.

57TH STREET BOOKS
BOOKS

Map p318 (📞773-684-1300; www.semcoop.com; 1301 E 57th St; ⏰10am-8pm; 🚇6, Ⓜ Metra to 55th-56th-57th) A serious university demands a serious bookstore, and as you descend the stairs to this basement-level shop you'll know you're in the right place. Its labyrinth of low-slung rooms makes up the kind of old-fashioned bookstore that goes way deeper than the popular titles. It has excellent staff picks. Seminary Co-op Bookstore is its sister shop selling academic tomes.

POWELL'S
BOOKS

Map p318 (📞773-955-7780; www.powellschicago.com; 1501 E 57th St; ⏰9am-11pm; 🚇6, Ⓜ Metra to 55th-56th-57th) This leading store for used books can get you just about any title ever published. Shelf after heaving shelf prop up the well-arranged stock. Staff sometimes put a box of free books outside by the entrance. They may be semi-tattered or in a foreign language, but then again, you may find a treasure to take away.

🏃 SPORTS & ACTIVITIES

CHICAGO WHITE SOX
BASEBALL

Map p317 (📞866-769-4263; www.whitesox.com; 333 W 35th St; Red Line to Sox-35th) The Sox are the Cubs' South Side rivals and play in the more modern 'Cell,' aka US Cellular Field. Tickets are usually cheaper and easier to get than at Wrigley Field; games on Sundays and Mondays offer the best deals. The Sox also come up with more promotions (free hot dogs, fireworks etc) to lure fans.

Because sellouts aren't usually an issue, you can stroll up to the ballpark box office on game day and buy a ticket. The Cell sports a couple of cool features, such as the Bullpen Bar, where you sip your beer practically on the field; and the pet check, which allows dog owners to bring Fido to the game and drop him off with a babysitter for a fee.

63RD STREET BEACH BEACH

(www.cpdbeaches.com; 6300 S Lake Shore Dr; ☐6, Ⓜ Metra to 63rd) This expanse of sand abutting Jackson Park (p195) contains a stately restored beach house with dramatic breezeways. It's next to a yacht harbor, and exudes a charm lacking at beaches with more modern – and mundane – facilities. Kids love the splashy, interactive water fountains. There are a couple of bars and grills for refreshments. Lifeguards patrol in summer.

57TH STREET BEACH BEACH

Map p318 (www.cpdbeaches.com; 5700 S Lake Shore Dr; ☐6, Ⓜ Metra to 55th-56th-57th) Just across Lake Shore Dr from the Museum of Science & Industry, 57th St Beach features an expanse of clean, golden sand. Surfers say it's the best beach to hang ten.

JACKSON PARK GOLF COURSE GOLF

(☎773-667-0524; www.cpdgolf.com; 6401 S Richards Dr; ☐6, Ⓜ Metra to 63rd) The district's only 18-hole course is moderately challenging. Public fees range from $28 to $31. Reservations are recommended. There's also a driving range.

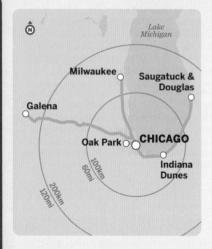

Day Trips from Chicago

Oak Park p207
Tour Frank Lloyd Wright's studio and see a slew of homes he designed for his neighbors. Ernest Hemingway's birthplace is here, too.

Indiana Dunes p208
Sunny beaches, woodsy trails, ranger-guided walks and towering sand dunes feature at this national and state park combination.

Milwaukee p210
Wisconsin's biggest city has a stellar lineup of beer, motorcycles, world-class art and a ballpark of racing sausages.

Saugatuck & Douglas p212
The artsy towns boom in summer thanks to their golden beaches, piney breezes, fruit pies and welcome-one, welcome-all mind-set.

Galena p213
Quaint it is, with perfectly preserved, Civil War-era streets set amid rolling, cow-dotted hills by the Mississippi River.

Oak Park

Explore

This suburb spawned two famous sons: novelist Ernest Hemingway was born here, and architect Frank Lloyd Wright lived and worked here for 20 years. The town's main sights revolve around the two men. For Hemingway, a low-key museum and his birthplace provide an intriguing peek at his formative years. For Wright, the studio where he developed the Prairie style is the big draw, as is a slew of surrounding houses he designed for his neighbors. Ten of them cluster within a mile along Forest and Chicago Aves (gawking must occur from the sidewalk since they're privately owned). You could easily spend an afternoon here.

The Best...

➡ **Sight** Frank Lloyd Wright Home & Studio

➡ **Place to Eat** Hemmingway's Bistro

Top Tip

Explore on the cheap by buying an architectural site map ($4.25) from the Wright Home & Studio shop, which gives the locations of all Wright-designed abodes in the area.

Getting There & Away

➡ **Car** Take I-290 west, exiting north on Harlem Ave; take Harlem Ave north to Lake St and turn right. There's a parking garage a few blocks down the road.

➡ **El** From downtown Chicago, take the CTA Green Line to the Oak Park station (one-way $3, 25 minutes), then walk north on Oak Park Ave. It's about a quarter mile to the Hemingway sights and a mile to the Wright home. The train traverses some bleak neighborhoods before emerging into Oak Park's wide-lawn splendor.

Need to Know

➡ **Area Code** 708

➡ **Location** 10 miles west of the Loop

➡ **Oak Park Visitors Center** (☑888-625-7275; www.visitoakpark.com; 1010 W Lake St; ⊙10am-5pm)

◉ SIGHTS

FRANK LLOYD WRIGHT HOME & STUDIO   ARCHITECTURE

(☑312-994-4000; www.flwright.org; 951 Chicago Ave; adult/child $17/14; ⊙10am-4pm) This is where Wright lived and worked from 1889 to 1909. Tour frequency varies, from every 20 minutes on summer weekends to every hour or so in winter. The hour-long walk-through reveals a fascinating place, filled with the details that made Wright's style distinctive. It costs $5 extra to take pictures inside. The studio also offers guided neighborhood walking tours ($15), as well as a self-guided audio version ($15).

ERNEST HEMINGWAY MUSEUM   MUSEUM

(☑708-848-2222; www.ehfop.org; 200 N Oak Park Ave; adult/child $15/13; ⊙1-5pm Wed-Fri & Sun, 10am-5pm Sat) Despite Hemingway allegedly calling Oak Park a 'village of wide lawns and narrow minds,' the town still pays homage to him at this museum. Exhibits begin with his middle-class Oak Park background and the innocent years before he went off to find adventure. The ensuing displays focus on his writings in Spain and during WWII. Admission also provides entry to his birthplace home across the street.

MOORE HOUSE   ARCHITECTURE

(333 N Forest Ave) During Wright's 20 years in Oak Park, he designed a whole heap of houses. Moore House is particularly noteworthy. First built in 1895, it's Wright's bizarre interpretation of an English manor house. In his later years, Wright called the house 'repugnant' and said he had only taken the commission because he needed the money. He claimed that he walked out of his way to avoid passing it.

UNITY TEMPLE   ARCHITECTURE

(☑708-383-8873; www.flwright.org; 875 Lake St; adult/child $10/8; ⊙10:30am-4:30pm Mon-Fri, 10am-2pm Sat, 1-4pm Sun) It's one of Frank Lloyd Wright's architectural wonders, built in 1908. Explore at your leisure on a self-guided look around, or check the schedule for guided tours. A recent restoration helps the building shine.

✕ EATING & DRINKING

HEMMINGWAY'S BISTRO   FRENCH $$$

(☑708-524-0806; www.hemmingwaysbistro.com; 211 N Oak Park Ave; mains $21-32; ⊙7am-10pm) Fork in to all the French classics – coq

DAY TRIPS FROM CHICAGO OAK PARK

WORTH A DETOUR

ROUTE 66

America's 'Mother Road' kicks off in downtown Chicago on Adams St, just west of Michigan Ave. Within a 3.5-hour drive you can see some vintage bits. Sadly, most of the original Route 66 has been superseded by I-55 in Illinois, though the old road still exists in scattered sections often paralleling the interstate. Keep an eye out for brown 'Historic Route 66' signs, which pop up at crucial junctions to mark the way.

The first primo stop rises from the cornfields 60 miles south of Chicago in Wilmington. Here the **Gemini Giant** (810 E Baltimore St) – a 28ft fiberglass spaceman – stands guard outside the Launching Pad Drive In. The restaurant is now shuttered, but the statue remains a quintessential photo op. To reach it, leave I-55 at exit 241, and follow Hwy 44 south a short distance to Hwy 53, which rolls into town.

Motor 45 miles onward to Pontiac and the tchotchke-and-photo-filled **Route 66 Hall of Fame** (☑815-844-4566; 110 W Howard St; ☺9am-5pm) `FREE`. Cruise another 50 miles to Shirley and **Funk's Grove** (☑309-874-3360; www.funksmaplesirup.com; ☺9am-5pm Mon-Fri, from 10am Sat, from 1pm Sun), a pretty 19th-century maple-syrup farm and nature preserve (exit 154 off I-55).

Ten miles later you'll reach the throwback hamlet of Atlanta. Pull up a chair at the **Palms Grill Cafe** (☑217-648-2233; www.thepalmsgrillcafe.com; 110 SW Arch St; mains $6-10; ☺10am-8pm Mon-Thu, 8am-9pm Fri & Sat, 10am-3pm Sun), where thick slabs of gooseberry, sour cream raisin and other retro pies tempt from the glass case. Then walk across the street to snap a photo with *Tall Paul*, a sky-high statue of Paul Bunyan clutching a hot dog.

The state capital of Springfield, 50 miles further on, has several more sights, including the **Cozy Dog Drive In** (www.cozydogdrivein.com; 2935 S 6th St; mains $2-5; ☺8am-8pm Mon-Sat), reputed birthplace of the corn dog.

For more information, see **Illinois Route 66 Scenic Byway** (www.illinoisroute66.org). And should you decide to keep on truckin', it's a lazy 2200 miles onward to the route's end in Los Angeles.

au vin, caussoulet, bouillabaisse – at this cozy little bistro across from the Hemingway Museum. If nothing else, drop in and sit at the bar for a glass of wine.

Indiana Dunes

Explore

Sunny beaches, rustling grasses and woodsy campgrounds are Indiana Dunes' claim to fame. The area is hugely popular on summer days with sunbathers from Chicago and towns throughout northern Indiana. In addition to its beaches, the area is noted for its plant variety: everything from cacti to pine trees sprouts here. Sweet hiking trails meander up the dunes and through the woodlands. Visit in the morning and linger on into the afternoon.

The Best...

➡ **Sight** Indiana Dunes National Lakeshore

➡ **Place to Eat** Great Lakes Cafe
➡ **Place to Drink** Flamingo Pizza

Top Tip

The best place to start is the **Visitor Center** (☑219-926-7561; Hwy 49; ☺8:30am-6:30pm Jun-Aug, to 4:30pm Sep-May). It can provide beach details; a schedule of ranger-guided walks and activities; and hiking, biking and birding maps.

Getting There & Away

➡ **Car** Take I-90 east out of Chicago to Indiana (be prepared to pay about $7.50 worth of tolls). After Gary, take exit 21 to merge onto I-94 east (toward Detroit). Soon after, take exit 22B to merge onto US 20 toward Porter. Parking is difficult on weekends; try West Beach (per car $6). Driving takes one hour.

➡ **Metra** South Shore Line trains make the journey from Millennium Station in the Loop. It's about 75 minutes to the Dune Park or Beverly Shores stops (one-way $8.25 to $9.25). Note both stations are about a mile-and-a-half walk from the beach.

Need to Know

→ **Area Code** ☏219

→ **Location** 45 miles southeast of the Loop

→ **Porter County Convention & Visitors Bureau** (www.indianadunes.com)

SIGHTS

INDIANA DUNES NATIONAL LAKESHORE   NATIONAL PARK

(☏219-926-7561; www.nps.gov/indu) FREE The dunes stretch along 15 miles of Lake Michigan shoreline. Swimming is allowed anywhere along the sand. A short walk away from the beaches, several hiking paths crisscross the dunes and woodlands. The best are the **Bailly-Chellberg Trail** (2.5 miles) that winds by a still operating 1870s farm, and the **Heron Rookery Trail** (2 miles), where blue herons flock. Oddly, all this natural bounty lies smack-dab next to smoke-belching factories, which you'll also see at various vantage points.

INDIANA DUNES STATE PARK   STATE PARK

(☏219-926-1952; www.dnr.in.gov/parklake; per car $12) The state park is a 2100-acre, shore-side pocket within the national lakeshore; it's located at the end of Hwy 49, near Chesterton. It has more amenities, but also more regulation and crowds (plus the vehicle entry fee). Wintertime brings out the cross-country skiers; summertime brings out the hikers. Seven trails zigzag over the landscape; No 4 up Mt Tom rewards with Chicago skyline views.

✗ EATING & DRINKING

GREAT LAKES CAFE   DINER $

(201 Mississippi St; mains $6-9; ☺5am-3pm Mon-Fri, 6am-1pm Sat; ♿) This colorful Greek family diner sits right in front of a steel mill, whose workers pile in for the cheap, hearty pancakes, meatloaf, butterfly shrimp, bacon-pecan brownies and whatever else features on the dry-erase board of daily specials. It's located a short distance off the highway, before you reach the national lakeshore.

LUCREZIA   ITALIAN $$$

(☏219-926-5829; www.lucreziacafe.com; 428 S Calumet Rd; mains $16-28; ☺11am-10pm Sun-

Thu, to 11pm Fri & Sat) It's a homey favorite for Italian staples, in Chesterton.

FLAMINGO PIZZA   BAR

(☏219-938-0323; 8341 Locust Ave; ☺11am-10pm Mon-Wed, to midnight Thu-Sun) Yes, you can get pizza, but the bar is what beckons: a cozy watering hole where you sit elbow-to-elbow with locals. The good beers and lake perch are a bonus to the ambience. Located near West Beach.

SPORTS & ACTIVITIES

WEST BEACH   BEACH

(per car $6) West Beach, nearest to Gary, draws fewer crowds than the other beaches and features a number of nature hikes and trails. It's also the only beach with lifeguards. There's a snack bar and cool Chicago vistas.

CAMP STOP GENERAL STORE   BICYCLE RENTAL

(☏219-878-1382; 2 W Dunes Hwy; bike rental per 3hr/day $12/20; ☺9am-9pm Mon-Sat, to 6pm Sun) The store serving the park's campground also rents bikes. It's located across the tracks from the Beverly Shores train stop. From here, it's a short ride to the nearest beach. Be sure to turn left onto Lake Front Dr for a quick detour past the 'Century of Progress homes,' five offbeat remnants from the 1933 Chicago's World's Fair.

⌊≡⌋ SLEEPING

DUNEWOOD CAMPGROUND   CAMPGROUND $

(☏219-395-8914; www.nps.gov/indu; campsites $18; ☺Apr-Oct) The Indiana Dunes National Lakeshore's seasonal campsites are rustic (no electricity) and first come, first served (no reservations).

INDIANA DUNES STATE PARK CAMPGROUND   CAMPGROUND $

(☏866-622-6746; www.camp.in.gov; campsites $23-36; ☺year-round) These campsites are modern and close to the beach. Reserve in advance in summertime.

TRYON FARM GUESTHOUSE   B&B $$

(☏219-879-3618; www.tryonfarmguesthouse. com; r incl breakfast $190; ❄@☎♿) This

Indiana Dunes

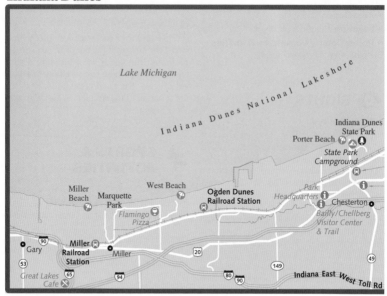

four-room B&B nestles in a turn-of-the-century farmhouse near Michigan City. It's part of a larger conservation community, in which 50 families share farm duties and an organic garden.

Milwaukee

Explore

Beer, brats and bowling? Of course Milwaukee has them. But attractions like the Calatrava-designed art museum, bad-to-the-bone Harley-Davidson Museum, and stylish eating and shopping 'hoods have added a groovy layer to Wisconsin's largest city. In summertime, festivals let loose revelry by the lake. And where else will you see racing sausages? Milwaukee rocks any time, but especially during weekends.

The Best...

➜ **Sight** Harley-Davidson Museum
➜ **Place to Eat** Comet Cafe
➜ **Place to Drink** Best Place (p212)

Top Tip

Many bars and restaurants host a traditional fish fry on Friday. Join locals celebrating the work week's end over a communal meal of beer-battered cod, french fries and coleslaw.

Getting There & Away

➜ **Car** Take I-90/94 west from downtown Chicago, and follow I-94 when it splits off. The interstate goes all the way into Milwaukee. Travel time is around two hours; tolls cost around $6.

➜ **Train** Traveling on **Amtrak** (☑414-271-0840; www.amtrakhiawatha.com; 433 W St Paul Ave) is often the quickest mode given the snail-crawl pace of highway traffic. The Hiawatha train runs seven times per day to/from Chicago ($25, 1½ hours). The main station is downtown.

Getting Around

➜ **Bus** The **Milwaukee County Transit System** (www.ridemcts.com; fare $2.25) provides efficient local bus service. Bus 31 goes to Miller Brewery; bus 90 goes to Miller Park. Catch them along Wisconsin Ave.

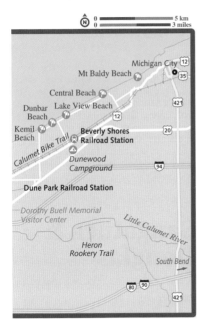

soars open and closed every day at 10am, noon and 5pm (8pm on Thursday), which is wild to watch; head to the suspension bridge outside for the best view. There are fabulous folk and outsider art galleries, and a sizable collection of Georgia O'Keeffe paintings. A 2015 renovation added photography and new media galleries to the trove.

MILLER BREWING COMPANY   BREWERY

(☑414-931-2337; www.millercoors.com; 4251 W State St; ⊙10:30am-4:30pm Mon-Sat, to 3:30pm Sun Jun-Aug, to 3:30pm Mon-Sat Sep-May) **FREE** Pabst and Schlitz have moved on, but Miller preserves Milwaukee's beer legacy. Join the legions lined up for the free tours. Though the mass-produced beer may not be your favorite, the factory impresses with its sheer scale: you'll visit the packaging plant, where 2000 cans are filled each minute, and the warehouse, where a half-million cases await shipment. And then there's the generous tasting session at the tour's end, where you can down three full-size samples. Don't forget your ID.

LAKEFRONT BREWERY   BREWERY

(☑414-372-8800; www.lakefrontbrewery.com; 1872 N Commerce St; 1hr tours $8; ⊙11am-8pm Mon-Thu, to 9pm Fri, 9am-9pm Sat, 10am-5pm Sun) Well-loved Lakefront Brewery, across the river from Brady St, has afternoon tours, but the swellest time to visit is on Friday nights when there's a fish fry, 16 beers to try and a polka band letting loose. Tour times vary throughout the week, but there's usually at least a 2pm and 3pm walk-through.

Need to Know

➡ **Area Code** ☑414

➡ **Location** 92 miles north of Chicago

➡ **Milwaukee Convention & Visitors Bureau** (☑800-554-1448; www.visitmilwaukee.org)

⊙ SIGHTS

★HARLEY-DAVIDSON MUSEUM   MUSEUM

(☑877-436-8738; www.h-dmuseum.com; 400 W Canal St; adult/child $20/10; ⊙9am-6pm Fri-Wed, to 8pm Thu May-Sep, from 10am Oct-Apr) Hundreds of motorcycles show the differing styles through the decades, including the flashy rides of Elvis and Evel Knievel. You can sit in the saddle of various bikes (on the bottom floor, in the Experience Gallery) and take badass photos. Even nonbikers will enjoy the interactive exhibits and tough, leather-clad crowds.

MILWAUKEE ART MUSEUM   MUSEUM

(☑414-224-3200; www.mam.org; 700 N Art Museum Dr; adult/child $17/free; ⊙10am-5pm daily, to 8pm Fri; 🛪) You have to see this lakeside institution, which features a stunning winglike addition by Santiago Calatrava. It

✖ EATING & DRINKING

★COMET CAFE   AMERICAN $

(☑414-273-7677; www.thecometcafe.com; 1947 N Farwell Ave; mains $8-13; ⊙10am-10pm Mon-Fri, from 9am Sat & Sun; 🖋) Students, young families, older couples and bearded, tattooed types pile in to the rock-and-roll Comet for gravy-smothered meatloaf, mac 'n' cheese, vegan gyros and hangover brunch dishes. It's a craft-beer-pouring bar on one side and a retro-boothed diner on the other. Be sure to try one of the giant cupcakes for dessert.

MILWAUKEE PUBLIC MARKET   MARKET $

(☑414-336-1111; www.milwaukeepublicmarket. org; 400 N Water St; ⊙10am-8pm Mon-Fri, 8am-7pm Sat, 10am-6pm Sun; 🛪) Located in the Third Ward, it stocks mostly prepared foods: cheese, chocolate, beer, tacos and frozen custard. Take them upstairs where there are tables, free wi-fi and $1 used books.

BEST PLACE
BAR

(www.bestplacemilwaukee.com; 901 W Junau Ave; ☺noon-6pm Mon, noon-10pm Wed & Thu, 10:30am-10pm Fri & Sat, 10:30am-6pm Sun) Join the locals knocking back beers and massive whiskey pours at this small tavern in the former Pabst Brewery headquarters. A fireplace warms the cozy, dark-wood room; original murals depicting Pabst's history adorn the walls. Staff give daily tours ($8, including a 16oz Pabst or Schlitz tap brew) that explore the building.

UBER TAP ROOM
BAR

(☑414-755-2424; www.ubertaproom.com; 1048 N Old World 3rd St; ☺11am-8pm Sun-Wed, to 10pm Thu, to 11pm Fri & Sat) It's touristy, in the thick of Old World 3rd St and attached to the Wisconsin Cheese Mart, but it's a great place to sample local fare. Thirty Wisconsin beers flow from the taps, and cheese from the state's dairy bounty accompanies. Themed plates (spicy cheeses, stinky cheeses etc) cost $11 to $14.

🛏 SLEEPING

★ **BREWHOUSE INN & SUITES**   HOTEL $$

(☑414-810-3350; www.brewhousesuites.com; 1215 N 10th St; r $199-249; P❄@🛜) This 90-room hotel opened in 2013 in the exquisitely renovated old Pabst Brewery complex. Each of the large chambers has steampunk decor, a kitchenette and free wi-fi. Continental breakfast is included. It's at downtown's far west edge, about a half-mile walk from sausagey Old World 3rd St and a good 2 miles from the festival grounds. Parking costs $26.

IRON HORSE HOTEL
HOTEL $$$

(☑888-543-4766; www.theironhorsehotel.com; 500 W Florida St; r $220-320; P❄🛜) This boutique hotel near the Harley museum is geared toward motorcycle enthusiasts, with covered parking for bikes. Most of the loft-style rooms retain the post-and-beam, exposed-brick interior of what was once a bedding factory. Parking costs $30.

🏃 SPORTS & ACTIVITIES

MILLER PARK
BASEBALL

(www.brewers.com; 1 Brewers Way) The Brewers play baseball at fab Miller Park, which has a retractable roof and real grass. The 'Racing Sausages' star in the middle of the sixth inning. To the uninitiated, that's five people in foam-rubber meat costumes – including Hot Dog, Bratwurst and Chorizo – who sprint around the ballpark's perimeter, vying for sausage supremacy. It's located near S 46th St.

Saugatuck & Douglas

Explore

Saugatuck is one of Michigan's most popular resort areas, known for its strong arts community, numerous B&Bs and gay-friendly vibe. Douglas is its twin city a mile or so to the south, and they've pretty much sprawled into one. It's a touristy but funky place, with ice-cream-licking families, yuppie boaters and martini-drinking gay couples sharing the waterfront. Galleries and shops fill the compact downtown core. Weekends bring out the masses.

The Best...

⇒ **Activity** Saugatuck Chain Ferry
⇒ **Place to Eat** Crane's Pie Pantry
⇒ **Place to Drink** Saugatuck Brewing Company

Top Tip

Don't forget that Michigan is on Eastern Standard Time, one hour ahead of Chicago.

Getting There & Away

⇒ **Car** Take I-90 east toward Indiana for about 30 miles. After Gary, merge onto I-94 east, and stay on it for 65 miles. After Benton Harbor merge onto I-196/US 31 north, and take it for about 40 miles, until the Saugatuck/Douglas exit. Travel time is around 2½ hours; tolls cost around $7.50.

WINERIES & ANTIQUES AROUND SAUGATUCK

The roads around Saugatuck are ripe for exploration. **Antiquing** prevails on the Blue Star Hwy running south for 20 miles. The odd shops often look like just a bunch of junk in someone's front yard, but pull up at the right time and that old traffic light or Victorian sled can be yours for a song. **Blueberry U-pick farms** share this stretch of road and make a juicy stop, too. And several wineries cluster in the area. The **Lake Michigan Shore Wine Trail** (www.miwinetrail.com) provides a map of vineyards and tasting rooms. Most are signposted off the highway.

Need to Know

→ **Area Code** 269
→ **Location** 140 miles northeast of Chicago
→ **Saugatuck/Douglas CVB** (www.saugatuck.com)

EATING & DRINKING

CRANE'S PIE PANTRY BAKERY $
(269-561-2297; www.cranespiepantry.com; 6054 124th Ave; pie slices $4.50; 9am-8pm Mon-Thu, 9am-9pm Fri & Sat, 11am-8pm Sun) Buy a bulging slice, or pick apples and peaches in the surrounding orchards. Crane's is in Fennville, 3 miles south on the Blue Star Hwy, then 4 miles inland on Hwy 89.

PHIL'S BAR & GRILLE AMERICAN $$
(269-857-1555; www.philsbarandgrille.com; 215 Butler St; mains $18-29; 11:30am-10pm Sun-Thu, to 11pm Fri & Sat) This humming pub turns out terrific 'broasted' (combining broiling and roasting) chicken, fish tacos, lamb lollipops and gumbo in a cozy, wood-floored room.

SAUGATUCK BREWING COMPANY BREWERY
(269-857-7222; www.saugatuckbrewing.com; 2948 Blue Star Hwy; 11:30am-10pm Sun-Fri, to 11pm Sat) Locals like to hang out and sip the housemade suds.

SPORTS & ACTIVITIES

SAUGATUCK CHAIN FERRY BOATING
(end of Mary St; one-way $1; 9am-9pm late May-early Sep) The best thing to do in Saugatuck is also the most affordable. Jump aboard the clackety chain ferry, and the operator will pull you across the Kalamazoo River.

MT BALDHEAD WALKING
Huff up the stairs of this 200ft-high sand dune for a stellar view. Then race down the other side to Oval Beach. Get here via the chain ferry; walk right (north) from the dock.

OVAL BEACH BEACH
(Oval Beach Rd; 9am-10pm) Lifeguards patrol the long expanse of fine sand. There are bathrooms and concession stands, though not enough to spoil the peaceful, dune-laden scene. It costs $8 to park. Or arrive the adventurous way, via chain ferry and a trek over Mt Baldhead.

SLEEPING

BAYSIDE INN INN $$
(269-857-4321; www.baysideinn.net; 618 Water St; r $160-260;) This former boathouse has 10 rooms on Saugatuck's waterfront.

PINES MOTORLODGE MOTEL $$
(269-857-5211; www.thepinesmotorlodge.com; 56 Blue Star Hwy; r $139-249;) Retro-cool tiki lamps, pinewood furniture and communal lawn chairs add up to a fun, social ambience amid the firs in Douglas.

Galena

Explore

Wee Galena spreads across wooded hillsides near the Mississippi River, amid rolling, barn-dotted farmland. Redbrick mansions line the streets, left over from the town's heyday in the mid-1800s, when local lead mines made it rich. Even with all the touristy B&Bs, fudge and antique shops, there's no denying Galena's beauty. Throw in cool kayak trips and back-road drives, and you've got a lovely, slow-paced getaway. Summer and fall weekends see the most action.

The Best...

➤ **Sight** Ulysses S Grant Home
➤ **Place to Eat** Fritz and Frites
➤ **Place to Drink** VFW Hall

Top Tip

When entering town on US 20, turn onto Park Ave, then Bouthillier St to reach the free parking lot beside the old train depot. Most sights, shops and restaurants are walkable from here.

Getting There & Away

➤ **Car** Take I-90 west out of Chicago (tolls apply). Just before Rockford, follow US 51 and I-39 heading south for 3 miles, and then merge onto US 20 west, which runs all the way into hilly Galena. The drive takes about three hours.

Need to Know

➤ **Area Code** ☎815
➤ **Location** 165 miles northwest of Chicago
➤ **Galena CVB** (www.galena.org)

◉ SIGHTS

ULYSSES S GRANT HOME MUSEUM
(☎815-777-3310; www.granthome.com; 500 Bouthillier St; adult/child $5/3; ⏰9am-4:45pm Wed-Sun Apr-Oct, reduced hours Nov-Mar) The 1860 abode was a gift from local Republicans to the victorious general at the Civil War's end. Grant lived here until he became the country's 18th president.

✕ EATING & DRINKING

FRITZ AND FRITES FRENCH, GERMAN $$
(☎815-777-2004; www.fritzandfrites.com; 317 N Main St; mains $17-22; ⏰4-9pm Tue-Sun) This romantic little bistro serves a compact menu of both German and French classics. Dig in to mussels with champagne sauce or maybe a tender schnitzel.

111 MAIN AMERICAN $$
(☎815-777-8030; www.oneelevenmain.com; 111 N Main St; mains $18-28; ⏰4-9pm Mon-Thu,

11am-10pm Fri & Sat, 11am-9pm Sun) Pot roast, pork and beans, and other Midwestern favorites arrive at the table, using ingredients sourced from local farms.

VFW HALL BAR
(100 S Main St; ⏰10am-11pm) The VFW Hall provides an opportunity to sip cheap beer and watch TV alongside veterans of long-ago wars. Don't be shy: as the sign out front says, the public is welcome.

🏃 SPORTS & ACTIVITIES

FEVER RIVER OUTFITTERS OUTDOORS
(☎815-776-9425; www.feverriveroutfitters.com; 525 S Main St; ⏰10am-5pm, closed Tue-Thu early Sep-late May) Outdoors enthusiasts should head to this shop, which rents canoes, kayaks, bicycles and snowshoes. It also offers guided tours, such as 9-mile kayak trips ($45 per person, equipment included) on the Mississippi River's backwaters.

STAGECOACH TRAIL SCENIC DRIVE
The Stagecoach Trail is a 26-mile ride on a narrow, twisty road en route to Warren. Pick it up by taking Main St northeast through downtown; at the second stop sign go right (you'll see a trail marker). And yes, it really was part of the old stagecoach route between Galena and Chicago.

SHENANDOAH RIDING CENTER HORSEBACK RIDING
(☎815-777-9550; www.theshenandoahriding center.com; 200 N Brodrecht Rd; 1hr ride $45) Saddle up at Shenandoah. It offers trail rides through the valley for all levels of riders. The stables are 8 miles east of Galena.

🛏 SLEEPING

GRANT HILLS MOTEL MOTEL $
(☎877-421-0924; www.granthills.com; 9372 US 20; r $80-100; ❄🛜🛝) The motel is a no-frills option 1.5 miles east of town, with countryside views and a horseshoe pitch.

DESOTO HOUSE HOTEL HOTEL $$
(☎815-777-0090; www.desotohouse.com; 230 S Main St; r $160-225; ❄🛜) 🐾 Grant and Lincoln stayed in the well-furnished rooms, and you can too. The hotel dates from 1855.

🛏️ Sleeping

Chicago's lodgings rise high in the sky, many in architectural landmarks. Snooze in the building that gave birth to the skyscraper, in one of Mies van der Rohe's boxy structures, or in a century-old art-deco masterpiece. Huge business hotels, B&Bs and hostels blanket the cityscape too. But nothing comes cheap...

Seasons & Prices

The high-season apex is June to August, when festivals and tourism peak. But Chicago hosts loads of business conventions, so demand – and prices – can skyrocket during odd times the rest of the year too. Book well in advance to avoid unpleasant surprises. Prices are lowest December to February.

Hotels

There are roughly 100,000 hotel rooms in Chicago, seemingly on every corner in the Loop, Near North and the Gold Coast in particular. All big-box chains have outposts (usually several) here. Most are geared to conventioneers. Groovy boutique hotels abound, as do uberluxury hotels catering to rock stars and business tycoons.

B&Bs

Chicago has several B&Bs and they're typically cheaper than big hotels. Set in elegant old row houses and greystones, they cluster in Wicker Park and Lake View. They're generally casual, with self-serve breakfast. Many have two- to three-night minimum stays.

Hostels

Chicago has one Hostelling International (www.hiusa.org) property and several independent hostels that do not require membership. There has been a boom of the latter in fun, outlying neighborhoods such as Wicker Park and Wrigleyville. Browse listings at www.hostels.com and www.hostelworld.com.

Apartments

Vacation rentals in apartments are a good deal in Chicago, especially if your stay coincides with a big convention that ratchets up hotel prices. Try Vacation Rental By Owner (www.vrbo.com) and Airbnb (www.airbnb.com).

Amenities

In-room wi-fi, air-con and a private bathroom are standard, unless noted otherwise.

TOP-END

On-site concierge services, fitness and business centers, restaurants, bars and room service are all par for the course. There's often a fee for in-room wi-fi ($10 to $15), while it's free in the lobby. Breakfast is rarely included.

MIDRANGE

Rooms have a phone, cable TV and free wi-fi; many also have a mini-refrigerator, microwave and hairdryer. Often a small fitness center is on-site. Rates often include a continental breakfast.

BUDGET

Budget accommodations generally means hostels. Expect bunk-bed dorms, shared bathrooms, free wi-fi and continental breakfast. Staff often organize outings to local sights and entertainment venues.

Pets

A fair number of Chicago hotels allow pets, but many charge a $50 to $100 nonrefundable cleaning fee. Some places, however, not only permit pets, but waive fees and/or provide special programs for four-legged friends.

NEED TO KNOW

Price Ranges
The following price ranges refer to a double room in high season.

$ less than $100

$$ $100–$250

$$$ more than $250

Tax
Room tax is 17.4%.

Parking Costs
Figure on $55 to $65 per night downtown for in-and-out privileges.

Tipping
Hotel bellhops $2 per bag

Housekeeping staff $2 to $5 daily

Parking valets At least $2

Room service 15% to 20%

Concierges Up to $20 (for securing last-minute restaurant reservations, sold-out show tickets etc)

Check-In & Check-Out Times
Normally 3pm for check-in and 11am for check-out. Many places will allow early check-in if the room is available (or will store your luggage if not).

Useful Websites
Lonely Planet (www.lonelyplanet.com/hotels) Recommendations and bookings.

Chicago Bed & Breakfast Association (www.chicago-bed-breakfast.com) Represents some 15 properties.

Hotel Tonight (www.hoteltonight.com) National discounter with last-minute deals; book via the free app.

Lonely Planet's Top Choices

Acme Hotel (p221) Downtown's grooviest boutique, complete with lava lights.

Hotel Burnham (p218) History, architecture and yoga gear mash up in slick rooms.

Virgin Hotel (p218) The first outpost of billionaire Richard Branson's cheeky hotel chain impresses.

Holiday Jones (p228) From plaid rooms to an on-site cafe, it wafts the buzzy Wicker Park vibe.

Hampton Inn Chicago Downtown/N Loop (p218) Historic art-deco building where you'll feel like a Route 66 road tripper.

Longman & Eagle (p229) Six wood-floored, vintage-stylish rooms that sit above a Michelin-starred gastropub.

Best by Budget

$
Freehand Chicago (p220) Super-hip hostel-hotel hybrid with spiffy, high-tech dorms.

Urban Holiday Lofts (p228) Live like a local in Bucktown, surrounded by cool cafes.

HI-Chicago (p218) You can't beat the Loop location and free city tours.

Wrigley Hostel (p226) Youthful facility that is spitting distance from the famed ballpark and nightlife.

$$
Hotel Lincoln (p226) Fun, from 'wall of bad art' kitsch to pedicab service.

Willows Hotel (p226) Peachy rooms fill this dapper little property.

Buckingham Athletic Club Hotel (p218) Expansive rooms

and a gym with lap pool, hiding downtown.

Wicker Park Inn (p229) Sunny pastel-colored B&B with sweet breakfast offerings.

$$$
Guesthouse Hotel (p227) Enormous modern suites near Andersonville's hip shops and taverns.

Radisson Blu Aqua Hotel (p219) Mod, blond-wood rooms with balconies and views.

Drake Hotel (p225) Historic gilded property at the head of the Magnificent Mile.

Best for Architecture Buffs

Hotel Burnham (p218) In the landmark Reliance Building, which laid the groundwork for modern skyscraper design.

Radisson Blu Aqua Hotel (p219) In the undulating Aqua Tower, the world's tallest structure designed by a woman.

Renaissance Blackstone Hotel (p230) In a neoclassical, beaux-arts beauty known as the 'hotel of presidents.'

Hard Rock Hotel Chicago (p219) In the art-deco, champagne-bottle-esque Carbide & Carbon building.

Best for Families

Embassy Suites Chicago – Lakefront (p223) Large rooms a few blocks from Navy Pier.

Days Inn Lincoln Park North (p227) Good-value digs near the park, zoo and beaches.

Residence Inn Chicago Downtown (p224) Laundry, kitchen and location near American Girl and Lego shops.

Where to Stay

Neighborhood	For	Against
The Loop	Cool boutique and architectural hotels. Convenient to the parks, festival grounds, museums and Theater District. Easy transportation access to anywhere in the city.	Limited eating and drinking options after dark.
Near North & Navy Pier	The most lodging-packed 'hood. Bars, restaurants and big-box stores are everywhere.	Lots of chain hotels. Can be crowded, noisy and pricey.
Gold Coast	Chichi environs. Close to both downtown and the lakefront. Shopping bonanza at your doorstep.	Expensive.
Lincoln Park & Old Town	Characterful lodgings. A short walk to the park, zoo and beaches. Fun nightlife.	A bit removed from downtown's sights.
Lake View & Wrigleyville	Good-value boutique hotels and B&Bs surrounded by rollicking bars, restaurants and music clubs.	Main areas can be congested and rowdy at night.
Andersonville & Uptown	Tranquillity in a residential, gay-friendly neighborhood.	Far from the top-draw sights.
Wicker Park & Bucktown	Hostels and B&Bs away from the tourist masses. Area has a real neighborhood feel. Near buzzy nightlife and trendy shops.	About a 15-minute El ride to get downtown and some properties are a 15-minute walk from the El station.
Logan Square & Humboldt Park	Authentic neighborhood vibe. Indie-cool cafes, bars and shops nearby.	Isolated from downtown and the lakefront.
Near West Side & Pilsen	Near restaurant-laden Greektown and the West Loop's hot eateries.	Lonely area at night, cut off from the Loop by the highway.
South Loop & Near South Side	Well positioned near the Museum Campus, Grant Park, lakefront and Loop attractions. Prices can be cheaper than elsewhere in town.	Not lively at night; bars and restaurants are in short supply.
Hyde Park & South Side	Low prices.	Far-flung from downtown and just about everything else.

SLEEPING

🛏 The Loop

HI-CHICAGO
HOSTEL $

Map p286 (☎312-360-0300; www.hichicago. org; 24 E Congress Pkwy; dm $35-55; P ❄ @ 🛜; MBrown, Orange, Purple, Pink Line to Library) Chicago's most stalwart hostel is immaculate, conveniently placed in the Loop, and offers bonuses such as a staffed information desk, free volunteer-led tours, free continental breakfast and discount passes to museums and shows. The simple dorm rooms have eight or 10 beds, and most have attached baths. There are co-ed dorms, as well as gender-segregated ones.

The fully equipped kitchen allows for DIY meal making. The giant common area buzzes with guests using the free wi-fi (available throughout the building), playing ping-pong and chatting up the concierge to plan their day. Linens are provided, but bring your own lock.

HAMPTON INN CHICAGO DOWNTOWN/N LOOP
HOTEL $$

Map p286 (☎312-419-9014; www.hamptonchi cago.com; 68 E Wacker Pl; r $200-280; P ❄ 🛜; MBrown, Orange, Green, Purple, Pink Line to State/Lake) Opened in spring 2015, this unique property makes you feel like a road tripper of yore. Set in the 1928 art-deco Chicago Motor Club Building, the lobby sports a vintage Ford and a cool USA mural map from the era. The dark-wood-paneled rooms strike the right balance of retro vibe and modern amenities. Free wi-fi and hot breakfast included.

The central location puts you near the river, Magnificent Mile shops and Millennium Park.

BUCKINGHAM ATHLETIC CLUB HOTEL
BOUTIQUE HOTEL $$

Map p286 (☎312-663-8910; www.thebucking hamclub.com; 440 S LaSalle St; r $175-300; P ❄ 🛜 🏊; MBrown, Orange, Purple, Pink Line to LaSalle) Tucked onto the 40th floor of the Chicago Stock Exchange building, this 21-room hotel is not easy to find. The benefit if you do? It's quiet (on weekends and evenings especially) and has expansive views south of town. Elegant rooms here are so spacious they'd be considered suites elsewhere. Lots of freebies add to the Buckingham's beauty, including free access to the namesake gym with lap pool.

There's free continental breakfast and free wi-fi, to boot.

HAMPTON MAJESTIC CHICAGO THEATER DISTRICT
HOTEL $$

Map p286 (☎312-332-5052; www.hamptonmajes tic.com; 22 W Monroe St; r $189-279; P ❄ @ 🛜; MRed, Blue Line to Monroe) You know what you're getting at a Hampton, and it's a solid deal at this property, which sits atop the landmark PrivateBank Theatre. The 135 rooms are painted a dramatic deep red and are furnished with downy-white beds. Freebies include a simple hot breakfast buffet each morning, cookies in the evening, a small fitness center and free wi-fi. It's surprisingly quiet and intimate for being above a Broadway venue.

CENTRAL LOOP HOTEL
HOTEL $$

Map p286 (☎312-601-3525; www.central loophotel.com; 111 W Adams St; r $149-249; P ❄ @ 🛜; MBrown, Orange, Purple, Pink Line to Quincy) The Central Loop is in a good location (the name doesn't lie) and has good prices if you're stuck paying rack rates. It's accessorized for business-oriented guests, though not so useful for families given the smallish size of the rooms. A fine pub pours drinks downstairs. The owners have a similar property called **Club Quarters** (75 E Wacker Dr) at the Loop's northern fringe.

★HOTEL BURNHAM
BOUTIQUE HOTEL $$$

Map p286 (☎312-782-1111; www.burnham hotel.com; 1 W Washington St; r $239-389; P ❄ @ 🛜 🛏 🐾; MBlue Line to Washington) The proprietors brag that the Burnham has the highest guest return rates in Chicago; it's easy to see why. Housed in the landmark 1890s Reliance Building (precedent for the modern skyscraper), its super-slick design woos architecture buffs. Big windows and pops of whimsical, bright-hued art liven up the warm wood decor. A free wine happy hour takes place each evening.

For an only-in-Chicago experience, try to nab room 809, where Al Capone's dentist and partner in crime drilled teeth.

VIRGIN HOTEL
HOTEL $$$

Map p286 (☎312-940-4400; www.virginho tels.com; 203 N Wabash Ave; r $240-380; P ❄ @ 🛜 🐾; MBrown, Orange, Green, Purple, Pink Line to State/Lake) Billionaire Richard Branson transformed the 27-story, art-deco Dearborn Bank Building into the first outpost of his cheeky new hotel chain. The airy, suite-like rooms have speedy free wi-fi and low-cost minibar items, plus a bed that can double as a work desk. An app controls the thermostat, TV and other electronics. Guests receive earplugs, handy for dulling noise from nearby El trains.

RADISSON BLU AQUA HOTEL   HOTEL $$$

Map p286 (312-565-5258; www.radisson blu.com/aquahotel-chicago; 221 N Columbus Dr; r $269-349; P❄@🎧🏊; MBrown, Orange, Green, Purple, Pink Line to State/Lake) Radisson Blu's clean-lined rooms occupy floors 1 to 18 of the rippling, 82-story Aqua Tower, designed by local starchitect Jeanne Gang. Chambers come in two styles: the Scandinavian-like 'naturally cool,' with light wood floors and aqua-hued bathrooms; and 'mansion house' rooms with darker colors. Most rooms have pretty city or park views. Upgrading to a room with a balcony (around $25) is worth it.

There's free wi-fi throughout. Service is top-notch, as is the fitness center with indoor and outdoor pools, a running track and half basketball court.

HOTEL MONACO   BOUTIQUE HOTEL $$$

Map p286 (312-960-8500; www.monaco -chicago.com; 225 N Wabash Ave; r $269-399; P❄@🎧🏊🐾; MBrown, Orange, Green, Purple, Pink Line to State/Lake) Free goldfish on request and a geometric, deco-inspired interior help polish the Monaco's cool-daddy-o vibe. Rooms are big and boldly colored, with at least one window providing a nook to sit and watch the street action below. Amenities such as dog beds for pooches, child-safety kits for families, and a fitness facility and free wi-fi for businessfolk, ensure the Monaco draws a mixed crowd. There's a free wine happy hour each evening (as per all Kimpton-brand properties).

WIT   BOUTIQUE HOTEL $$$

Map p286 (312-467-0200; www.thewithotel. com; 201 N State St; r $255-385; P❄@🎧; MBrown, Orange, Green, Purple, Pink Line to State/Lake) One of the Loop's hottest properties, the design-savvy Wit draws holidaying hipsters and business travelers with its view-tastic rooms, swanky rooftop bar and private movie theater. The green-glass tower glints in a sweet spot between the Theater District and the river. Each chamber features vast windows and eco-amenities such as dual-flush toilets and energy-efficient heating and lighting.

Wi-fi is free in the lobby, though there's a fee for in-room service. The hotel is part of the Doubletree chain.

SILVERSMITH   HISTORIC HOTEL $$$

Map p286 (312-372-7696; www.silversmith chicagohotel.com; 10 S Wabash Ave; r $239-329; P❄@🎧; MRed, Blue Line to Monroe) This Loop architectural gem was built in 1897. Although the exterior was designed by Daniel Burnham's architecture firm, the hotel's interior recalls Frank Lloyd Wright: the chunky wood furniture has a distinct Prairie School charm. Too bad that windows overlook the El tracks or face right onto another building. Ah well, it's a small price to pay for the core Loop location.

The Art Institute and Millennium Park are steps away. Wi-fi is free.

HOTEL ALLEGRO   HOTEL $$$

Map p286 (312-236-0123; www.allegro chicago.com; 171 W Randolph St; r $229-359; P❄@🎧🐾🏊; MBrown, Orange, Purple, Pink Line to Washington) Hotel Allegro is part of the fun and flirty Kimpton chain. The 483 rooms sport a retro luxury-cruise-ship look, with funky patterned wallpaper and carpet in royal blue and snowy white tones. It's dramatic, which makes sense for a hotel right next to the Cadillac Palace Theatre and its Broadway crowd.

Flat-screen TVs, free wi-fi, free evening wine receptions and free yoga gear round out the stylish package.

PALMER HOUSE HILTON   HISTORIC HOTEL $$$

Map p286 (312-726-7500; www.palmerhouse hiltonhotel.com; 17 E Monroe St; r $179-369; P❄@🎧🏊🐾; MRed, Blue Line to Monroe) The Palmer House has been around since 1875 and the lobby still has an 'Oh my God' opulence – Tiffany chandeliers, ceiling frescoes – that makes a look-see imperative. The 1600-plus guest rooms give off a more updated vibe: most are spacious, done up in funky chartreuse-and-red decor, with geometric-print drapes and carpet. The Art Institute and Millennium Park are within spitting distance.

Chicago millionaire Potter Palmer set many worldwide records when he opened the property (first to use electric lighting, first to have in-room telephones, invention of the brownie…). Today it remains the nation's oldest hotel in continual operation. Its huge size makes it a convention favorite, which is why prices fluctuate wildly. Wi-fi costs $13 per day.

HARD ROCK HOTEL CHICAGO   HOTEL $$$

Map p286 (312-334-6767; www.hardrockho telchicago.com; 230 N Michigan Ave; r $249-399; P❄@🎧; MBrown, Orange, Green, Purple,

Pink Line to State/Lake) The Hard Rock tries hard to prove it rocks – DJs work the lobby lounge, staff will loan you an electric guitar to wail in your room, rock star photos pop up everywhere (including the bathroom, where you might find, say, The Beatles staring out over your toilet). Considering that, the standard-sized, steel-gray rooms are relatively staid. The young and stylish clientele doesn't seem to mind though. And the architecture is stunning: the hotel sits inside the landmark art-deco Carbide & Carbon Building, supposedly modeled after a gold-foiled champagne bottle. Wi-fi costs $13.50 per day.

HOTEL BLAKE CHICAGO BOUTIQUE HOTEL $$$

Map p286 (⏺312-986-1234; www.hotelblake.com; 500 S Dearborn St; r $169-339; P ❄ @ ☎; MBlue Line to LaSalle) The old customs house building has found new life as a boutique hotel at the Loop's southern edge. It's a unique location midway between downtown's core and the Museum Campus, though not much goes on in the evenings. The modern, black-and-red furnishings are spread out in the well-sized rooms; the bathrooms are flat-out huge. Wi-fi is free.

Breakfast is not included, but there's a good cafe on-site for omelets and creative French-toast dishes. If rates swing up to the high end of the spectrum, you'll probably get better bang for your buck elsewhere.

FAIRMONT HOTEL $$$

Map p286 (⏺312-565-8000; www.themillenniumparkhotel.com; 200 N Columbus Dr; r $279-499; P ❄ @ ☎; MBrown, Orange, Green, Purple, Pink Line to State/Lake) Millennium Park here you come. All 687 luxury rooms and suites here are as close to the statues and fountains as you can stay. Upgrade to a deluxe room to get a park or lake view. Those near the top of the hotel's 45 stories are the best.

Accents such as Asian ceramics combine with French Empire chairs to create soft – if a bit stodgy – surrounds. Allergy sufferers can book one of the 22 hypoallergenic rooms. Wi-fi costs $14 per day; premium (faster) wi-fi takes it up to $24.

SWISSÔTEL CHICAGO HOTEL $$$

Map p286 (⏺312-565-0565; www.swissotelchicago.com; 323 E Wacker Dr; r $239-319; P ❄ @ ☎ ⛱ ♿; MBrown, Orange, Green, Purple, Pink Line to Randolph) Water vistas are just part of the attraction at this triangular-shaped, mirrored-glass high-rise at the confluence of river and lake. Business folk like the rooms' ample, well-appointed workstations. Families love the oversized layouts,

separate shower and tub, and special kids' suites with colorful furnishings and toys. The hotel shows up a lot on discount booking sites. Summer weekends sell out fast.

The fitness center with indoor pool is a fine perk. Wi-fi costs $15 per day.

HYATT REGENCY CHICAGO HOTEL $$$

Map p286 (⏺312-565-1234; www.chicagoregency.hyatt.com; 151 E Wacker Dr; r $179-319; P ❄ @ ☎; MBrown, Orange, Green, Purple, Pink Line to State/Lake) With 2019 rooms and four restaurants and bars, the riverside Hyatt Regency is Chicago's biggest hotel and typically filled with conventioneers. Rooms are vanilla but, thanks to a recent renovation, they're now vanilla with new beds, chairs, bathroom fixtures and tech-savvy work spaces. Lots of specials keep all those rooms filled during nonconvention times. Wi-fi is free. Drinkers rejoice that the hotel has the longest free-standing bar in North America (so it claims).

RENAISSANCE CHICAGO DOWNTOWN HOTEL HOTEL $$$

Map p286 (⏺312-372-7200; http://renaissance-hotels.marriott.com; 1 W Wacker Dr; r $289-489; P ❄ @ ☎ ⛱; MBrown, Orange, Green, Purple, Pink Line to State/Lake) Don't be fooled by the bland exterior. Step into the lobby, where modern art, sink-right-in couches and lively earth tones exude warmth and style. Rooms are pretty typical contemporary stuff, but those with a water view (about $50 extra) have bay windows overlooking the skyline and the adjacent river. Conventioneers populate most of the 513 rooms. Wi-fi costs $15 per day.

W CHICAGO CITY CENTER HOTEL $$$

Map p286 (⏺312-332-1200; www.wchicagocitycenter.com; 172 W Adams St; r $269-409; P ❄ @ ☎; MBrown, Orange, Purple, Pink Line to Quincy) You expect urban-hip from the W brand and that's what you get here. The small, sleek black-and-white rooms can seem stark, but the bedding is ubercomfy. The soaring 'living room' (lobby/bar) feels a little like a dance club, especially when the bass-heavy music gets pumping. Excellent concierge staff can work miracles for reservations. Wi-fi costs $15 per day.

🛏 Near North & Navy Pier

FREEHAND CHICAGO HOSTEL, HOTEL $

Map p290 (⏺312-940-3699; www.thefreehand.com/chicago; 19 E Ohio St; dm $35-70, r $220-310; ❄ ☎; MRed Line to Grand) This is an outpost of Miami's super-hip hostel-hotel hybrid. Rooms are small but stylish, finished with warm woods, bright tiles and Central American–tinged fabrics. Travelers are split evenly between the private rooms and eight-person, bunk-bed dorms (way spiffier than in most hostels, with privacy curtains around each bed). Everyone mingles in the shaggy, totem-pole-filled common area and in the on-site Broken Shaker bar. No surprise: the Freehand sits in the thick of trendy shops, eateries and nightlife venues.

★ACME HOTEL   BOUTIQUE HOTEL **$$**
Map p290 (☏312-894-0800; www.acmehotel company.com; 15 E Ohio St; r $189-299; P❄@⊛; MRed Line to Grand) Urban bohemians love the Acme for its indie-cool style at (usually) affordable rates. The 130 rooms mix industrial fixtures with retro lamps, mid-century furniture and funky modern art. They're wired up with free wi-fi, good speakers, smart TVs and easy connections to stream your own music and movies. Graffiti, neon and lava lights decorate the common areas. The handy location puts you between the Michigan Ave shopping haven (a few blocks east) and the Theater District (about a half-mile south).

IVY HOTEL   BOUTIQUE HOTEL **$$**
Map p290 (☏312-335-5444; www.exploreivy.com; 233 E Ontario St; r $179-279; P❄@⊛; MRed Line to Grand) The 63-room Ivy parcels out its chambers so there are just five per floor, making it feel exceptionally intimate. The sleek and chic rooms are decent sized and offer platform beds, bathrooms with big soaking tubs and ecofriendly bamboo flooring. It often shows up on booking sites with good deals, so take advantage. Wi-fi is free.

HOTEL FELIX   HOTEL **$$**
Map p290 (☏312-447-3440; www.hotelfelixchi cago.com; 111 W Huron St; r $139-279; P❄@⊛; MRed Line to Chicago) ✒ The 225-room, 12-story Felix is downtown's first hotel to earn ecofriendly LEED certification (Leadership in Energy and Environmental Design; silver status, to be exact). The earth-toned, mod-furnished rooms are small but efficiently and comfortably designed. It's more of a place for urban hipsters than families, but who doesn't enjoy soft Egyptian-cotton sheets, free wi-fi and a wine-soaked French cafe on-site?

BEST WESTERN RIVER NORTH   HOTEL **$$**
Map p290 (☏312-467-0800; www.river northhotel.com; 125 W Ohio St; r $179-279;

P❄@⊛⛵⛟; MRed Line to Grand) Well-maintained rooms with maple veneer beds and desks, together with low-cost parking (per night $25) and an indoor pool and sundeck overlooking the city, make the Best Western good value for the area. Families in particular dig the straightforward, seven-story hotel given its proximity to several kid-friendly restaurants.

GODFREY HOTEL   HOTEL **$$**
Map p290 (☏312-649-2000; www.godfreyhotel chicago.com; 127 W Huron St; r $175-275; P❄❄@⊛; MRed Line to Chicago) The Godfrey's Cubist-inspired exterior looks amazing. Inside, the large, mod-industrial rooms are more comfy than you'd think, with a snug bed, wet bar and ergonomic workstation. South-facing rooms offer swell city views. Guests are mostly the young and stylish. Request a room on a higher floor to avoid noise from the popular 4th-floor lounge. Free wi-fi.

DOUBLETREE
MAGNIFICENT MILE   HOTEL **$$**
Map p290 (☏312-787-6100; www.doubletree magmile.com; 300 E Ohio St; r $179-299; P❄@⊛⛵⛟; MRed Line to Grand) Relax on your window seat and look out at the sliver of a lake view many rooms have here, near Navy Pier. The average-size rooms are sort of modern generic (ie white, black and gray decor, with ruby-red accents), but there is a large fitness room and a nifty rooftop outdoor pool. Wi-fi costs $10 per day per device.

The three-star property pops up at lower rates on discount booking websites quite often.

AC HOTEL CHICAGO
DOWNTOWN   HOTEL **$$**
Map p290 (☏312-981-6600; www.marriott.com; 630 N Rush St; r $190-330; P❄@⊛⛵; MRed Line to Grand) This eight-story, Marriott-brand property targets millennials and business travelers. The crisp, earth-toned rooms are on the small side, but they have a decent work space, large flat-screen TV, coffeemaker and mini refrigerator. It's a great location, within easy walking distance to loads of food and drink options. Basic wi-fi is free; enhanced wi-fi for video streaming costs $10 per day.

HOTEL CASS   BOUTIQUE HOTEL **$$**
Map p290 (☏312-787-4030; www.casshotel. com; 640 N Wabash Ave; r $189-309; P❄@⊛; MRed Line to Grand) This vintage 1920s building is now a Holiday Inn Express–affiliated

boutique. Small room spaces are maximized with modern flair: hanging flat-screen TVs, mod C-shaped tables, armless couches and accents in bright pops of celery green. The breakfast bar includes bacon, eggs and a few other hot items. Wi-fi is free.

HILTON GARDEN INN   HOTEL $$
Map p290 (☑312-595-0000; www.hiltongarden inn.com; 10 E Grand Ave; r $189-279; ⓟ✳@⚡✕♿; Ⓜ Red Line to Grand) Part of the stalwart chain, this outpost near the Magnificent Mile caters to business travelers, families and holidaying couples in equal measure. Rooms are decent sized and good quality, with free wi-fi. Meaty smells waft up from the Weber Grill restaurant downstairs. Rates vary wildly, so you may get a steal.

OHIO HOUSE MOTEL   MOTEL $$
Map p290 (☑312-943-6000; www.ohiohousemo tel.com; 600 N LaSalle St; r $139-179; ⓟ✳@⚡; Ⓜ Red Line to Grand) First the good news about this retro 1960s motel: free parking! And a trendy, fried-chicken-serving diner on-site. And a great location close to transportation and restaurants to the east (though it's still ragged to the west). Free wi-fi, too... Now the less-good news: the rooms are basic, kind of dingy and thin-walled. Still, it's a killer deal for the area.

RED ROOF INN   HOTEL $$
Map p290 (☑312-787-3580; www.redroofinn downtownchicago.com; 162 E Ontario St; r $149-279; ⓟ✳@⚡; Ⓜ Red Line to Grand) If you snag one of the lower rates it might be worth your while to stay at this basic hotel, which is steps from the Michigan Ave shopping bonanza. But just how much money are you willing to pay for faded, stuffy rooms with barely enough space to walk around two beds? Wi-fi is free.

INN OF CHICAGO   HOTEL $$
Map p290 (☑312-787-3100; www.innofchicago. com; 162 E Ohio St; r $165-239; ⓟ✳@⚡; Ⓜ Red Line to Grand) This hotel tries hard to be trendy with a clubby lobby and cocktail lounge. Rooms come in 'contemporary' style (lime-green accents, mod *Jetsons*-like chair) or 'traditional' style (beige-striped wallpaper, office-like furniture). They're all pretty darn small. Wi-fi costs $5 to $15 per day, depending on speed. All in all, the Inn is not particularly good value, but it often has rooms when other places are sold out. It's an OK option in that case (or if you find a low price on a booking site).

HOTEL PALOMAR   HOTEL $$$
Map p290 (☑312-755-9703; www.hotelpalo mar-chicago.com; 505 N State St; r $220-409; ⓟ✳@⚡✕♿; Ⓜ Red Line to Grand) This is another excellent property in the Kimpton chain (joining the Burnham, Monaco and Allegro, all in the Loop). Note of distinction: the 17-story, 261-room Palomar has a green roof, Chicago's first for a hotel. Arty decor – little sculptures, original paintings on the wall – add to the fashionable but business-like scheme. There's an indoor rooftop pool and a free wine hour each evening.

ALOFT CHICAGO CITY CENTER   HOTEL $$$
Map p290 (☑312-661-1000; www.aloftchica gocitycenter.com; 515 N Clark St; r $159-379; ⓟ✳@⚡; Ⓜ Red Line to Grand) This relatively new Aloft offers the chain's typical compact, efficiently designed, minimalist rooms. They sport a bookish, library look here, with big windows and all the electronics you need. The clubby, game-filled lobby (another Aloft staple) is prime for mingling. So is Beatrix, a popular comfort-food restaurant and bakery that's on-site. Wi-fi is free.

If the hotel is full, well, it happens to be attached to two other new properties that might be options: family-oriented Fairfield Inn & Suites and business-focused Hyatt Place.

JAMES   HOTEL $$$
Map p290 (☑312-337-1000; www.jameshotels. com; 55 E Ontario St; r $279-409; ⓟ✳@⚡⚡; Ⓜ Red Line to Grand) Low and loungey chairs sidle up to oversized tripod lamps. Porthole windows allow you to peep through sliding bathroom doors. Hep cats and fans of midcentury modern design love it here. But everyone can appreciate the little luxuries: organic bath products, Turkish cotton towels, a bar that has half bottles instead of minis, a real-deal gym, free wi-fi...

A gracious staff helps work out any service kinks, such as rooms not being ready on time.

KINZIE HOTEL   BOUTIQUE HOTEL $$$
Map p290 (☑312-395-9000; www.kinziehotel. com; 20 W Kinzie St; r $259-359; ⓟ✳@⚡⚡; Ⓜ Red Line to Grand) There's lots to love at the Kinzie beyond the modern-design-driven, warm-toned, good-sized rooms. Each floor lays out its own sumptuous spread of pastries, fruit and yogurt every morning. In the evening you can munch free hors d'oeuvres and sip two free cocktails in the lounge. Rooms have 42in HDTVs with loads of channels and a small work desk. Wi-fi is free. The

swell location puts you near the river, Michigan Ave shopping and House of Blues.

PENINSULA
HOTEL $$$

Map p290 (☑312-337-2888; www.peninsula.com; 108 E Superior St; r from $450; [P][❄][@][🛜][≋]; [M]Red Line to Chicago) The over-the-top Peninsula is among Chicago's top addresses. Equestrian statues and marquetry furnishings decorate the neoclassical rooms. Two-story walls of glass enclose the pool, where you can swim after your essence-of-rubies spa facial. How's the service? Buttoned down. This is where Hollywood stars check in when they come to town.

LANGHAM HOTEL
HOTEL $$$

Map p290 (☑312-923-9988; www.chicago.langhamhotels.com; 330 N Wabash Ave; r from $450; [P][❄][@][🛜][≋]; [M]Red Line to Grand) Early starchitect Ludwig Mies van der Rohe originally designed the 52-story, black-box building. His grandson remade the lower floors into the Langham in 2013. The megaswank, 316-room property features some of the biggest chambers in the city; they start at 516 sq ft and go up from there. Groovy sculptures and modern art dot the common areas.

The building's upper floors house the American Medical Association. There's free wi-fi throughout.

HAMPTON INN & SUITES CHICAGO DOWNTOWN
HOTEL $$$

Map p290 (☑312-832-0330; www.hamptonsuiteschicago.com; 33 W Illinois St; r $199-349; [P][❄][@][🛜][≋][♿]; [M]Red Line to Grand) Thick oak desks and angular leaded-glass lamps give the lobby a Prairie School feel. The Frank Lloyd Wright influence is less apparent in the tidy, contemporary rooms. One-bedroom suites have full kitchens; all rooms have super comfy beds. The 12-story property offers Hampton's requisite free wi-fi, a small indoor pool and hot (if spare) breakfast buffet. Families and older couples love it here.

INTERCONTINENTAL CHICAGO
HOTEL $$$

Map p290 (☑312-944-4100; www.icchicagohotel.com; 505 N Michigan Ave; r $269-429; [P][❄][@][🛜][≋]; [M]Red Line to Grand) The InterContinental is split in two. The Executive Tower's 315 rooms are its historic core. The spacious chambers got a makeover in 2015 and are bright and clean lined, done up in whites, grays and jewel-toned accents. The Grand Tower is the hotel's newer portion. Its 477 rooms have spiffy fabrics and lots of USB ports for the many business travelers who stay here. The ornate original tower was built in 1929 as the Medinah Athletic Club. Period architecture and decor grace the premises, best known for the mosaic-tiled indoor pool where Hollywood goddess Esther Williams swam. Ask the concierge for the iPod audio tour that lets you explore the building.

EMBASSY SUITES CHICAGO – LAKEFRONT
HOTEL $$$

Map p290 (☑312-836-5900; www.chicagoembassysuiteslakefront.com; 511 N Columbus Dr; ste $229-359; [P][❄][@][🛜][≋][♿]; [M]Red Line to Grand) The Embassy Lakefront displays the chain's typical hallmarks: all the units are two-room suites (living room with sofa bed in front, bedroom in back); there's always a cooked-to-order bacon, egg and pancake breakfast each morning; there's free wine each evening; and there's an indoor, kiddie-mobbed pool. Families dig the location between Michigan Ave and Navy Pier.

It may leave little to the imagination, but this Embassy outpost does a fine job with all the basics. Wi-fi costs $10 to $15 per day (higher fee equals higher speed) for up to three devices.

EMBASSY SUITES CHICAGO – DOWNTOWN
HOTEL $$$

Map p290 (☑312-943-3800; www.embassysuiteschicago.com; 600 N State St; ste $209-349; [P][❄][@][🛜][≋][♿]; [M]Red Line to Grand) This hotel rises a mere half-mile west of its sibling the Embassy Suites Lakefront (yes, the latter is closer to the water). It's the same deal – large rooms, free cooked-to-order breakfast, indoor pool etc – particularly beloved by families. Wi-fi costs $10 per device. The Downtown property sometimes has slightly cheaper prices than the Lakefront one.

PARK HYATT
HOTEL $$$

Map p290 (☑312-335-1234; www.parkchicago.hyatt.com; 800 N Michigan Ave; r from $425; [P][❄][@][🛜][≋]; [M]Red Line to Chicago) Want every inch of your suite covered in rose petals, with candles lit and your bath water run? They've done it before at this ask-and-it-shall-be-granted luxury flagship of the locally based Hyatt chain. From the miniature TVs in the bathroom to the butler and the courtesy car service, no expense has been spared.

Bow-shaped tubs hide behind rolling window shades in some rooms, so you can soak and still admire the view. C'mon – if it's good enough for U2 when they rock through town, you know it's got street cred.

WHEN CONVENTIONS COME TO TOWN

When huge conventions trample through town, beware. You'll be competing with an extra 30,000 people or so for hotel rooms, which will skyrocket in price. In general, spring and fall are the busiest convention times. Check Choose Chicago's convention calendar (www.choosechicago.com/meeting-professionals/convention-calendar) to see what's on when. The following are some of the largest events, at which times room prices will make you weep:

➡ International Home & Housewares Show – three nights in mid-March

➡ National Restaurant Association – three nights in mid-May

➡ American Society of Clinical Oncologists (ASCO) – five nights in late May/early June

➡ Radiological Society of North America – five nights in late November/early December

WARWICK
ALLERTON HOTEL   HISTORIC HOTEL $$$

Map p290 (☑312-440-1500; www.warwickhotels.com; 701 N Michigan Ave; r $189-332; P❄@🛜; MRed Line to Chicago) High atop the Italianate redbrick facade shines the red neon Allerton Tip Top sign, a reminder of the hotel's past. From the 1920s to the '50s, the penthouse Tip Top Club was a happening place. All the big bands and early radio stars played here. Thankfully, the Allerton's rooms have leaped into modern times with marble bathrooms, flat-screen TVs and comfy bedding.

Standard rooms are by no means large (and the 'classic' rooms are downright tiny), but they can be a bargain off-peak. It's a prime location right on the Mag Mile. Wi-fi costs $10 per day.

W CHICAGO LAKESHORE   HOTEL $$$

Map p290 (☑312-943-9200; www.wchicago-lakeshore.com; 644 N Lake Shore Dr; r from $300; P❄@🛜🏊; ❑66) The W has an earthy aesthetic that feels entirely appropriate here on the lakefront. You can see the water from telescopes by the windows in the elevator bays, from 'spectacular' rooms and 'marvelous' suites. Navy Pier and ocean-like expanses stretch before you while you run on the treadmill or lie on the pool deck.

Wi-fi costs $15 per day.

CHICAGO MARRIOTT HOTEL   HOTEL $$$

Map p290 (☑312-836-0100; www.marriott.com; 540 N Michigan Ave; r $189-359; P❄@🛜🏊; MRed Line to Grand) A Magnificent Mile address is the primary drawcard of this 46-story behemoth. The standard rooms are smaller than what you'd expect at these rates. The downy duvets and flat-screen TVs will do, though.

TRUMP HOTEL & TOWER   HOTEL $$$

Map p290 (☑312-588-8000; www.trumphotelcollection.com; 401 N Wabash Ave; r from $450; P❄@🛜♿; MBrown, Orange, Green, Purple, Pink Line to State) Donald opened his glassy Chicago handiwork, which rose to be the city's second-tallest building, in 2008. The masculine, earth-toned rooms are high in the sky with floor-to-ceiling windows, and most have kitchens full of stainless-steel appliances. The views are sweet, and service is as polished as you'd expect.

🛏 Gold Coast

HOTEL INDIGO   BOUTIQUE HOTEL $$

Map p294 (☑312-787-4980; www.ihg.com/hotelindigo; 1244 N Dearborn St; r $159-279; P❄@🛜; MRed Line to Clark/Division) The Indigo feels more like your perky friend's apartment than a hotel. Smallish rooms feature hardwood floors, white furniture and neon-green, orange and yellow accent fabrics, while a macro photo wall mural of something, er, indigo (like blueberries) watches over it all. The location is quiet for the Gold Coast, yet it's within walking distance of shopping, nightlife and the lakefront. Free wi-fi.

RESIDENCE INN
CHICAGO DOWNTOWN   HOTEL $$

Map p294 (☑312-943-9800; www.marriott.com; 201 E Walton St; r $179-289; P❄@🛜♿; MRed Line to Chicago) What to say about a generic extended-stay hotel... Well, it's got all the extras families crave: DIY kitchens, laundry facilities, free wi-fi and hot breakfast buffet. They'll even run out and buy groceries for you. Studios, one bedroom and two bedrooms available. No pool though – sorry, kids (though Oak St Beach is nearby).

TREMONT HOTEL
HOTEL **$$**

Map p294 (☎312-751-1900; www.tremontchica
go.com; 100 E Chestnut St; r $159-289; P ✳ 🛱;
M Red Line to Chicago) Here are the Tremont's
pros: you're steps from the Magnificent
Mile in a ritzy neighborhood and the prop-
erty often turns up dirt cheap on booking
sites. Do the rooms tend toward faded up-
holstery and peeling wallpaper? Yes, but
you can help the situation by asking for a
room with good natural light at check-in.

Old-school touches, like the parlor that's
studded with leather chairs and has a fire-
place, evoke nostalgia, as does the on-site
meaty restaurant of former Bears coach
Mike Ditka. Look elsewhere if room prices
slide toward the high end of the range. Star-
wood Hotels–affiliated.

WHITEHALL HOTEL
HISTORIC HOTEL **$$**

Map p294 (☎312-944-6300; www.thewhite
hallhotel.com; 105 E Delaware Pl; r $179-289;
P ✳ @ 🛱; M Red Line to Chicago) This old-
world hotel offers cozy rooms with vintage mahogany furniture and earth-toned
wallpaper and carpeting. It's popular with
wedding parties; you'll often see gown-clad
beauties flowing by. Michigan Ave is su-
perbly close. Free wi-fi.

DRAKE HOTEL
HISTORIC HOTEL **$$$**

Map p294 (☎312-787-2200; www.thedrakehotel.
com; 140 E Walton St; r $229-349; P ✳ @ 🛱;
M Red Line to Chicago) Queen Elizabeth, Dean
Martin, Princess Di...the Reagans, the
Bushes, the Clintons... Who hasn't stayed at
the elegant Drake Hotel since it opened in
1920? The chandelier-strewn grande dame
commands a terrific location at the north
end of Michigan Ave, near Oak St Beach.
While the public spaces are gilded eyepop-
pers, the rooms are more everyday (though
well-sized and comfy).

North-facing rooms have awesome lake
views; they're worth the extra cost. Guests
tend to be older or members of the many
weddings the Drake hosts. Wi-fi costs $13
per day.

SOFITEL CHICAGO
WATER TOWER
HOTEL **$$$**

Map p294 (☎312-324-4000; www.sofitel-chicago.
com; 20 E Chestnut St; r $199-350; P ✳ @ 🛱;
M Red Line to Chicago) The Sofitel looks a little
like some state-of-the-art Apple computing
device from the outside, its triangular glass
tower leaning gracefully forward into space.
Inside, stylish staff members tend to stylish
30- and 40-something guests, including
many Europeans, who appreciate the minimalist vibe and sizable rooms (think blond
wood and rectangular lines). Wi-fi is free to
$15 per day, depending on speed.

WALDORF ASTORIA CHICAGO
HOTEL **$$$**

Map p294 (☎312-646-1300; www.waldorfastoria
chicagohotel.com; 11 E Walton St; r from $400;
P ✳ @ 🛱 🏊 ✳; M Red Line to Chicago) The
Waldorf routinely tops the list for Chicago's
best uberluxury hotel. It models itself on
1920s Parisian glamour and, we gotta say, it
delivers. Rooms are large – they have to be,
to hold the fireplaces, the bars, the marble
soaking tubs, the beds with 460-thread-
count sheets and the fully wired work spac-
es and other techno gadgets.

There's a fancy gym with a lap pool, a
high-rolling bar and a couple of spiffy res-
taurants. Wi-fi is free.

RAFFAELLO HOTEL
BOUTIQUE HOTEL **$$$**

Map p294 (☎312-943-5000; www.chicagoraffael
lo.com; 201 E Delaware Pl; r $179-319; P ⟳ ✳ @ 🛱;
M Red Line to Chicago) If only you could live in
the creamy, silk-draped modernity of these
rooms. Oh, wait, you can – they're condominiums, too. Suites have microwaves and
minifridges in marble cooking centers,
plus roomy seating areas or separate living
rooms. King and double rooms are smaller,
but they have similar upscale amenities,
such as rainforest shower heads and high-
thread-count linens. Free wi-fi.

A smart rooftop lounge and Italian seafood restaurant tempt on-site.

PUBLIC
BOUTIQUE HOTEL **$$$**

Map p294 (☎312-787-3700; www.publichotels.
com; 1301 N State Pkwy; r $189-325; P ✳ 🛱;
M Red Line to Clark/Division) Pop-hotelier Ian
Schrager took over the old Ambassador
East Hotel and gave it a minimalist-chic
touch. Rooms are done up in a 'no-color
palette' (aka light beige). Walls are bare ex-
cept for a giant flat-screen TV, an oversized
clock and cow photos (a nod to Chicago's
historic stockyards). Stylish urbanites are
digging it in droves. Wi-fi is free.

You'll get the vibe as soon as you enter
the swanky white lobby, which leads to the
'library' with its limestone fireplace and
beautiful people sipping coffee by day and
vino by night. Or make like Frank Sinatra
and Mick Jagger by hitting the glamorous
Pump Room bar-restaurant.

WESTIN MICHIGAN AVENUE
HOTEL **$$$**

Map p294 (☎312-943-7200; www.thewestinmich
iganavenue.com; 909 N Michigan Ave, entrance on
E Delaware Pl; r $199-339; P ✳ @ 🛱; M Red Line

SAVING STRATEGIES

In peak season it's hard to find a room for less than $225 per night. Here are a few ways to cut costs:

Ditch the car Most downtown properties charge $55 to $65 per night for parking. Lodgings in outlying neighborhoods, such as Lake View and Wicker Park, often have free or lower cost parking lots (closer to $25 per night).

Bidding sites Try Priceline (www.priceline.com) or Hotwire (www.hotwire.com). 'River North' and 'Mag Mile' yield the most listings. Certain properties turn up often at well-reduced rates.

Free wi-fi While free wi-fi is common, many business-oriented hotels still charge for it ($10 to $15 daily).

Leave downtown Prices decrease as you move out to Lincoln Park, Lake View, Wicker Park and the South Loop.

---

to Chicago) The Magnificent Mile location – we're talking smack on the Mag Mile, by all the high-end shops – is the main selling point. While the Westin's rooms are decent sized and offer comfy beds, they feel like being in an office cubicle with their beige, corporate vibe. Indeed, the 752 rooms often fill with convention goers.

The good news is rates drop in off-peak times to keep the many rooms filled. Wi-fi costs $13 per day. Lake views are available for a premium.

🛏 Lincoln Park & Old Town

CHICAGO GETAWAY HOSTEL   HOSTEL **$**
Map p296 (☑773-929-5380; www.getawayhostel. com; 616 W Arlington Pl; dm $32-36, r from $90; 🅿❄@🛜; 🚌22, Ⓜ Brown, Purple, Red Line to Fullerton) The fun, social Getaway Hostel attracts mostly a 20-something-age crowd who strum the house guitars, lounge on leather couches, sip beer on the patio and head out to nightlife-rich Clark and Halsted Sts (the hostel is equidistant between the two). Staff organizes outings, such as pub crawls, throughout the week. Continental breakfast and wi-fi are free.

Rooms have a fresh, bright-hued coat of paint. Dorms are single sex, sleeping six to 12 people. The private rooms are small and either have a full bathroom, a half bathroom or share one down the hall.

HOTEL LINCOLN   BOUTIQUE HOTEL **$$**
Map p296 (☑312-254-4700; www.hotellincolnchi cago.com; 1816 N Clark St; r $179-319; 🅿❄@🛜; 🚌22) The boutique Lincoln is all about kitschy fun, as the lobby's 'wall of bad art' and front desk patched together from

flea market dresser drawers attest. Standard rooms are small, but vintage-cool and colorful; many have sweet views. Leafy Lincoln Park and the city's largest farmers market sprawl across the street.

A hotel pedicab provides transport to nearby North Avenue Beach. Bike rentals are also available.

🛏 Lake View & Wrigleyville

WRIGLEY HOSTEL   HOSTEL **$**
Map p300 (☑773-598-4471; www.wrigleyhostel. com; 3512 N Sheffield Ave; dm $30-55, r from $99; 🅿❄@🛜; Ⓜ Red Line to Addison) This unobtrusive hostel, located in a converted brick apartment block, is practically within home-run distance of Wrigley Field (and its rowdy nightlife). The blue-and-green-painted dorms come in co-ed or women-only configurations with four to 10 beds. Small private rooms are also available. Bathrooms, some with vintage claw-foot tubs, are shared on each floor. There's free breakfast (pancakes and fruit) and free, strong-signaled wi-fi property-wide.

The common room rocks a pool table, leather couches, bar stools and a sound system into which you can hook your iPod. The hostel also organizes trips to local blues and honky-tonk clubs. Bike rental costs $20 per day; it's about a mile to the lakefront trail.

WILLOWS HOTEL   BOUTIQUE HOTEL **$$**
Map p300 (☑773-528-8400; www.willowshotel chicago.com; 555 W Surf St; r $159-265; 🅿❄🛜; 🚌22) Small and stylish, the Willows wins an architectural gold star. The chic little lobby provides a swell refuge of overstuffed chairs by the fireplace, while the 55 rooms,

done up in shades of peach and soft green, evoke a 19th-century French countryside feel. Continental breakfast is included. It's well located near loads of casual restaurants, bars and shops, as well as the lakefront parklands.

DAYS INN LINCOLN PARK NORTH   HOTEL $$

Map p300 (☑773-525-7010; www.daysinnchi cago.net; 644 W Diversey Pkwy; r $130-189; P❋@☎♿; ☒22) This well-maintained chain hotel in Lincoln Park is a favorite of both families and touring indie bands, providing good service and perks like a free hot breakfast and on-site fitness center. It's an easy amble to the lakefront's parks and beaches, and a 15-minute bus ride to downtown. It's right at the hustle-bustle intersection of Broadway, Clark and Diversey streets.

MAJESTIC HOTEL   BOUTIQUE HOTEL $$

Map p300 (☑773-404-3499; www.majestic -chicago.com; 528 W Brompton Ave; r $159-265; P❋☎; ☒151) Nestled into a row of residential housing, the Majestic is walking distance to Wrigley Field, Boystown and the lakefront. From the lobby fireplace and dark-wood furnishings to the handsome, paisley-swirled decor, the interior has the cozy feel of an English manor. Free wi-fi and continental breakfast are included. Rooms are slightly larger than those at sibling hotels, the City Suites and Willows (both also in the neighborhood), and the location is quieter and more remote.

CITY SUITES HOTEL   BOUTIQUE HOTEL $$

Map p300 (☑773-404-3400; www.chicagocity suites.com; 933 W Belmont Ave; r $159-265; P❋☎; Ⓜ Red, Brown, Purple Line to Belmont) The mod, art-deco-tinged rooms and lobby buzzing just off Belmont Ave are vaguely reminiscent of a European city hotel. The El races right by the building, so light sleepers should ask for a room away from the tracks. Perks include free wi-fi throughout, free continental breakfast and a pass to a nearby fitness club.

Compared with the Majestic and Willows, the owners' other two properties nearby, the City Suites skews toward a bit of a younger and livelier crowd.

BEST WESTERN
HAWTHORNE TERRACE   HOTEL $$

Map p300 (☑773-244-3434; www.hawthorne terrace.com; 3434 N Broadway; r $159-239; P❋@☎; ☒36) The earthy Hawthorne Terrace attracts the most mixed crowd of the neighborhood's hotels. Sporty Cubs fans check in next to gay groups, with everyone primed to go out and have some fun. Standard-issue furnishings fill the rooms, but the free wi-fi, microwaves and minifridges are nice perks, along with the continental breakfast and a small fitness room.

The 1920s Federal-style apartment building may not be the newest place around, but it retains a classic appeal inside and out.

OLD CHICAGO INN   B&B $$

Map p300 (☑773-472-2278; www.oldchicagoinn. com; 3222 N Sheffield Ave; r $120-175; ❋☎; Ⓜ Red, Brown, Purple Line to Belmont) Sure the street din may seep into this century-old, 10-room greystone building, but that's the price you pay for being in a high-energy nightlife hub. Most of the chambers have wood floors and vintage accents; a few rooms share a bathroom. In addition to continental breakfast, you get a free dinner at the owner's pub, Trader Todd's, two doors down. There's free wi-fi and on-street parking (though you may have to search a bit).

VILLA TOSCANA   B&B $$

Map p300 (☑773-404-2416; www.thevillatoscana. com; 3447 N Halsted St; r $129-159; ❋☎; Ⓜ Red Line to Addison) This 1890s Victorian home sits smack on the busiest of Boystown streets. Wander through the leafy front garden and you're transported. Purple silks evoke Morocco in one room, toile recalls France in another. All eight diminutive lodgings (five with private bath) are often booked, so plan ahead. Enjoy breakfast pastries on the rear sundeck in nice weather. Free wi-fi.

🛏 Andersonville & Uptown

HOUSE 5863   B&B $$

(☑773-682-5217; www.house5863.com; 5863 N Glenwood Ave; r $109-189; P❋☎; Ⓜ Red Line to Thorndale) Hip and urban, House 5863 is a thoroughly modern B&B located in an old apartment building. You'll find no frilly ruffles in the five rooms, just clean-lined furnishings and abstract art. Lounge on the black leather sofa in the common living room and watch the plasma TV, or use the free wi-fi throughout. The self-serve breakfast is a bountiful continental one.

GUESTHOUSE HOTEL   BOUTIQUE HOTEL $$$

Map p302 (☑773-564-9568; www.theguest househotel.com; 4872 N Clark St; ste $219-379;

AIRPORT ACCOMMODATIONS

Got an early flight to catch? Given the crazy Chicago traffic, or long El commute (45 minutes from the Loop), resting your head at one of the dozens of airport hotels may be your best bet. Most run free 24-hour airport shuttles.

O'Hare

Aloft Chicago O'Hare (☑847-671-4444; www.aloftchicagoohare.com; 9700 Balmoral Ave, Rosemont; r $129-189; P❄@⚡; MBlue Line to Rosemont) It offers the chain's usual petite, industrial-toned rooms and sociable, game-filled lobby. It's about 3.5 miles from the airport.

O'Hare Hilton (☑773-686-8000; www.hilton.com; O'Hare International Airport; r $149-289; P❄@⚡⚲; MBlue Line to O'Hare) Attached to the airport via an underground tunnel. Relax in the sauna, take a refreshing dip in the indoor pool and then retire to your soundproofed contemporary room.

Midway

Hilton Garden Inn (☑708-496-2700; www.hiltongardeninn.com; 6530 S Cicero Ave, Bedford Park; r $149-219; P❄@⚡; MOrange Line to Midway) It's in the Midway Hotel Center complex of nine hotels.

Sleep Inn (☑708-594-0001; www.sleepinn.com; 6650 S Cicero Ave, Bedford Park; r $89-159; P❄@⚡; MOrange Line to Midway) Slightly cheaper than Hilton Garden Inn, but in the same complex. The modern modular rooms are perfectly acceptable. Free hot breakfast is a nice touch.

P↻❄@⚡✋🐾; ☐22, MRed Line to Lawrence) The Guesthouse is comprised of 25 former condominiums that have been converted into huge suites, each with a full kitchen, washer-dryer and private balcony. Choose from a one-, two- or three-bedroom setup. The more expensive suites have a fireplace and extra bathroom. A two- or three-night minimum stay is required (though exceptions are made for last-minute and off-season bookings).

Gracious staff can arrange grocery delivery. Andersonville's slew of bars and restaurants are a short walk up Clark St.

🛏 Wicker Park, Bucktown & Ukrainian Village

HOLIDAY JONES HOSTEL $
Map p304 (☑866-639-0573; www.holidayjones.com; 1659 W Division St; dm/r from $29/85; ↻❄@⚡; MBlue Line to Division) Holiday Jones has the same owners as nearby Urban Holiday Lofts. Rooms are compact but tidy, with fresh paint and splashes of plaid (via the bedding and wallpaper). Gender-segregated dorms have three to six bunk beds. Some private rooms have en suite bathrooms. There is a big sociable common room with couches and a flat-screen TV, plus free wi-fi, continental breakfast,

linens and lockers. An empanada restaurant that serves beer and wine is attached to the lobby.

URBAN HOLIDAY LOFTS HOSTEL $
Map p304 (☑312-532-6949; www.urbanholidaylofts.com; 2014 W Wabansia Ave; dm $30-55, r from $85; ❄@⚡; MBlue Line to Damen) An international crowd fills the mix of dorms (with four to eight beds) and private rooms in this building of converted loft condos. Exposed-brick walls, hardwood floors and bunks with plump bedding feature in all 25 rooms. It's close to the El train station and in the thick of Wicker Park's nightlife. Continental breakfast is included.

The common room bustles with folks using the kitchen facilities, shooting pool and playing arcade games. Loads of bars and cafes beckon in the surrounding blocks. If the hostel is full, try Holiday Jones, the Lofts' sibling property in the neighborhood (on Division St).

IHSP CHICAGO HOSTEL HOSTEL $
Map p304 (☑312-731-4234; www.ihspusa.com; 1616 N Damen Ave, 2nd floor; incl breakfast dm $35-45, r from $105; P❄@⚡; MBlue Line to Damen) Set on Damen Ave, this hostel couldn't be any closer to the neighborhood's cache of hipster shops and eateries. The rooms hold one to 12 beds in various

dorm and private-room configurations. The flimsy metal bunks and thin-walled bathrooms don't seem to deter the young global backpackers, who head up to the viewtastic rooftop deck to grill, drink and socialize.

Freebies include a DIY pancake breakfast, wi-fi and a game room with Wii and foosball. The social hostel organizes frequent outings. There's limited parking for $10 per night.

WICKER PARK INN B&B $$
Map p304 (☑773-486-2743; www.wickerparkinn.com; 1329 N Wicker Park Ave; r $159-225; ✳🛜♿; MBlue Line to Damen) This classic brick row house is steps away from rockin' restaurants and nightlife. The sunny rooms aren't huge, but all have hardwood floors, soothing pastel color schemes and small desk spaces where you can use the free wi-fi. Breakfast is rich in baked goods and fruit. Across the street, two apartments with kitchens provide a self-contained experience. Rooms have varying minimum-stay requirements.

HOUSE OF TWO URNS
BED & BREAKFAST B&B $$
Map p304 (☑773-235-1408; www.twourns.com; 1239 N Greenview Ave; r $139-259; P✳🛜; MBlue Line to Division) Artists own these two houses at Wicker Park's edge, so it's no surprise both are fancifully furnished with old cameras, cobalt glass and other offbeat antiques, as well as original art. Rooms are more homey than luxurious. All have private bathrooms (though in a couple of cases they are not en suite). Higher-priced rooms have a Jacuzzi tub and include free off-street parking.

Guests all gather in the main dining room for a cooked breakfast, though you can request self-serve continental morning munchies. The helpful hosts also lend out umbrellas, provide free snacks and share their large DVD collection. Children over age 10 are welcome.

RUBY ROOM INN $$
Map p304 (☑773-235-2323; www.rubyroom.com; 1743-5 W Division St; r $125-195; ✳🛜; MBlue Line to Division) Take a meditation class, go on a guided intuitive journey or get your chakras massaged. Ruby Room is primarily a spa and 'healing sanctuary.' Eight simplified rooms are boiled down to the essence of comfort. No TVs, no telephones, no elevator, no breakfast. Instead, expect 500-thread-count sheets, pristine white interiors, pillow-top mattresses and free wi-fi. No children under 12.

🛏 Logan Square & Humboldt Park

LONGMAN & EAGLE INN $$
Map p308 (☑773-276-7110; www.longmananddeagle.com; 2657 N Kedzie Ave; r $95-200; ✳🛜; MBlue Line to Logan Sq) Check in at the Michelin-starred tavern downstairs, then head to your wood-floored, vintage-stylish accommodations on the floor above. The six rooms aren't particularly soundproofed, but after using your whiskey tokens in the bar, you probably won't care. Artwork by local artists decorates each room.

🛏 Near West Side & Pilsen

CHICAGO PARTHENON HOSTEL HOSTEL $
Map p310 (☑312-258-1399; www.chicagoparthenonhostel.com; 310 S Halsted St; dm/r from $30/62; ✳🛜; MBlue Line to UIC-Halsted) Guests young and old check in to this hostel that sits next to the Parthenon Restaurant in Greektown. It's a bit more out of the way and basic than other Chicago hostels; then again, prices are usually lower. Tidy dorms and private rooms come in myriad configurations; the typical single-sex dorm has eight beds with the bathroom down the hall.

There's not much in the way of common areas (though renovations are on the horizon). The free continental breakfast is a nice start to the day. Dorm dwellers must pay $2 extra for towels. Wi-fi is free but spotty.

CHICAGO MARRIOTT
AT MEDICAL DISTRICT/UIC HOTEL $$
Map p310 (☑312-491-1234; www.marriott.com; 625 S Ashland Ave; r $119-269; P✳@🛜; MBlue Line to Medical District) This hotel works best if you're visiting the medical center complex nearby. A complimentary bus shuttles you to the hospital door, to the University of Illinois at Chicago or to Little Italy – anywhere within a mile radius. Rooms are standard with HDTVs, work-friendly desks and a minifridge. Wi-fi costs $10 to $14 per day.

🛏 South Loop & Near South Side

HYATT REGENCY
MCCORMICK PLACE HOTEL $$
Map p314 (☑312-567-1234; www.mccormickplace.hyatt.com; 2233 S Martin Luther King Jr Dr; r $189-279; P✳@🛜♿; MGreen Line to

Cermack-McCormick Pl) If you're manning a trade show booth at McCormick Place, you can't beat the short walk to your bed in this attached hotel, where lobby monitors keep track of meeting schedules. However, if you're not a conventioneer, even the skyline views and comfy beds may not be reason enough to stay in this isolated 1258-room behemoth, 2.5 miles south of the Loop.

ESSEX INN
HOTEL **$$**

Map p314 (☑312-939-2800; www.essexinn.com; 800 S Michigan Ave; r $159-249; P✷@🛜🏊♿; MRed Line to Harrison) The Essex has been a family-favorite neighborhood staple for years. The oldish rooms are nothing fancy, but they are decent sized with flat-screen TVs, free wi-fi, minifridges and desks. Sweet perks include the 4th-floor rooftop garden to soak up the sun and the giant glass-enclosed pool and garden with lake views. An upscale hotelier recently bought the property, so big changes are expected. Until then, be wary of paying upper-end rack rates (more than $210 or so), since the quality doesn't match that price point.

BEST WESTERN GRANT PARK
HOTEL **$$**

Map p314 (☑866-360-5113; www.bwgrantparkhotel.com; 1100 S Michigan Ave; r $159-269; P✷@🛜♿; MRed, Green, Orange Line to Roosevelt) This very basic Best Western attracts for its location near the Museum Campus. Though the lobby's gone modern, rooms have standard faux-oak and floral-bedspread decor. Outside convention time, it can be a bargain. But if the rates ratchet up, remember you're getting a no-frills room for that price.

TRAVELODGE CHICAGO DOWNTOWN
HOTEL **$$**

Map p314 (☑312-427-8000; www.travelodgechicago.com; 65 E Harrison St; r $139-179; P✷🛜; MRed Line to Harrison) The Travelodge's mid-priced competitors in the South Loop typically offer better quality with more amenities, but if you're just looking for the lowest rates in the neighborhood, Travelodge likely has them. What do you say about lackluster motel-like rooms? Um, they're there.

RENAISSANCE BLACKSTONE HOTEL
HISTORIC HOTEL **$$$**

Map p314 (☑312-447-0955; www.blackstonerenaissance.com; 636 S Michigan Ave; r $199-319; P✷@🛜♿; MRed Line to Harrison) This 1910 neoclassical, beaux-arts landmark is known as the 'hotel of presidents' (more than a dozen have slumbered here). The 23-story beauty now caters to a highfalutin business crowd. Rooms are urban stylish (downy bedding, white-marbled bathrooms, abstract artworks); several have lake views (about $50 extra). Check out the painting-filled Art Hall on the 5th floor. Wi-fi costs $15 per day.

HILTON CHICAGO
HISTORIC HOTEL **$$$**

Map p314 (☑312-922-4400; www.hilton.com; 720 S Michigan Ave; r $179-319; P✷@🛜♿; MRed Line to Harrison) When built in 1927, this was the world's largest hotel with some 3000 rooms (and a hospital, and a theater...). Renovations brought that total down to 1544, but the gilt grandeur and crystal-dripping class have remained. The rooms are standard-issue Hilton types, with heavy drapes, cherrywood decor and comfy beds. A lakeview upgrade (about $30) makes a nice enhancement. Wi-fi costs $13 per day.

Anecdotes abound at the Hilton: in the 1940s it served as an army barracks; and at the height of the 1968 Democratic National Convention riots, police tossed protesters through the front plate-glass windows.

🛏 Hyde Park & South Side

BENEDICTINE B&B
B&B **$$**

Map p317 (☑773-927-7424; www.chicagomonk.org; 3111 S Aberdeen St; r from $180; 🚌8) Monks run this B&B that consists of two simple apartments offering loads of space and kitchen facilities. One is a two-bedroom garden apartment with a deck and self-serve breakfast; the other is a three-bedroom loft with breakfast prepared by the monks. It's in Bridgeport, about 1.5 miles from US Cellular Field. You'll fare best if you have a car.

LA QUINTA CHICAGO – LAKE SHORE
MOTEL **$$**

Map p318 (☑773-324-3000; www.laquintachicagolakeshore.com; 4900 S Lake Shore Dr; r $129-179; P✷@🛜♿🐾; 🚌6) Despite fresh paint, new furniture and other renovations, this four-story motel remains a bit scruffy (dimly lit, thin doors). Focus instead on the lakeside location, free parking and outdoor pool. A free shuttle takes you up to Michigan Ave, or you can hop on the bus for the 15-minute ride. Continental breakfast included.

Understand Chicago

Chicago Today

Downtown is thriving, with new skyscrapers, ambitious renovation projects, burgeoning technology industries and a celebrated restaurant scene. Meanwhile, other parts of the city struggle with entrenched matters of poverty, gangs and gun violence. So there are two Chicagos, and the ever-present issue is how to bring the peripheral city on par with the booming core. The mayor has his hands full with this task. Budget woes and recent scandals have made the road rocky.

Best on Film

Ferris Bueller's Day Off (1986) A teen truant discovers the joys of the city, from Wrigley Field to the Art Institute. Classic Chicago locations.
The Untouchables (1987) Native son David Mamet wrote the screenplay for this nail-biter about Eliot Ness' takedown of Al Capone.
The Blues Brothers (1980) Second City alums John Belushi and Dan Aykroyd star in the cult classic of two bluesmen on the run.

Best in Print

The Man with the Golden Arm (Nelson Algren; 1949) This tale of a drug-addicted kid on Division St won the 1950 National Book Award.
The Adventures of Augie March (Saul Bellow; 1953) Huck Finn–esque story of a destitute boy growing up in Depression-era Chicago.
The Jungle (Upton Sinclair; 1906) Immigrant life in Chicago's brutal South Side meatpacking plants.
Chicago: A Novel (Brian Doyle; 2016) A young writer chronicles his time in the 'real Chicago' with a colorful cast of characters.

Shiny Downtown

Chicago's core has boomed in recent years. Between 2000 and 2010, the city's downtown added residents faster than any other urban center in America. Developers built stacks of glossy condos that are filled to brimming, and more are on the way – like the 93-story Vista Tower, designed by star local architect Jeanne Gang and set to become the city's third-tallest skyscraper, with $18-million apartments inside. Add in the many new companies that have moved downtown (ConAgra, Motorola, GE Healthcare, Gogo), jobs at their highest level in almost two decades, and all the downtown civic projects in action (Navy Pier, McCormick Place, the Riverwalk), and you have a shining zone of affluence.

Guns & Gangs

There's a flip side to the city center's prosperity. In outlying neighborhoods, especially on the south and west sides where mostly ethnic poor and working-class Chicagoans live, more than 35,000 properties stand vacant and the population is dwindling. Part of the decrease has to do with the demise of the troubled public housing high-rises, which have all been razed. Many residents are also leaving due to high levels of violent crime.

In 2015, there were nearly 470 homicides in Chicago, and more than 2900 people were shot, mostly in gang-related rivalries. That's more than any other US city. Some blame lax state gun laws. Others link Chicago's crime to its history of entrenched segregation, which has left generations of south- and west-side families stuck in poverty and prime for the lure of gangs. Adding to the problem is mistrust between police and these communities, which came to a boil in the recent case of Laquan McDonald.

McDonald was an African American teenager shot 16 times as he was walking away from a Chicago police officer. The incident was caught on police video, but the video was withheld for more than a year, until a journalist got it released under the Freedom of Information Act in late 2015. Allegations of a police cover-up exploded and sparked waves of protests that went on for months afterward. The police officer was eventually charged with murder.

Politics

Mayor Rahm Emanuel's first term in office from 2011 to 2014 had some bumps. He took over from Richard M Daley, the city's longest-reigning mayor, who left after 22 years on the job. Emanuel got handed a whopping budget deficit and began his term by cutting or consolidating city services like garbage collection, which irked the labor unions, traditional backers of his Democratic Party. He also ticked off the teachers' union by canceling contracted pay increases, lengthening the school day and closing 50 neighborhood schools.

These grievances and more came home to roost during Emanuel's 2015 reelection bid. For the first time in Chicago history, the incumbent mayor didn't receive more than 50% of the vote, so a runoff election was held between the top two contenders. Emanuel won, but it was clear many citizens weren't pleased with his job performance. Roughly six months later, the Laquan McDonald police shooting scandal broke, and then the mayor's problems really took off. Many locals called for his resignation, claiming he was in on a cover-up. Emanuel has had his hands full since trying to revamp the police department, stem violence, fix the city's budget crisis and show neglected south- and west-side communities that their concerns matter as much as those in the visible downtown areas.

Food & Technology

Fifteen years ago no one came to Chicago for the food. Then, chef by chef, restaurant by restaurant, the city built a gastronomic scene. Suddenly international critics were dubbing Chicago one of the globe's top eating destinations, and locals such as Grant Achatz, Rick Bayless and Stephanie Izard were winning James Beard awards. Now the Beard awards ceremony is held here (at least through 2017) and it's no surprise when it crowns a Chicago restaurant as best in the nation (such as Achatz' Alinea in 2016).

The city has also been carving out a role as a technology hub. Hundreds of digital start-ups have moved into the River North and West Loop alongside Groupon's headquarters and Google's big local facility. Many companies cluster in the offices of 1871, a 50,000-sq-ft center for designers, engineers and entrepreneurs in the Merchandise Mart.

if Chicago were 100 people

33 would be African American
32 would be Caucasian
29 would be Latino
5 would be Asian
1 would be Native American & Alaska Native

belief systems
(% of population)

Catholic 39
Protestant 37
Jewish 3
Buddhist
Hindu
Unaffiliated 15
Other 4

population per sq mile

CHICAGO   USA

† ≈ 85 people

History

Much of Chicago's past is downright legendary. You've probably heard about Mrs O'Leary's cow that kicked over a lantern that started the Great Fire that torched the city. And about a gent named Al Capone who wielded a mean machine gun during an unsavory era of booze-fueled vice. And about the 'machine' that has controlled local politics for decades. Throw in the invention of the skyscraper and Ferris wheel, and you've got a whopper of a tale.

To see where Fort Dearborn once stood downtown, look for plaques in the sidewalk marking the spot at the corner of Michigan Ave and Wacker Dr.

Early Days: Onions & Forts

The Potawatomi Indians were the first folks in town, and they gave the name 'Checagou' – or Wild Onions – to the area around the Chicago River's mouth. Needless to say, they weren't particularly pleased when the first settlers arrived in 1803. The newcomers built Fort Dearborn on the river's south bank, on marshy ground under what is today's Michigan Ave Bridge.

The Potawatomi's resentment toward their new neighbors mounted, and bad things ensued. In 1812, the Potawatomi Indians – in cahoots with the British (their allies in the War of 1812) – slaughtered 52 settlers fleeing the fort. The killings took place near what is today Chicago Women's Park. During the war, this had been a strategy employed throughout the frontier: the British sought the allegiance of various Indian tribes through trade and other deals, and the Indians paid them back by killing American settlers.

After the war ended, everyone let bygones be bygones for the sake of the fur trade.

Real Estate Boom

Chicago was incorporated as a town in 1833, with a population of 340. Within three years land speculation rocked the local real estate market; lots that sold for $33 in 1829 now went for $100,000. Construction on the Illinois & Michigan Canal – a state project linking the Great Lakes to the Illinois River and thus to the Mississippi River and the Atlantic

TIMELINE	Late 1600s	1779	1803
	The Potawatomi Indians settle in. They paddle birchbark canoes, fish and ponder a name for the place. How about Checagou (Wild Onions), after the local plants growing here?	Jean Baptiste Point du Sable sails down from Québec and sets up a fur-trading post on the Chicago River. He is the city's first settler.	More settlers arrive and build Fort Dearborn at the river's mouth. The Potawatomi locals are not pleased by their new neighbors. They kill the settlers nine years later.

coast – fueled the boom. Swarms of laborers swelled the population to more than 4100 by 1837, and Chicago became a city.

Within 10 years, more than 20,000 people lived in what had become the region's dominant city. The rich Illinois soil supported thousands of farmers, and industrialist Cyrus Hall McCormick moved his reaper factory to the city to serve them.

In 1848 the canal opened. Shipping flowed through the area and had a marked economic effect on the city. A great financial institution, the Chicago Board of Trade, opened to handle the sale of grain by Illinois farmers, who now had greatly improved access to eastern markets.

Bring on the Bacon

By the end of the 1850s, immigrants had poured into the city, drawn by jobs on the new railroads that served the ever-growing agricultural trade. Twenty million bushels of produce were shipped through Chicago annually by then. The population topped 100,000.

Like other northern cities, Chicago profited from the Civil War, which boosted business in the burgeoning steel and toolmaking industries. In 1865, the same year the war ended, the Union Stockyards opened on the South Side. Chicago's rail network and the invention of the iced refrigerator car meant that meat could be shipped for long distances, satiating hungry carnivores all the way east to New York and beyond. The stockyards soon became the major meat supplier to the nation. But besides bringing great wealth to a few and jobs to many, the yards were also a source of water pollution.

Stop the Bacon!

The stockyard effluvia polluted not only the Chicago River but also Lake Michigan. Flowing into the lake, the fouled waters spoiled the city's source of fresh water and caused cholera and other epidemics that killed thousands. In 1869 the Water Tower and Pumping Station built a 2-mile tunnel into Lake Michigan and began bringing water into the city from there; it was hoped that this set-up would skirt the contaminated areas. Alas, the idea proved resoundingly inadequate, and outbreaks of illness continued.

Two years later, engineers deepened the Illinois & Michigan Canal so they could alter the Chicago River's course and make it flow south, away from the city. Sending waste and sewage down the reversed river provided relief for Chicago residents and helped ease lake pollution, but it was not a welcome change for those living near what had become the city's drainpipe.

Historical Reads

Boss: Richard J Daley of Chicago (Mike Royko)

Sin in the Second City (Karen Abbott)

Get Capone (Jonathan Eig)

The South Side (Natalie Y Moore)

HISTORY BRING ON THE BACON

By the early 1870s Chicago's stockyards processed more than one million hogs a year and almost as many cattle. In his novel *The Jungle*, Upton Sinclair described the slaughterhouses as the place to 'hear the hog-squeal of the universe.'

1837	1860	1865	1869
Chicago incorporates as a city (population 4170). It's a happenin' place, having skyrocketed from just 340 people four years earlier. Within 10 years 16,000 folks call the city home.	The Republican Party holds its national political convention in Chicago and selects Abraham Lincoln, a lawyer from Springfield, IL, as its presidential candidate.	The Union Stockyards open. Thanks to new train tracks and refrigerated railcars, Chicago can send its bacon afar and becomes the world's butchering and meatpacking hub.	The city builds the Water Tower and Pumping Station to help bring clean water in from Lake Michigan, since pollution from the stockyards was contaminating the usual supply.

Burn Baby Burn – Chicago Inferno

On October 8, 1871, the Chicago fire started just southwest of downtown. For more than 125 years, legend has had it that a cow owned by a certain Mrs O'Leary kicked over a lantern, which ignited some hay, which ignited some lumber, which ignited the whole town. The image of the hapless heifer has endured despite evidence that the fire was actually the fault of Daniel 'Peg Leg' Sullivan, who dropped by the barn on an errand, accidentally started the fire himself and then tried to blame it on the bovine.

However it started, the results were devastating. The fire burned for three days, killing 300 people, destroying 18,000 buildings and leaving 90,000 people homeless. The dry conditions and mostly wood buildings set the stage for the runaway conflagration. The primitive, horse-drawn firefighting equipment could do little to keep up. Almost every structure was destroyed or gutted in the area bounded by the river on the west, what's now Roosevelt Rd to the south and Fullerton Ave to the north.

The Chicago City Council officially passed a resolution in 1997 absolving the O'Leary family (and their cow) of blame for the Great Chicago Fire.

Birth of the Skyscraper

Despite the human tragedy, the fire taught the city some valuable lessons – namely, don't build everything from wood. Chicago reconstructed with modern materials, and created space for new industrial and commercial buildings.

The world's best architects poured into the city during the 1880s and '90s to take advantage of the situation. They had a blank canvas to work with, a city giving them lots of dough, and pretty much the green light to use their imaginations to the fullest. The world's first skyscraper soon popped up in 1885. Several other important buildings also rose during the era, spawning the Chicago School of architecture. Daniel Burnham was one of the premier designers running the show, and he encouraged architects to think big and go beyond traditional limits of design.

Labor Riots

Labor unrest had been brewing in the city for a while. In 1876, organized strikes began in the railroad yards as workers demanded an eight-hour workday and rest breaks. The turbulence spread to the McCormick Reaper Works, which was then Chicago's largest factory. The police and federal troops broke up the strikes, killing 18 civilians and injuring hundreds more.

1871	1880s	1885	1886
The Great Fire torches the entire inner city. Mrs O'Leary's cow takes the blame, though it's eventually determined that Daniel 'Peg Leg' Sullivan kicked over the lantern that started the blaze.	People start calling Chicago the 'Windy City' – not because of its blustery weather, but because of its big-mouthed local citizenry who constantly brag about the town's greatness.	The world's first steel-frame 'skyscraper,' the Home Insurance Building, rises up. It's 10 stories (138ft) tall and paves the way for big things to come.	Workers fight for an eight-hour workday and decent pay with a rally at Haymarket Sq. The police come, bombs explode, anarchists take the blame, and the labor movement is born.

By then, May 1 had become the official day of protest for labor groups in Chicago. On that day in 1886, around 60,000 workers went on strike, once again demanding an eight-hour workday. As usual, police attacked the strikers at locations throughout the city. Three days later, self-described anarchists staged a protest in Haymarket Sq; out of nowhere a bomb exploded, killing seven police officers. The government reacted strongly to what became known as the Haymarket Riot. Eight anarchists were convicted of 'general conspiracy to murder' and four were hanged, although only two had been present at the incident and the bomber was never identified. A sculpture marks the square today.

Top History Sites

Graceland Cemetery

Water Tower

Haymarket Square

Biograph Theater

Nuclear Energy sculpture

The White City Debuts

The 1893 World's Expo marked Chicago's showy debut on the international stage. The event centered on a grand complex of specially built structures lying just south of Hyde Park. They were painted white and were brilliantly lit by electric searchlights, which is how the 'White City' tag came to be. Designed by architectural luminaries such as Daniel Burnham, Louis Sullivan and Frederick Law Olmsted, the fairgrounds were meant to show how parks, streets and buildings could be designed in a harmonious manner that would enrich the chaotic urban environment.

Open for only five months, the exposition attracted 27 million visitors, many of whom rode the newly built El train to and from the Loop. The fair offered wonders heretofore unknown to the world: long-distance phone calls, the first moving pictures (courtesy of Thomas Alva Edison's Kinetoscope), the first Ferris wheel and the first zipper. It was at this fair that Pabst beer won the blue ribbon that has been part of its name ever since.

The glimmering 1893 World's Expo buildings were short lived, having been built out of a rough equivalent of plaster of paris. Only the Fine Arts Building survived, which was revamped into today's Museum of Science & Industry.

The entire assemblage made a huge impact worldwide, and the fair's architects were deluged with commissions to redesign cities.

The Great Migration

Between 1910 and 1930 more than two million African Americans moved from the rural South in what came to be known as the Great Migration. Chicago played a pivotal role in this massive population shift, both as an impetus and as a destination. Articles in the African American–owned and nationally circulated *Chicago Defender* proclaimed the city a workers' paradise and a place free from the horrors of Southern racism. These lures, coupled with glitzy images of thriving neighborhoods like Bronzeville, inspired thousands to relocate.

1890s	1893	1900	1908
Socialite Bertha Palmer makes trips to Paris, buying Monets, Renoirs and other impressionist works before they achieve acclaim. Her collection later forms the core of the Art Institute.	The World's Expo opens near Hyde Park, and Chicago grabs the global spotlight for the wonders it unveils, including the Ferris wheel, movies, Cracker Jack and Pabst beer.	In an engineering feat, Chicago reverses the flow of the Chicago River, forever ingratiating itself with its downstate neighbors as waste now streams in their direction.	Chicago Cubs win the World Series. But curses involving goats, fans named Bartman and general all-round crappy teams keep them winless for the next 108 years. And counting...

Chicago's African American population zoomed from 44,103 in 1910 to 109,458 in 1920 and continued growing. The migrants, often poorly educated sharecroppers with big dreams, found a reality not as rosy as promised. Employers were ready with the promised jobs, but many hoped to rid their factories of white unionized workers by replacing them with African Americans, which exacerbated racial tensions. Blacks were also restricted by openly prejudicial real estate practices that kept them from buying homes anywhere except for certain South Side communities. The South Side remains predominantly black to this day.

Da Mayor No 1: Richard J Daley

In the 1930s Chicago's Democratic Party created the legendary 'machine' that would control local politics for the next 50 years. Its zenith of power began with the election of Richard J Daley in 1955. Initially thought to be a mere party functionary, Daley was reelected mayor five times before dying while still in office in 1976. With an uncanny understanding of machine politics and how to use it to halt dissent, he dominated the city in a way no mayor had before. His word was law, and the city council routinely approved all his actions, lest a dissenter find his or her ward deprived of vital city services.

Under 'the Boss's' rule, corruption was rampant. A 1957 *Life* magazine report called Chicago's police the most corrupt in the nation. Although

---

CAPONE'S CHICAGO

Al Capone came to Chicago from New York in 1919. He quickly moved up the ranks and was the city's mob boss from 1924 to 1931, until Eliot Ness brought him down on tax evasion charges. Ness was the federal agent whose task force earned the name 'The Untouchables' because its members were supposedly impervious to bribes.

The success of the Chicago mob was fueled by Prohibition. Gangs made fortunes dealing in illegal beer, gin and other intoxicants. Infamous Capone sites to see include:

➡ **Green Mill** (p133) The speakeasy in the basement was a Capone favorite.

➡ **Holy Name Cathedral** (p71) Capone ordered a couple of hits that took place near the church.

➡ **Mt Carmel Cemetery** (cnr Roosevelt & S Wolf Rds, Hillside) Capone is buried in this cemetery in suburban Hillside, west of Chicago. His simple gravestone reads, 'Alphonse Capone, 1899–1947, My Jesus Mercy.'

➡ **St Valentine's Day Massacre Site** (p99) Capone's thugs killed seven members of Bugs Moran's gang here.

1909	1915	1929	1931
Daniel Burnham counsels Chicago's leaders on architecture. He tells them to think big and not be constrained by the usual boundaries.	The *Eastland* steamboat, filled with picnickers, capsizes in the Chicago River while still tied to the dock by LaSalle St Bridge; 844 people die, though the water is only 20ft deep.	Prohibition conflict boils over when seven people are killed in a shoot-out between gangsters Al Capone and Bugs Moran. The day becomes known as the St Valentine's Day Massacre.	After years of running the Chicago Outfit and supplying the nation with illegal booze, Capone goes to jail for tax evasion.

A BOMB IS BORN

On December 2, 1942, Enrico Fermi and a group of fellow scientists achieved the world's first controlled release of nuclear energy. The scene was a dank squash court under the abandoned football stadium in the heart of the University of Chicago. So began the atomic age.

The nuclear reactor was supposed to have been built in a remote corner of a forest preserve 20 miles away, but a labor strike had stopped work. The impatient scientists went ahead on campus, despite the objections of many who thought the thing might blow up and take a good part of the city with it.

Daley and the machine howled with indignation over the article, further exposés by the press revealed that some police and politicians were in cahoots with various crime rings.

Hippies & Riots Come to Town

In August 1968 Chicago hosted the Democratic National Convention, which degenerated into a fiasco of such proportions that its legacy dogged the city for decades.

With the war in Vietnam escalating and general unrest quickly spreading through the USA, the convention became a focal point for protest groups of all stripes. Enter Abbie Hoffman, Jerry Rubin, Rennie Davis, Tom Hayden, John Froines, Lee Weiner and David Dellinger – the soon-to-become 'Chicago Seven.' They called for a mobilization of 500,000 protesters to converge on Chicago. As the odds of confrontation became high, many moderate protesters decided not to attend. When the convention opened, there were just a few thousand young protesters in the city. But Daley and his allies spread rumors to the media to bolster the case for their aggressive preparations, including a claim that LSD would be dumped into the city's water supply.

The force amassed amounted to 11,900 Chicago police officers, 7500 Army troops, 7500 Illinois National Guardsmen and 1000 Secret Service agents for the August 25 to 30 convention. The first few nights police staged raids on protesters attempting to camp in Lincoln Park. They then moved in with tear gas and billy clubs, singling out some individuals – including several news reporters – for savage attacks.

The action then shifted to Grant Park, across from the Conrad Hilton (now the Hilton Chicago), where the main presidential candidates were staying. Protesters attempted to march to the site, and the

Chicago Inventions

Roller skates (1884)

Ferris wheel (1893)

Hostess Twinkies (1930)

Pinball (1930)

Spray paint (1949)

Lava Lite lava lamps (1965)

House music (1977)

1933	1942	1955	1960
Prohibition is repealed and beer flows again. The Democratic Party comes to power with a well-organized (and often corrupt) 'machine' that controls city politics for decades to come.	The first nuclear chain reaction occurs at the University of Chicago. Enrico Fermi and his Manhattan Project pals high-five each other for pulling it off – and not blowing up the city in the process.	Mayor Daley number one takes office, solidifying the Democratic Party's reign.	McCormick Place opens and is immediately hailed as the 'Mistake on the Lake.' More than 40 years later, nearby Soldier Field hones in on the title after its renovation.

police again met them with tear gas and nightsticks and threw many protestors through the hotel's plate-glass windows. The media widely covered the incident, which investigators later termed a 'police riot.'

Polishing the Rust

In the early 1970s, the city's economy was hitting the skids. In 1971 financial pressures caused the last of the Chicago stockyards to close, marking the end of one of the city's most infamous enterprises. Factories and steel mills were also shutting down as companies moved to the suburbs or southern USA, where taxes and wages were lower. Chicago and much of the Midwest earned the moniker 'Rust Belt,' describing the area's shrunken economies and rusting factories.

But two events happened in the 1970s that were harbingers of the city's more promising future. The world's tallest building (at the time) – the Sears Tower (later renamed Willis Tower) – opened in the Loop in 1974, beginning a development trend that would spur the creation of thousands of high-paying white-collar jobs. And in 1975, the Water Tower Place shopping mall brought new life to N Michigan Ave.

The city's first and only female mayor – the colorful Jane Byrne – took the helm in 1979. Byrne's reign was followed by that of Harold Washington, Chicago's first African American mayor, in 1983. His legacy was the success of the African American politicians who followed him. Democrat Carol Moseley-Braun's election to the US senate in 1992 can be credited in part to Washington's political trailblazing. Barack Obama is another name that comes to mind.

Da Mayor No 2: Richie M Daley

In 1989 Chicago elected Richard M Daley, the son of Richard J Daley, to finish the remaining two years of Harold Washington's mayoral term (Washington died in office). Like his father, Daley had an uncanny instinct for city politics. He made nice with state officials, who handed over hundreds of millions of public dollars. Among the projects that bore fruit were an O'Hare airport expansion, a huge addition to the McCormick Place Convention Center and the reconstruction of Navy Pier.

Despite falling to the third-largest US city, population-wise, in the 1990 census (behind New York and LA), Chicago enjoyed a good decade in the '90s. In 1991 the Chicago Bulls won the first of six national basketball championships. The 1994 World Cup soccer opening ceremony focused international attention on the city. And in 1996 a 28-year-old demon was exorcised when the Democratic National Convention returned to Chicago. Officials spent millions of dollars spiffing up the

Figures Who Changed History

....

Daniel Burnham – Chicago Plan architect

....

Al Capone – gangster who left corruption legacy

....

Chess Brothers – electric blues promoters

....

Richard J Daley – city politics have never been the same

1964	1968	1974	1983
The Rolling Stones come to jam with bluesman Muddy Waters at Chess Records. They consider the studio hallowed ground.	The Democratic National Convention debacle occurs. Around 27,000 police, army regulars and national guardsmen beat a few thousand hippie protestors.	Chicago pops the last girder into the Sears Tower, which becomes the world's tallest building at 110 stories (1454ft) and remains the record holder for the next quarter century.	Harold Washington, Chicago's first African American mayor, wins election. He paves the way for other politicians down the road, like Barack Obama.

city, and thousands of cops underwent sensitivity training on how to deal with protestors. The convention went off like a dream and left Chicagoans believing they were on a roll.

And when you're on a roll, who else do you thank but the guy who seems to have made it all possible? Daley won his reelection bids in 1991, 1995, 1999, 2003 and 2007, pretty much by a landslide every time. That's not to say the guy didn't have issues, including the 2003 bulldozing of Meigs Field airport and the 2005 'Hired Truck scandal,' in which city staff had been accepting bribes in exchange for lucrative contracts. By 2011, Daley had had enough; he chose not to run for reelection. He had been Chicago's mayor for a record-setting 22 years.

The Post-Daley Years

Enter Rahm Emanuel, President Obama's former chief of staff. He ran for mayor in 2011 and crushed the competition, pledging change, transparency and an end to corruption. But that's all easier said than done. Emanuel has had to deal with rising rates of violent crime, cases of police misconduct, crises in the public schools and more.

1989	2008	2011	2015
Mayor Daley number two takes office. His reign is highlighted by midnight bulldozings and shiny park unveilings. He ends up in charge of the city even longer than his father.	Local boy Barack Obama stands in the electric air of Grant Park and gives his acceptance speech as President of the United States. Chicagoans swell with pride.	Mayor Richard M Daley leaves office after 22 years, having decided not to run for reelection. Rahm Emanuel, Obama's former chief of staff, takes the reins.	Cover-up allegations follow the delayed release of a video showing teenager Laquan McDonald being shot 16 times by a Chicago policeman; protestors take to the streets.

Architecture

The Great Fire of 1871 sparked an architectural revolution in Chicago. It created a blank slate where new ideas could be tested. Daniel Burnham, one of the prime designers during the era, encouraged architects to think big and not be put off by traditional limits. Chicago has been a hotbed for skyscraper design ever since.

First Chicago School (1872–99)

Though the 1871 fire didn't seem like an opportunity at the time, it made Chicago what it is today. The chance to reshape the city's burned downtown drew young, ambitious architects including Dankmar Adler, Daniel Burnham, John Root and Louis Sullivan. These men saw the scorched Loop as a sandbox for innovation, and they rapidly built bigger, better commercial structures over the low roughshod buildings that immediately went up after the fire. These men and their colleagues

Above Rookery (p54)

made up the First Chicago School (some say they practiced the Commercial style), which stressed economy, simplicity and function. Using steel frames and elevators, their pinnacle achievement was the modern skyscraper.

The earliest buildings of the First Chicago School, such as the Auditorium Theatre (p65), used thick bases to support towering walls above. William Le Baron Jenney, the architect who constructed the world's first iron-and-steel-framed building in the mid-1880s, had a studio in Chicago, where he trained a crop of architects who pushed the city skyward through internal frames.

In the Loop, the Monadnock Building (p54) gives you a practical sense of how quickly these innovations were catching on: the original northern half of the building consists of more traditional load-bearing walls measuring 6ft thick at ground level, while the southern half, constructed only two years later, uses the then-revolutionary metal frame for drastically thinner walls that go just as high.

No matter how pragmatic these First Chicago School architects were in their inspiration and motivation, the steel-framed boxes they erected rarely suffered from lack of adornment. Maverick firms like Adler & Sullivan and Burnham & Root used a simple, bold geometric language to rebuild downtown in style. Steel skeletons were clad in exterior masonry, often with highly decorative terra-cotta panels – which were, perhaps most importantly, fireproof – embellished with designs taken from neoclassicism or nature. When gazing up at these early skyscrapers, notice their strong vertical lines crossed grid-like by horizontal bands and topped by ledge-like ornamental cornices, contrasted with the sweeping lines of jutting bay windows, curved corners and grand entrances from the street.

Prairie School (1895–1915)

It was the protégé of Louis Sullivan, Frank Lloyd Wright, who would endow Chicago with its most distinctive style, the Prairie School. Wright, a spottily educated ladies' man from a Wisconsin farm town, was the residential designer for Adler & Sullivan until 1893, when his architectural commissions outside the firm led to his dismissal. Forced into his own practice, he eventually set up a small studio in suburban Oak Park and by 1901 had built 50 public buildings and private homes around the Chicago metro area.

Over the next 15 years, Wright's 'Prairie Houses' contrasted the grand edifices of the First Chicago School with more modest charms. His unique residential buildings emphasize low-slung structures with dominant horizon lines, hipped (shallowly sloped) roofs, overhanging eaves and unadorned open-plan spaces that mirrored the flat Midwestern landscape. To blend visually, such natural, neutral materials as brick, limestone and stucco were often used. Much in sympathy with the turn-of-the-20th-century arts-and-crafts style, Wright's 'organic architecture' was likewise anti-industrial, inspired by and aiming to exist harmoniously with nature.

Of all the Prairie Houses by Wright's hand, the Robie House (p194) is the most dramatic and successful. It's a measuring stick by which all other buildings in the style are often compared, and is alone worth the trip to Hyde Park. A bit of Wright's early work is nearer to the city center – Bronzeville's Robert W Roloson Houses (p202), which were designed in 1894 while Wright still worked for Adler & Sullivan and are his only set of row houses; and the airy atrium of the Loop's landmark Rookery (p54). Wright's notable colleagues in the Prairie style include George W Maher, Walter Burley Griffin and Marion Mahony Griffin, the latter one of the USA's first licensed female architects.

With shimmering glass walls soaring skyward, the proto-modernist skyscraper Reliance Building was restored in 1999, more than a century after it was erected. Today you can sleep inside this opulent landmark at the Hotel Burnham.

Dome in the Chicago Cultural Center (p52)

Beaux Arts (1893–1920)

While the First Chicago School and Prairie School were forward-looking inventions that grew from the marshy shores of Lake Michigan, beaux arts – named for the École des Beaux-Arts in Paris – took after a French fad that stressed antiquity. Proud local builders like Louis Sullivan hated the style. Even so, these buildings are pleasing today for their eclectic mixed bag of classical Roman and Greek elements, including stately columns, cornices and facades crowded with statuary.

The popularity of the style was spurred on by the colossal French neoclassical structures of Daniel Burnham's 'White City,' built for the 1893 World's Exposition, which also erected the Palace of Fine Arts, now housing the Museum of Science & Industry (p193). After Burnham's smash hit at the Expo, beaux arts became the city's dominant architectural paradigm for the next two decades, making a welcome contrast to the dirty, overcrowded slums that had come with Chicago's urban expansion.

Beaux arts also propelled the 'City Beautiful' urban planning movement, for which Burnham was an evangelist. Published in 1909, Burnham's own *Plan of Chicago* called for a more splendorous, scenic and well-ordered cityscape. Although much of the Burnham Plan was never actually implemented, many public parks were reclaimed along the lakeshore and a network of diagonal streets newly built, both features that still define the city today.

The impressive echoes of Burnham's White City are evidenced in some of the city's best-known civic landmarks, including downtown's Art Institute (p49) and the Chicago Cultural Center (p265). The latter began in 1897 as the Chicago Public Library, housing a donated collection of some 8000 books sent by British citizens after the Great Fire

The local public TV station offers a great, free mobile guide and audio tour of downtown architecture. It's available at http://interactive.wttw.com/loop.

Magnificent Mile (N Michigan Avenue; p70)

of 1871. (Many books were even autographed by the donors, including Queen Victoria, Charles Darwin and Alfred Lord Tennyson.) While the books have since been moved to the Harold Washington Library, the magnificent gilded ceilings, inlaid marble mosaics, stained-glass domes and classical details of the original beaux-arts building remain.

Art Deco (1920–39)

After the decline in popularity of beaux arts, Chicago's architects found inspiration from another French movement: art deco. The art-deco style may have been as ornamental as beaux arts, but instead of classical columns and statues, it took on sharp angles, geometric elements, reflective surfaces and a modern palette of blacks, silvers and greens.

Sadly, there are few remaining buildings in the Loop that characterize this style, which withered before WWII. An exception is the 1929 Carbide & Carbon Building, designed by Daniel Burnham's two sons, and now housing the Hard Rock Hotel Chicago (p219). Pull yourself away from the rock-and-roll memorabilia to check out the building's polished black granite, green terra-cotta and gold-leaf accented crown, rumored to be intended to look like a foil-wrapped champagne bottle. Another downtown deco landmark is the 1930 Chicago Board of Trade (p55), which remained the city's tallest skyscraper until 1965 when the Richard J Daley Center opened.

Opposite the eclectic Wrigley Building on Chicago's Magnificent Mile, the 1925 neo-Gothic Tribune Tower is uniquely inlaid with stones from the Taj Mahal, the Great Pyramid, Notre Dame, the Great Wall of China, Lincoln's Tomb, the Alamo and more.

Second Chicago School (1946–79)

The city once again led the architectural world in the 1950s as German immigrant Ludwig Mies van der Rohe pioneered the Second Chicago School. Having previously drafted buildings in Europe alongside fellow German innovator Walter Gropius and Swiss-French modernist Le

FIVE CHICAGO ARCHITECTS TO KNOW

Louis Sullivan Chicago's architectural founding father, a revolutionary of steel-frame high-rises.

Frank Lloyd Wright Sullivan's student, who catapulted the Prairie style to global renown.

Daniel Burnham The man with the Plan that preserved Chicago's lakefront.

Ludwig Mies van der Rohe His 'less is more' motto and simple, boxy designs grounded modern skyscrapers.

Jeanne Gang Her Aqua Tower is currently the world's tallest building designed by a woman.

Corbusier, Mies was influenced by both Bauhaus and the International Style. Under Mies' direction, the steel frame that once revolutionized Chicago's skyline once again became seminal, though now no longer hidden on the inside of walls.

The functional, stripped-bare style of the Second Chicago School was all about exposed metal and glass, and represents most people's image of the modern skyscraper. The Loop's best example of this is the **Chicago Federal Center** (Map p286; 219 & 230 S Dearborn St; Ⓜ Blue Line to Jackson), Mies' masterstroke, which demonstrates both the open, universal spaces and starkly minimalist vertical I beams he favored.

Chicago Architecture Today

In the last half of the 20th century, the Chicago architectural partnership of Skidmore, Owings & Merrill came to dominate the cityscape. Further developing Mies' ideas, they stretched the modern skyscraper even higher with the John Hancock Center in 1969, and again in 1974 with the Sears Tower, which kept its crown as the world's tallest building for almost a quarter century. Now called the Willis Tower (p51), it remained the USA's tallest building until surpassed by NYC's One World Trade Center in 2013. This same prominent architectural firm continues to hold sway on the global stage, most recently as the designer of Dubai's Burj Khalifa, the world's tallest building since it opened in 2010.

The late '90s sparked a slew of development downtown, not all of it pretty. Local architects and developers were taken to task for betraying Chicago with a crop of unsightly condos and town-house developments. Blame the big, bad '80s, when downtown real estate prices were stratospheric, and largely unchecked development sprawled both north and south of the Loop.

So far, the 21st century has been marked by great architectural triumphs – including Millennium Park (p46) and Frank Gehry's sculpted steel Jay Pritzker Pavilion (p47) – and great controversies, such as the failed Chicago Spire (p70) and the love-it-or-hate-it Trump Tower (p74), now the city's second-tallest building. Jeanne Gang's Aqua Tower (p55), with its spectacularly undulating wavelike balconies, was named the 2010 skyscraper of the year by Emporis, and she continues to build impressive structures throughout the city. Meanwhile Chicago remains one of the nation's leaders in ecofriendly, LEED-certified construction, helping to keep its architectural reputation sky-high.

Fans of the band Wilco or *The Jetsons* cartoon won't want to miss snapping a photo of 1960s mod Marina City, with its giant corn-cob-shaped towers.

Sports

Chicago is the USA's greatest sports town. There – we said it. Why? It's not because every professional sports team is winning championships these days, but because of the undying passion of the city's sports fans. Listen in at the office water cooler and the talk is all about the Bears or the Blackhawks. Eavesdrop on a conversation between neighbors as they tidy their yards, and the chatter revolves around the Cubs or the White Sox.

Many Teams, One Unified City of Fans

Almost every Chicagoan declares a firm allegiance to at least one of the city's teams, and the place goes absolutely nuts when one of them hits the big time. Take the Blackhawks' Stanley Cup win in 2015: some two million people poured into the city's streets for a raucous victory parade. When the White Sox won the World Series in 2005? Similar scene, only with a ticker-tape parade that also included F-16 fighter planes, Journey's Steve Perry and Oprah, all strangely woven together. And when the Bears went to the Super Bowl in 2007, the city couldn't talk about anything else. Businesses with coat-and-tie dress codes were suddenly requiring staff to wear blue-and-orange jerseys to the office.

Die-hard sports fandom is an accepted way of life here. This is a city that sees no conflict of interest in taking one of its most revered cultural icons – the Art Institute's lion sculptures – and plopping giant fiberglass Blackhawks helmets on them when the local team wins the Stanley Cup. The creatures also donned Bears helmets and White Sox caps when those teams played in recent championships. Even the city's staid skyscrapers get into the spirit, arranging their window lights to spell 'Go Hawks' or 'Go Cubs' when those teams make a run for the championship play-offs.

Baseball

Chicago is one of only a few US cities to boast two Major League Baseball (MLB) teams. The Cubs are the North Side squad, with enthusiastic attendance year after year despite generally disappointing play (though

Chicago Sports Blogs

....

Bleed Cubbie Blue (www.bleedcubbie blue.com)

....

South Side Sox (www.southside sox.com)

....

Windy City Gridiron (www. windycitygridiron. com)

....

Blog-A-Bull (www. blogabull.com)

ALTERNATE WAYS TO GET CUBS TICKETS

If you can't get tickets from the Cubs directly, you can always try the frightfully named 'scalpers.' These guys stand across from the Wrigley Field entrance (on Clark St's west side and Addison St's south side). They typically charge above face value for tickets – until the third inning or so, when tickets can be yours for a pittance. Private fans also try to unload tickets they can't use, usually at face value. Look for the sad-faced people walking around and asking, 'Anyone need tickets?'

Another option is to inquire about rooftop seats (ie those not in the park, but rather on the rooftops of the surrounding houses on Sheffield and Waveland Aves). They're usually booked out by groups, but not always, and they include food and drinks as part of the deal; check www.wrigleyrooftopsllc.com.

that might be changing...). The White Sox are the working man's team on the South Side, and thumb their nose at all the hoopla across town.

The two ballparks are also a study in contrasts: traditional Wrigley Field (p111), aka 'the Friendly Confines,' is baseball's second-oldest park and is about as charming as they get. US Cellular Field, or 'the Cell,' is the new breed of stadium with modern amenities like a chock-full food court and fireworks exploding if the Sox hit a home run after dark.

Basketball

The Bulls, once the stuff of legend, haven't posed much of a threat since the late 1990s, when Michael Jordan led the team. Controversial team owner Jerry Reinsdorf allowed Jordan, revered coach Phil Jackson, Scottie Pippen and other key parts of the Bulls juggernaut to leave after the 1997–98 championship year. Since then the team, which plays at United Center (p165), has yo-yoed from awful to stellar to just so-so.

TOP 10 CHICAGO SPORTS HEROES

Should you find yourself in a sports bar anywhere in the Windy City, a misty-eyed mention of any of the names below will help you bond with fellow drinkers. Heck, someone might even buy you a beer.

Mike Ditka The Chicago Bears star (and current Chicago restaurateur), Ditka is the only person to have won a Super Bowl as a player, assistant coach and head coach. His mustache is legendary.

Michael Jordan The Chicago Bulls great ended his career of 15 seasons with the highest per-game scoring average in National Basketball Association (NBA) history.

Ryne Sandberg The Cubs second baseman played a record 123 consecutive games without an error. In 2005, he became the fourth Cubs player ever to have his number (23) retired.

Dick Butkus Elected to the Pro Football Hall of Fame in 1979, the Bears' linebacker recovered a record-breaking number of fumbles during his career. *Sports Illustrated* once called him 'the Most Feared Man in the Game.'

Walter Payton This 1970s and '80s Chicago Bears great is ranked second on the National Football League (NFL) all-time rushing list, and fourth in all-time rushing touchdowns.

Ernie Banks Voted the National League's most valuable player (MVP) twice (1958 and '59) and a 14-time All-Star, 'Mr Cub' was the first player to have his number (14) retired by the Cubs. A swell statue of him stands near Wrigley Field's main entrance on Clark St.

Stan Mikita The Czech-born hockey star played his entire career (1959–80) with the Chicago Blackhawks, often alongside superstar teammate Bobby Hull, aka 'the Golden Jet,' considered one of hockey's all-time greats.

Ozzie Guillén Former White Sox coach and player known for his outspoken and politically incorrect comments, Ozzie nonetheless brought the World Series trophy to Chicago in 2005 – the first big baseball win in almost a century.

Scottie Pippen Leading the Bulls through champion seasons throughout the 1990s, Pippen is known for pioneering the unofficial 'point forward' position on the basketball court.

Frank Thomas Nicknamed 'the Big Hurt' for his ability to smack balls right out of the park, this White Sox player holds the club's all-time home-run record. His number (35) was retired in 2010.

The Chicago Bears versus the Denver Broncos at Soldier Field (p181)

Football

Once upon a time the Chicago Bears were one of the most revered National Football League (NFL) franchises. Owner and coach George Halas epitomized the team's no-nonsense, take-no-prisoners approach. The tradition continued with players such as Walter Payton, Dick Butkus and Mike Singletary and coach Mike Ditka. In 1986 the Bears won the Super Bowl with a splendid collection of misfits and characters, such as Jim McMahon and William 'the Refrigerator' Perry, who enthralled the entire city. The team has been up and down ever since, eventually making it to – and then promptly losing – Super Bowl XLI in 2007. No matter what, fans still fill the stands at sometimes snowy Soldier Field (p181).

Hockey

What a difference a management change can make. After languishing at the bottom of Chicago's pro-sport pantheon for the past few decades, the Blackhawks have skated into prominence with a young winning team and TV and radio deals that put them back in the mainstream, largely thanks to franchise president John McDonough. Oh, and they won the NHL's Stanley Cup in 2010, their first trophy since 1961 – and then repeated that feat in 2013 and 2015. The Hawks slapshot pucks at United Center (p165).

Soccer

Thanks to support from the city's large Latino and European communities, the city's soccer team, Chicago Fire, attracts a decent-sized fan base, despite being largely ignored by the mainstream media. The team has made the Major League Soccer (MLS) play-offs several times in recent years, and last won the championship in 1998. Watch 'em kick at suburban Toyota Park (p204).

Don't leave town without a Mike Ditka or Harry Caray T-shirt from Strange Cargo (p122); Cubs baseball cap or mini–Wrigley Field street sign from Sports World (p123); Ozzie Guillén bobblehead doll or custom T-shirt from US Cellular Field (p204); or a Cubs, Bears or Hawks jersey for your pooch from Barker & Meowsky (p107).

Chicago Dining

For years epicures wrote off Chicago as a culinary backwater. Then a funny thing happened: the city won a heap of James Beard awards, and foodie magazines like *Saveur* ranked it among the nation's top restaurant scenes. So get ready: from 24-course meals of 'molecular gastronomy' to deep-dish pizza slices, and from porterhouse steaks to locavore salads, this town serves up a plateful. An unapologetically rich clash of high gastronomy and comfort food, at once traditional and visionary – that's Chicago dining.

Top Chicago Cookbooks

....

More Mexican Everyday by Rick Bayless

....

Cooking Like a Master Chef by Graham Elliot

....

Cookie Love by Mindy Segal

....

Girl in the Kitchen by Stephanie Izard

From Midwestern Farms to Urban Kitchens

Plenty of meat gets carved in this city, a lasting legacy from when Chicago was the world's slaughterhouse capital. Steakhouses are a dime a dozen downtown, and new gastropubs and taverns with charcuterie menus seem to open weekly. That's not to say vegetarians and vegans don't get their due, with an increasing number of stylish options, including Mana Food Bar (p141) and Green Zebra (p145).

A dynamic vanguard of Chicago chefs led by Grant Achatz has helmed the trend of molecular gastronomy – a catch-all term for meal preparation that's more like a science experiment. (What exactly does a 'pillow of lavender air' taste like?) Less haute, locavore fare has come into its own as many restaurants and star chefs now source from nearby Midwestern farms and Lincoln Park's seasonal outdoor Green City Market (p98).

If getting an authentic taste of the city ranks high on your agenda, break out of downtown. The West Loop, Wicker Park and Bucktown neighborhoods have heaps of tempting eateries at their cores. Logan Square, Humboldt Park and Ukrainian Village are more off the beaten path, but deliver perhaps the most inventive fare of all – and usually at more affordable prices too.

If you're willing to trek further still, immigrant enclaves dish out Vietnamese sandwiches and Thai noodles (Uptown), Mexican tacos and tortas (Pilsen), Swedish pastries (Andersonville), Indian and Pakistani curries (Far North Side's Devon Ave) and much more of the least expensive, most genuine dishes Chicago has to offer.

For street food that breaks all the rules – c'mon, you know you're craving a meat-loaf cupcake or a chicken tikka masala taco, right? – track down Chicago's food trucks online at Chicago Food Truck Finder (www.chicagofoodtruckfinder.com) or Roaming Hunger (http://roaminghunger.com/chi).

Chicago's Best-Loved Specialties

Deep-dish pizza is Chicago's most famous concoction. These behemoths are nothing like the flat circular disks known as pizza in the rest of the world. Here pies are made in a special cast-iron pan – kind of like a skillet without a handle – so the dough, stuffed with molten American-style

FIVE CHICAGO CHEFS TO KNOW

Rick Bayless He's everywhere: on TV, cooking at the White House, tending the organic garden where he grows the restaurants' herbs, and tending Xoco (p74), Topolobampo/Frontera Grill (p77) and Cruz Blanca (p174).

Grant Achatz Made 'molecular gastronomy' a culinary catchphrase at stratospherically priced Alinea (p103); his other hot spots include Next (p172) and Aviary (p174).

Graham Elliot The tattooed contrarian of the group, turning the usual rules upside down at the West Loop's Graham Elliot Bistro (p172).

Stephanie Izard Gaining fame as the first woman to win *Top Chef*, this sustainable farm-to-table fan's Girl & the Goat (p172), Little Goat (p167) and Duck Duck Goat (p171) are West Loop landmarks.

Paul Kahan The son of a Chicago smokehouse and deli owner, this classically influenced chef makes waves at Dove's Luncheonette (p141), Avec (p171), Blackbird (p172), Publican (p172) and Big Star Taqueria (p139), among others.

mozzarella cheese, chunky tomato sauce and other typical ingredients like sausage, is oven baked. The flagship Pizzeria Uno (p76) claims to have invented deep-dish pizza in the 1940s, but this, like many other fanatical conversations about food (and sports) in the Windy City, will inspire debate.

No less iconic is the Chicago-style hot dog. A real-deal specimen uses a local Vienna Beef weenie and requires a poppy-seed bun and a litany of toppings (including onions, tomatoes, a dill pickle and neon-green relish). And remember rule numero uno: no ketchup! For gourmet versions (rabbit sausage with anchovy hazelnut butter sauce, anyone?) and stalwart classics (beer-soaked brats), swing by Hot G Dog (p128) in Andersonville.

Another renowned Chicago specialty is the Italian beef sandwich, and it stacks up like this: thin-sliced, slow-cooked roast beef that's sopped in natural gravy and *giardiniera* (spicy pickled vegetables), then heaped on a hoagie roll. Local Italian immigrants on the South Side invented it as a low-budget way to feed factory workers during the Depression era. Try it while you're here – Mr Beef (p74) makes a popular one – because you'll be hard-pressed to find one elsewhere on the planet.

Less well known, but equally messy and delicious, is the *jibarito* sandwich, developed at a local Puerto Rican eatery. It consists of steak covered in garlicky mayo and served between thick, crispy-fried plantain slices, which form the 'bread.' Many Latin American cafes in the Humboldt Park neighborhood, such as Papa's Cache Sabroso (p155), have it on the menu.

And who could leave the Midwest without trying some pie, maybe Amish Country–style 'shoofly' molasses, juicy strawberry-rhubarb or Dutch apple layered with sour-cream custard and nutty streusel? Take a sugar-loaded tasting flight at Hoosier Mama Pie Company (p144) in Ukrainian Village – you might just devour an entire pie.

Foodie Websites

Eater Chicago (http://chicago. eater.com)

LTH Forum (www. lthforum.com)

Fooditor (www. fooditor.com)

Food Media

Chicago is rarely impressed by snooty food trends, so it follows that Chicagoans are a self-reliant bunch when it comes to picking where to eat. Case in point? The oft-discussed *Check, Please!* (http://checkplease. wttw.com), a local TV program airing on Public Broadcasting Service

Blackbird (p172)

(PBS) affiliate WTTW (channel 11), which sends dining citizens to restaurants across the spectrum to get their straightforward critiques. The show has been flooded with tens of thousands of applications from would-be food critics – not shocking in a city where a discussion about pizza can end in fisticuffs. See for yourself what locals have to say in the show's entertaining video archives online. An episode from 2001 features a young state senator named Barack Obama recommending Hyde Park's now-defunct Dixie Kitchen & Bait Shop.

Chicago's Best (http://chicagosbesttv.com) is a similar TV program, only here locals write in and recommend bites for the show's hosts to try. Episodes are also archived online.

City of Chains

It's strangely fitting that Ray Kroc opened the first McDonald's franchise restaurant in a Chicago suburb, because today top-flight Chicago restaurateurs love to expand their turf to multiple locations. Sometimes – as is the case with Giordano's (p75) pizzeria and high-class pasta kitchen Rosebud (p173) – it's a good thing. In general, though, secondary outlets of local franchises such as the Billy Goat Tavern (p74) are more like the unfortunate sequel to a great movie. When possible, stick with the original location.

Music & the Arts

Contrasts fuel the city's creative engine: high-concept installations occupy erstwhile warehouses, while poetry readings are nearly a contact sport. The city's dedication to populist ideals – most visible at free summer music festivals and in ubiquitous public art – lets artists push boundaries in front of unusually broad audiences. Few US cities can boast such engaging, affordable options for art lovers, and none can do so with such little pretension.

Visual Arts

Nowhere is it easier to see the great chasms and curious bridges of the city's artistic ethos than in the visual arts. Take the recent work of painter and sculptor Kerry James Marshall, who plays with comics and superheroes; or cartoonist Chris Ware, who draws graphic novels with architectural perfectionism. Photographer Rashid Johnson evokes

Above Pritzker Pavilion (p47)

19th-century photographic techniques and elements of hip-hop, while Dzine (pronounced 'design') draws inspiration from Chicago's graffiti movement, lowrider cars and urban street fashion to create outdoor sculptural works, large-scale paintings and art installations that fuse high and low culture.

Such transgressive boundary crossings may well have rankled the fat-cat industrialists who raised marble halls for European art over a century ago, but Chicago's public has long embraced pioneering forms. Consider society matron Bertha Palmer, who fostered the city's artistic edge in the late 1800s when she collected impressionist paintings in Europe that later became the Art Institute's core. Since then, Chicago's artists have contributed to every major international movement – from Archibald Motley Jr's portraits of roaring South Side jazz clubs in the 1920s to today's locals such as Theaster Gates, an installation artist and founder of the Stony Island Arts Bank (p195); and multimedia provocateur Matthew Hoffman.

Chicago's five gallery districts show more of the current scene. River North is the most entrenched, where top international names show off their works; it also has the largest concentration of galleries. The West Loop is a hotbed of edgy, avant-garde art that garners international praise. Bucktown and Wicker Park are rife with alternative spaces and emerging talent. Pilsen hosts several small, artist-run spaces that have erratic hours. And the South Side neighborhood of Bridgeport has become a player with cool-cat galleries in a warren of old warehouses on W 35th St.

Music

The birthplace of electric blues and house music, Chicago also fosters a vibrant independent rock scene, boundary-leaping jazz cats and world-class orchestras and chamber groups. From top to bottom, local musicians embody the best characteristics of the city itself: they're resourceful and hardworking, sweating it out in muggy blues clubs, sunny outdoor amphitheaters, DIY punk bars and everyplace in between.

CHICAGO'S MONUMENTAL PUBLIC ART

Chicago has a standard-setting public policy that made it an international center for public art: in 1978, the city council approved an ordinance stipulating that more than 1% of costs for constructing or renovating municipal buildings be set aside for the commission or purchase of original artworks. The result? A public art collection that's as much a part of the city's character as its groundbreaking architecture.

The most prominent public artworks go well beyond the staring eyes of the Picasso (p53) at Daley Plaza or Millennium Park's Cloud Gate (p46) (aka 'the Bean'). Sculptor Alexander Calder has three major works in the city, all completed in 1974. The most visible is the arching red Flamingo (p53) at Federal Plaza. The Universe is hardly out of the way for most visitors – its colorful kinetic shapes grace the lobby of Willis Tower. Flying Dragon floats in the Art Institute's North Stanley McCormick Memorial Garden. Joan Miró's Chicago (p53) sculpture – originally titled The Sun, The Moon and One Star – is also conveniently in the Loop, as is Jean Dubuffet's Monument with Standing Beast (p53) sculpture and an expansive mosaic by Marc Chagall titled Four Seasons (p53).

To find more free public artwork locations all around town, visit www.cityofchicago.org/publicart.

Sign on the Chicago Theatre (p63)

Chicago Blues

The most famous of Chicago's musical styles comes in one color: blue. After the Great Migration of African Americans out of the rural South, Delta bluesmen set up on Chicago's street corners and in the open-air markets of Maxwell St during the 1930s, when Robert Johnson first recorded 'Sweet Home Chicago.'

What distinguishes Chicago's regional blues style from Johnson's original ode is simple: volume. Chicago blues is defined by the plugged-in electric guitars typified by genre fathers Muddy Waters and Howlin' Wolf. Bluesmen from the 1950s and '60s, such as Willie Dixon, Junior Wells and Elmore James, and later champions like Buddy Guy, Koko Taylor and Otis Rush, became national stars.

These days, Chicago's blues clubs are still playing much the same song they were decades ago, but it's a proud one – synonymous with screaming guitars, rolling bass and R&B-inflected rhythms.

House Music

Chicago's other big taste-making musical export took root in the early '80s at a now-defunct West Loop nightclub called the Warehouse, where DJ Frankie Knuckles got tired of spinning disco and added samples of European electronic music and beats from that new-fangled invention, the stand-alone drum machine. Uninterested in appealing to commercial radio, the tracks used deep, pounding bass beats and instrumental samples made for dancing.

House music DJs such as Derrick Carter and Larry Heard revolutionized the form and huge second-wave stars like Felix da Housecat, DJ Sneak and acid-house artist Armando took Chicago's thump worldwide. The club scene was all about big beats, wild parties and drugged-out

Top Chicago Blues Tracks

'Sweet Home Chicago,' Robert Johnson

'Red Rooster,' Howlin' Wolf

'Wang Dang Doodle,' Koko Taylor

'Mannish Boy,' Muddy Waters

'We're Ready,' Junior Wells & Buddy Guy

Winter Garden, Harold Washington Library Center (p55)

dancing until the late '90s, when police cracked down. In recent years, the house-music scene has matured – no more rave kids with glow sticks – while still continuing to innovate.

Jazz, Folk, Rock, Hip-Hop & Gospel

For innovative, cutting-edge and avant-garde jazz, the name to know is AACM (aka the Association for the Advancement of Creative Musicians), a Chicago-based nonprofit organization formed in 1965 that has been a big inspiration for African American musicians. Contemporary jazz scene makers include saxophonist Ken Vandermark, a MacArthur 'genius' grant recipient; and Grammy-winning 'vocalese' singer Kurt Elling, who got his first big break at Uptown's Green Mill.

Chicago's underground rock community has filled an important niche in recent decades with established indie labels such as Bloodshot, Thrill Jockey, Drag City and Touch & Go. The reigning king of Chicago rock is (arguably) still Wilco.

For hip-hop, Kanye West put Chicago on the map. He grew up in the city; his mom was the former head of Chicago State University's English department. Love him or hate him, he opened the door for fresh underground names like Lupe Fiasco, Twista and Kid Sister. Chance the Rapper, usually seen wearing his White Sox ballcap, is the native son headliner these days.

Folk troubadours hold down open-mike nights and play at the North Side's Old Town School of Folk Music, while gospel choirs raise the roof at South Side churches. A worthy destination for old-school Sunday morning gospel is Greater Salem Baptist Church (p200), where famed gospel singer Mahalia Jackson was a faithful member until her death in 1972.

Literature & Spoken Word

Nelson Algren is perhaps the city's most famous writer. He lived in Wicker Park (p137) and wrote about the underbelly: drunks, prostitutes, drug addicts and street toughs. He won the 1950 National Book Award for the *The Man with the Golden Arm* about a drug addict on Division St. Saul Bellow grew up in Humboldt Park and taught at the University of Chicago. He won the 1954 National Book Award for *The Adventures of Augie March*, which is set in the city. These days Hyde Parker Sara Paretsky carries the torch. She writes a bestselling series of novels about female private investigator VI Warshawski, who solves crimes in Chicago.

The city is home to the nation's gold standard of poetic journals, *Poetry*. Long a bellwether for the academic establishment, the journal got a financial boost in 2003 when pharmaceutical heiress and philanthropist Ruth Lilly bequeathed almost $200 million to its publisher, renamed the Poetry Foundation (p74). The group sponsors big-name readings and events around town.

Small independent book publisher **Featherproof** (www.featherproof. com) showcases local urban authors by printing idiosyncratic fiction books, many with a humorous slant. You can also check out emerging writers in **Another Chicago Magazine** (www.anotherchicagomagazine. net), whose self-effacing title perfectly exemplifies the literary scene's underdog spirit. And, of course, nothing could be more unlike the scholarly verse of *Poetry* than spending a night at the venerated Uptown Poetry Slam (p133).

For author readings and other literary events around the city, browse the *Chicago Reader* (www.chicagoreader.com), or turn up for the **Printers Row Lit Fest** (www.printersrowlitfest.org) in June or the **Chicago Humanities Festival** (☏312-494-9509; www.chicagohumanities.org) in October/November.

The whole city reads together as part of the Chicago Public Library's 'One Book, One Chicago' book-club program. Even the mayor turns the pages of books by Chicago writers, such as *The Third Coast* by Thomas Dyja and Sandra Cisneros' *The House on Mango Street*.

ESSENTIAL CHICAGO RECORD LABELS

Chicago record labels have long been trailblazing leaders in new musical sounds, from the 1950s through today.

Chess Records When the blues left the Delta and migrated north, its sweet Chicago home became Chess Records, founded by Polish immigrant brothers Leonard and Phil Chess. The label also served as a catalyst for early rock-and-roll stars. You can visit Chess' original studios at Willie Dixon's Blues Heaven (p184).

Delmark Records (www.delmark.com) The oldest independent jazz and blues label in the country was founded in 1953 by Bob Koester after selling out-of-print blues and jazz records from his college dorm room.

Wax Trax! It's hard to say what would have happened to 1980s punk, new-wave and industrial music without this local label, which tirelessly worked to import European giants and issue fledgling domestic acts such as Ministry.

Thrill Jockey (www.thrilljockey.com) Started by NYC transplant Bettina Richards, this label is a celebrated nexus for indie bands. But it isn't limited to the 'postrock' sounds that made it famous, having signed genre-bending jazz greats to experimental electronica artists.

Bloodshot (www.bloodshotrecords.com) Left-of-center American roots music label fuses indie and punk rock with old-school country, alt-country or (the label's preferred moniker) insurgent country.

Theater & Comedy

Chicago's theater scene draws international acclaim. Steppenwolf Theatre (p105) has been cultivating stunning talent and groundbreaking programming since 1976. Hollywood heavyweights Joan Allen, John Malkovich and Gary Sinise are Steppenwolf members, and they exemplify Chicago's bare-knuckled, physical style of acting. Goodman Theatre (p63) and Lookingglass Theatre Company (p92) are award-winning drama houses with big, shiny theaters downtown. Many smaller theater companies are transient, setting up DIY productions in whatever space they can get their hands on – and their sheer volume of makeshift productions defies every convention.

Along with Wonder Bread, spray paint and house music, add improvised ('improv') comedy to the heap of Chicago's wide-reaching cultural contributions. Were it not for Chicago's Second City comedy troupe – which evolved from intentionally unstructured skits by the Compass Players, a mid-1950s group of University of Chicago undergrads – the proverbial chicken might still be crossing the road of American comedy.

The Compass Players' original gag of incorporating audience suggestions into quick-witted comedy became standard fare after 1959 at Second City (p105) theater. Its tongue-in-cheek name adopted from *New Yorker* articles mocking Chicago, Second City has produced some of the country's most capable funny-bone ticklers including John Belushi, Stephen Colbert, Tina Fey and Steve Carell.

Best Chicago Non-Fiction Books

....

One More Time, Mike Royko

Working, Studs Terkel

....

The Devil in the White City, Erik Larson

....

The Third Coast, Thomas Dyja

Dance

Like many of the city's other expressive hallmarks, jazz dance is an art form based on jarring contradictions. At its core, it relies on exceedingly controlled yet fluidly expressive motion, a style whose invention is credited to legendary Chicago dance teacher Gus Giordano. Exhilarating performances by his namesake company, **Giordano Dance Chicago** (☑312-922-1332; www.giordanodance.org), these days overseen by his daughter Nan, will quickly annihilate any associations with campy 'jazz hands' or 'razzle dazzle.'

Chicago's cultural landscape is crowded with A-list dance companies. At the forefront is the Joffrey Ballet (p64), which relocated here from NYC in 1995. The renowned Hubbard Street Dance Chicago (p63) keeps the attention of the international community with its modern moves.

In the Loop, Columbia College supplies dancers and choreographers to innovative fledgling companies that set up shop in performance spaces around the city. The *Chicago Reader* (www.chicagoreader.com) and *See Chicago Dance* (www.seechicagodance.com) cover the scene and list events.

Cinema & Television

Cinespace (www.chicagofilmstudios.com), a short distance west of Pilsen in Douglas Park, is where the action is. It's the largest soundstage in the US outside of Hollywood and a prime filming location. TV shows including *Empire*, *Chicago Fire* and *Chicago PD* shoot there, as do big-budget movies such as *Transformers* when they come to town.

You can always check with the **Chicago Film Office** (http://www.cityofchicago.org/city/en/depts/dca/provdrs/chicago_film_office.html) to see what might be filming when you're in town. Better yet, check the 'Casting Calls' section and see if there's a role for you.

Survival Guide

Transportation

ARRIVING IN CHICAGO

Most visitors arrive by air. The city has two airports: O'Hare International Airport and Chicago Midway Airport. O'Hare is larger and handles most of the international flights, as well as domestic flights. It is one of the world's busiest airports, with delays galore should the weather go awry. Chicago Midway Airport handles domestic services plus some flights to Canada and Mexico, and is a bit closer to the Loop. Both airports have easy El train links into the city.

Bus services are a popular means of getting to Chicago from nearby cities such as Minneapolis, Indianapolis and Detroit. Tickets are cheap, the routes are direct to the city center, and the buses usually have free wi-fi and power outlets.

It's also easy to reach Chicago by train from major cities across the country. Union Station is a hub for regional and national Amtrak services.

Flights, cars and tours can be booked online at lonelyplanet.com/bookings.

O'Hare International Airport

O'Hare International Airport (ORD; www.flychicago.com) is 17 miles northwest of the Loop. It's the headquarters for United Airlines and a hub for American Airlines. Most non-US airlines and international flights use Terminal 5 (except Lufthansa and flights from Canada). The domestic terminals are 1, 2 and 3. ATMs and currency exchanges are available throughout. Wi-fi costs $8 per day.

Train

The airport has its own El train station on the Blue Line operated by the **Chicago Transit Authority** (CTA; ☑312-836-7000; www.transitchicago.com). Trains run 24/7 and cost $5. The station is a long walk from the flight terminals. Follow the signs to baggage claim, then ones that are variously marked as 'Trains to City' and 'CTA.' Trains depart every 10 minutes or so and reach downtown in 40 minutes. Unless you are staying right in the Loop, you will likely have to transfer (or hail a taxi) to complete your journey.

Shuttle Van

Airport Express (☑888-284-3826; www.airportexpress.com) shared-van service goes downtown for $32 per person. Vans run between 4am and 11:30pm; they leave every 15 minutes. It takes 60

CLIMATE CHANGE & TRAVEL

Every form of transport that relies on carbon-based fuel generates CO_2, the main cause of human-induced climate change. Modern travel is dependent on airplanes, which might use less fuel per mile per person than most cars but travel much greater distances. The altitude at which aircraft emit gases (including CO_2) and particles also contributes to their climate change impact. Many websites offer 'carbon calculators' that allow people to estimate the carbon emissions generated by their journey and, for those who wish to do so, to offset the impact of the greenhouse gases emitted with contributions to portfolios of climate-friendly initiatives throughout the world. Lonely Planet offsets the carbon footprint of all staff and author travel.

minutes or more, depending on traffic and where your hotel is in the drop-off order. Look for ticket counters by baggage claim.

Taxi

Rides to the center take 30 minutes and cost around $50. Taxi queues can be lengthy, and the ride can take longer than the train, depending on traffic. Taxi stands are outside baggage claim at each terminal.

Chicago Midway Airport

Chicago Midway Airport (MDW; www.flychicago.com) is 11 miles southwest of the Loop. It has three concourses: A, B and C. Southwest Airlines uses B; most other airlines go out of A. There's a currency exchange in A and ATMs throughout. Wi-fi costs $8 per day.

Train

The airport has its own El train station on the Orange Line operated by the **Chicago Transit Authority** (☑312-836-7000; www.transitchicago.com). Trains operate between 4am and 1am and cost $3. They depart every 10 minutes or so and reach downtown in 30 minutes. The station is a fairly long haul from the concourses. Follow the signs for 'Trains to City' and 'CTA.'

Shuttle Van

The **Airport Express** (☑888-284-3826; www.airportexpress.com) door-to-door shuttle goes downtown for $27. Vans run between 4am and 10:30pm. It takes approximately 50 minutes. Look for ticket counters by baggage claim.

Taxi

Rides to the center take 20 minutes or longer (depending on traffic) and cost $35

to $40. Taxis queue outside the main entrance.

Union Station

Grand, Doric-columned **Union Station** (www.chicagounionstation.com; 225 S Canal St; M Blue Line to Clinton) is the city's rail hub, located at the Loop's western edge. **Amtrak** (☑800-872-7245; www.amtrak.com) has more connections here than anywhere else in the country.

→ For public transportation onward, the Blue Line Clinton stop is a few blocks south (though not a good option at night). The Brown, Orange, Purple and Pink Line station at Quincy is about a half-mile east.

→ Taxis queue along Canal St outside the station entrance.

Bus Stations

Megabus (Map p286; ☑877-462-6342; www.megabus.com/us; cnr S Canal St & W Jackson Blvd; 🛜; M Blue Line to Clinton) travels to and from major Midwestern cities. Prices are often less, and quality and efficiency better, than Greyhound on these routes. Buses arrive and depart near Union Station, on Canal St (east side) between Jackson Blvd and Van Buren St. There are no terminals: drop-offs and pickups are streetside. All purchases must be made online in advance (you cannot buy a ticket from the driver).

Greyhound (Map p310; ☑312-408-5821; www.greyhound.com; 630 W Harrison St; M Blue Line to Clinton) travels nationwide. The main station is two blocks southwest of the CTA Blue Line Clinton stop. The station is open 24 hours, but it's pretty desolate late at night. It's not an ideal walk to the El at night.

GETTING AROUND CHICAGO

The **Chicago Transit Authority** (☑312-836-7000; www.transitchicago.com) has El and bus schedules on its website, as well as a useful trip-planning feature (which basically harnesses Google). Or click 'Transit Tracker' to find out when the next train or bus is due to arrive.

Train

Elevated/subway trains are part of the city's public transportation system. Metra commuter trains venture out into the suburbs.

Elevated/Subway

The El (it stands for 'elevated,' though many trains also run underground) is fast, frequent and will get you to most sights and neighborhoods.

Two of the eight color-coded lines – the Red Line, and the Blue Line to O'Hare airport – operate 24 hours a day. The other lines run from 4am to 1am daily, about every 10 minutes or so.

The standard fare is $3 (except from O'Hare, where it costs $5) and includes two transfers. Enter the turnstile using a Ventra Ticket, which is sold from vending machines at train stations.

You can also buy a Ventra Card, aka a rechargeable fare card, at stations. It has a one-time $5 fee that gets refunded once you register the card. It knocks around 75¢ off the cost of each ride.

Unlimited ride passes (one/three/seven days $10/20/28) are another handy option. Get them at rail stations and drug stores.

For maps and route planning, check the website of the Chicago Transit Authority. The 'Transit Tracker' section tells you when the next train or bus is due to arrive at your station.

Metra

Metra (312-836-7000; www.metrarail.com; fares $3.50-10.50, all-weekend pass $8) commuter trains traverse 12 routes serving the suburbs from four terminals ringing the Loop: LaSalle St Station, Millennium Station, Union Station and Richard B Ogilvie Transportation Center (a few blocks north of Union Station). Some train lines run daily, while others operate only during weekday rush hours. Buy tickets from agents and machines at major stations.

Bus

City buses operate from early morning until late evening. The fare is $2 ($2.25 if you want a transfer). You can use a Ventra Card or pay the driver with exact change. Buses are particularly useful for reaching the Museum Campus, Hyde Park and Lincoln Park's zoo.

Bicycle

Chicago is a cycling-savvy city with a well-used bike-share program. Riders can take bikes free of charge onto El trains, except during rush hour (7am to 9am and 4pm to 6pm Monday to Friday). Most buses are equipped with a bike rack on the front that accommodates two bikes at a time. **Divvy** (855-553-4889; www.divvybikes.com) has 4700 sky-blue bikes at 470-odd stations around town. Kiosks issue 24-hour passes ($10) on the spot. Insert a credit card, get your ride code, then unlock a bike. The first 30 minutes are free; after that, rates rise fast if you don't dock the bike.

Bike rentals for longer rides (with accoutrements

such as helmets and locks) start at around $18 for two hours.

Try **Bike Chicago** (Map p286; 312-729-1000; www.bikechicago.com; 239 E Randolph St; bikes per hour/day from $9/30; 6:30am-10pm Mon-Fri, 8am-10pm Sat & Sun Jun-Aug, reduced hours rest of year; Brown, Orange, Green, Purple, Pink Line to Randolph) or **Bobby's Bike Hike** (Map p290; 312-245-9300; www.bobbysbikehike.com; 540 N Lake Shore Dr; per hour/day from $10/34; 8:30am-8pm Mon-Fri, 8am-8pm Sat & Sun Jun-Aug, 9am-7pm Mar-May & Sep-Nov; Red Line to Grand). They also rent children's bikes, and offer discounts if you book online.

Taxi

Taxis are plentiful in the Loop, north to Andersonville and northwest to Wicker Park/Bucktown. Hail them with a wave of the hand. Fares are meter-based and start at $3.25 when you get into the cab, then it's $2.25 per mile. The first extra passenger costs $1; extra passengers after that are 50¢ apiece. Add 10% to 15% for a tip. All major companies accept credit cards. The ride-share company Uber is also popular in Chicago.

Reliable companies:

Flash Cab (773-561-4444; www.flashcab.com)

Yellow Cab (312-829-4222; www.yellowcabchicago.com)

Boat

Two different water-taxi companies provide an interesting alternative to walking or busing between major sights.

Shoreline Water Taxi (312-222-9328; www.shorelinesightseeing.com; one-way adult $6-8, child $3-4; 10am-6:30pm late May-early Sep) transports you on its Lake Taxi from Navy Pier (at the

southwestern corner) to the South Loop's Shedd Aquarium. The River Taxi connects Polk Bros Park (just west of Navy Pier) to Willis Tower (via the Adams St bridge's southeast side).

Chicago Water Taxi (312-337-1446; www.chicagowatertaxi.com; one-way $4-6, weekday/weekend all-day pass $8/10) plies the river from the Michigan Ave bridge (northwest side, by the Wrigley Building) to Madison St (near the Metra Ogilvie Transportation Center), stopping at LaSalle/Clark en route. In summer it continues on to Chinatown.

Car

Driving in Chicago is no fun. Traffic snarls not only at rush hours, but also just about every hour in between. Especially for short trips in town, use public transportation to spare yourself the headache.

Parking

➡ Meter spots and on-street parking are plentiful in outlying areas, but the Loop, Near North, Lincoln Park and Lake View neighborhoods can require serious circling before you find a spot.

➡ Note that 'meter' is a bit of a misnomer – you actually feed coins or a credit card into a pay box that serves the entire block. Decide how much time you want, then the box spits out a receipt to display on the car's dashboard. Per-hour costs range from $2 in outlying areas to $6.50 in the Loop. In many areas, you do not have to pay between 10pm and 8am. Check the pay box's instructions.

➡ Downtown garages cost about $40 per day, but will save you time and traffic tickets.

Millennium Park Garage (www.millenniumgarages.com;

5 S Columbus Dr; per 3/24hr $28/35) is one of the cheapest.

➡ Some meter-free neighborhoods require resident parking passes, some don't. Read signs carefully.

➡ Never park in a spot or red-curbed area marked 'Tow-Away.' Your car *will* be towed.

Road Rules

➡ The speed limit is 30mph unless posted otherwise.

➡ You must wear your seat belt and restrain kids under eight years in child-safety seats.

➡ Driving while using a hand-held cell phone is illegal.

➡ Be aware that many intersections have cameras that snap a photo if you go through a red light or speed. A $100 ticket arrives in your mailbox not long thereafter.

Auto Associations

For emergency road service and towing, members can call the American Automobile Association (www.aaa.com). It has reciprocal membership agreements with several international auto clubs.

Car-Share Services

The car-share service **Zipcar** (☎866-494-7227; www.zipcar.com) is popular in Chicago. Hourly/daily rates are $8.50/74 weekdays and $9.25/79 on weekends. That includes gas and insurance and good parking spaces around town. You need to become a member first ($70 annually plus $25 application fee).

Rental

All major car-rental agencies are in Chicago. Rates fluctuate radically. In general, it's more expensive to rent at the airport than downtown. To rent a car you typically need to be at least 25 years old, hold a valid driver's license and have a major credit card.

Unless stated otherwise, these companies have outlets at both Chicago airports and downtown.

Alamo (☎800-462-5266; www.alamo.com)

Avis (☎800-331-1212; www.avis.com)

Budget (☎800-527-0700; www.budget.com)

Dollar (☎800-800-4000; www.dollar.com) At the airports only.

Enterprise (☎800-867-4595; www.enterprise.com)

Hertz (☎800-654-3131; www.hertz.com)

National (☎800-227-7368; www.nationalcar.com)

Thrifty (☎800-527-7075; www.thrifty.com)

TOURS

Chicago offers loads of tours. Jaunts by boat, foot or bus are popular. They provide a fine introduction to the city, particularly if you're short on time. Bicycle rental companies such as Bike Chicago and Bobby's Bike Hike also run worthy excursions. Outdoor-oriented tours usually operate from April to November only. Many companies offer discounts if you book online.

Chicago Architecture Foundation (CAF; Map p286; ☎312-922-3432; www.architecture.org; 224 S Michigan Ave; tours $15-50; MBrown, Orange, Green, Purple, Pink Line to Adams) The gold-standard boat tours ($44) sail from the river dock (Map

---

BOAT TOURS

Boat tours are the most popular way to see the city. Most run April to November, several times daily. The **Chicago Architecture Foundation** (CAF; Map p286; ☎312-922-3432; www.architecture.org; 224 S Michigan Ave; tours $15-50; MBrown, Orange, Green, Purple, Pink Line to Adams) does the best job, but several other companies offer similar tours from the docks at Michigan Ave. They cruise the river and lakefront for around 90 minutes; costs are $36/18 per adult/child on average. Check online to see what works for your schedule and budget.

Mercury Cruises (Map p286; ☎312-332-1353; www.mercurycruises.com; tours adult/child $34/12; ⊙late Apr-early Oct; MBrown, Orange, Green, Purple, Pink Line to State/Lake)

Shoreline Sightseeing (Map p293; ☎312-222-9328; www.shorelinesightseeing.com; 75min tours adult/child from $35/18; MRed Line to Grand, then trolley)

Wendella Boats (Map p290; ☎312-337-1446; www.wendellaboats.com; 400 N Michigan Ave; 90min tours adult/child $36/17; MRed Line to Grand)

Other fun boat tours depart from Navy Pier, such as **Seadog Speedboats** (Map p293; ☎888-636-7737; www.seadogcruises.com; 600 E Grand Ave; tours $24-38; MRed Line to Grand, then trolley), where you'll likely get splashed, and **Windy** (Map p293; ☎312-451-2700; www.tallshipwindy.com; 600 E Grand Ave; 60-75min tours adult/child $30/10; MRed Line to Grand, then trolley), a kid-favorite four-masted schooner.

p286; Ⓜ Brown, Orange, Green, Purple, Pink Line to State/Lake) on the southeast side of the Michigan Ave Bridge. The popular Historic Skyscrapers walking tours ($20) leave from the main downtown address. Weekday lunchtime tours ($15) explore individual landmark buildings and meet on-site. CAF sponsors bus, bike and El train tours, too. Buy tickets online or at CAF; boat tickets can also be purchased at the dock.

Chicago by Foot (☎312-612-0826; www.freetoursbyfoot.com/chicago) Guides for this pay-what-you-want walking tour offer engaging stories and historical details on different jaunts covering the Loop, Gold Coast, Lincoln Park's gangster sites and much more. Most takers pay around $10 per person. Reserve in advance to guarantee a spot; walk-up guests are welcome if space is available (chancy).

Chicago Detours (☎312-350-1131; www.chicagodetours.com; tours from $22) It offers engrossing, detail-rich tours (mostly walking, but also some by bus) that take in Chicago's architecture, history and culture. The Historic Pub Crawl Tour is a popular one.

Chicago Greeter (Map p286; www.chicagogreeter.com) This company pairs you with a local city dweller who takes you on a personal two- to four-hour tour customized by theme (architecture, history, gay and lesbian, and more) or neighborhood. Travel is by foot and/or public transportation. Reserve at least 10 business days in advance online. Departure locations vary.

Chicago History Museum Tours (Map p296;☎312-642-4600; www.chicagohistory.org; tours $20-55) The museum counts El (elevated/subway system) jaunts, cycling routes and cemetery walks among its excellent tour arsenal. Departure points and times vary.

InstaGreeter (Map p286; www.chicagogreeter.com/instagreeter; 77 E Randolph St; ◷10am-3pm Fri & Sat, 11am-2pm Sun; Ⓜ Brown, Orange, Green, Purple, Pink Line to Randolph) Provides one-hour Loop tours on the spot from the Chicago Cultural Center. Meet in the Randolph St lobby. In summer, free tours of Millennium Park also depart from here daily at 11:30am and 1pm; first-come, first-served for these, so arrive early.

Seadog Speedboats (Map p293;☎888-636-7737; www.seadogcruises.com; 600 E Grand Ave; tours $24-38; Ⓜ Red Line to Grand, then trolley) Seadog offers several boat tours, including a high-speed, jet-propelled thrill ride (on which you'll likely get wet) and a slower-moving (but still speedy!) cruise along the lakefront. Tours range from 30 to 75 minutes.

Untouchable Gangster Tours (Map p290;☎773-881-1195; www.gangstertour.com; 600 N Clark St; 2hr tours $30; Ⓜ Red Line to Grand) Comic, costumed actors take you by van to some of Chicago's famous gangster sights. There's usually a tour at 11am daily, plus 1pm daily in summer, with additional offerings Friday through Sunday. Departs from outside McDonald's.

Weird Chicago Tours (Map p290;☎888-446-7859; www.weirdchicago.com; 600 N Clark St; 3hr tours $35; ◷Fri-Sun; Ⓜ Red Line to Grand) Drives by ghost, gangster and red-light sites. Departs from outside McDonald's.

Windy (Map p293;☎312-451-2700; www.tallshipwindy.com; 600 E Grand Ave; 60-75min tours adult/child $30/10; Ⓜ Red Line to Grand, then trolley) The four-masted schooner sets sail from Navy Pier. Trips have different themes (pirates, architecture, sailing skills etc). With only the sound of the wind in your ears, these tours are the most relaxing way to see the skyline from offshore.

Directory A–Z

Customs Regulations

For a complete list of US customs regulations, visit the official portal for US Customs and Border Protection (www.cbp.gov).

Duty-free allowance per person is as follows:

➡ 1L of liquor (provided you are at least 21 years old)

➡ 100 cigars and 200 cigarettes (if you are at least 18)

➡ $200 worth of gifts and purchases ($800 if a returning US citizen)

If you arrive with $10,000 in US or foreign currency, it must be declared.

There are heavy penalties for attempting to import illegal drugs. Fruit, vegetables and other food must be declared.

Discount Cards

➡ The **Go Chicago Card** (www.smartdestinations.com/chicago) allows you to visit an unlimited number of attractions for a flat fee. It's good for one, two, three or five consecutive days.

➡ The company also offers a three-choice or five-choice 'Explorer Pass' where you pick among 26 options for sights. It's valid for 30 days.

➡ **CityPass** (www.citypass.com/chicago) gives access to five of the city's top draws, including the Art Institute, Shedd Aquarium and Willis Tower, over nine days. It's less flexible than Go Chicago's pass, but cheaper for those wanting a more leisurely sightseeing pace.

➡ All of the above let you skip the regular queues at sights.

Electricity

120V/60Hz

120V/60Hz

Emergency

Nonemergency police matters ☑311

Police, fire, ambulance ☑911

Internet Access

➡ Wi-fi is common in lodgings across the price spectrum; many places also have a computer terminal for you to use.

➡ Many bars, cafes and public buildings, such as the Chicago Cultural Center, offer free wi-fi.

➡ Outlets of the Chicago Public Library (www.chipublib.org) offer free wi-fi. There are no passwords required or time limits. Libraries also offer free computer terminals for one hour; get a 'day pass' at the counter.

→ For a list of wi-fi hot spots, visit Wi-Fi Free Spot (www. wififreespot.com).

Legal Matters

→ If you are arrested, you are allowed to remain silent, though never walk away from an officer; you are entitled to have access to an attorney. The legal system presumes you're innocent until proven guilty. All arrested persons have the right to make one phone call. If you don't have a lawyer or family member to help you, call your embassy or consulate. The police will give you the number on request.

→ The blood alcohol limit is 0.8%. Driving under the influence of alcohol or drugs is a serious offense, subject to stiff fines and even imprisonment.

→ Possession of any illicit drug, including cocaine, ecstasy, LSD, heroin, hashish or more than an ounce of pot, is a felony potentially punishable by a lengthy jail sentence.

→ The city recently decriminalized possession of small amounts of marijuana. However, if you're caught with 15g or less of pot, you can be ticketed for $250 to $500.

→ It's against the law to have an open container of any alcoholic beverage in public. However, this is overlooked during most concerts at Millennium Park, as well as at Navy Pier if you buy from one of the vendors on-site.

Medical Services

Chicago has no unexpected health dangers. But if you do find yourself in need of medical care, recommended facilities include the following:

Advocate Illinois Masonic Medical Center (773-975-1600; www.advocatehealth. com/immc; 836 W Wellington Ave; ⓜBrown, Purple Line to Wellington) Hospital located in Lake View.

Lurie Children's Hospital (www.luriechildrens.org; 225 E Chicago Ave; ⊙24hr; ⓜRed Line to Chicago) Brand-new downtown facility.

Northwestern Memorial Hospital (312-926-5188; www. nmh.org; 251 E Erie St; ⊙24hr; ⓜRed Line to Chicago) Well-respected downtown hospital.

Stroger Cook County Hospital (312-864-1300; www. cookcountyhhs.org; 1969 W Ogden Ave; ⊙24hr; ⓜBlue Line to Illinois Medical District) Public hospital serving low-income patients; 2.5 miles west of the Loop.

Pharmacies

Walgreens pharmacies are located all around the city. Convenient branches are located on **Michigan Ave** (312-664-8686; 757 N Michigan Ave; ⊙24hr; ⓜRed Line to Chicago) and **W Monroe St** (312-346-5727; 79 W Monroe St; ⊙7am-7pm Mon-Fri; ⓜRed, Blue Line to Monroe). CVS is another local chain with branches throughout town.

Money

The US dollar ($) is the currency.

ATMs

ATMs are everywhere in Chicago. They are available 24/7 at banks, airports and convenience shops. Most ATMs link into worldwide networks (Plus, Cirrus, Exchange etc). ATMs typically charge a service fee of $3 or more per transaction, and your home bank may impose additional charges.

Credit Cards

Visa, MasterCard and American Express are widely accepted at hotels, restaurants, bars and shops.

Money Changers

Although the airports have exchange bureaus, better rates can usually be obtained in the city.

Travelex (312-807-4941; www.travelex.com; 19 S LaSalle St; ⊙8am-5pm Mon-Fri; ⓜBlue Line to Monroe)

World's Money Exchange (312-641-2151; www. wmeinc.com; 203 N LaSalle St; ⊙8:45am-4:45pm Mon-Fri; ⓜBrown, Orange, Green, Purple, Pink, Blue Line to Clark/Lake)

Tipping

Tipping is not optional; only withhold tips in cases of outrageously bad service.

Airport & hotel porters $2 per bag, minimum per cart $5.

Bartenders 15% per round, minimum per drink $1.

Housekeeping staff $2 to $5 per night.

Restaurant servers 15% to 20%, unless gratuity already included on bill.

Taxi drivers 10% to 15%, rounded up to the next dollar.

Parking valets At least $2 when you're handed back the keys.

Opening Hours

Typical normal opening times are as follows:

Banks & businesses 9am to 5pm Monday to Friday

Bars 5pm to 2am (3am on Saturday); some licensed until 4am (5am on Saturday)

Nightclubs 10pm to 4am; often closed Monday through Wednesday

Restaurants Breakfast 7am or 8am to 11am, lunch 11am or 11:30am to 2:30pm, dinner 5pm or 6pm to 10pm Sunday to Thursday, to 11pm or midnight Friday and Saturday

Shops 11am to 7pm Monday to Saturday, noon to 6pm Sunday

Post

The US Postal Service (www.usps.com) is reliable and inexpensive. The postal rates for 1st-class mail within the USA are 47¢ for letters weighing up to 1oz (21¢ for each additional ounce) and 34¢ for postcards. International airmail rates are $1.15 for a 1oz letter or postcard. Convenient post offices:

Fort Dearborn Station (Map p290; 540 N Dearborn St; ⊙8:30am-6pm Mon-Fri, 9am-3pm Sat, 10am-2pm Sun)

Loop Post Office (Map p286; ☏312-983-8000; 211 S Clark St; ⊙7am-6pm Mon-Fri; ⓂBrown, Orange, Purple, Pink Line to Quincy)

Main Post Office (Map p286; ☏312-983-8130; 433 W Harrison St; ⊙8:30am-midnight Mon-Fri, 9am-11pm Sat, 10am-9pm Sun; ⓂBlue Line to Clinton)

Public Holidays

Banks, schools, offices and most shops close on these days:

New Year's Day January 1

Martin Luther King Jr Day Third Monday in January

President's Day Third Monday in February

Pulaski Day First Monday in March (observed mostly by city offices)

Memorial Day Last Monday in May

Independence Day July 4

Labor Day First Monday in September

Columbus Day Second Monday in October

Veteran's Day November 11

Thanksgiving Day Fourth Thursday in November

Christmas Day December 25

Safe Travel

➤ You've probably heard about Chicago's high murder rate, but know this is mostly concentrated in certain far west and far south neighborhoods.

➤ Overall, serious crime in Chicago has been dropping in recent years, and major tourist areas are all reasonably safe.

➤ That doesn't mean you shouldn't take normal, big-city precautions, especially solo at night. Many crimes involve cell phone theft, so be subtle when using yours.

Taxes & Refunds

Taxes are usually not included in the stated price. The basic sales tax in Chicago is 10.25%. Restaurant tax is 11.25% in most parts of town. Hotel tax is 17.4%.

Telephone

Calls from a regular landline or cell phone are usually cheaper than a hotel phone. Pay phones are thin on the ground.

Cell Phones

Most US cell phones – aside from iPhones – operate on CDMA, not the European standard of GSM. Be sure to double-check compatibility with your phone service provider. Roaming costs, especially for data, can be enormous if you're not careful.

It might be cheaper to buy a prepaid SIM card for the USA, like those sold by AT&T, which you can insert into your international cell phone to get a local phone number and voicemail.

You can also buy inexpensive, no-contract (prepaid) phones with a local number and a set number of minutes, which can be topped up. Virgin Mobile, T-Mobile, AT&T and other providers offer phones starting at $30, with a package of minutes starting around $40 for 400 minutes.

Electronics store chain **Best Buy** (Map p294; ☏312-397-2146; www.bestbuy.com; 875 N Michigan Ave; ⊙10am-9pm Mon-Sat, to 8pm Sun; ⓂRed Line to Chicago) sells these phones, as well as international SIM cards. Another good place to poke around is on Devon Ave, where several shops sell cell-phone equipment to a mostly Indian and European clientele.

Phone Codes

US country code ☏1

Chicago area codes ☏312, ☏773, ☏872

Making international calls
Dial ☏011 + country code + area code + local number

Calling other US area codes or Canada Dial ☏1 + area code + seven-digit local number

Calling within Chicago Dial ☏1 + area code + seven-digit local number. It works the same whether you're calling a landline or cell phone.

Phonecards

Private prepaid phonecards are available from convenience stores, supermarkets and pharmacies. AT&T sells a reliable phonecard that is widely available.

Time

Chicago is on Central Standard Time, six hours behind Greenwich Mean Time. Daylight Saving Time is observed between mid-March and early November.

Chicago is one hour behind Eastern Standard Time, which encompasses nearby Michigan and Indiana (apart from the northwestern corner of Indiana, which follows Chicago time). The border between the two zones is just east of the city.

When it's noon in Chicago, it's 1pm in New York City, 6pm in London, 3am the next day in Sydney and 5am the next day in Auckland.

Tourist Information

Visitor Center (Map p286; www.choosechicago.com; 111 N State St; ☉10am-8pm Mon-Fri, to 9pm Sat, 11am-7pm Sun; Ⓜ Brown, Orange, Green, Purple, Pink Line to Randolph) This isn't a particularly useful place, but has a smattering of brochures and maps. Concierges can answer basic questions. Located in Macy's basement.

Travelers with Disabilities

➡ Most museums and major sights are wheelchair accessible, as are most large hotels and restaurants.

➡ All city buses are wheelchair accessible, but about one-third of El stations are not.

➡ Easy Access Chicago (www.easyaccesschicago.org) is a free resource that lists museums, tours, restaurants and lodgings, and provides mobility, vision and hearing accessibility information for each place.

➡ The **Mayor's Office for People with Disabilities** (☏312-744-7050, TTY 312-744-4964; www.cityofchicago.org/disabilities) can answer questions about the availability of services in the city.

Visas

➡ The Visa Waiver Program (VWP) allows nationals from 36 countries (including most EU countries, Japan, Australia and New Zealand) to enter the US without a visa for up to 90 days.

➡ VWP visitors require a machine-readable passport and approval under the Electronic System For Travel Authorization at least three days before arrival. There is a $14 fee for processing and authorization (payable online). Once approved, the registration is valid for two years.

➡ Those who need a visa – ie anyone staying longer than 90 days, or from a non-VWP country – should apply at the US consulate in their home country.

➡ Check with the US Department of State (www.travel.state.gov) for updates and details on entry requirements.

Behind the Scenes

SEND US YOUR FEEDBACK

We love to hear from travelers – your comments keep us on our toes and help make our books better. Our well-traveled team reads every word on what you loved or loathed about this book. Although we cannot reply individually to your submissions, we always guarantee that your feedback goes straight to the appropriate authors, in time for the next edition. Each person who sends us information is thanked in the next edition – the most useful submissions are rewarded with a selection of digital PDF chapters.

Visit **lonelyplanet.com/contact** to submit your updates and suggestions or to ask for help. Our award-winning website also features inspirational travel stories, news and discussions.

Note: We may edit, reproduce and incorporate your comments in Lonely Planet products such as guidebooks, websites and digital products, so let us know if you don't want your comments reproduced or your name acknowledged. For a copy of our privacy policy visit lonelyplanet.com/privacy.

OUR READERS

Many thanks to the travelers who used the last edition and wrote to us with helpful hints, useful advice and interesting anecdotes:

Seth Blumenthal, Su Elliot, Elizabeth Hambourger, Fey Martin, Cornelia Pabijan, Hilary Phillips, Valentina Sarracco, Bárbara Viana

WRITER THANKS

Karla Zimmerman

Many thanks to Carmine Cervi, Tressa Ferrella, Dan Hartley, David Lynch, Kari Lydersen, Cathy McKee and all of my other friends who took the time to share their favorite local spots. Thanks most to Eric Markowitz, the world's best partner-for-life, who indulges my beer- and donut-filled ramblings with an endless supply of good humor.

ACKNOWLEDGEMENTS

Cover photograph: Anish Kapoor's *Cloud Gate* sculpture, Nick Ledger/AWL©.

THIS BOOK

This 8th edition of Lonely Planet's *Chicago* guidebook was researched, written and curated by Karla Zimmerman. Karla and Sara Benson wrote and researched the previous edition. This guidebook was produced by the following:

Destination Editor Rebecca Warren
Product Editors Carolyn Boicos, Grace Dobell
Senior Cartographer Alison Lyall
Book Designers Jessica Rose, Wendy Wright
Assisting Editors Michelle Bennett, Robyn Loughnane, Charlotte Orr, Saralinda Turner
Cover Researcher Naomi Parker
Thanks to Katie Connolly, Kate James, Andi Jones, Virginia Moreno, Claire Naylor, Karyn Noble, Victoria Smith, Tony Wheeler

Index

🍷 DRINKING & NIGHTLIFE

☆ ENTERTAINMENT

Chicago Maps

Sights

- Beach
- Bird Sanctuary
- Buddhist
- Castle/Palace
- Christian
- Confucian
- Hindu
- Islamic
- Jain
- Jewish
- Monument
- Museum/Gallery/Historic Building
- Ruin
- Shinto
- Sikh
- Taoist
- Winery/Vineyard
- Zoo/Wildlife Sanctuary
- Other Sight

Activities, Courses & Tours

- Bodysurfing
- Diving
- Canoeing/Kayaking
- Course/Tour
- Sento Hot Baths/Onsen
- Skiing
- Snorkeling
- Surfing
- Swimming/Pool
- Walking
- Windsurfing
- Other Activity

Sleeping

- Sleeping
- Camping

Eating

- Eating

Drinking & Nightlife

- Drinking & Nightlife
- Cafe

Entertainment

- Entertainment

Shopping

- Shopping

Information

- Bank
- Embassy/Consulate
- Hospital/Medical
- Internet
- Police
- Post Office
- Telephone
- Toilet
- Tourist Information
- Other Information

Geographic

- Beach
- Gate
- Hut/Shelter
- Lighthouse
- Lookout
- Mountain/Volcano
- Oasis
- Park
- Pass
- Picnic Area
- Waterfall

Population

- Capital (National)
- Capital (State/Province)
- City/Large Town
- Town/Village

Transport

- Airport
- BART station
- Border crossing
- Boston T station
- Bus
- Cable car/Funicular
- Cycling
- Ferry
- Metro/Muni station
- Monorail
- Parking
- Petrol station
- Subway/SkyTrain station
- Taxi
- Train station/Railway
- Tram
- Underground station
- Other Transport

Note: Not all symbols displayed above appear on the maps in this book

Routes

- Tollway
- Freeway
- Primary
- Secondary
- Tertiary
- Lane
- Unsealed road
- Road under construction
- Plaza/Mall
- Steps
- Tunnel
- Pedestrian overpass
- Walking Tour
- Walking Tour detour
- Path/Walking Trail

Boundaries

- International
- State/Province
- Disputed
- Regional/Suburb
- Marine Park
- Cliff
- Wall

Hydrography

- River, Creek
- Intermittent River
- Canal
- Water
- Dry/Salt/Intermittent Lake
- Reef

Areas

- Airport/Runway
- Beach/Desert
- Cemetery (Christian)
- Cemetery (Other)
- Glacier
- Mudflat
- Park/Forest
- Sight (Building)
- Sportsground
- Swamp/Mangrove

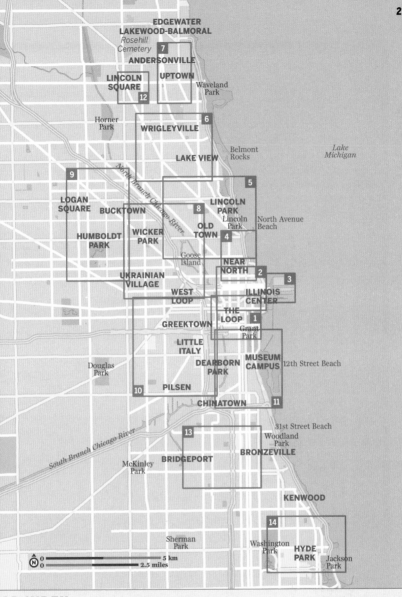

EDGEWATER
LAKEWOOD-BALMORAL
Rosehill
Cemetery 7
ANDERSONVILLE
LINCOLN
SQUARE
12 UPTOWN
Waveland
Park

Horner
Park
6
WRIGLEYVILLE
LAKE VIEW
Belmont
Rocks
Lake
Michigan

9
North Branch Chicago River
LOGAN
SQUARE
BUCKTOWN
8
LINCOLN
PARK
5

HUMBOLDT
PARK
WICKER
PARK
OLD
TOWN
4
Lincoln
Park
North Avenue
Beach

Goose
Island
NEAR
NORTH
2
3

UKRAINIAN
VILLAGE
WEST
LOOP
ILLINOIS
CENTER

THE
LOOP
1
GREEKTOWN
Grant
Park

LITTLE
ITALY
DEARBORN
PARK
MUSEUM
CAMPUS
12th Street Beach

Douglas
Park
10
PILSEN
CHINATOWN
11

31st Street Beach
13
Woodland
Park
BRONZEVILLE

McKinley
Park
BRIDGEPORT

KENWOOD

14
Sherman
Park
Washington
Park
HYDE
PARK
Jackson
Park

N 0   5 km
   0   2.5 miles

MAP INDEX

THE LOOP

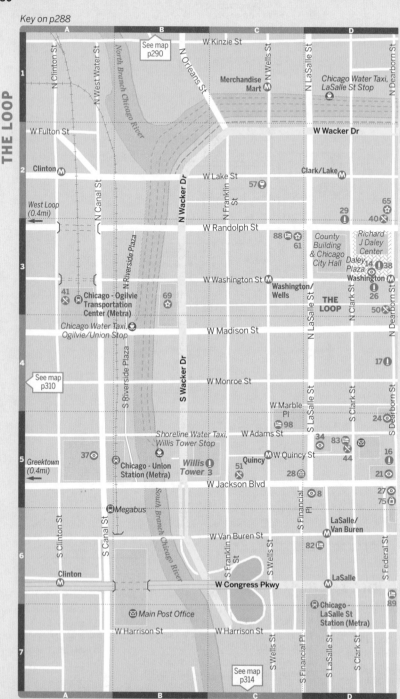

Key on p288

See map p290

W Kinzie St

N Clinton St

N West Water St

North Branch Chicago River

N Orleans St

Merchandise Mart

N Wells St

N LaSalle St

Chicago Water Taxi, LaSalle St Stop

N Dearborn St

W Fulton St

W Wacker Dr

Clinton

West Loop (0.4mi)

N Canal St

N Wacker Dr

W Lake St

57

Clark/Lake

65

W Randolph St

29
40

County Building & Chicago City Hall

Richard J Daley Center

88
61

Daley Plaza

14 38

Washington

26

Chicago - Ogilvie Transportation Center (Metra)

41

N Riverside Plaza

69

W Washington St

Washington/ Wells

THE LOOP

50

Chicago Water Taxi, Ogilvie/Union Stop

W Madison St

N LaSalle St

N Clark St

N Dearborn St

See map p310

S Riverside Plaza

S Wacker Dr

W Monroe St

17

W Marble Pl

98

24

Shoreline Water Taxi, Willis Tower Stop

W Adams St

34
83
44

16

Greektown (0.4mi)

37

Chicago - Union Station (Metra)

Willis Tower 3

Quincy

51

W Quincy St

28

21

W Jackson Blvd

S Clinton St

S Canal St

South Branch Chicago River

Megabus

W Van Buren St

S Financial Pl

S Franklin St

S Wells St

27
8
75

LaSalle/ Van Buren

82

Clinton

W Congress Pkwy

LaSalle

S Federal St

89

Main Post Office

Chicago - LaSalle St Station (Metra)

W Harrison St

W Harrison St

S Wells St

S Financial Pl

S LaSalle St

S Clark St

See map p314

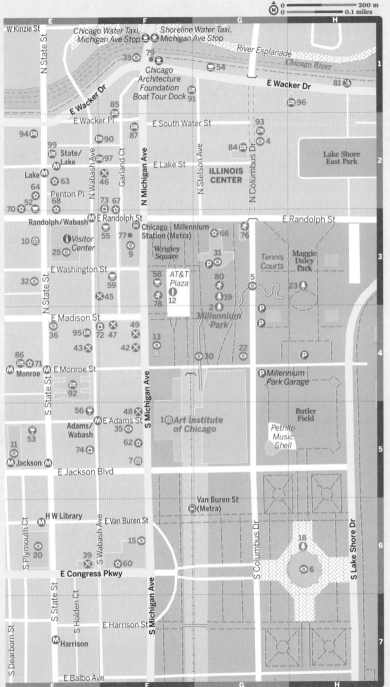

N

0   200 m
0   0.1 miles

W Kinzie St

Chicago Water Taxi,
Michigan Ave Stop

Shoreline Water Taxi,
Michigan Ave Stop

River Esplanade

Chicago River

E Wacker Dr

33

79

54

81

N State St

E Wacker Dr

Chicago
Architecture
Foundation
Boat Tour Dock

91

96

85

E Wacker Pl

E South Water St

93

94

99

90

87

84

4

State/
Lake

N Wabash Ave

97

Garland Ct

E Lake St

N Stetson Ave

N Columbus Dr

ILLINOIS
CENTER

Lake

63

46

N Michigan Ave

Lake Shore
East Park

64

52

Penton Pl

68

73 67

70

Randolph/Wabash

E Randolph St

E Randolph St

10

Visitor
Center

55

77

Chicago
Station (Metra)

Millennium

66

76

25

9

Wrigley
Square

31

Tennis
Courts

Maggie
Daley
Park

E Washington St

32

58

AT&T
Plaza

80

5

23

N State St

59

12

19

45

78

2

43

36

E Madison St

49

Millennium
Park

86

95 72 47

13

71

42

22

Monroe

E Monroe St

30

92

Millennium
Park Garage

56

48

Butler
Field

Adams/
Wabash

E Adams St

35

1 Art Institute
of Chicago

Petrillo
Music
Shell

74

62

11

53

7

Jackson

E Jackson Blvd

S Michigan Ave

S Columbus Dr

S Lake Shore Dr

H W Library

E Van Buren St

Van Buren St
(Metra)

S Plymouth Ct

20

S Wabash Ave

15

18

39

60

6

E Congress Pkwy

S State St

S Holden Ct

E Harrison St

S Michigan Ave

S Dearborn St

Harrison

E Balbo Ave

THE LOOP *Map on p286*

THE LOOP

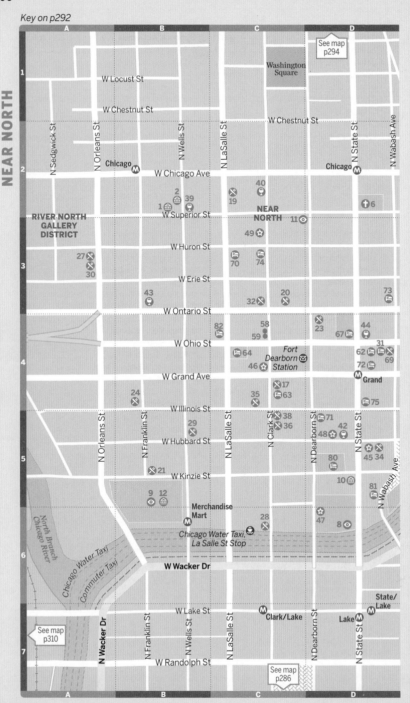

NEAR NORTH

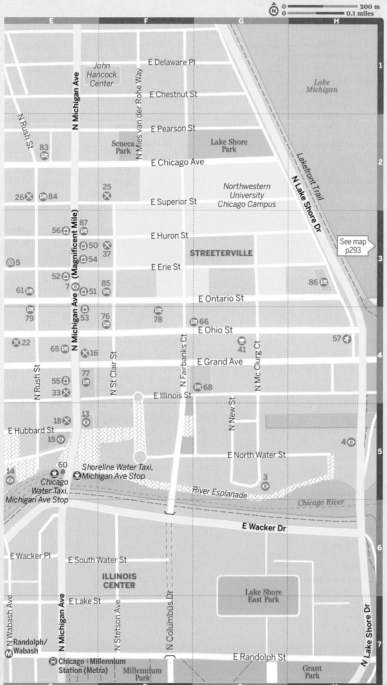

See map p293

NEAR NORTH *Map on p290*

GOLD COAST

See map p296

N 0 — 200 m
0 — 0.1 miles

Lincoln Park

W North Ave
E North Blvd

3

N North Park Ave
N Wieland St
N Wells St
N LaSalle St
N Clark St
N Dearborn St
N State Pkwy
N Astor St

8

7 W Burton Pl

W Burton Pl

Lakefront Trail

E Schiller St
4

W Schiller St

10

E Banks St

N Lake Shore Dr

22
24

N Astor St

W Goethe St
E Goethe St

39

E Scott St

27

Clark/Division
M

W Division St
E Division St

Oak Street Beach

N Clark St
W Elm St
23

N Dearborn St
E Elm St

E Cedar St

W Maple St
E Bellevue Pl

18
33 34

25
14

29 16
E Oak St

Wateriders (1mi)
20
15
38

N Franklin St
N Wells St
N LaSalle St

30
E Walton St

43

9
28
44

11
Washington Square
45

19
21 42
360°
Chicago
John Hancock Center

17

Water Tower Place

N Rush St

E Delaware Pl

31
5
36

W Chestnut St
E Chestnut St

W Chestnut St

35

W Institute Pl
6
32
26

Chicago
M
W Chicago Ave
Chicago
M

N State St
N Wabash Ave

E Pearson St

12

N Michigan Ave

E Chicago Ave

See map p290

GOLD COAST

Lake
Michigan

37
Lakefront Trail
N Lake Shore Dr
E Lake Shore Dr

E Walton St
41
40
13
N Dewitt Pl
N Mies van der Rohe Way

Museum of
Contemporary
Art
2
Lake Shore
Park
Seneca
Park

LINCOLN PARK & OLD TOWN

Key on p298

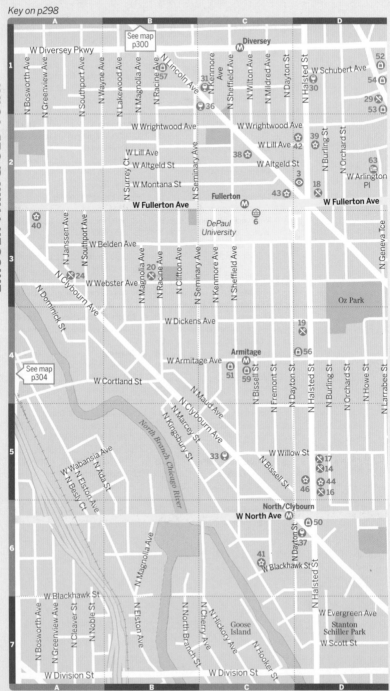

See map p300

See map p304

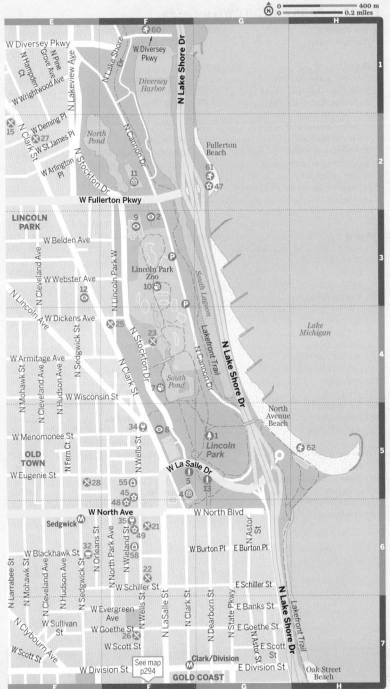

LINCOLN PARK & OLD TOWN *Map on p296*

LAKE VIEW & WRIGLEYVILLE *Map on p300*

LAKE VIEW & WRIGLEYVILLE

Key on p299

LAKE VIEW & WRIGLEYVILLE

Corn Productions (0.1mi);
Lincoln Square (0.4mi)

W Belle Plaine Ave

W Belle Plaine Ave

W Cuyler Ave

18

23

Irving Park

W Irving Park Rd

W Irving Park Rd

N Lincoln Ave

W Byron St

31

W Byron St

32
38

N Ravenswood Ave

W Grace St

W Grace St

13

40

N Hoyne Ave

N Damen Ave

N Hermitage Ave

N Paulina St

N Marshfield Ave

N Ashland Ave

N Southport Ave

W Waveland Ave

Waveland
Bowl (0.3mi)

W Waveland Ave

W Addison St

Addison

W Addison St

51

W Cornelia Ave

W Cornelia Ave

14

Paulina

Southport

W Roscoe St

15

W Roscoe St

W Henderson St

30

W School St

N Southport Ave

W School St

W Melrose St

W Melrose St

34

W Belmont Ave

W Belmont Ave

41

Hungry Brain (0.3mi);
Constellation (0.4mi)

W Fletcher St

47

W Fletcher St

N Ravenswood Ave

N Paulina St

N Ashland Ave

W Barry Ave

W Barry Ave

N Hoyne Ave

N Damen Ave

W Nelson St

W Wellington Ave

44

N Lincoln Ave

N Clybourn Ave

W Oakdale Ave

36

W George St

Diversey-River Bowl (0.1mi)

W Wolfram St

W Diversey Ave

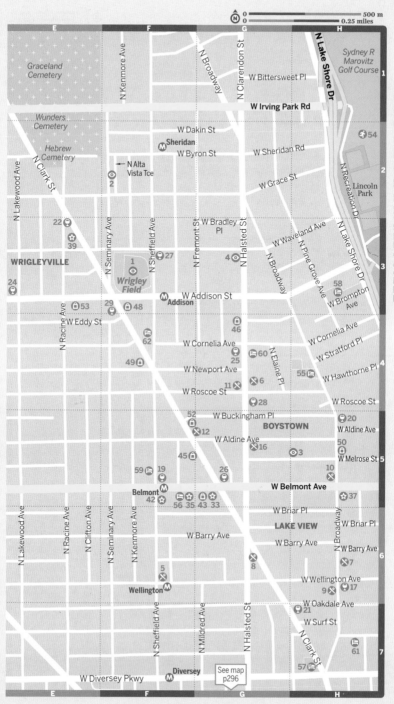

0   500 m
0   0.25 miles

Graceland
Cemetery

Wunders
Cemetery

Hebrew
Cemetery

N Kenmore Ave

N Broadway

N Clarendon St

W Bittersweet Pl

N Lake Shore Dr

Sydney R
Marovitz
Golf Course

W Irving Park Rd

W Dakin St

Sheridan

W Byron St

W Sheridan Rd

54

N Alta
Vista Tce

2

W Grace St

N Recreation Dr

Lincoln
Park

N Clark St

N Lakewood Ave

N Seminary Ave

N Sheffield Ave

N Fremont St

W Bradley
Pl

N Halsted St

W Waveland Ave

N Pine Grove Ave

N Broadway

N Lake Shore Dr

22

39

1

Wrigley
Field

27

4

58

W Brompton
Ave

WRIGLEYVILLE

24

N Racine Ave

Addison

W Addison St

W Cornelia Ave

W Stratford Pl

53

29

48

W Eddy St

62

46

W Cornelia Ave

55

W Hawthorne Pl

25

60

N Elaine Pl

49

W Newport Ave

11

6

W Roscoe St

28

W Roscoe St

52

W Buckingham Pl

20

W Aldine Ave

12

BOYSTOWN

50

W Aldine Ave

16

3

W Melrose St

45

26

10

59

19

W Belmont Ave

Belmont

42

56 35 43 33

37

W Briar Pl

LAKE VIEW

N Broadway

W Briar Pl

N Lakewood Ave

N Racine Ave

N Clifton Ave

N Seminary Ave

N Kenmore Ave

W Barry Ave

W Barry Ave

N Barry Ave

5

8

7

Wellington

W Wellington Ave

9

17

21

W Oakdale Ave

N Sheffield Ave

N Mildred Ave

N Halsted St

W Surf St

N Clark St

61

Diversey

See map
p296

57

W Diversey Pkwy

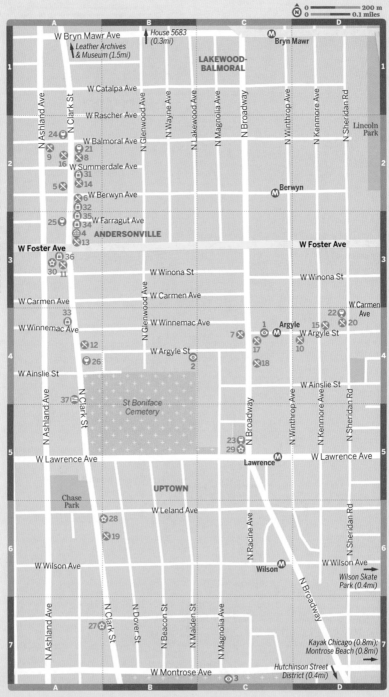

ANDERSONVILLE & UPTOWN

0 — 200 m
0 — 0.1 miles

W Bryn Mawr Ave

House 5683
(0.3mi)

Bryn Mawr

Leather Archives
& Museum (1.5mi)

LAKEWOOD-
BALMORAL

W Catalpa Ave

W Rascher Ave

Lincoln
Park

N Ashland Ave
N Clark St
N Glenwood Ave
N Wayne Ave
N Lakewood Ave
N Magnolia Ave
N Broadway
N Winthrop Ave
N Kenmore Ave
N Sheridan Rd

24

W Balmoral Ave

9
16
21
8

W Summerdale Ave

Berwyn

31
5
14

W Berwyn Ave

6
32

25
35
34

W Farragut Ave

4
13

ANDERSONVILLE

W Foster Ave

W Foster Ave

36
30
11

W Winona St

W Winona St

W Carmen Ave

N Glenwood Ave

W Carmen Ave

W Carmen
Ave

33

W Winnemac Ave

22
15
20

W Winnemac Ave

1

Argyle

12

7

W Argyle St

10

17

26

W Argyle St

2

18

W Ainslie St

W Ainslie St

N Ashland Ave
N Clark St
N Broadway
N Winthrop Ave
N Kenmore Ave
N Sheridan Rd

37

St Boniface
Cemetery

23
29

W Lawrence Ave

Lawrence

W Lawrence Ave

UPTOWN

Chase
Park

W Leland Ave

N Racine Ave

N Sheridan Rd

28

19

Wilson

W Wilson Ave

W Wilson Ave

Wilson Skate
Park (0.4mi)

N Ashland Ave
N Clark St
N Dover St
N Beacon St
N Malden St
N Magnolia Ave

N Broadway

27

Kayak Chicago (0.8mi);
Montrose Beach (0.8mi)

W Montrose Ave

3

Hutchinson Street
District (0.4mi)

ANDERSONVILLE & UPTOWN

Sights   (p127)
1 Argyle Street C4
2 Essanay Studios..B4
3 Graceland Cemetery C7
4 Swedish American Museum Center A3

Eating   (p127)
5 Acre A2
6 Andie's...A2
7 Ba Le Bakery C4
8 Big Jones...A2
9 First Slice A2
10 Hai Yen D4
11 Hopleaf..A3
12 Hot G Dog...A4
13 Jin Ju...A3
14 Kopi, A Traveler's Cafe...............................A2
15 Nha Hang Viet Nam...................................D4
16 Swedish Bakery A2
17 Tank Noodle C4
18 Thai Pastry...C4
19 Tiztal Cafe..B6
20 Tweet..D4

Drinking & Nightlife   (p132)
21 @mosphere A2

22 Big Chicks...D4
23 Crew C5
24 Hamburger Mary's A2
25 Simon's A3
26 SoFo Tap A4

Entertainment   (p133)
27 Black Ensemble Theater A7
28 Carol's Pub...B6
29 Green Mill C5
30 Neo-Futurists...A3
   Paper Machete ....(see 29)
   Uptown Poetry Slam........................(see 29)

Shopping   (p133)
31 Alamo Shoes...A2
32 Andersonville Galleria................................A2
33 Early to Bed..A4
34 Scout...A3
35 Women & Children First A3
36 Woolly Mammoth Antiques &
   Oddities...A3

Sleeping   (p227)
37 Guesthouse Hotel......................................A4

ANDERSONVILLE & UPTOWN

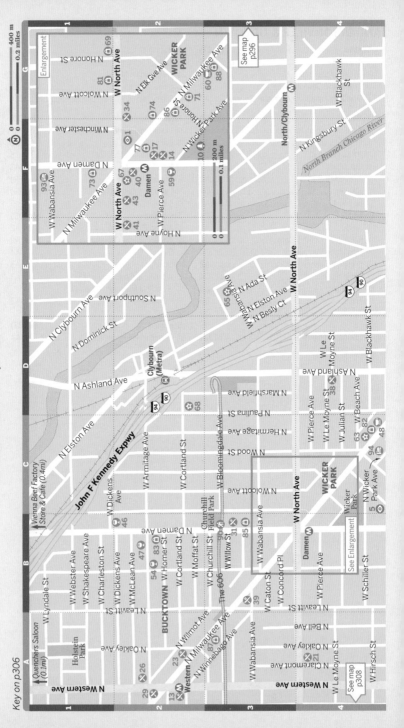

WICKER PARK, BUCKTOWN & UKRAINIAN VILLAGE

Key on p306

0 — 400 m
0 — 0.2 miles

Enlargement

WICKER PARK

See map p296

G

F

E

D

C

B

A

N Honore St
69
81
W North Ave
N Elk Gve Ave
34
74
86
N Milwaukee Ave
71
60
88
N Wolcott Ave
N Winchester Ave
1
77
N Honore St
17
14
N Wicker Park Ave
10
N Damen Ave
67
73
40
43
59
Damen
W North Ave
W Pierce Ave
41
N Hoyne Ave
93
W Wabansia Ave
N Milwaukee Ave

200 m
0.1 miles

North Branch Chicago River

North/Clybourn
N Kingsbury St
W Blackhawk St

W North Ave

N Ada St
65
N Wabansia Ave
N Elston Ave
N Besly Ct

94
90

W Blackhawk St

Clybourn
(Metra)

N Ashland Ave

N Southport Ave
N Clybourn Ave
N Dominick St

John F Kennedy Expwy

N Elston Ave

94
90

68

N Bloomingdale Ave
N Hermitage Ave
N Paulina St
N Wood St
N Marshfield Ave

W Le Moyne St
W Pierce Ave
W Julian St
N Ashland Ave
63
38
82
48
94

W Armitage Ave
W Cortland St
W Dickens Ave

Vienna Beef Factory
Store & Cafe (0.4mi)

W Webster Ave
W Shakespeare Ave
W Charleston St
W Dickens Ave
W McLean Ave

46
83
47

BUCKTOWN

N Elston Ave
N Damen Ave
N Leavitt St
N Winnebago Ave
N Milwaukee Ave
N Wilmot Ave

The 606

54

Churchill
Field Park

90
31
85

W Willow St
W Wabansia Ave
N Wolcott Ave

WICKER PARK

W North Ave

Wicker
Park

Damen

N Wicker
Park Ave
5

See Enlargement

N Winchester Ave
W Cortland St
W Moffat St
W Churchill St

39
W Caton St
W Concord Pl
N Leavitt St
N Bell Ave
N Oakley Ave
W Wabansia Ave
N Claremont Ave

Quenchers Saloon
(0.1mi)

Holstein
Park

W Lyndale St
W Webster Ave
W Shakespeare St
W Charleston St
W Dickens Ave
N Oakley Ave

26
23
12
29
13
Western
N Western Ave

W Cortland St
W Pierce Ave
N Pierce Ave
W Schiller St

W Le Moyne St
W Hirsch St

See map
p308

N Western Ave

See map p310

WICKER PARK, BUCKTOWN & UKRAINIAN VILLAGE

WICKER PARK, BUCKTOWN & UKRAINIAN VILLAGE Map on p304

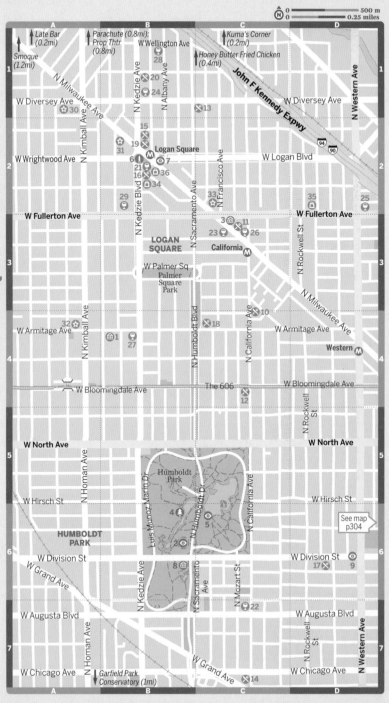

LOGAN SQUARE & HUMBOLDT PARK

0 — 500 m
0 — 0.25 miles

Late Bar (0.2mi)
Parachute (0.8mi); Prop Thtr (0.8mi)
Kuma's Corner (0.2mi)
Smoque (1.2mi)
W Wellington Ave
Honey Butter Fried Chicken (0.4mi)
John F Kennedy Expwy
N Western Ave
W Diversey Ave
30
N Kedzie Ave
N Albany Ave
20
24
28
W Diversey Ave
13
N Milwaukee Ave
94
90
15
W Wrightwood Ave
19
Logan Square
31
N Kimball Ave
6
21
7
W Logan Blvd
16
36
34
N Francisco Ave
N Sacramento Ave
29
33
35
25
W Fullerton Ave
W Fullerton Ave
3
N Kedzie Blvd
11
23
26
N Rockwell St
LOGAN SQUARE
California
W Palmer Sq
Palmer Square Park
N Humboldt Blvd
N Milwaukee Ave
W Armitage Ave
32
10
N Kimball Ave
18
W Armitage Ave
N California Ave
1
27
Western
The 606
W Bloomingdale Ave
W Bloomingdale Ave
12
N Rockwell St
W North Ave
W North Ave
N Homan Ave
Humboldt Park
N California Ave
W Hirsch St
W Hirsch St
Luis Munoz Marin Dr
N Humboldt Dr
See map p304
4
HUMBOLDT PARK
5
W Division St
17
9
W Division St
W Grand Ave
8
N Kedzie Ave
N Sacramento Ave
N Mozart St
W Augusta Blvd
22
W Augusta Blvd
N Homan Ave
N Rockwell St
N Western Ave
W Chicago Ave
Garfield Park Conservatory (1mi)
W Grand Ave
14
W Chicago Ave
N California Ave

LOGAN SQUARE & HUMBOLDT PARK

NEAR WEST SIDE & PILSEN

0 0
500 m
0.25 miles

See map
p290

Blommer Chocolate
Store (0.1mi)

Clinton

Chicago - Ogilvie
Transportation
Center (Metra)

See map
p286

WEST
LOOP

Dan Ryan Expwy

GREEKTOWN

UIC-Halsted

Greyhound

Morgan

Racine

Illinois
Medical
District

LITTLE
ITALY

Dwight D Eisenhower Expwy

Union
Park

Arrigo Park

Illinois
Medical
District

See map
p304

W Ogden Ave

N Ogden Ave

W Taylor St
3
26
56
W DeKoven St

See map p314

W 14th Pl
W 15th St

S Ruble St
S Desplaines St
S Jefferson St
S Clinton St

Dan Ryan Expwy

34
38
S Union Ave

Chinatown (0.75 mi)

South Branch Chicago River

University of Illinois at Chicago

W Roosevelt Rd

S Halsted St

Halsted St (Metra)

2

W Cullerton St
S Sangamon St

33
51

S Canal Port Ave
S Peoria St

W Cermak Rd

28
12
17
S May St
S Aberdeen St

W Maxwell St

W 14th Pl
W 15th St

W 16th St
W 18th St
50
48
18
W 19th St

S Carpenter St
S May St
S Racine Ave

PILSEN

S Aplport St
20
S Throop St

38
W Taylor St

S Blue Island Ave
S Racine Ave

S Loomis St
S Loomis St

Duck Inn (0.5mi)

36

W 14th St
S Loomis St

S Laflin St
16
55

10

S Ashland Ave
S Ashland Ave

Lagunitas Brewing Company (0.8mi)

W Taylor St
W Roosevelt Rd
W Washburne Ave
S Wolcott Ave
W 13th St
W Hastings St

S Paulina St

18th St

W 18th Pl
W 19th St

4

W Roosevelt Rd

W 16th St
S Wood St
W 17th St
W 18th St

Harrison Park
8

S Damen Ave

Hoyne

W 21st St
W 21st Pl

W Cermak Rd

Working Bikes Cooperative (0.5mi)

NEAR WEST SIDE & PILSEN *Map on p310*

SOUTH LOOP & NEAR SOUTH SIDE *Map on p314*

SOUTH LOOP & NEAR SOUTH SIDE

SOUTH LOOP & NEAR SOUTH SIDE

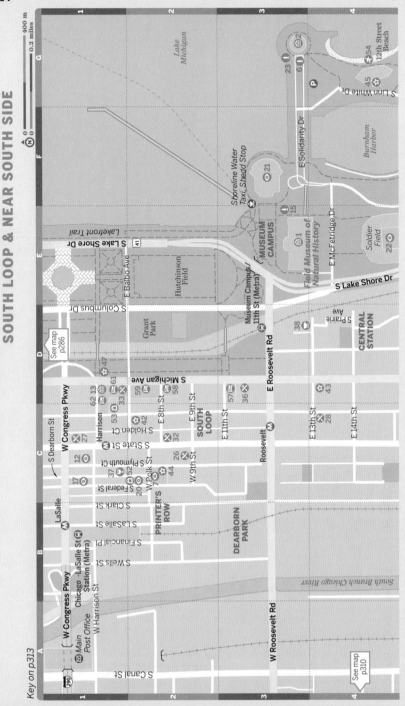

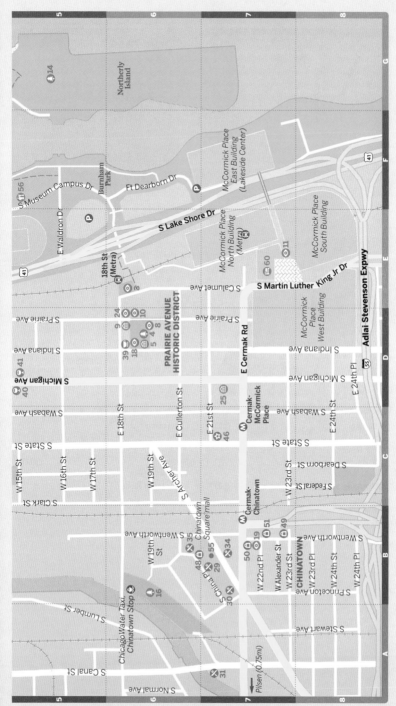

Northerly Island

Northerly Island

S Museum Campus Dr
E Waldron Dr
Burnham Park
Ft Dearborn Dr

S Lake Shore Dr

McCormick Place East Building (Lakeside Center)

McCormick Place North Building (Metra)

McCormick Place South Building

18th St (Metra)

S Calumet Ave

S Martin Luther King Jr Dr

McCormick Place West Building

Adlai Stevenson Expwy

PRAIRIE AVENUE HISTORIC DISTRICT

S Prairie Ave
S Indiana Ave
S Prairie Ave
S Indiana Ave

E Cermak Rd

E 18th St
E Cullerton St
E 21st St

S Wabash Ave

S Michigan Ave

E 24th Pl

S Michigan Ave
S Wabash Ave

S Indiana Ave

S State St
S Dearborn St
S Federal St

Cermak-McCormick Place

Cermak-Chinatown

W 15th St
W 16th St
W 17th St
W 19th St

Chinatown Square mall

S Wentworth Ave

S Archer Ave

W 19th St

S China Pl

Chicago Water Taxi Chinatown Stop

S Lumber St

CHINATOWN

S Princeton Ave
S Wentworth Ave

W 22nd Pl
W Alexander St
W 23rd St
W 23rd Pl
W 24th St
W 24th Pl

S Canal St
S Normal Ave
S Stewart Ave

Pilsen (0.75mi)

S Clark St
S State St
S Dearborn St
S 23rd St

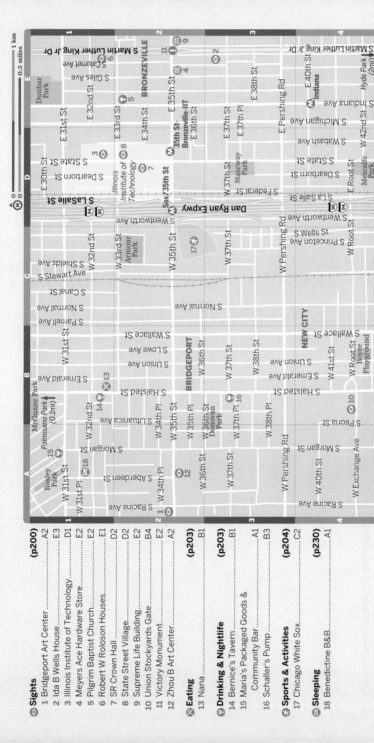

BRIDGEPORT & BRONZEVILLE

HYDE PARK & SOUTH SIDE

400 m
0.2 miles

Lake
Michigan

Promontory
Point

Lakefront Trail

Burnham
Park

S Lake Shore Dr

S Lake Shore Dr

S Chicago Beach Dr

S East End Ave

S Everett Ave

E 55th St

E 56th St

S Hyde Park Blvd

E 57th Dr

E 54th St

Museum of
Science &
Industry

S Cornell Ave

S Cornell Ave

53rd St
(Metra)

S Cornell Ave

Jackson
Park

S Stony Island Ave

S Lake Park Ave

55th–56th–
57th St (Metra)

S Lake Park Ave

S Harper Ave

S Harper Ave

S Blackstone Ave

S Blackstone Ave

S Dorchester Ave

S Dorchester Ave

Kenwood
Park

S Kenwood Ave

E 49th St

E 50th St

E Hyde Park Blvd

E 52nd St

E 53rd St

E 54th St

S Ridgewood
Ct

HYDE
PARK

E 55th Pl

S Kimbark Ave

S Woodlawn Ave

S Woodlawn Ave

S Greenwood Ave

KENWOOD

S Greenwood Ave

Muddy Waters'
House (0.6mi)

S University Ave

S Ellis Ave

S Ellis Ave

S Ingleside Ave

S Drexel Ave

E Drexel Sq

E 52nd St

E 53rd St

E 54th St

E 55th St

University
of Chicago

E 56th St

E 57th St

S Maryland Ave

S Drexel Blvd

S Cottage Grove Ave

S Cottage Grove Ave

Bronzeville
(2mi)

E 50th Pl

E 51st St

Payne Dr

E 57th St

Washington
Park

Payne Dr

S Champlain Ave

S St Lawrence Ave

◎ **Top Sights** (p193)

1 Museum of Science & Industry	F4
2 Robie House	C5

◎ **Sights** (p195)

3 4944 S Woodlawn Ave	C1
4 Bond Chapel	C5
5 DuSable Museum of African American History	A4
6 Elijah Muhammad House	C1
7 Garden of the Phoenix	E5
8 Hyde Park Art Center	E1
9 Hyde Park Hair Salon	D2
10 Jackson Park	E5
11 KAM Synagogue	C2
12 Nuclear Energy Sculpture	C4
13 Obama's House	C2
14 Oriental Institute	C5
15 Rockefeller Memorial Chapel	C5
16 Smart Museum of Art	C4
17 University of Chicago	B4
18 William Rainey Harper Memorial Library	C5

✕ **Eating** (p202)

19 Medici	D4
20 Valois Cafeteria	E2

● **Drinking & Nightlife** (p203)

21 Jimmy's Woodlawn Tap	C3

✪ **Entertainment** (p204)

22 Court Theatre	C4
23 Promontory	E2

🛍 **Shopping** (p204)

24 57th Street Books	D4
25 Powell's	E4
26 Seminary Co-op Bookstore	C4

✪ **Sports & Activities** (p205)

27 57th Street Beach	F4

🛏 **Sleeping** (p230)

28 La Quinta Chicago – Lake Shore	E1

63rd Street Beach (0.5mi);
Jackson Park
Golf Course (0.7mi)

Our Story

A beat-up old car, a few dollars in the pocket and a sense of adventure. In 1972 that's all Tony and Maureen Wheeler needed for the trip of a lifetime – across Europe and Asia overland to Australia. It took several months, and at the end – broke but inspired – they sat at their kitchen table writing and stapling together their first travel guide, *Across Asia on the Cheap*. Within a week they'd sold 1500 copies. Lonely Planet was born.

Today, Lonely Planet has offices in Franklin, London, Melbourne, Oakland, Dublin, Beijing and Delhi, with more than 600 staff and writers. We share Tony's belief that 'a great guidebook should do three things: inform, educate and amuse'.

Our Writer

Karla Zimmerman

Karla lives in Chicago, where she has been eating deep-dish pizza (Giordano's preferred) and yelling at the Cubs for more than 25 years. She never tires of the city's sky-high architecture, global neighborhoods and character-filled dive bars, though she does tire of its wind-bashed winters. Karla writes about travel for books, magazines and websites. She has written several Lonely Planet guides, covering the USA, Canada, Caribbean and Europe. To learn more, follow her on Instagram and Twitter (@karlazimmerman).

Published by Lonely Planet Global Limited
CRN 554153
8th edition – Feb 2017
ISBN 978 1 78657 227 1
© Lonely Planet 2017   Photographs © as indicated 2017
10 9 8 7 6 5 4 3 2 1
Printed in China